The

OF HISTORY

Post-Contemporary Interventions

Series Editors: Stanley Fish and Fredric Jameson

THE
SPECTACLE
OF HISTORY

Speech, Text,

and Memory

at the Iran-contra

Hearings

Michael Lynch

and David Bogen

Duke University Press

Durham and London

1996

© 1996 Duke University Press

Printed in the United States of America on acid-free paper ∞

Designed by Cherie H. Westmoreland

Typeset in Melior with Copperplate display by Keystone Typesetters, Inc.

Library of Congress Cataloging-in-Publication Data appear on
the last printed page of this book.

CONTENTS

PREFACE

This study began in a playful way during the summer of 1987 when both of us were affiliated with Boston University. Shortly after the Iran-contra hearings were televised, we struck up a conversation about how the witnesses seemed to have difficulty recalling key matters of fact until their interrogators produced written records to "refresh" their recollections. No doubt, this is a common enough occurrence in courtrooms and tribunals, but it seemed especially salient to the conduct of the hearings. We agreed that we ought to look into the matter. Shortly afterward, we obtained videotaped copies of the telecast of the testimony of North and Poindexter, and we began a series of more or less weekly meetings in which we played portions of the tapes and discussed a variety of things that we found interesting. Often during these sessions we would stop the tape, and with North's freeze-framed visage hovering over us like a specter, we would heatedly discuss and debate whatever came to mind while viewing the immediate testimony. Needless to say, this was not a methodical procedure, but it was enjoyable and engrossing. These regular, and sometimes irregular, meetings continued over the next few years. Although we toyed with numerous themes, we kept returning to the issue that initially piqued our interest: the interplay between spoken personal testimony and written organizational records. At the time, ML was studying how natural scientists compose and make use of visual representations, and DB was beginning a dissertation that critically examined Habermas's theory of communicative action in relation to detailed studies of natural language use. Although the testimony at the hearings was not directly related to these projects, in a more general way the videotapes, together with written sources on the Iran-contra affair, provided rich materials for exploring our interests in the practical and communicative production of master narratives. Above all, given the momentous buildup that accompanied the hearings, and especially the spectacle of North's testimony, there seemed to be good reason to figure that a close study of the testimony might provide clear insight into the (de)construction of an event that was unmistakably historical.

Within a year or so, we began to develop our scattered notes and squibs into more systematic accounts on the production of history and the contextual uses of memory in testimony. We had no intention of writing a book on the subject until we were encouraged to do so after presenting a paper at a conference in 1989. This seemed like a neat idea, as North might say. Gradually, and while pursuing other research projects, we wrote and revised a manuscript that discussed a set of themes on the interplay among history, testimony, speech, and writing. Meanwhile, the Iran-contra affair became old news, and its scandalous significance seemed to diminish with time. It did not completely disappear, however, as new twists in the plot resurfaced during the special prosecutor's criminal investigations and North's run for a U.S. Senate seat in 1994. Despite, and indeed because of, their diminishing news value, the Iran-contra hearings remained highly interesting for our purposes. The outlines and significance of the Iran-contra affair remained disturbingly unresolved, and this lack of resolution was foreshadowed in the details of the testimony we kept reviewing.

Throughout this book we focus on only a small and highly selective portion of the public record because we believe that an intensive study of the testimony should provide unique insight into the production of a historical event (an event that already has been written about from many other angles). We feel that the fragmentary details we examine resonate with themes—history, spectacle, interrogation, stories, memory, intertextuality, and lying—that have a place in countless other discussions, debates, and research programs in the humanities and social sciences. We believe that the organization of this book in terms of these themes will help to illuminate the production of an event that provided both the historical circumstance and product of the Iran-contra testimony, and we hope that readers who bear with us will gain a novel understanding of how the familiar conceptual themes and distinctions we discuss entered into the production of that event.

For giving us the opportunity to present our materials and analyses, we gratefully recognize the Temple University Conference on Discourse Analysis, the annual meetings of the International Association of Philosophy and Literature (IAPL), the American Sociological Association, the Society for Phenomenology and the Human Sciences, the World Congress of International Sociological Association, and the History of Science Society. We also were invited to present our research at colloquia sponsored by the Institute for Research on Learning in Palo Alto, the Oregon Humanities Center at the University of Oregon, Michigan State University, UCLA, UC Santa Barbara, Loughborough University, Brunel University, and the University of York. We are grateful to the colleagues who helped arrange these meetings and to many others who offered their comments, unpublished writings, criticisms, and editorial advice. They include Bob Anderson, Dede Boden, Graham Button, Paul Drew, Harold Garfinkel, Tim Halkowski, Brigitte Jordan, John Lee, Gene Lerner, Ken Liberman, Doug Macbeth, Doug Maynard, John O'Neill, Anita Pomerantz, Joseph Schneider, Steven Shapin, Wes Sharrock, John Stuhr, Lucy Suchman, Rod Watson, Jack Whalen, Martha Woodmansee, and Steve Woolgar. There also were many others we have neglected to mention. We are especially grateful to our former colleagues at Boston University, particularly Jeff Coulter, Dusan Bjelic, Tim Costelloe, Eileen Crist, Ed Parsons, Jeff Stetson, George Psathas, and other graduate students and faculty members in the Sociology Department who supplied us with helpful advice, criticism, and support. We would like to thank Thos Niles for preparing the photographs used as figures in the book. We also owe our thanks to Stanley Fish and Reynolds Smith of Duke University Press for encouraging us to write this book, and Bob Mirandon, for his outstanding copyediting. Finally, we should not forget John Silber, the philosopher-king of Boston University, who administered a "living lesson in the museum of order," which is inscribed, in ways we cannot begin to acknowledge, in these pages.

TRANSCRIPTION CONVENTIONS

Some of the transcripts presented in this book use symbols or typographic conventions developed by Gail Jefferson, and used widely in conversation analysis, to denote lapses of time (silences, pauses, lapses, gaps), overlapping utterances, and selected aspects of pace, pitch, prosody, pronunciation, and stress. When used intensively, these can make a transcript difficult to read, especially for readers unfamiliar with the genre.

Numbers in parentheses: (0.8) Pauses, gaps, silences measured in seconds and tenths of seconds. Measures are approximate.

Period in parentheses: (.) "Micro-pause" of less than two-tenths of a second.

Letters, words, or phrases in single parentheses: (tch) Sounds, words, or phrases that are indistinct or otherwise difficult for the transcriber to make out from the recording.

Double parentheses: ((throat clear)) Commentary describing nonlexical or nonverbal actions evident on the tape, which the transcriber deems relevant to mention.

Degree sign: °let's see° Barely audible sound, whisper, or word.

Colons: you:: A stretched sound within, or at the end of, a word.

Equals signs: =That's correct "Latching" of utterance; utterance follows unusually quickly after the immediately preceding utterance.

Square brackets: Marking of points where talk by different speakers overlaps. Left brackets mark the beginnings of overlaps, and right brackets the ends. In many of our transcripts, we do not mark ends of overlaps. So, for example:

> Joan: tch Ye[ah]
>
>   [
>
> Linda: [But,]

Italics: I *did.* Voiced stress on word, phrase, or sound. Stress sometimes does not correspond to written syllables.

Hyphen stroke: a- a call Word or sound is cut off.

Arrow in margin: → Indication of a significant line or utterance for the analysis.

INTRODUCTION

It is a well-known feature of historical inquiries that an event can be reconstructed in countless ways. Chronologies can begin earlier or later and can be fleshed out with variable amounts of detail; characters can be added or elided; agency and blame can be assigned to different parties. It also is well-known that certain details and identities can become set features of an official or conventional history. An innovative historian will look for ways to disclose suppressed evidence, discover forgotten characters, or otherwise revise the conventionally accepted elements of such a narrative. In this book we examine history-producing work in both of these aspects: the piecing together of narrative elements to compose an official history, and the creative disruption of that history. Our main interest does not center on the work of professional historians. Instead, we investigate the discourse of a public tribunal and the history-producing work of parties to that official investigation. This tribunal—the Iran-contra hearings—was itself a historic occasion on which a substantive event in recent U.S. history was both investigated and problematized. In our view, the hearings produced a vivid instance of a battle over the writing of history. Questions about what happened and who was responsible for the events in question were part of a relentless discursive struggle. In the pages that follow, we give a blow-by-blow description of selected moments in that struggle which made for the high drama of those hearings. By describing the public spectacle of the Iran-contra hearings, we hope to gain insight into the situated practices through which historical events are composed and decomposed.

A SCANDAL AND ITS INVESTIGATION

In January 1987 the U.S. Congress set up the Joint House-Senate Select Committee on Secret Military Assistance to Iran and the Nicaraguan Opposition. This committee was given the mandate to investigate a series of events that came to be known as "the Iran-contra affair," "the Iran-contra scandal," or simply "Iran-contra." By the time the committee convened its hearings, the outlines of the Iran-contra scandal were fairly well established. It had been a major news story for several months, and already subjected to a number of official and unofficial investigations. A conventionally accepted basic narrative had begun to coalesce, and the key players in the unfolding drama—the investigators, the instigators, and a huge media audience—were exposed to a story of an emerging historical event.[1]

The story of the Iran-contra affair begins in the late summer of 1985 when members of the White House National Security Council (NSC) staff, including President Ronald Reagan's National Security Advisers Robert McFarlane and John Poindexter,[2] collaborated with a shadowy collection of international arms salesmen, mercenaries, and U.S., Israeli, and Iranian officials to arrange a series of covert sales of U.S. weapons to Iran. Marine Lt. Col. Oliver North, acting in a civilian capacity as an NSC staff member, was a key coordinator of these operations. It was widely believed that the operations were conducted with the knowledge, approval, and complicity of the president, vice president, several leading Cabinet members, and the director and other officials of the Central Intelligence Agency. The motives and extent of these officials' involvement remained in doubt, but it was clear that members of the relevant intelligence oversight committees of the U.S. Congress had not been notified about these transactions. The sales involved TOW (antitank) and Hawk (ground-to-air) missiles. They were authorized with the expectation that they would result in the release of American hostages held in Lebanon by Islamic fundamentalist groups. These sales, and the connection between the sales and the release of the hostages, violated repeatedly stated U.S. policies against aiding "terrorist" nations (among which Iran was prominently included) and against paying ransom for hostages. The administration defended the arms sales by saying that they were designed to establish a cooperative relationship with "moderate" political factions that might come to power in Iran after the death of the Ayatollah Khomeini, but relevant notes, memos, and records compiled at the time indicated that securing the release of the hostages was a prominent, if not the exclusive, purpose of the arms sales.

In 1986, NSC operatives began "diverting" some of the profits from the Iranian arms sales to aid the contra forces seeking to overthrow the Sandinista government in Nicaragua. This diversion was one of several methods for "privately" aiding the contras at a time when Congress had cut off all "lethal aid" to them and had prohibited agents from U.S. intelligence services from assisting them. In October 1986, Sandinista forces in Nicaragua shot down an airplane and captured an American, Eugene Hassenfus, who admitted that the plane had been dropping weapons and other supplies to the contras. Documents aboard the aircraft linked the mission to the CIA and to officials at the White House. This connection was initially denied by White House spokespersons and by CIA chief William Casey.

In early November a Lebanese weekly *Al Shiraa* published an exposé of the U.S.-Iran missile deals, describing a particular mission in May 1986 involving former National Security Adviser Robert McFarlane. This report was initially denounced by the White House as a fabrication, but it soon became apparent to members of the press and the government that further revelations concerning the sales were likely to follow and that some form of official investigation into these events would be required. In late November, Attorney General Edwin Meese and members of his staff began an in-house investigation of the arms sales. Despite the fact that North and other NSC staff members were able to destroy great numbers of relevant documents before the Meese investigation, the attorney general's inquiries uncovered documentary evidence detailing the diversion of arms sale profits to assist the Nicaraguan contras. Faced with an erupting scandal, Reagan called a press conference, and on November 25, 1986, he and Attorney General Meese announced that Poindexter was resigning and North had been fired. Further governmental inquiries were initiated shortly afterward, and a special prosecutor was appointed to begin investigations of possible criminal violations by North, Poindexter, and other officials.

At the outset of the congressional investigation the historical import of the Iran-contra affair seemed monumental. It was a major scandal whose full exposure portended the end of a popular presidential reign, or, at the very least, a reigning in of a shadow government that had apparently taken over the affairs of state. At first, a number of key officials—most notably the president and vice president—maintained that until November 1986 they had had little or no direct knowledge of the nature and scope of Oliver North's covert activities. However, in the midst of growing objections to these earlier denials, President Reagan grudgingly acknowledged that "mistakes had been made."[3] By some accounts, the arms sales and diversion of funds constituted violations of law of sufficient magnitude to warrant impeachment of the president and the criminal prosecution of several senior White House officials. After several months of investigation, including much wrangling with the White House and the CIA over the release of documents, and extended negotiations with North, Poindexter, and their respective legal staffs regarding the conditions of partial immunity from criminal prosecution under which they agreed to testify, the House-Senate joint committee hearings convened.

This was the situation up until May 1987 when the committee began its televised hearings. During that summer the story took a dramatic turn when North testified before the committee from July 7–14. Although many other witnesses testified at the tribunal, North's appearance became the center of a public spectacle. A battery of cameras and microphones monitored his every move while he recounted his involvement in the events. The entire setup was arranged as a conspicuous civics lesson in which North and his interrogators all expressed an orientation to "the truth" about secret and deceptive dealings.[4] In the words of one of North's interrogators, it was "a principal purpose" of the hearings "to replace secrecy and deception with disclosure and truth."[5]

North and Poindexter (who testified immediately after him) both stated that, to their knowledge, President Reagan had not been aware of the diversion of proceeds from the Iranian arms sales, and Poindexter took responsibility for approving the action. By itself, this testimony was unsurprising, but what was more significant was the way that North's performance before the cameras touched off an unexpected outpouring of popular attention and support. He became an instant media figure, the subject of a carnival—"Olliemania"—in which a covert agent and admitted liar was dubbed "the hero America needs." Several committee members and numerous commentators and members of the audience were appalled, but it soon became clear that the tribunal had been transformed into an event of a different order.

The hearings, and North's testimony in particular, were rich with quotable phrases and memorable images. North appeared in his U.S. Marine Corps uniform, bedecked with medals. As he testified, he struck classic theatrical poses evoking themes from adventure films, his protean face giving off expressions of valor, contrition, indignation, pride, and sincerity. His voice occasionally cracked in a manner recalling James Stewart's film appearance before a hostile Congress in *Mr. Smith Goes to Washington* (1939). At other times North's phrases and gestures seemed reminiscent of John Wayne, and twice in his testimony he wove the title of a movie starring Clint Eastwood into a forceful assertion of truthfulness and tainted heroism.[6] In part through North's theatrical achievements, but also as a product of the incessant publicity, the tribunal became a story in and of itself, overshadowing its historic task of producing an official version of the Iran-contra affair. From the beginning, the story of the hearings, and the stories told *in* the hearings, resonated with intertextual connections and ceremonial precedents, not the least of which was "Watergate."[7]

By the time the committee issued its final report in November 1987, the Iran-contra affair had begun to settle down into history as an event that might have brought down a presidency but failed to do so. Although the echoes and reverberations of the scandal continued to haunt the careers and lives of many of the key players, it was widely suspected that the investigative efforts of the joint congressional committee had been blocked, inhibited, or otherwise thwarted by the parties under investigation. This is where we end the story. However, the saga of Ollie North and many other echoes of the hearings are likely to reverberate for years to come.

THE SOCIAL PRODUCTION OF HISTORY

We should make clear that it is not our intent to get to the bottom of the scandal in order to explain who really authorized the covert weapons deals with Iran and who ultimately was responsible for diverting the profits from those sales to aid the Nicaraguan contras. We are far more interested in the fact that what really happened was, and remains to this day, obscure and contestable. Accordingly, our central task in this study is to examine how the social production of testimony at the Iran-contra hearings gave rise to the irresolute features of the events in question. We shall delve into the procedures and maneuvers through which testimony was solicited, verified, challenged, and equivocated. This examination extends beyond the analysis of talk and includes a focus on how written documents were located, retrieved, and interpreted by the parties whose actions composed the testimony.

Throughout this book we present excerpts from the videotaped record of the hearings. We focus on the interrogation of Oliver North because his testimony was a key moment in an extended battle over the disclosure and recitation of the historical facts in question. The fact that this battle reached no determinate resolution, and the history that resulted was equivocal, subject to continuing doubts, and caught up in partisan controversy, makes it no less interesting. Indeed, for our purposes, this circumstance is even more interesting than if the hearings had resulted in a consensus. The disputatiousness at the hearings made it clear in a more general way that public knowledge of the historical event was contingent upon a historically embedded production of truth. The hearings were thus a paradigm case of the "social construction" of history.

Considerable debate and confusion in the human sciences surround the issue of how and to what extent natural and cultural facts can be said to be "socially constructed." Increasingly, we are informed that virtually anything that can be said to be *objectively given*—including even the laws of physics and the rules of mathematics—is in fact a social construction.[8] According to a familiar argument, a thing (an event, activity, or formal structure) can be real only when it is made real, and thereafter presumed real, by agents in a social context. Contexts of reality construction are culturally and historically specific, and so it may seem that the facts and meanings that emerge from them are also variable, relative, or even arbitrary.[9] As Stanley Fish summarizes it, constructionist views of law, discourse, and science hold that "the present arrangement of things— including, in addition to the lines of power and influence, the categories of knowledge with their attendant specification of factuality or truth—is not natural or given, but is conventional and has been instituted by the operation of historical and political (in the sense of interested) forces, even though it now wears the face of 'common sense.' "[10] This certainly applies to histories of the Iran-contra affair. Some versions of that event may seem more transparently political than others, but we see no reason to suppose that any version (including our own) simply reports the facts of history.

In academic discourse, the term "construction" tends to be used in equivocal ways. A critical use of the term implies a devious and intentional manipulation of the facts, whereas the more general sense of construction can refer to any mode of practical activity whatsoever, whether honestly or dishonestly intended, and whether defensible or indefensible in terms of local standards of judgment and competence. Frequently, when a general constructionist stance is adopted in a social-scientific, legal, or literary study, a normative sense of the word nevertheless remains in force, and the construction in question is made out to be a scandal or transgression. This view begs the question of how the normative standards implied by the criticism were themselves constructed.[11] If one assumes that no objective or historical knowledge can ever be "unconstructed," then to say that something held out to be a fact really is a social construction does not imply that the fact should be dismissed as an illusion or condemned as a product of political machinations. Instead, any criticism applies to a metaphysical conception of the factual origins of all (genuine) knowledge, and this conception has no direct bearing on mundane considerations about the real or illusory status of particular objects or events. To use a concrete analogy, a highway can be built well or poorly; it may remain solid for decades or fall apart soon after being laid (for example, because a construction company secretly controlled by the Mafia substituted an inferior grade of concrete for the kind officially required). In either case, the highway holds together or falls apart as a construction. More generally, to say that a particular practice or body of knowledge is constructed or manufactured carries no special criticism, unless one supposes the possibility that the object in question could be "unconstructed."[12] Accordingly, in this study when we say a historical event was constructed, we are not suggesting that something untoward was done, although it certainly may have been. Whether valid or not, particular judgments about conspiracies, deceptive strategies, and the like were embedded in the substantive events in question and do not follow from a general social constructionist position.

It should be no surprise to anyone that the versions of the Iran-contra affair that resulted from the official and unofficial investigations of that event were constructed. The spectacle of North's testimony at the Iran-contra hearings made it stunningly clear at the time that "history" was being assembled in a contested field. Many reasons can be found to complain about the way the official investigation was conducted,[13] but the fact that the investigation constructed an event is not by itself an interesting issue, at least not as far as this book is concerned. We are more interested in the infrastructure of that construction, the practical methods through which the event was assembled, contested, and stabilized. To avoid possible confusion about what we are trying to say, we prefer to speak of the social *production* of history.[14]

Our approach to the North testimony follows the general precepts of ethnomethodological studies of practical reasoning and ordinary action, and we extend that work to the study of social practices that were featured in the production of a historical event (see Methodological Appendix for a more elaborate discussion of our postanalytic approach to ethnomethodology). Consistent with the ethnomethodological initiatives of Harold Garfinkel and Harvey Sacks, our central aim is to use an intensive investigation of video materials as a basis for addressing (and "respecifying") a series of general questions about lying and truth, testimony, interrogation, stories, memory, and documentary records. All of these subjects pertain to the relationship between biography and history, a topic that makes up a (if not *the*) central problem of sociological theory.[15] Close study of the video text of the Iran-contra hearings will enable us to challenge general assumptions about these topics that have been handed down through traditions of social theory and cultural inquiry.

There are alternatives to the approach we are taking. One would be to deconstruct the official histories written by various government committees and commissions to reveal the limits of the inquiries and the notable omissions from the reports. Another would be to get access to the backroom machinations through which administration participants and committee investigators negotiated the eventual outcome. Short of getting inside the White House and the other private chambers in which meetings, rehearsals, strategy sessions, etc., took place, we could have tried to reconstruct the relevant events through interviews with key participants and a close study of relevant documents. Still another approach would be to focus on the audience's response by consulting poll results and other indicators of mass opinion. Although we have not entirely disregarded such approaches and evidences, we must admit to a lack of privileged access to the facts. It was never our intention to attain such access, as the aims of our inquiry differ from those of the investigative bodies that attempted to define what actually happened, and that themselves contributed to the further production of the historical events they set out to describe. Like millions of others in the mass audience, we witnessed a televised spectacle of an official tribunal. We gained no special access to the events we witnessed. Instead, we were privy to the accumulation of an immense popular archive of official and journalistic accounts, analyses, criticisms, testimonies, published transcripts, and evidential documents that shaped the history of the Iran-contra affair. What we have in hand is the record of the spectacle itself—the video text aired on national television during the hearings and the many public commentaries on it that circulated widely at the time. By repeatedly examining selected fragments of this intertextual spectacle, we have tried to gain insight into its discursive production.

We characterize this work as empirical, but not empiricist. While we have little use for social-science methods that use the management of data sets to supplant commonsense understandings of social affairs, we nonetheless see a point to making a painstaking effort to come to terms with the details of the audiovisual record of the hearings. The Iran-contra hearings initially held our interest precisely because they seemed to embody a struggle over historical truth and interpretation that resonated with recent debates about history among philosophers and social scientists. As the hearings unfolded, it became clear that many key questions raised at the tribunal were, and would continue to be, undecidable. Consequently, we directed our attention away from speculations regarding the "real truth" of the historical accounts offered and debated during the Iran-contra testimony and toward the less elusive and yet more complex matter of the *produced undecidability* of the records and testimony that made up the evidence under scrutiny. To colleagues who would have us deconstruct the testimony and media reports in order to expose and denounce substantive abuses of power and a manipulation of public opinion, we will insist that in this case the most effective deconstructionists were on the administration's side.

Videotapes of the testimony provided a rich textual basis for examining the vicissitudes of truth-finding in interrogative settings. It is our contention that a close examination of these tapes shows *in detail* how the official investigation's spade was turned whenever committee interrogators attempted to dig beneath the "plausible denials" given by North and his colleagues. Through the examination of this vivid demonstration of the contingencies of testimony we aim to shed new light on broader questions of how testimony is related to evidence, and, more generally, of how speech is related to writing.[16]

WRITING HISTORY

This book addresses the social-organizational procedures and tactics through which a history of the Iran-contra affair was produced. Such procedures and tactics include, among others, the iteration of stories, the analysis of testimonies, and the enrollment of sympathetic or supportive audiences. When treated in this way, just *what* a history is about is intertwined on several fronts with just *how* it is written. In the case of the Iran-contra affair, the anticipation of such a history was evident in the way "plausible deniability" was explicitly built into the writing, destruction, and interpretation of documentary evidence. As many who watched the hearings learned, the term plausible deniability originated with intelligence agencies whose covert actions were taken under the cover of legitimate transactions. The actions, together with the documentary evidence they produced, were designed to be equivocal. Such a design enabled the agents to deny involvement by using the self-same evidence to demonstrate the legitimate (or, at the very least, unremarkable) nature of their activities. The official investigation was complicated immeasurably by the acknowledged fact that many of the documents used by the committee for purposes of eliciting and verifying testimony were designed to enable deniability. Consequently, both the denials of substantive knowledge and the interrogatory challenges to those denials that were voiced by the interlocutors during the hearings were subject to the contingencies and slippages of plausible deniability.

In our view, no essential point separates the history of the Iran-contra affair and the various official investigations through which that history was written. The reflexive relationship between history and writing operated with such density around the issue of plausible deniability that the archive of records and testimonies examined by the various fact-finding bodies could not be viewed by any wide-awake observer as a neutral record of the various covert activities at issue. In this sense, the public archive of the Iran-contra affair was itself shaped by the alleged covert activities it was being used to investigate and describe. (For instance, by the much-publicized shredding of documents by Oliver North and his NSC staff in November 1986, by White House resistance to the disclosure of classified documents, and by false chronologies put out by the key actors in the affair.) In light of these considerations, the continuing history of the Iran-contra affair was a history of struggle over the very documents through which that history was—and, in many ways, still is—being written.

DECONSTRUCTION AS A PRACTICAL ACCOMPLISHMENT

The terms "deconstruction" and "discourse analysis" have become so popular in the social sciences and humanities that they now threaten to weave together an entire range of previously incompatible approaches to textual materials.[17] Concepts of "text," "narrative," and "discourse" have been extended beyond the more tangible or mundane forms of written or spoken material. They now cover virtually every modality of communicative action, including fragments of writing, interchanges of speech, proverbial or paradigmatic statements, intertextual assemblages, heterogeneous complexes of practice and architecture, coherent ideologies, and grand narratives that epitomize an era. Despite occasional rumors that deconstructionism has played itself out in the literary circles where it got its start, social scientists continue to promote it as a novel, even radical, approach to analysis.[18] In sociology, deconstructionist and discourse-analytic strategies have often been used to put a new face on some well-established lines of neo-Marxist, feminist, interactionalist, and structuralist research.[19] In the absence of a widespread acquaintance among social scientists with the traditions in hermeneutics and linguistic philosophy from which deconstruction developed, deconstructionist social science often is enlisted in the service of older traditions of criticism in which texts are shown to "reflect" and promote a priori configurations of power, social inequality, partisan interest, and institutional order that make up the "social context" of the text.[20] Often lost in the bargain is the fact that the Heideggerian hermeneutics that Derrida transformed attacks the very forms of causal and quasi-causal contextual explanation so prevalent in the social sciences.[21] If instead of being a time-bound reflection of a set of substantive intentions and partisan objectives, a text's intelligibility can emerge from readings in the actual absence of the author (and often in the actual ignorance of the author's historical circumstances) then no single social context stands behind the text to guarantee its intelligibility. Moreover, in line with Derrida's conception of texts as iterable and intelligible documents that are displaced—or orphaned—from the conditions of their authorship, the relationship between any particular reading and the original context of the writing is undecidable. That is, no original meaning attaches to the text and acts as a fixed standard for assessing the correctness of any subsequent reading. A reader can, of course, try to reconstruct an author, an author's intentions, an author's cultural circumstances, or an author's ideological orientation from within the text (indeed, such reconstructions may be inevitable byproducts of any reading), but to explain what is read by reference to such reconstructed personages and contextualizations is to get things exactly backward.

Undecidability is often thought to pose horrific methodological problems for any systematic effort to make consistent sense of a text or body of texts. Biblical scholarship, law, science, and even everyday communicative understanding might seem impossible given the polysemous properties of signs, traces, and inscriptions (not to speak of more extended documents). As we conceive the issue, however, undecidability is not necessarily, or even ordinarily, a problem. People manifestly do understand what others say and write, with particular misunderstandings being set off against a backdrop of relatively unproblematic agreement. Undecidability becomes an essential (as opposed to an occasional) problem only when framed by the formalist belief that textual meaning must somehow attach to a context-free order of signs. To turn away from the idea that an original intent remains embedded in the words of a document does not disallow the familiar practices through which defeasible, provisional, and yet adequate understandings are read from, or found within, particular texts and fragments. Nor does such a pragmatic understanding of textual materials stand in ironic contrast to an idealized concept of meaning, any more than a secular source of authority must stand in ironic contrast to a deity's transcendental powers.

As mentioned, prominent in the Iran-contra hearings was the relationship between spoken testimony and various written documents used as evidence. Throughout this study we rely on the work of witnesses and interrogators as a guide for recasting, in ethnomethodological terms, the more general relationship between speech and writing. Our aim is to consider, by respecifying the terms of a philosophical dispute that has come to regard speech and writing as distinct orders of discourse, how the relationship between particular testimonies and evidentiary writings were managed, and, hence, how speech and writing were irremediably intertwined at the moment of interrogation. This approach transforms a theoretical distinction between speech and writing into a theme made perspicuous by a particular occasion of action. We shall argue that the distinction between speech and writing was practically significant and discursively embedded in the interrogative work of soliciting and examining spoken testimony by reference to a cumulative "record" of the Iran-contra affair. The specifications of conventional history—dates, places, times, named characters, bounded actions and events—contrast point-by-point to the locally organized and biographically relevant stories told in testimony. Members of the joint Senate-House committee were responsible for a final report, which was to be published after the close of the hearings. The committee's literary task included much more than composing this summary report; this task pervaded the hearings themselves. Throughout, the cumulative record of the affair and the mass of committee documents were actively brought into play. Witnesses were often questioned with reference to the documents and earlier testimonies that were available in the record. Not only were witnesses' utterances heard by reference to what might later be written about them, but they were solicited and assessed in relation to a record that was being written as the witness spoke.

Committee investigators treated written records as actual or potential constraints on what a witness could say, or not say, credibly. They treated these records as resources for formulating interrogative questions and as sources of leverage for probing witnesses, testing their answers, and holding those answers accountable to conventional standards of accuracy and sincerity. On the other hand, the fragmentary notes, documents, and other writings used by the committee were not simply transparent bits of factual evidence. Examinations of these documents provided the witness with opportunities to specify the situational and intentional contexts of those writings. Like any reasonably clever deconstructionist, North did not always go along with the official interpretive program. For the most part, the committee interrogators aimed to use written documents as representations of real-worldly events. North and the other witnesses were able to dissociate their testimony from particular texts by, among other things, exploiting undecidable features of the authorship, intention, and original meaning of the orphaned texts collected by the investigators.

The administration's defenders claimed that the Iran-contra affair was nothing more than a political dispute and not a scandal resulting from the discovery of serious transgressions. When giving testimony at the hearings, North and his lawyer, Brendan Sullivan, worked vigorously to turn the interrogation into a scene in which an accused hero was being confronted by a powerful group of bureaucrats. The pragmatic conditions for such a transformation were negotiated in part by Sullivan and North before the hearings, but these conditions were articulated and expanded during the hearings themselves. North's discursive triumphs, and the allowances that were made for them by the committee, were not simply a consequence of his conversational virtuosity. The clearing for his oft-quoted sound bytes and video posturings was secured through aggressive maneuverings by his legal staff and allies on the committee. And he was aided immeasurably by his quick identification as the "hero that America needs" by various press agents.

North and his lawyers used the tension between evidence and testimony as a resource for problematizing a civics lesson forecast by the tribunal's explicit procedural design and its historical precedent (the Watergate hearings). By exploiting equivocalities in documents already designed, erased, or shredded in order to preserve plausible deniability, and by enlisting the themes of right-wing popular culture, North managed to convert the spectacle of the hearings into a forum for his dubious heroism. While it may seem perverse to call him and his allies "applied deconstructionists," it is clear that North, his colleagues in the CIA and NSC staffs, his legal representatives, and his employers at the White House, all worked doggedly (and with success) to problematize the committee's treatment of particular documents as factual evidence.[22] Their substantive methods of deconstruction included the recording, collecting, redacting, and shredding of materials that formed the documentary basis of the subsequent investigations. The result was a body of testimony that supported at least two plausible yet incommensurable versions of events. As it turned out, the committee produced two reports, a majority report consisting of a chronology of events followed by a set of recommendations, and a shorter minority report that, on selected topics, specified an alternative version. The very existence of this second version substantiated the claim that the hearings were essentially a political dispute and not a bipartisan investigation of "the facts."

Our aim in this study is to describe, and not to undermine, the production of history. In this case, the committee majority's task of writing the official history of a scandal already was undermined by a deconstructionist effort on the part of the majority's opposition. Consequently, deconstruction does not identify our own methodological agenda, but instead it is a perspicuous feature of the struggle we describe. We shall assume an ability to describe and exhibit recognizable features of the video text we have chosen to examine. In this effort we shall inevitably engage in constructive (i.e., productive) practices, such as using the video text as a proxy for the live performances of interrogators and witnesses, and selectively using written transcripts to exhibit recurrent discursive actions. Our descriptive claims and expository devices can, of course, be criticized in their own right. They are no less subject to a skeptical mode of deconstruction than any other investigation. Although it is commonplace in the social sciences to lay out a set of methodological procedures that provide reasonable foundations for the selection and interpretation of data, in this study we trust that readers will be able to discern our methods by reference to what we say about the subject matter. Our methods are organized around, and take many of their initiatives from, the complexity and circumstances of the case at hand. Although it is fashionable to attribute latent epistemologies to a text or practice being analyzed, ethnomethodology's approach to practical action and practical reasoning is more in line with the Aristotelian concept of "phronesis." Unlike episteme—the geometrical method of deducing proofs from axioms—phronesis takes its departure from the conventional recognizability of a perspicuous case. The presumption is that a community of readers will grasp enough of the details in question, with no need to justify such understanding on ultimate grounds, so that relevant maxims and precedents can be brought to bear on the case and extended to others like it. The failure of such a method to live up to the universal standards of procedure and proof associated with Euclidean geometry carries no necessary stigma. Indeed, it can be argued that science and mathematics do not fully exemplify episteme, and that at the moment of their production all inquiries involve an effort to come to terms with relevant circumstances. Ethnomethodology makes a topic of cases under inquiry in law, medicine, science, and daily life. This does not necessarily place the ethnomethodologist at a metaphysical or epistemological advantage vis-à-vis the practical actions studied, since any analysis of such actions is itself responsible for coming to terms with the circumstantially specific and immanently recognizable features of the case before it.[23]

When discussing questions and answers, modes of verbal recollection, stories, documents, and the relevance of truth in testimony, it should be obvious that we are not making use of a discrete analytical method that defines the general structures of narrative or that specifies criteria and decision rules that enable us to say, for instance, that a particular utterance is in fact a "question." In the course of our discussions we shall criticize some of the extant structural theories of discourse. It is not our intention, however, to replace one structural theory with another. Instead, we shall rely on our readers to know, for instance, what questions look like, and to use such commonplace understandings to recognize from transcribed examples some of the nonobvious and subtle ways in which testimony is organized. Everything we shall examine is, in its own field of production, a vernacular achievement: a production in a language common to the speakers and various constituencies that make up the audience; a production whose analytical elements—questions, stories, recollections, documentary exhibits, and the like—are themselves organized as vernacular objects designed to be used and recognized by masters of the common language. Practical problems, and sometimes fierce contests, concerning the sense and identity of such vernacular objects often arise in an adversarial discourse, but unless we aim to solve such problems and adjudicate such disputes we should have no reason to stipulate normative or analytical criteria that set up a more rigorous or enlightened vantage point.[24] In view of the fact that so much social-scientific, literary, and philosophical effort has been devoted to getting to the bottom of discourse, our aim of sticking to the surface of the text may strike some readers as curious. It is our view, however, that any deeper readings would have to ignore the complexity and texture of the surface events, and thus they would fail to explicate how an order of activities is achieved as a contingent, moment-by-moment production. As in any study, the substantiation of our preliminary argument is to be found by reading and assessing the chapters that follow.

The book is organized into seven chapters, each of which takes up a specific theme related to the interplay of truth, history, discourse, and memory at the hearings. The book also contains a Methodological Appendix, which surveys some relevant aspects of ethnomethodology and conversation analysis as they bear upon the discourse at the hearings. We placed such discussions in the appendix to avoid sidetracking the substantive and thematic continuity of the chapters.

Chapter 1 discusses one of the most salient issues at the hearings, the matter of lying. North admitted to having lied in the past when he testified at the hearings, but he attempted to justify his lies as necessary for protecting "the American people" against the nation's "enemies." He also suggested that such dangers might apply to his present testimony, although he also professed to be telling the truth. What North said in words was only part of the story. As many journalists reported, his bodily comportment (military poses, fascinating facial displays, and committed expressions) visibly exuded sincerity, and he and his legal staff brilliantly exploited the

spatio-temporal frame of the televisual production to challenge the committee's mandate to produce a bipartisan account of a historical event. The
analysis in chapter 1 examines how North's testimony relentlessly tied
questions about truth and lying to questions about political struggle, including the struggle then under way between himself and his interrogators.

Chapter 2 takes up the topic of history. Following the new historiogra-
phers and others, we argue that historical writing depends on conventional
methods for constituting significant, relevant, intelligible, and coherent
narratives. Unlike others who concentrate mainly on the problems of professional historical writing, we locate the problem of writing history with
the Iran-contra committee's mandate to get the facts and write a report.
Moreover, we argue that the tasks and difficulties of writing history pervaded the hearings, both thematically and organizationally, as testimony
was given for the record and was held answerable to a massive accumulation of documents and prior testimonies. Our analysis shows that the often
contentious dialogues in the televised portions of the hearings highlighted
some of the methodological difficulties faced by the committee while it
tried to convert testimonies into a coherent master narrative.

Chapter 3 examines the public spectacle at the hearings. We focus particularly on the first day of North's testimony because many of the early
exchanges established North's on-camera persona and adumbrated the
themes he and his interrogators continued to debate. Moreover, those
opening moments laid the groundwork for converting an interrogation of a
prime suspect into a political debate. Borrowing from Foucault's illuminating discussions of the "ceremonial of truth" and the "examination," we
conceptualize the hearings as a public spectacle in which the body of the
witness (the televised talking head) "provides the synthesis of the reality of
the deeds and the truth of the investigation, of the documents of the case
and the statements of the [witness]."[25] Despite the different historical eras,
Foucault's vivid explication of the spectacle of the scaffold suggests some
features of the contemporary televised hearing, particularly its design as a
civics lesson. In addition, just as the unstable field of rituals and stigmata
on the scaffold at the public execution provided the condemned criminal
with the opportunity to go to his death as a redeemed hero, rebellious
martyr, repentant soul, or unrepentant scoundrel, so the publicly televised
ceremonial of truth—arranged to get to the bottom of a political scan-

dal—provided North with opportunities to construct counternarratives in which he stood as a righteous hero, victim of unwarranted accusations, and scapegoat.

Chapter 4 outlines the pragmatic structure of interrogation. Interrogation is formally structured according to a rule that prescribes the counsel to ask questions and the witness to respond directly to each question in turn. An examination of recorded testimony shows, however, that interlocutors use this rule in an occasional and sometimes contentious way. Many of counsel's utterances are stated flatly as assertions that build toward accusations and/or challenges to the witness's testimony. In cross-examination and related modes of adversary interrogation, a series of questions can produce a dilemma for the witness. Each question is designed to solicit confirmation of the adversarial case and to dramatize the implausibility of disconfirmation. As North's testimony demonstrates, however, witnesses have resources to resist and evade this dilemma. North challenges the terms of the questions, qualifies his answers, and uses such "answers" as an occasion for developing long statements and speeches combating the interrogator's claims and entitlements.

Chapter 5 examines stories told in testimony. A witness narrates stories about events in question, which in some respects are organized like stories told in ordinary conversation. In both instances, the stories typically place the speaker within the narrative field (often as hero, or main character) and elaborate events centered on the speaker/character's place in the scene of action. Such stories also are marked by the current occasion of the telling: the situation, the addressees' identities and actions, and the topical relevancies supplied by previous stories. The speaker typically is the main character, or a close relation to the main character, and the story otherwise displays the speaker's special access to the events and identities in the narrative. Such stories centered on the speaker/character differ systematically from a master narrative of what actually happened. This difference was a dynamic part of the interrogation of North and other key witnesses. The potential rupture between biography and history was a key site for a contentious struggle between the principals in the hearings.

Chapter 6 looks at recall as a discursive production in testimony. In our treatment, a witness's avowals of recall are not simply the verbal endproducts of chains of cognitive acquisition, storage, and retrieval. What North's (and also Poindexter's) testimony makes clear is that verbal formats for recalling, or failing to recall, memories are *moves* within testimony. One thing done in testimony by disavowals of recall is nicely summed up by North's phrase: "I'm not saying that I did, I don't say that I didn't." Failures to recall provide a way out of the witness's dilemma (as discussed in chapter 4). However, the use of such disavowals is also constrained by standards of what ought to be remembered under the circumstances. This constraint is less than ironclad, and when the audience is divided along highly partisan lines, it becomes especially difficult to define unequivocal standards of reasonability.

Chapter 7 continues on the topic of memory, focusing on the relationship between spoken testimony and the memoranda collected by the committee. Interrogators use written exhibits to leverage testimony out of the witness. Much of the interrogation focused on detailed features of particular documents, such as the famous "diversion memoranda" with which President Reagan may have authorized profits from covert arms sales to be diverted to aid the Nicaraguan contras at a time when government aid had been prohibited by Congress. The interrogatory dialogues about this document and others exhibited a kind of pragmatic and situated hermeneutic as the interlocutors explored the heterogeneous surfaces of the documents. Relevant issues included authorship and authority for writing, organizational place and dispersion of texts, responsibilities for reading and signing, histories of particular marks and signatures, and references to identities and entitlements to read them. The voluminous mass of documents itself became an issue insofar as North/Sullivan professed unfamiliarity with particular documents from that mass, thus setting up North's avowals of imprecise and "unrefreshed" recall of the events in question. No less significantly, some documents, such as those that North may have shredded, were referenced in their absence. Insofar as what North "recalled" in his testimony was leveraged from records, the missing memoranda were part and parcel of his imprecise memory, and his motives for shredding and for failing to recall relevant details that the documents might have included became terminally contentious.

In the conclusion we take stock of the indecisive aftermath of the hearings and suggest that the most tangible outcome was a civics lesson in the logic of sleaze. "Sleaze," of course, is a pejorative term for corruption. We use it somewhat more playfully, to describe a kind of lubricant operating at the interface between the legal-rational machinery of the state and the situated production of contingent events. In contrast to trust, which supports and vindicates binary values, sleaze negates them while resisting clear resolution in terms of truth or falsity, rightness or wrongness, and guilt or innocence. As our analyses of testimony demonstrate, the binary logic of the committee's truth-finding machinery was unable to handle the plausibly deniable fragments of evidence, heroic counternarratives, and irresolvable testimony. This is not the whole story, but we believe that this case study provides a starting point for a history of the present that focuses on cultural sites in which residues of a classical spectacle are revived by novel arrangements of the technology of surveillance.

1. THE SINCERE LIAR

In the seventeenth century it was accepted that honesty and sincerity could not be communicated. Anyone claiming to be honest would at the same time give off the impression that there might be doubts about it.
—Niklas Luhmann[1]

"I'm not trying to dissemble at all with you."—Oliver North

The Iran-contra story is largely about lies, secrecy, and deception. Oliver North and the other principal characters in the story admitted to withholding evidence, writing false chronologies, and shredding documents. They described elaborate methods for securing and hiding caches of funds and conducting covert operations under pretext. Most interestingly for our purposes, they admitted that these activities were designed to enable "plausible deniability." In other words, according to North's testimony, rather than simply hiding their activities from scrutiny, he and his White House and CIA colleagues prospectively constructed a field of evidence to mislead future inquiries. They anticipated the possibility of an official investigation or other threat of exposure, and they set up their pretexts, alibis, and paper trails accordingly. The testimony about these practices, together with a set of problems associated with the interpretation of such testimony, provide a striking exhibit of how actions *in* history reflexively become entangled with the investigation *of* history.

Naturally enough, the investigating committee, the journalists who covered the hearings, and many members of the audience remained curious as to whether North and his fellow operatives were coming clean in their testimony or continuing to dissemble, dissimulate, and withhold significant evidence. This issue came to a head early during the first day of North's testimony on July 7, 1987, when House majority counsel John Nields directly challenged North for having difficulty recalling any details about the records from his office he destroyed shortly after the scandal became public.

Nields: Well that's the whole reason for shredding documents, isn't it, Colonel North, so that you can later say you don't remember, (0.4) whether you had 'em, and you don't remember what's in 'em.

North: No, Mister Nields, the reason for shredding documents, and the reason the Government of the United States gave me a shredder, I mean I didn't buy it myself, was to destroy documents that were no longer relevant, that did not apply or that should not be divulged. And again I want to go back to the whole intent of the covert operation. Part of (in- eh) a covert operation is to offer plausible deniability of the association of the government of the United States with the activity, part of it is to deceive our adversaries. Part of it is to insure that those people who are at great peril, carrying out those activities are not further endangered. All of those are good and sufficient reasons to destroy documents. And that's why the government buys shredders by the tens and dozens. And gives them to people running covert operations. Not so that they can have convenient memories. I came here to tell you the truth. To tell you:: and this committee, and the American people the truth, and I'm trying to do that Mister Nields, °hh and I don't like the insinuation that I'm up here having a convenient memory lapse, like perhaps some others have had.

Nields: Colonel North, you shredded these documents on the Twenty-first of November, Nineteen-eighty-six, isn't that true? (1.2)

North: Try me again on the date. (1.0)

Nields: Friday, the Twenty-first of November, Nineteen-eighty-six. (1.8)

Nields: I started shredding documents as early as:: uh my return from Europe in October (0.4)

North: I have absolutely no recollection (0.2) when those documents were des- were shredded. None whatsoever.=

Nields: =There's been testimony before the committee that you engaged in shredding of documents on November the Twenty-first, Nineteen-eighty-six.

North: [(as-)

        [

Nields: [Do you deny that?

North: I do *not* deny that I engaged in shredding on November Twenty-first. (1.2) I will also tell this committee that I engaged in shredding (.) almost every day that I had a shredder. And that I put things in burn bags when I didn't. (0.8) So, every single day that I was at the National Security Counsel Staff, some documents were destroyed. (0.6) And I don't want you to- to have the impression (0.2) that (.) those documents that I referred to (0.2) seeking approval, disappeared on the Twenty-first, 'cause I can't say that.

This exchange is rich with pragmatic moves that recurred throughout North's testimony: failures to recall significant details, temporal reframings of acknowledged actions and events, and self-righteous proclamations in response to questions and challenges. We shall revisit these moves at length, but for the present we shall observe only how North denies what Nields suggests is the "whole reason" for his apparent inability to remember significant details of the matter in question. Nields's initial challenge suggests that history was being fabricated from both ends: from a retrospective vantage point in the present, and from an anticipatory one in the past. North's present testimony fails to recall certain details from his past, and as an actor in the past he may have shredded documentary evidence of those same details. North counteracts this scenario by giving an alternative rationale for his shredding-as-usual on the date in question. Not only that, he expresses strong indignation at the very suggestion that he could be dissimulating, and, in a memorable evocation of truthfulness and patriotism, he reaffirms his will to tell the truth.

Sequences of testimony like this one create a number of analytic temptations, two of which immediately come to mind. First, it is tempting to declare that North certainly is lying, and then to give an account of how his lies can be made visible through an inspection of his words and body behavior, together with a reconstruction of what he must have known. Second, there is the temptation to politicize the question of lying by subordinating truth to a clash of ideologies. These analytic paths are temptations not because they are likely to lead to error, but because they would be all too easy to pursue with the materials at hand. The problem with yielding to such temptations is that one settles presumptively what often remains contentious and unresolved at the surface of the testimony. In contrast, we want to investigate how the parties to the testimony employed the distinction between truth and lying, and how they articulated the opposition between politics and value neutrality.

LIES, TRUTH-TELLING, AND TESTIMONY

During North's unsuccessful run for a U.S. Senate seat in Virginia in 1994, virtually every journalist, writer, and commentator who did not agree with his politics, as well as many others who did, went on record to say that he lied or deliberately concealed what he knew during the Iran-contra hear-

ings, and many accused him of being a pathological liar. Notable in this
context was Robert McFarlane's characterization of North as "an Elmer
Gantry without peer . . . a man not suited for public life." Nevertheless, the
widely shared suspicion that North lied, or even that he was an inveterate
liar, does not equip us to inspect the record of his 1987 testimony in order
to find just when and just how he was lying. We say this not to admit a
failure of analysis (or of nerve), but to identify a salient feature of the
testimony itself. The conclusion that North or any of the other witnesses
lied, or must have lied, at some point in the testimony settles very little,
and it reveals even less about the way credibility is built up or undermined
in testimony. Like others who viewed the Iran-contra hearings, we were
able to see that some of the things North said were corroborated by other
testimonies and documents, while others were not, and we have read a
number of accounts that impugned North's credibility on matters of trivial,
as well as major, importance. Judgments nevertheless differ about the extent, justifiability, and consequences of his lying. For some people the
acknowledged and alleged lying mattered a great deal, but for others not at
all. North's own admissions during his 1987 testimony that he lied in the
past certainly did *not* diminish his credibility for major elements of the
U.S. public. Instead, the forthright way he made those admissions apparently enhanced his credibility, although perhaps only for those in the audience who were inclined to support him on other grounds. Given the
traditional conception of the man of honor whose social standing essentially depends on a steadfast truthfulness, this is a curious matter. It would
be all too easy to condemn North as a hypocrite, and to dismiss his supporters as a band of fanatical ideologues, but to do so would obscure the fact
that he and his allies managed to sustain a counterdrama of truthfulness
and sincerity even while North disclosed an elaborate scheme of lies and
deceptions designed to thwart the very sort of inquiry the committee was
conducting. Both as a logical and historical matter, this tangled relationship between deception and revelation is far more interesting to explore
than the mere fact of North's lying.

Although we shall recount some stories about North's lying, and we shall
delve into some of the reasons given for suspecting or concluding that he
lied, we do not intend to conduct a rump perjury trial under academic
auspices. We are not nearly as well equipped for such a task as was Special
Prosecutor Lawrence Walsh, who headed an extensive criminal investiga-

tion of North and several of the story's other main characters.[2] Walsh did successfully convict North for lying to congress, but not in his testimony at the hearings, and even those convictions were overturned on appeal. We are more prepared (and inclined) to explore how truth, lies, and related matters were made relevant and practically managed in and through the testimony. Consequently, we shall describe how the parties to the hearings produced and contested the factual, moral, and political grounds for truth-telling and lying.

Although the concept of lying calls into play questions about truth or falsity, the grammatical relationship between truth-telling and lying is not a simple binary opposition between making true and false statements. In ordinary English usage, "to lie" is to commit an act. There is no equivalent verb "to truth." One can tell the truth, be truthful, speak truthfully, or withhold the truth, but "truth" is not a verb; it is grammatically positioned beyond the compass of an act. In contrast, lies and lying actively distort, cover up, or depart from a more natural, omnirelevant truth.[3] Because of the way this picture of truth and lying is deeply entrenched in language, it is not equivalent to a belief or theory of meaning that can be changed or overthrown through argument. It pervades the very syntax of argumentative conduct.

As usually defined, a lie involves two essential ingredients: (1) a contradiction (or notable difference) between a statement and the relevant facts, and (2) a judgment that the speaker knows the relevant facts and deliberately acts to conceal or misrepresent them.[4] This definition presupposes the possibility of distinguishing the facts of the matter from what is said about them and deciding that the speaker knows the difference and intends to mislead the recipient(s) of the lie. An element of responsibility thus is associated with lying, whereas responsibility for truth-telling is made explicit only in circumstances where doubt or special difficulty might arise. Truth has default status.[5]

The picture gets more complicated when we consider the family of concepts associated with lying in ethical, legal, and ordinary discourse: fabrication (simulation), deceptiveness, mendacity, dissembling, and dissimulation. These terms bring into play different modes of operation and variable degrees of culpability. At the Iran-contra hearings the term most often used in connection with lying in testimony was to "dissemble" (to speak in a way that conceals the reality of the events in question). Although dissembling or dissimulation (concealing one's motives or knowledge) should be prohibited under the oath to tell the whole truth in testimony, they nevertheless tend to be associated with lesser degrees of guilt and less severe accusations. Richard Nixon, for example, is said to have objected to the charge that he lied, while being willing to acknowledge that dissembling—concealing his opinions, motives, and knowledge—was an inevitable part of his dealings with other world leaders.[6]

In courtrooms, congressional hearings, and many other areas of modern life, the criteria formulated by John Locke continue to describe heuristic grounds for assessing credibility: "the number of witnesses, their integrity, their skill at presenting evidence, and its agreement with the circumstances, and lastly, the presence or absence of contrary testimony."[7] In practice, it can be difficult, and at times impossible, to tell the difference between truthful and untruthful testimony. Such difficulty is part and parcel of courtroom drama. A typical courtroom trial includes conflicting testimonies given before jurors who are supposed to have no knowledge of "what really happened" aside from what they gather from the evidence presented to them in situ. In some cases, most notoriously with rape trials, the only eyewitness accounts of what happened are supplied by the conflicting testimonies of the implicated parties, and when the defendant chooses not to testify, credibility judgments are focused on the alleged victim. In such cases, a witness's performance on the stand is crucial.

Unlike the jurors at North's 1989 criminal trial who were selected under the condition that they were substantially uninformed of North's involvements in the highly publicized Iran-contra affair, the members of the Senate and House committees were well informed about, and sometimes implicated in, the events being investigated. Like courtroom jurors, however, they professed to have no direct knowledge of many of the covert actions that North described in his testimony, and as uninvolved parties they made various efforts to corroborate his testimony with other testimonies, written documents, photographs, and other forms of evidence. Like jurors, they had little alternative but to accept or reject the witness's testimony on the basis of surface or face-value assessments of credibility and plausibility. As we will discuss, in chapters on the organization of questions, answers, and the discursive production of "recollections," the production and assessment of testimony involves binary yes-or-no judgments. At the same time, however, interrogators, witnesses, and their overhearers contend with a slippery field of discourse in which efforts to *exclude the middle* between the binary poles of yes or no, true or false, and guilty or not guilty become difficult to bring off.

NORTH'S CHARACTER AND NORTH'S LIES

The strong suspicion that North lied during the hearings can be supported by citing his own admissions about his past actions. He admitted to having intentionally misinformed members of Congress during meetings a year before the hearings. He also admitted to shredding many of the files in his office prior to, and even during, the attorney general's investigation of the emerging scandal in November 1986, and he explicitly described an entire containment strategy devised by the late CIA chief William Casey. According to this fall guy plan, North (and, if necessary, someone a step higher in the NSC staff hierarchy) would take the blame for the most scandalous aspects of the administration's covert weapons sales and fund-raising activities. Although North disclosed this plan in his testimony, he and his immediate boss, John Poindexter, may have continued to enact it. As specified in the plan, albeit not necessarily because of the plan, Poindexter eventually took responsibility for authorizing the diversion of funds to the contras. The records that survived the shredder and that were released to the committee did not contradict Poindexter's testimony. Casey, the alleged author of the plan, died of a brain tumor just as the hearings began. In this and related aspects of the Iran-contra story, the disclosure of strategies did not negate the possibility of their continued enactment.

After the hearings, North's credibility was further impugned by the fact that he was convicted on three criminal charges, two of which had to do with deceiving Congress and destroying evidence.[8] However, these convictions were overturned on appeal because of the possibility that evidence North gave under immunity at the hearings had influenced the testimony of witnesses at his criminal trial. Numerous other lies are documented in books and articles about the Iran-contra affair. Theodore Draper, for example, musters documentary evidence to support his charge that North lied in a "most unconscionable" way when he told the attorney general in 1986 that the Israelis initially suggested the idea of diverting funds from Iranian arms sales to aid the contras.[9]

In addition to chronicling the official lies that North told in the capacity

of a government operative, several writers noted that he seemed to have a
general penchant for fictionalizing his supposedly heroic past. In an un-
authorized biography of North published shortly after the Iran-contra hearings, Ben Bradlee Jr. noted:

> Aside from North's admitted lying to Congress about the contras, his admit-
> ted lying to the Iranians, his admitted falsifying of the Iran initiative chro-
> nology, his admitted shredding of documents and his admitted lying to vari-
> ous administration officials as the Iran-contra affair unraveled in November
> of 1986, there are stories, statements or claims that he has made to vari-
> ous people while at the National Security Council that are either untrue,
> strongly denied, or unconfirmable and thought to be untrue.[10]

Bradlee then recounts several of these lies, including North's gross exag-
gerations of how often he met with the president (including an apparently
fictitious evening spent together in the White House living quarters watching television coverage of the U.S. invasion of Grenada), stories about
meetings and conversations with important officials such as Kissinger and
Philip Habib (who denied that such meetings ever happened), tales of
derring-do such as North's piloting a small plane and making a hair-raising
rescue of wounded Salvadoran soldiers under fire from guerrillas, and
even a story about how his dog died. "Ollie told numerous people, including the FBI, that the dog had been poisoned—presumably by those whom
he said had been threatening his life. But one of North's neighbors told the
Los Angeles Times that the dog had actually just died of cancer. 'It got old
and died,' the neighbor said. 'Ollie told everybody it died for effect.'"[11]

Constantine Menges, one of North's former NSC colleagues, also recounted a number of incidents such as the following story attributed to
Jacqueline Tillman, a staff colleague, who concluded that North not only
was a liar, but "delusional, power-hungry":

> In the summer of 1984 Tillman told me a disturbing story. A journalist friend
> of hers had described, in colorful detail, certain events that occurred during
> Secretary of State George Shultz's flight to Nicaragua in June 1984. In a
> casual office chat, she had related the events to Ollie. About two weeks later,
> Ollie told her the same stories and said that a journalist who had been on
> Shultz's plane had related this to him.
>
> Startled, Tillman reminded Ollie that she had originally told him this

story. Yet Ollie insisted, for about 20 minutes, that this had been his rather than her experience. When she told me about this, she was worried for him: Ollie seemed to be having trouble distinguishing between his fantasies and objective reality.[12]

This story has an unusual twist. Tillman charges not only that North lied, but that he preempted her entitlement to mediate a story first told to her, and he later denied that he had done so. In Menges's account, Tillman originally heard the story from a journalist and relayed it secondhand, while North, instead of telling the story thirdhand, eliminated Tillman's mediation and told it as his secondhand story. According to Tillman's objections, North's heroic biography is inflated through a kind of hostile takeover of the storytelling entitlements of others; he absorbs others' experiences into his own inflated biography. Like the actor-president he served, who reportedly recalled the actions of characters in World War II films as though they were his own deeds, North was accused of collapsing the distinction between fiction and real life, or more precisely, assimilating the experience of a character in a story into recollections of his own past.[13]

Many of these anecdotes impugn North's credibility on the basis of stories told by others who presumably had no reason to fabricate them. North, or one of his defenders, could of course try to discount each story by attributing professional jealousy, journalistic bias, and political hostility to the particular sources. Although each anecdote may have little weight on its own, the inventories of lies that Bradlee, Menges, and others have chronicled portray a consistent picture of North as someone actively constructing a heroic biography in which he is a man of great influence within a circle of powerful insiders, and that he is someone who is continually threatened by equally powerful adversaries. Moreover, the suggestion that he had trouble distinguishing between "his fantasies and objective reality" raises the possibility that he is the sort of person who would testify forthrightly and unself-consciously about events that never occurred and deeds he never performed. The case against North is strengthened by the fact that many of those who have impugned his credibility are not his "liberal" detractors. They include, for example, columnist George Will, who is quoted as saying "[h]e is completely unable to tell what the truth is," and a conservative activist, Woody Holton, who avows, "[t]he simple fact is that you cannot believe what he tells you." When North's 1994 campaign for the

U.S. Senate began to look as if it could be successful, even former President Reagan and Nancy Reagan impugned his credibility.[14]

Given the significance of truth-telling in communications from important officials about matters of national interest, many investigators and media commentators expressed concern about the dissembling, dissimulation, secrecy, shredding, and fabrication of chronologies that featured so prominently in the Iran-contra story. For many, this proliferation of lying and deception signaled a breakdown of the public trust traditionally deemed so necessary for order in a civil, democratic society; it also seemed relevant to contemporary worries about an increasing public cynicism about politics and politicians.[15] If poll results are to be believed, however, the publicity about North's (alleged) lies did not, and still does not, seem to have dampened the enthusiasm expressed about him and his views among a substantial proportion of U.S. citizens. A *USA Today* poll taken at the time of the hearings had 58,863 of the national newspaper's readers agreeing that Ollie was "honest, and deserved a medal," while only 1,756 put him down as "a liar" who "ought to go to jail." This, of course, is not a representative sample, and the results may tell us more about the readership of the newspaper than the population at large. However, perhaps it does indicate something about North's nascent constituency and the media vehicles through which its views were expressed. A *Newsweek* poll taken shortly after the hearings indicated a somewhat more nuanced picture. A majority of the people polled agreed that North was not "telling the whole truth," but they also tended to agree that he was acting in the line of duty to protect others and not himself.[16] A majority also agreed with a characterization of North as "well-meaning," even though he "did things that were illegal." Despite North's admissions of lying, and despite suspicions that he continued to lie at the hearings, his testimony apparently enhanced his credibility for a large proportion of his audience. In a typical example of North hagiography, the editors of *U.S. News and World Report* celebrated the miraculous transformation of North's reputation from a shadowy operative and suspected liar to a media hero.

> That North and his combative attorney, Brendan Sullivan, had managed this coup is a bit of a media miracle. In the seven months he had lived in self-imposed silence about his role in the Iran-Contra affair, North had become the subject of public accusations, intense speculation and an underground

whispering campaign that had turned his public image into that of a petty chiseler, inveterate liar, political naif and international cowboy. He was portrayed as a lean, mean, fighting machine gone haywire, running his own foreign policy from a third-floor office in the Old Executive Office Building, oblivious to policy, protocols, and presidential directives, not to mention public law.

But in his six days of gripping congressional testimony, North gave future witnesses a textbook performance on how to change a public persona and recraft a personal image. Simply put, he not only was a national hero, he became a national sensation accomplishing a stunning role reversal from the accused to the accuser that outdid in its breathtaking speed even Richard Nixon's recovery with his legendary "Checkers" speech.[17]

By all indications, North's image has held up over the years. A poll taken during North's 1994 Senate campaign indicated that 45 percent of the sample had favorable feelings toward him. (This also indicated that a large proportion of the sample did not express this opinion, and news commentaries in the aftermath of the 1994 election frequently mentioned that his lying was one of the most frequently given reasons by those not voting for him.) When quoted by the press, his supporters tended to express far more cynicism about "establishment" figures in the federal government and national press corps than about North. In addition to the tokens of support collected by polling organizations, large amounts of money have flowed North's way. According to one estimate, North's senatorial campaign accumulated $25 million before his Republican primary victory, and without significant business backing. He is said to earn $1.7 million per year from speaking engagements and his two books. Estimates of his personal assets top $3 million, and his estate on Shenandoah Mountain is valued at $1.2 million.[18]

It is tempting to regard North's popular support as inauthentic, as the result of media manipulation of a credulous mass by a rhetorically adept, telegenic liar-hero. Although much can be said in favor of such an interpretation, it misses something we consider crucial to the political logic of testimony. This is the differential distribution of assessments of truth, honesty, and rightness, and of expressions and relations of trust, which became prominent both within North's testimony and by reference to it. These distributions were not simply present as stable divisions within the body

politic, they were actively mobilized in and through the discursive struggle between interrogator and witness. Journalists coined the expression
"Ollie's army" to describe the vocal constituency recruited immediately
after North's first day of testimony. No other army was officially mentioned, so one might get the picture of an unopposed army's march through
undefended civilian territory. North and his support team tended to emphasize a different balance of forces, as his attorney, Brendan Sullivan,
repeatedly mentioned the committee's immense resources and powers.
North made populist appeals to his band of militia, opposing them to powers of an elite organization. North's justifications for lying turned on a
rhetorical instantiation of the Foucauldian equation of truth with political
struggle and of power with war. As Foucault expresses his inversion of
Clauswitz's aphorism: "power is war, a war continued by other means."[19]
Considered as a contingent achievement, rather than a general hypothesis,
this equation invites us to examine just how it was brought off in the
testimony. In what follows, we examine how questions about truth and
deception were subordinated to reflexive political assessments of the hearings themselves.

THE LIAR PARADOX

North presented his interlocutors on the committee with a mundane variant of the classic liar paradox, which Saul Kripke summarizes: "If, as the
author of the Epistle of Titus supposes (Titus I, 12), a Cretan prophet, 'even
a prophet of their own,' asserted that 'the Cretans are always liars,' and if
'this testimony is true' of all other Cretan utterances, then it seems that the
Cretan prophet's words are true if and only if they are false. And any
treatment of the concept of truth must somehow circumvent this paradox."[20] The traditional conception of this paradox dissolves when more
mundane relevancies are considered, but it does serve to introduce some
relevant aspects of North's admitted lying.[21] The paradox hinges upon an
understanding of the expression "the Cretans are always liars" as referring
to every utterance that has a truth value which is made by a Cretan. In a
more ordinary sense, however, to call someone a liar does not imply that
every statement made by that person is false.[22] Instead, the assumption that
the statement is spoken by a liar becomes salient as a background condition for assigning to the statement the possible status of a lie. At worst, the

assertion "the Cretans are always liars" when said (nonironically) by a Cretan may be viewed with suspicion by someone who knows the reputation of its source, but it would not be paradoxical in any strict sense. To sustain the logician's paradox, we are required to understand the words "always liars" to mean that every statement said by every Cretan is without exception untrue, and this simply is not required by a more ordinary sense of those words (not to speak of the difficulties it would create for communication among the Cretans).[23] When understood in this way, the paradox is not amenable to a truth-conditional analysis. This lack of amenability to analysis does not imply that ordinary language is deficient or self-contradictory with respect to the concept of truth.[24]

This mundane conception of the liar paradox dissolves the logical strictures necessary for setting up the paradox in the first place, but it also enables us to specify how a suspected (or admitted) liar like North may "circumvent" (to borrow Kripke's term but not his sense of the task) any implication of self-contradiction in his present testimony. The suspicion that an admitted liar is currently telling a lie is subject to judgments of relevance. For example, a person may be reputed to lie persistently in the context of a marital relationship, but not to lie when conducting certain business transactions. What such a person says may be accepted without question when the present occasion evidently has no relation to other occasions in which the speaker has been known to lie. Moreover, even when the present occasion may seem to be like others in which the speaker was known to lie, the speaker may allay such suspicions with assurances about how the present occasion is "really different" *this time.*

Accordingly, even if we were to suppose that North lied frequently while testifying at the hearings, it would not allow us to say that his testimony was untrue at every point, and we assume that this inability was endemic to the situation. North testified at the hearings under partial immunity from criminal prosecution, but he was not immune from charges of perjury. For a number of reasons, including that of his legal liability, whether or not he was lying to his interrogators was pertinent. The question surfaced several times during the hearings, as well as in many commentaries about them. But while he acknowledged lying in the past, these very admissions were presented, and by all indications accepted, as sincere and truthful testimony.

North freely and righteously admitted that he told lies that were associated with good reasons. Even when acknowledging that lying to Congress on an earlier occasion was wrong, he declared that the lies were motivated out of a concern to protect his clandestine activities from publicity that would "damage national interests" and threaten the lives of agents abroad. In North's summary formulation, it was a choice between "lies or lives." He used other justifications for false testimony, which could have applied to the present one. During his first morning of testimony, while being interrogated by House majority counsel John Nields, North characterized the present hearings in a way that could justify dissimulation. Nields had just suggested that certain of the covert activities in which North was involved were "designed to be kept a secret from the American people."[25]

North: I- I think what- what is important, uh Mister Nields is that- we somehow arrive at some kind of an understanding right here and now, as to what a covert operation is. If we could find a way to insulate with a bubble over these *hear*ings that are being broadcast in Moscow, uh- a- and *talk* about covert operations to the American people without it getting into the hands of our adversaries, I'm sure we would *do* that.

Shortly afterward, he elaborated further on what a covert operation is:

North: By their very nature covert operations or special activities are a lie. There is great deceit, deception practiced in the conduct of covert operations. They are in essence a lie. . . . The effort to conduct these covert operations was made in such a way that our adversaries would not have knowledge of them, or that we could deny American association with it, or the association of this government with those activities. And that is not wrong.[26]

The term "bubble" in the above passage may be a technical reference to a particular room where high-security depositions were taken. Although North did not give a deposition before testifying, John Poindexter did. An account of Poindexter's deposition to the committee investigators includes a description of a kind of Foucauldian architecture: "a specially constructed ninth-floor Senate Office Building security vault called the bubble. Made with panels of aluminum on the outside, with an air conditioning system composed of special 'sound baffling' materials, it was so security-proof that laser devices would not penetrate it. The CIA used something like it for its special interrogations, and this bubble, like theirs, was filled with sophisticated electronic antibugging devices."[27] Given the fact that the hearings were not insulated by such a bubble, North might be heard as giving good reasons for withholding testimony at the present time. As might be expected, several members of the committee objected to North's suggestion that their tribunal might benefit the nation's "adversaries," but throughout the hearings some committee members supported North by making an issue of leaks of confidential information from congressional committees to the press, which then became available to Soviet, Iranian, Libyan, or other "enemy" agents.[28]

Lying to enemies is one of the several types of lies and justifications for lying discussed by Sissela Bok in her popular book on lying. Bok points out that even when no crisis or question of survival exists, "lies to enemies are traditionally accompanied by a special sense of self-evident justification."[29] She adds that liars' classifications of the recipients of their lies as enemies can be taken to paranoid extremes, where the liars "imagine that the public itself constitutes the conspiracy they combat."[30] Public acknowledgment of such lies is precluded by the inclusion of the public (or a proportion of the public that is impossible to segregate from a public communication) among the enemies to whom lies are directed. Bok warns that "the great likelihood of error and discrimination in the selection of who is to count as an enemy necessitates the greatest caution" because indiscriminate use of official lies can generate public cynicism about political leaders.[31] In the present case, whether or not the category "lies to enemies" can be extended from the likes of the Iranians and Soviets to elements of the U.S. Congress and the American people is the very matter in dispute among the parties to the hearings. Both North and his interrogators rhetorically enlist "the American people" on their side of the battlefield. In this case, Bok's warning about the consequences of overextending the category of enemies does not indicate an ethical criterion so much as a contested boundary in the dispute between North and his interrogators. While Bok's discussion nicely illuminates the theme that was in dispute—just how far official lying and secrecy should reasonably extend—in the absence of a nonpartisan adjudication of the dispute, the question of what counts as a relevant enemy for some lie remains a contingent part of the dispute itself.

Even though North did not place the committee squarely on the side of "our adversaries," many in the audience were more than willing to do so.[32] Thousands of angry letters denouncing and even threatening the interrogators for harassing this American hero were sent to congressional offices and newspaper editors. Whether directly or indirectly drawn, this rhetorical link between the committee and "our adversaries" created an interesting interpretative situation. If we juxtapose North's justifications for lying with his repeated and forceful insistence that he *is* telling the truth in his present testimony, we arrive at a variant of the liar paradox.

1. Lying is justified to prevent our adversaries from knowing our secrets.
2. Our adversaries have access to this very testimony.
3. I am not now lying.

This is not a paradox in any purely logical sense. According to this syllogism, the statement "I am not now lying" is not paradoxical in the classic sense of being self-contradictory as a matter of logical necessity. Rather, whenever premises (1) and (2) are accepted as applicable, the assertion "I am not now lying" becomes suspect. Moreover, any attempt to resolve the paradox brings into play fields of relevancy that supersede the problems associated with a strictly defined truth-conditional conception of the matter at hand. Premises (1) and (2) present an opposition between "us" and "our adversaries" that indexes a field of political relevancies for deciding whether or not it is justifiable to lie. The general rule of telling the truth is relativized with respect to that "friend-enemy grouping."[33] Assessing North's testimony then becomes a matter not only of assessing the truth of what he says, but of assessing the immediate relevance and acceptability of the political justifications he gives for lying. North does not strictly delineate the boundaries of the opposition between "us" and "our adversaries." For his audience, an entire array of questions about social categories can become relevant: Who are "our adversaries"? Which secrets should be withheld from these enemies? At any given moment in the course of testimony, should the witness withhold a particular secret he knows? To what extremes can the witness go in order to prevent disclosure by glossing over relevant details or dissembling to keep a particular secret? Consequently, judgments about truth and truthfulness are bound up with an assemblage of political judgments. Moreover, when we consider the interactional production of testimony, this is not a matter of an audience's judgment about what North says at a single point in time; it is, instead, part of an adversary struggle between interrogator and witness, in the presence of various over-hearing audiences to make out what he is saying.

LOCAL RELEVANCE AND CREDIBILITY

Even though the liar paradox never wholly applies in actual testimony, a witness who claims, "I am not now lying," can still face the problem of warding off reflexive implications of admitted lies on earlier, and arguably similar, occasions.[34] This recalls the parable of the boy who cried, "Wolf!" Note, however, that the prudential maxim exemplified by the parable—that the price of being a liar is that others will disbelieve you even when you tell the truth—presupposes that the audience's reaction on this occasion is governed by past occasions on which lies were told. Such serializing of events is, of course, a defeasible matter. Again, we are faced with the problem of relevance. The shepherd boy who cried "Wolf!" was disbelieved when, after falsely doing so before, he cried "Wolf!" once again. The relation between the present and past occasions is presumed to be transparent. We are given no hint in the parable about how the villagers would react to the boy's claims about matters that had little to do with sheep or wolves. Would it occur to anyone to disbelieve his claims about his family heritage or his sexual exploits? Perhaps, but, then again, perhaps not. When considered in the circumstances of testimony, questions of relevance and analogies between situations become part of a discursive contestation. Putting such relevancies and analogies in play, and taking them out of play, takes rhetorical, interactional work.

A poignant demonstration of the contingencies associated with the problem of relevance occurred toward the end of the morning session on the third day of North's testimony when House deputy counsel George Van Cleve asked him to respond to the implications of a litany of the lies that he had previously admitted telling. Van Cleve represented the Republican minority on the committee and conducted his interrogation in a conspicuously friendly way.

(1) Van Cleve: Colonel North, I have the- what I regard is the personal and painful task of asking you the following questions: You've admitted before this committee that you lied to representatives of the Iranians in order to try and release the hostages. Is that correct?

(2) North: I lied every time I met the Iranians.

(3) Van Cleve: And, you've admitted that you lied to General Secord with respect to conversations that you supposedly had with the President? Is that correct?

(4) North: In order to encourage him to stay with the project, yes.

(5) Van Cleve: And, you've admitted that you lied to the Congress. Is that correct?

(6) North: I have.

(7) Van Cleve: And, you admitted that you lied in creating false chronologies of these events. Is that correct?

(8) North: That is true.

(9) Van Cleve: And you've admitted that you created false documents that were intended to mislead investigators with respect to a gift that was made to you. Is that correct?

((North opens his mouth to speak, Sullivan leans over, and the two confer for about 20 seconds))

(10) North: No.

(11) Van Cleve: I think I understand the reason for your hesitation. You certainly have admitted that the documents themselves were completely false. Is that correct?

(12) North: That is correct.

(13) Van Cleve: And, they were intended to create a record of an event that never occurred. Is that correct?

(14) North: That is correct.

(15) Van Cleve: Can you assure this committee that you are not here now lying to protect your Commander in Chief?

(16) North: I am not lying to protect anybody, counsel. I came here to tell the truth. I told you that I was going to tell it to you, the good, the bad, and the ugly. Some of it has been ugly for me. I don't know how many other witnesses have gone through the ordeal that I have before arriving here and seeing their names smeared all over the newspapers, and by some members of this committee, but I committed when I raised my right hand and took an oath as a midshipman that I would tell the truth, and I took an oath when I arrived here before this committee to tell the truth, and I have done so, painful though it may be for me and for others. I have told you the truth, counsel, as best I can.

(17) Van Cleve: I have no further questions for this witness, Mr. Chairman.[35]

This sequence provided an occasion for counsel and witness to repeat topics, themes, and tropes from the previous two days of testimony. In a conspicuously less adversarial way than during House majority counsel Nields's earlier interrogation, Van Cleve gently raises the question of whether North might be lying here and now, in the present session (line 15). Van Cleve's recitation of lies is organized in a graded series of cases, roughly akin to the series of cases presented under taxonomic headings in medieval casuistical manuals. In these manuals, which provided confessors with precise guidelines for teaching ordinary people how to examine their consciences, each sin would be discussed in terms of a series of cases, starting with the clearest, and ending with more complex and difficult ones.[36] In the case we are discussing here, Van Cleve's list starts with the easiest lie for North to defend, and then moves to more difficult cases. For a second time—he had used it on the first morning of testimony as well—North recited the memorable phrase "the good, the bad, and the ugly" (line 16) while taking part in this confessional dialogue.[37]

The sequence begins with Van Cleve apologizing for the series of questions he is about to raise, and then going on to mention the matter of North's lying. The prefatory remarks about the "personal and painful task" of raising these questions mitigates what otherwise might come across as a grave insult to a "man of honor": the accusation of lying.[38] Van Cleve begins an interrogative sequence in which he presents a series of preliminary characterizations, assertions, and statements for the witness to confirm, leading up to a question about North's present testimony in line 16. In this sequence, North confirms each of Van Cleve's summaries of his previous testimony, with the exception of the question about the "false documents" pertaining to a gift (line 9), which Van Cleve reformulates (line 11) after North initially answers, "No." The sequence builds progressively to the culminating question. The progression of questions lays out an ethical continuum, starting with lies that have widely acknowledged justification (lying to enemies, lying to protect the lives of others), and then proceeding to lies that have more questionable justification (self-protection, avoiding political damage). The progression of questions begins with more defensible lies, which also were told in situations unlike the present circumstances. The progression then moves to less easily defended lies told in circumstances very much like the present inquiry. In this way the series of questions progressively homes in on the reflexive implications of North's immediate testimony.

Note the variation in North's answers. When asked about his lies to "the

Iranians" (line 1), he not only confirms the question, he upgrades the characterization supplied by the question: "I lied every time I met the Iranians." He says this without hesitation, and one can infer that he makes
this admission proudly, expressing what Bok describes as the "special
sense of self-evident justification" associated with this category of lie.
From North's earlier testimony, it is clear that he includes the Iranians
among the various "adversaries" who cannot and should not be told "the
truth."

North's confirmation of Van Cleve's question about lying to Secord (lines
3 and 4) takes a different tack. Here he confirms the question by appending
a clause that supplies a purpose: "In order to encourage him [Secord] to
stay with the project, yes." Although this answer does not negate or contest
the terms of the question, it situates the admitted lie in a mitigating circumstance. North simply confirms the next two questions (lines 5 through 8,
about lying to Congress and constructing false chronologies) without giving justificatory explanations. The absence of explanation here does not
necessarily mean that he was unable to defend these admitted lies. In his
testimony to Van Cleve and to Nields during the preceding two days of
interrogation, North had defended the actions in question. He cited the
authority of the "superiors" at the White House under whose directives he
claimed to be acting, and he also claimed to be motivated to protect the
lives of American hostages, secret agents, and collaborators in other countries; when pressed, he also admitted that these lies were designed to protect the administration from domestic and international political damage.
Bok observes that "lies to protect individuals and to cover up their secrets
can be told for increasingly dubious purposes to the detriment of all."[39] In
this case, Van Cleve's questions are arranged in a series that suggests increasingly dubious purposes for the lies in question, thus enabling the
witness to explain, and the audience to assess, just where justification ends
and detriment begins. Although the relevance and sincerity of these justifications were contested at the time, as North presented them they associated the lies in question with collective purposes, lines of legitimate authority, national interest, and altruistic motives.

Van Cleve continues with a question about falsifying documents concerning "a gift" (line 9), the gift apparently being a security fence pur-
chased for North from profits gained in arms-hostage transactions. This
question implies a different order of motive: covering up evidence of il-

legitimate personal gain or benefit. Notably, North confers extendedly with Sullivan before answering "No." Van Cleve pursues the question by re-phrasing it in two parts (lines 11, 13). The revised questions employ the passive voice, refer to "the document" and the "intention" under which it was composed (by unnamed authors), and no longer explicitly mention North's responsibility for writing the document in anticipation of an "in-vestigation." The question adheres to a conventional way of defining a lie as a false statement made with the intention to mislead, but it no longer mentions the agent or agency of the statement or the intention, and thus it does not include the formal elements of a direct accusation. North then confirms these revised questions without admitting or denying that it was he who created the false documents in question.

Van Cleve's culminating question—"Can you assure this committee that you are not here now lying to protect your Commander in Chief?" (line 15)—does not come across as an accusatory question, although it could easily be stated as such. The transcript does not do justice to Van Cleve's deferential voice and meek demeanor, which together with what he says emphasize the delicacy of his interrogative task. Compare his question to one asked earlier by Nields, which more directly impugns North's present testimony:

Nields: Well that's the whole reason for shredding documents, isn't it, Colonel
          North, so that you can later say you don't remember, (0.4) whether you had
          'em, and you don't remember what's in 'em.

In contrast to this more direct enunciation of a culpable motive ("the whole reason") for North's actions, Van Cleve presents North with a *possible* accusation to rebut, rather than an accusatory challenge emerging from the preceding testimony. He takes care not to accuse North directly; instead, he provides North with an opportunity to rebut an accusation arising from the analogy between earlier occasions of lying and the present circumstances. As Van Cleve presents it, he is not forcing this analogy, but is instead giving North an opportunity to "assure" the committee that its members should not draw inferences about his present testimony on the basis of what he admits about his past acts. Van Cleve's questions elucidate a recognizably fragile aspect of North's earlier testimony about scenes in which, as a char-acter in those scenes, he gave doubtful testimony. The fragility has to do with how, as Harvey Sacks put it, "the doubting that's been introduced could after all be applied . . . to the teller-character's [present] report of his own behavior."[40] Sacks describes cases in which storytellers impute disreputable actions and motives to other characters, while presenting themselves as innocent participants or mere bystanders, and he observes that audiences typically do not undermine such stories by explicitly questioning the teller's exemption from the reflexive implications of the story. Instead, through a kind of collusion, such a story gets treated "as a reasonable characterization of the world, without getting smashed, burst, dropped, ruined."[41] In his testimony, however, North is claiming to tell the truth while acknowledging that *he* lied to Congress on an earlier occasion. Moreover, in the present circumstances, skeptical challenges to a witness's motives and credibility are far more salient than in the sorts of polite conversation Sacks discusses. Consequently, Van Cleve's invitation to North to defend against a possible way to "undermine" his testimony is less of an attack on his credibility than the offer of an opportunity to defend against an inference that many others are likely already to have drawn.

North's culminating answer (line 16) provides more than a mere assurance, as it takes the form of a monological speech inserted into the wide-open dialogical space offered by Van Cleve's earlier question. The speech reiterates a defense North had elaborated throughout his earlier testimony. Although he keeps his face raised while reciting this speech—he is not evidently reading from the open notebook in front of him—the utterance seems composed of a series of stock lines, some of which undoubtedly were prepared in advance for the occasion. Again, "the good, the bad, and the ugly" is the most obvious fragment grafted from an extrinsic cultural text (a cliché, recalling a movie title in this case).

North also mentions two related ritual oaths: the "oath as a midshipman" that he presumably swore when attending Annapolis, and the oath "to tell the whole truth" he swore at the outset of the hearings. Both oaths explicitly commit the swearer to truthfulness. His citation of the midshipman's oath also underlines the salience of his military identity, an identity that he constantly evoked by the marine lieutenant colonel's uniform he wore for the occasion. North's mention of the oath raises potentially dangerous implications for his testimony. As many commentators pointed out, when acting as a member of the NSC staff, North was a civilian functionary, so that the uniform, and the military connotations of North's claims that he always acted under the authority of his superiors in the government, implied an inappropriate context for assessing his actions. Nevertheless, such connotations were in play, and they were available not only to build up his credibility, but also to impugn it. In the present instance, for example, it could be pointed out that by admitting that he lied to Congress and made false chronologies, in effect he admits to violating the midshipman's oath he had sworn to uphold. And, since one could easily recognize the similarity between the present occasion (a congressional hearing) and a past occasion where, as North just acknowledged, he lied to Congress, it might seem irresistible to conclude that North is (re)citing an oath that he had already violated and could just as easily be violating here and now for similar reasons. He is thus faced with a task of warding off inferences about the present situation that seem readily transferable from the analogous situations in his past. He attempts to avoid the issue by forcibly asserting that things are different this time around, and that he has gone to heroic and painful lengths to tell the truth and face the consequences. To recall, once again, North's "liar paradox," it now looks like this:

1. Lying is justified to prevent our adversaries from knowing our secrets.
2. Our adversaries have access to this very testimony.
3. I am not now lying. *And I really mean it, honest!*

THE SINCERE LIAR

What cannot be ignored about North's assertions of truthfulness is their performative force, that is, their display of sincerity. A written transcript gives only the barest indication of such force, as it badly recollects some of the more memorable features of the televisual field that embodied and expressed what North said and meant. This field was filled by a medal-bedecked uniform, animated by a body with military bearing, clean-cut grooming, a polite and deferential voice, occasionally erupting in moments of righteous indignation and combative speech, all of which were accented by bright blue eyes and labile eyebrows, inscribed on the clean horizontal lines of a symmetrical forehead. These elements of North's televisual physiognomy composed a dramatic symphony of truthfulness, righteousness, loyalty, sincerity, and—when called for—contrition. When we consider the totality of North's on-camera performance, we begin to appreciate that he is not just reiterating textual fragments (a title, an oath, a sound byte), he is pronouncing the words—"I have told you the truth, counsel, as best I can"—and, on several occasions, compounding and intensifying his swearing of the oath, much in the way children will do ("cross my heart and hope to die"). He even goes so far as to attack the very insinuation that he could be dissimulating.

> North: I came here to tell you the truth. To tell you:: and this committee, and the American people the truth, and I'm trying to do that Mister Nields, °hh and I don't like the insinuation that I'm up here having a convenient memory lapse, like perhaps some others have had.

The compounding of the oath is produced by repeating stock phrases (e.g., "I came here to tell the truth"); an emphatic or formalized use of key terms of reference like "you," "Mister Nields," "the American people"; a declaration of his will to tell the "truth"; and his stated objection to the very idea he could be doing otherwise. All of these intensifiers evidently underline his sincere commitment to the truth on *this* occasion. There is a conventional use of the expression "I *mean* it" (a use that tends to elude semantic and semiotic conceptions of meaning), which is relevant in such contexts as an emphatic (re)doubling of the assertive force of a statement that might otherwise be doubted: "I *really mean it* this time; I'm not kidding." In this case, the very intensity of swearing expresses a wholeness of involvement. We witness a character engrossed in an act without any sense of an (incompetent) actor's alienation from that character. If what he says "here and now" is a lie, it is said with such overt enthusiasm, conviction, and sincerity that any initial suspicion can be overwhelmed by the immediate force of the demonstration. And thus, if he does happen to be lying, he is doing so sincerely.

In general, a sincere lie can arise from any of several clinical, practical, or political conditions, some of which may remove or displace the act from the category of lying. For example, when the speaker is saying something untrue, but actually thinks it is true, the category of lying no longer applies: "A liar may come over time to believe in her own lie. If that happens she would no longer be a liar, and her untruths . . . should be much harder to detect."[42] Although one may question what the person says, her sincerity may remain intact. For example, in a quaint account of pathological liars written in the 1920s, William Healy and Mary Tenney Healy observe that "any of us may be so confronted by fabrications so consistent as to leave at one or several interviews the impression of truth."[43] They describe pathological liars as particularly skilled, poised, systematic, and charming in the way they go about lying. In a case they describe at some length, the crucial diagnostic moment occurs through "shrewd detective work." "Hazel's stories were successfully maintained for several days until a shrewd detective, who got her to tell some street numbers in Chicago ferreted out her family. She had denied the existence of them in Chicago, and, indeed, stated that her father and mother had died years previously. One of the most convincing things about her was her poise; she displayed an attitude of sincerity combined with a deep surprise when her word was questioned."[44] A liar's ability to remain free from such detection, and even to sustain credibility in the face of it, is enhanced when the audience has no reason to suspect the lie and has no access to corroborating or discrediting biographical information. The moral implications and practical difficulties become less problematic when the liar is not a very smooth actor, as we can appreciate from a clinical account of a class of prattlers, which describes them as "chattering people that might be confounded with pathological liars from the stories they tell in full detail. But they have no system which they develop, often change their subject and do not paint in a lifelike way because they do not believe their own stories or live them in a self-centered manner."[45] In this account, the prattler's transparent and awkward performance fails to secure entitlement to sincerity. In contrast, when the fantasy or fiction is transparently, warrantably, and conventionally part of an act, there no longer is any implication of lying. It would be strange to charge Laurence Olivier with misrepresenting himself when he plays Hamlet (the actor may be accused of misrepresenting the character, but that is a separate issue). If he plays the part well, the audience notices no incongruity between actor and fictional character. Assuming the audience accepts the legitimacy of the actor's engagement in fictional actions, it would be absurd to charge the actor with dissembling, since this is the whole point of his performance.

In other cases, a speaker may say something designed explicitly to mislead an audience or interrogator, while holding a "mental reservation" which supplements what is said with an unspoken "qualification" that would make it true. Sincerity is maintained by setting up a division be-

tween actual and virtual audiences. In post-Reformation England this practice was denounced by Henry Mason, an Anglican divine and author of
The New Art of Lying, who associated this "art" with "Jesuit casuists"
wishing to avoid persecution. According to Steven Shapin: "This 'new art'
was propagated, for example, to enable English Catholics to mislead Prot-
estant authorities without doing anything Rome was obliged to regard as
sinful. Accordingly, a priest might properly tell an English magistrate that
he was *not* a priest, by having the appropriate mental reservation—'so far as
I am obliged to tell you,' or 'not a Jewish priest'—at the moment he said
it."[46] It is significant here that the "mental reservation" is problematic for
the inquisitor, precisely because it is oriented to an alternative moral community, a community that perhaps is absent from the mundane scene but
whose virtual authority overhears the act plus the thought behind it. This
standard applies rather nicely for members of a religious community who
believe that God overhears their thoughts with greater authority than the
inquisitor at hand. As we shall see shortly, it also applies to a witness who
appeals to a virtual televisual community to stand in judgment of an interrogator's mundane right to hear the truth.[47] When accused of lying or
caught in a lie, the sincere liar can successfully turn the occasion into a
confrontation of opposing wills in which he defends himself without the
slightest hint that he could be anything but right. As Hare et al. have noted,
such a sincere liar "embraces a social norm in which others are viewed as
having malevolent intent toward him . . . he feels it is legitimate to manipu-
late and deceive them."[48] Here, we are reminded of the inferential link
North draws in his testimony between malevolent enemies abroad and the
committee interrogators demanding revelations from him.

We are not claiming that North actually was a sincere liar, but rather that
this possibility was much alive during the hearings and that his performance presented skeptical members of his audience with an interpretive
problem: namely, how to expose particular instances of deception or self-
deception. This is more than a matter of assessing the truth of statements,
and it can turn out to be a difficult problem even in cases where the subject
is said to confabulate incessantly and fantastically. The problem has to do
with the differential availability of the social circumstances and resources
necessary to expose the symptoms in question.[49] For a striking example of
this phenomenon, consider the following anecdote about a Mr. Thompson,
a man who was diagnosed with Korsikow's syndrome (a severe memory

disorder) and who was said to compensate for memory deficits by con-
fabulating stories.

> On one occasion, Mr. Thompson went for a trip, identifying himself at the
> front desk as "the Revd. William Thompson" ordering a taxi, and taking off
> for the day. The taxi-driver, whom we later spoke to, said he had never had
> so fascinating a passenger, for Mr. Thompson told him one story after an-
> other, amazing personal stories full of fantastic adventures. "He seemed to
> have been everywhere, done everything, met everyone. I could hardly be-
> lieve so much was possible in a single life," he said. "It is not exactly a single
> life," we answered.[50]

The description of Mr. Thompson's disordered world makes the patient
out to be a strikingly postmodern figure, a nomad migrating from scene to
scene in a decentered narrative landscape. "Deprived of continuity, of
a quiet, continuous inner narrative, he is driven to a sort of narrational
frenzy—hence his ceaseless tales, his confabulations, his mythomania. . . .
The world keeps disappearing, losing meaning, vanishing—and he must
seek meaning, *make* meaning, in a desperate way, continually inventing,
throwing bridges of meaning over abysses of meaninglessness, the chaos
that yawns continually beneath him."[51] This case is interesting, not only
because it illustrates a pathological syndrome, but because it gives us a
glimpse of an interactional habitat in which even the most outlandish
stories can remain plausible, at least for a while.[52] It is not just that the
circumscribed elements of the taxi ride lead the driver to mistake Mr.
Thompson for the heroic character he portrays. Mr. Thompson (or the syndrome acting through him) turns the taxi ride—a bracketed social space in
which identities and biographies are constructed on the fly—into a hyper-
normal adventure. Unlike the usual customer, who sits quietly in the back-
seat of the taxi, Mr. Thompson becomes an actor who is typecast for a
heroic performance in just such a space. Unleashed in such an optimal
situation, his controlled "narrational frenzy" outstrips his audience's ability to corroborate the story. Truth becomes embedded in a performance,
including expressions of earnestness and sincerity, cut off from biography
and history.

A simulation of sincerity performed under the right circumstances—that
is, a performance done with no recollection of a contradictory reality behind it—disables the conceptual resources necessary for the exposure of

deception, which, according to Habermas, depends on an a priori distinction between a surface statement and its intentional meaning: "An interpreter can interpret an action rationally in such a way that he thereby captures elements of deception or self-deception. He can expose the latently strategic character of a self-presentation by comparing the manifest content of the utterance, that is, what the actor says, with what the actor means."[53] The problem in the present case is that even though this distinction may be highly relevant, it is pragmatically inoperable. Imagine, for the moment, how we would decide that North is being deceptive, self-deceptive, sincere, or all of these things at once, when he says "I have told you the truth, counsel, as best I can." According to Habermas, we would expose the "latently strategic character" of this assertion by comparing its manifest content to what North means. But, what else does he mean, and how would we ever find out? When a speaker like North is a convincing actor, the very quality of the action militates against an audience's ability to distinguish meaning from content. No gap between what the actor says and what the actor means can be inspected; he insists forcefully that he means what he says.

Interrogation is largely built on the assumption that a witness will be compelled to respect consistency and avoid self-contradiction.[54] A venerable picture of truth-telling supports this conception by associating truth with simplicity and untruth with complexity and inelegance.[55] According to this picture, it should be difficult to sustain a network of lies over the course of an aggressive interrogation, because sooner or later the witness will be humbled by the task of inventing a detailed, logically coherent, and reasonable account that is consistent with previously acknowledged and corroborated facts. One of the rationales for having a witness testify in full view of a jury (or in this case, TV cameras) is that the play of bodily expressions will give off dramatic indications of whether or not the witness is existentially committed to what he or she is saying.[56] Without endorsing the metaphysics involved, contemporary social-psychological studies confirm the hold this classic picture has on conventional judgments of credibility. According to several studies of audience assessments of witness credibility, hesitant speech, shifting glances, breaks in the voice, "hypercorrect" speech, and many other nervous and furtive gestures (the steel balls rattling in Humphrey Bogart's hand during the climactic scene of *The Caine Mutiny* [1954]) tend to be viewed as indications of the speaker's wavering commitment to what he says.[57] Ekman supplies a reasoned basis for such behavioral judgments by describing some of the complications faced by a person who maintains a lie: the person may forget, and then contradict, what he or she said earlier, or may be caught off guard by a question and need to think of a credible answer on the spot. In such circumstances, the person's hesitancy, repeated self-corrections, circumlocutions, gaze aversion, nervous mannerisms, and other disruptions of fluency may be noticeable as signs of dissimulation.[58] It is as though the speaker's bodily comportment stands in judgment of what he says, and his alienated soul gives itself away. Ekman speaks of "leakage" in this context, where "some sign of the concealed emotion may escape efforts to inhibit or mask it." He focuses, for example, on features of the face like "Duchenne's smiles," where the muscles around the eyes express emotional signs that wholly or partly contradict what the muscles around the mouth are signaling.[59] In contrast, a sincere and meaningful enunciation absorbs the speaker in a total, fluid, coherent, and convincing performance.

Such bodily indications are part of a much larger field of visible bodily "commitments" to what the speaker apparently is doing and saying. For example, Charles Goodwin observes that speakers who are trying to recall a name or detail they apparently have forgotten will characteristically "assume a clearly recognizable, almost stereotyped, facial expression that shows visually that they are engaged in a word search. . . . Within this posture, gaze is not focused on anyone or anything in the local environment but instead assumes an out of focus 'middle-distance' look."[60] Sometimes, however, a speaker will turn to a recipient as a kind of silent invitation to join in the search. At the Iran-contra hearings, a witness's searches were often directed toward the notebooks at hand, and those texts became relevant to the interactional field. A convincing performance of such characteristic expressions of "forgetting," and being absorbed in a search for the elusive information, is part and parcel of a witness's evidently sincere testimony.

Because of the expansive, temporal and interactional fields in which the particular gestures and utterances are situated, there are no sure behavioral "indicators" of lying, of genuine failures to recall, or of other relevant individual "states." As Ekman points out, the "clues" he mentions are not signs of lying per se, because they can be attributed to conditions other than lying, and they can be suppressed or faked by a skillful and well-prepared dissembler. He warns the aspiring "lie catcher" not to make "Othello's error" of mistaking signs of fear for a liar's fear of being caught.[61] Acting skill can be all-important. A number of studies testify (not surprisingly) that children are more readily caught at lies than adults and that some people are especially skilled at dissimulating in testing situations. "Many adults are aware of the features which characterize a credible statement and are able to fabricate statements which appear credible."[62] Consequently, even when suspected or accused of lying, a confabulator can defeat or mitigate such an accusation by moving fluently and seamlessly across logical contradictions and factual gaps, as though with a sincere commitment to what is being said.

North's performative sincerity was not limited to the audiovisual spectacle. He recontextualized his acknowledged lies and other wrongdoings in a justificatory counternarrative that, according to his own testimony, was built into the preparation of the documents released as evidence to the committee and used to corroborate his testimony. Like a sincere liar, but not necessarily *as* one, North spoke with complete commitment and conviction, enunciating forcefully what he meant. Where there is no demonstrable gap between fantasy and reality, and no wavering commitment or contradictory division within the elements of the bodily spectacle, the very force of the speaker's conviction that his actions are "right," and that his utterances are "true" even when acknowledging lies, challenges the teleological foundation of the truth-finding engine of interrogation. As we elaborate in later chapters, the elements of the contemporary public hearing become subject to theatrical disruptions and politicized inversions. The old instabilities are reenacted within a modern technological theater. In the contemporary theater of televisual politics, gestures toward the traditional value of truth are a commonplace. At the same time, these gestures become absorbed within performance. Illusionist tricks are staged openly, but they are accepted by the audience as well-acted illusions. "The narrative is made up of many such understandings, tacit agreements, small and large, to overlook the observable in the interests of obtaining a dramatic story line."[63]

Televised tribunals like the Watergate and Iran-contra hearings have been likened to "a world without history" whose "characters did not have remembrable pasts."[64] The Iran-contra witnesses contributed to this sense of a media world without history. Although their "shredded memories" had a different etiology than Mr. Thompson's memory disorder, the Iran-contra witnesses had access to a relatively free space for manufacturing biographies, whether true or not. Especially in North's case, the intensive week-long media focus opened up a space that highlighted the significance of his immediate appearance and performance. It was noted, for example, that North's opportunities to play the hero were enhanced by the way the cameras framed him on the screen. According to an unnamed media consultant, "In the hearing room, North is down low, and the committee is perched up high—the classic confrontation of suspect and judge—but on television they're shooting Ollie from the heroic angle, from down low, so that he looks like a figure on Mt. Rushmore."[65] Needless to say, North's persona and the TV spectacle seemed made for each other. Initially, the networks received calls from many soap-opera viewers who complained that their favorite shows had been preempted. In the course of North's testimony, however, viewers quickly came to appreciate the live drama that was replacing their favorite shows.[66] Viewers who were unable to catch the live broadcast were able to witness replays of the more exciting moments (or sound bites) on the evening news or read about them in the morning papers. North's medal-bedecked talking torso, his stirring speeches, filmic citations, and classic poses were invariably given a central place in the endless replays of excerpts. In contrast, the cameras were said to be "unkind" to Nields and Arthur Liman, the two interrogators representing the committee majority. Liman's thinning hair and New York accent, and Nields's long hair, combed forward to mask a receding hairline, became emblematic targets of politically and culturally hostile letters sent to the committee.[67]

We are not here dealing with cultural media effects in a discrete and measurable sense, but with something like a media space that makes creative use of a popular archive containing a diverse set of files, film clips, old scrapbooks, ethnic and regional stereotypes, and news clippings. Actors recite lines and pull citations reminiscent of the standard genre of courtroom drama, they draw from an open variety of available precedents and prerehearsed repertoires, and they opportunistically insert disparate fragments into available discursive spaces to compose a pastiche of recognizable poses and speeches. They do not simply select wholesale from a stable cultural repository the particular lines, narratives, scripts, or poses expressed and exhibited from one moment to the next. They play to the viewers' televisual competence, to their familiarity with and mastery of the medium.[68] The production is flexible, situated, and context-sensitive; it does not trace back to a single discursive or normative source. So, for example, although many commentators pointed out that North evoked the image of James Stewart as Jefferson Smith confronting Congress in *Mr. Smith Goes to Washington,* it is difficult to draw a point-by-point correspondence between the two performances. At other times North's performance evoked fragments of John Wayne war movies, and even relatively recent film comedies starring Steve Martin: "raised eyebrows to suggest injured innocence; the eyebrows reversed, slanting downward, to suggest intense concentration; and, above all, the hilariously dated and arch vocabulary to suggest regular-guyness. . . . 'It was a matter of getting this kid smart.' . . . 'I think it was a neat idea.' "[69] "Ollie North Goes to Washington" was an original story, one that called into play the multifaceted and temporally situated elements of the Iran-contra affair. The singular historical circumstances of the hearings were intertwined with the way the story unfolded.

OBJECTIVITY AND POLITICIZATION

The hearings were explicitly organized for the purpose of practically and publicly demonstrating the truth about the historical events in question. Assuming that the parties who were closest to those events were less than eager to disclose actions and rationales for those actions that would expose them to prosecution, impeachment, or, at the least, severe political damage, their confessional admissions were especially important (and, of course, difficult to extract) for disclosing and validating elements of the Iran-contra story. In principle, and assuming the legitimacy of the undertakings that elicit them, confessional truths transcend partisan positions in an adversarial dispute. By yielding to particular statements supportive of the adversary's case, for all practical purposes the confession certifies those statements as facts. Uncoerced false confessions are not unknown, but the highly pathological association they evoke points to the presumptive role of confessions in interrogative procedures.[70] When no such compliance is present, a third party may be called on to make a summary judgment that breaks the deadlock. The institutionalization of a nonpartisan audience to witness the dispute lends legitimacy to such intervention. Nonpartisanship is a delicate matter since a judge or jury can be suspected of political or otherwise partisan bias. Such suspicions are officially (although not always effectively) mitigated by various selection procedures, solemn trappings, and formal oaths that symbolize or certify nonpartisanship. At the Iran-contra tribunal many features of the proceedings were parasitic upon the more familiar courtroom arena. The appointment of a bipartisan committee was designed to assure the appearance of a nonpartisan investigation. The media presentation of the hearings also included overt elements of "objective" journalism; detached commentaries and "balanced" interviews, with politicians and pundits speaking on behalf of each of the contending parties.

Despite these various displays and trappings of nonpartisanship, politics was never far out of the picture. The joint House and Senate committee membership was staffed by representatives of both parties. The cochairmen who presided over the tribunal were both from the Democratic party, which was the majority party in both the House and Senate. Sen. Inouye and Rep. Hamilton assumed quasijudicial positions when they opened and closed the sessions, heard objections, and made rulings, but they also were seen as representatives of the opposition party that stood to gain from the exposure of scandals in the Republican-controlled executive branch. According to Haynes Johnson's account of the hearings, Inouye and Hamilton were sincerely committed to bipartisanship, although they ran into a firestorm of complaints about their biased conduct while chairing the hearings. Johnson recounts a progression of counterattacks against the committee and committee interrogators starting with Richard Secord, the first witness called before the committee. Instant polls and radio talk shows publicized widespread public disapproval of the interrogation. Arthur Liman, who was noted as a canny interrogator, reported death threats and anti-Semitic attacks by callers, and by the time he finished North's interrogation, according to Johnson, "House Republicans on the committee were openly attacking Liman, almost without defense, as a partisan liberal Democrat biased against North and Ronald Reagan."[71] According to Johnson, Nields also was well aware of the popular reception North was getting: "Nields could understand what had happened. Here was this attractive person [North], with what appeared to be the world's most sincere pair of eyes, proudly wearing his country's uniform and being subjected to rude and accusatory questions and bravely responding with moving speeches."[72] The interrogators and committee members gradually backed away from using more aggressive interrogative methods, and North and the witnesses that followed him in the remaining weeks of the hearings were able to exploit the openings they were given. Disputes over such openings occurred from the start of North's interrogation, when North's counsel, Brendan Sullivan, requested that he be allowed to read a prepared statement.[73] Chairman Inouye ruled against this request, but after protests by Sullivan and several Republicans on the committee, he allowed it to be read two days later. In the statement North accused the committee of a one-sided, arbitrary exercise in power.

> I believe that this is a strange process that you are putting me and others through. Apparently, the President has chosen not to assert his prerogatives, and you have been permitted to make the rules. You called before you the officials of the Executive Branch. You put them under oath for what must be collectively thousands of hours of testimony. You dissect that testimony to find inconsistencies and declare some to be truthful and others to be liars. You make the rulings as to what is proper and what is not proper. You put the testimony which you think is helpful to your goals up before the people and leave others out. It's sort of like a baseball game in which you are both the player and the umpire. It's a game in which you call the balls and strikes and where you determine who is out and who is safe. And in the end you determine the score and declare yourself the winner.
>
> From where I sit, it is not the fairest process. One thing is, I think, for certain—that you will not investigate yourselves in this matter.[74]

In the face of such accusations by North (or in this case his speechwriters), Nields, Liman, and the Democrats on the committee took care not to formulate questions that might seem rude and accusatory.[75] They went to great lengths to show that they were not placing the witness in the position of an underdog with limited discursive rights. Consequently, over the course of the testimony North and his allies on the committee managed to enlist growing popular support by intensively working with the audiovisual elements of the spectacle to dismantle asymmetric elements of the truth-finding engine of interrogation. This reconfiguration of politicized rights and identities occurred through a progressive and contingent shifting of the very infrastructure of the spectacle.

As with many of the other relevant features of the scene, the politics was not simply present in the setting, but it was made relevant and visible as such through the actions of the participants. Bipartisan agreements were a significant basis for assigning factual status to the agreed-to matters, whereas disputes sustained along party lines tended to enhance the visibility of politics as usual. The mediation of these proceedings to a televisual audience, and the various expressions of audience reaction (newspaper polls and interviews, phone calls and telegrams, radio talk shows, etc.), fed back into the hearings as evidence of either public consensus or political divisiveness.

Under the circumstances, it was especially important for the majority party, which took a quasiprosecutorial role in the hearings, to demonstrate an orientation to a truth that was above partisan politics. The conclusion that the hearings were merely a political sideshow was more palatable to witnesses, members of the committee, and members of the audience who supported or were part of the administration. The fact that both sides could, and indeed did, invoke the American people, the Constitution, and the "truth," while impugning the truthfulness, fairness, and lawfulness of the other side's conduct, worked against the committee majority's effort to secure univocal authority.[76] The question of whether the hearings were fair and objective or merely political was not simply a matter of opinion about what occurred, as it animated the moment-to-moment conduct at the hearings. Many elements of the spectacle, including the utterance-by-utterance pragmatics of interrogation, became sites of reflexive struggle. The relation between truth and politics itself became part of the struggle. As noted, North's interrogators questioned the "rightness" of his lying under politically contentious circumstances, circumstances that by extension included the very hearings in which he was testifying. North admitted to lying for good political reasons. According to his testimony, when he previously lied to Congress and constructed false chronologies, he suspended his commitment to truth-telling in order to protect lives and spare the president from political damage. Consequently, North's lies, if performed sincerely for the reasons he gave, were "normatively regulated," albeit not regulated by a rule to tell the truth at all times.[77] The problem for the committee investigators was to ascertain whether North's actions were normatively justified by what he believed, and relatedly to decide whether those norms were legitimate. This became a contentious, overtly "political" matter. A speech or argument stated in the context of a debate is prototypically political, whereas a confession solicited in the context of an interrogatory pursuit of truth ideally produces a bipartisan agreement. Both possibilities were latent in the spectacle at the hearings, and both occasionally were realized.

North acknowledged that covert activities are "at essence a lie," but he also asserted that they were not wrong. The committee interrogators could have pursued the line of argument that covert actions are indeed lies and therefore wrong, but after very little public debate on the subject, the members determined not to dispute the general legitimacy of covert activities and decided instead to assess the legitimacy of particular operations conducted by North, Poindexter, Secord, Hakim, MacFarlane, and other agents and employees of the executive branch.[78] Consequently, the committee agreed that for purposes of conducting (some) international operations, secrecy and deception were warranted. The dispute centered on some particular aspects of the authorization, circumstance, and bureaucratic accountability of government-sponsored secrecy and deception. Among the things at stake were procedures for instituting the duty of executive branch officials to inform Congress about covert activities, but the committee majority did not challenge those officials' right to conduct such activities in the first place. While the majority of the committee held that North was out of bounds, they did not challenge the game itself. Covert activities—politically motivated lying and secrecy—were not in question. Consequently, public evaluations of North's testimony included evaluations of the "rightness" of lying in that testimony. By all indications—polls, interviews, letters, telegrams, Ollie North haircuts, T-shirts, bumper stickers, and the like—a large proportion of the audience figured that North was a right-acting and sincere guy. Apparently, if he lied, he did so successfully. His "success" was a contentious matter. As the separate accounts in the minority and majority reports by the committee indicated, judgments about the truthfulness of North's testimony, and about the moral significance of his (occasionally acknowledged) lies, were expressions of a divided polity. Moreover, the successful elicitation and high visibility of such divided public judgments became inseparable from the investigation of the Iran-contra affair, so that any subsequent claim about "what really happened" during that historical event was intelligible as a further contribution to an ongoing debate. No transcendent resolution was attained.

2. THE PRODUCTION

OF HISTORY

What deeds could man ever have done if he had not been enveloped in
the dust-cloud of the unhistorical? ... This condition ... is the cradle not
only of unjust action, but of every just and justifiable action in the
world. ... If the man of action, in Goethe's phrase, is without conscience,
he is also without knowledge: he forgets most things in order to do one,
he is unjust to what is behind him, and only recognizes one law—the law
of that which is to be.—Nietzsche[1]

Perhaps the most significant outcome of the Iran-contra hearings was that a
congressional investigation which initially promised to unearth a political
scandal extending to the highest reaches of government failed to do so. As
Howard Horwitz tersely observed, one of the central messages of the hearings was that "history was not, as it were, happening."[2] This is not to say
that the hearings produced no revelations, that nothing was learned, for
instance, about the CIA's involvement in covert weapons deals with Iran,
the use of proceeds from those weapons deals to aid the Nicaraguan contras, the workings of a paragovernmental organization including high-
ranking members of the CIA and the National Security Council, or the
depth of political cynicism that apparently pervaded those two institutions. However, given the proximate historical precedent of Watergate—a
political scandal that brought down a presidency—and given the serious-
ness and political volatility of the activities in which senior members of the
Reagan administration were engaged, the potential for political damage to
the administration was relatively well-contained. Thus, the most salient
and enduring feature of the Iran-contra hearings may well be that they
inscribed a distinctive array of discursive technologies for making and
managing history on the landscape of contemporary culture.

In this chapter we propose that the Iran-contra committee's difficulties
in writing an official history of the Iran-contra affair are related to more
general problems of writing historical narratives. Although guided by recent discussions on the literary construction and interpretation of history,
we are primarily interested in how the substantive enactment of histori-

cal events anticipated and attempted to influence what later was made of those events. The present chapter introduces a conception of history that highlights the work of writing, memorializing, collecting, and recollecting the documentary basis of historical investigations. A basic premise of our discussion is that by ignoring the practical methods by which histories are recounted, disputed, valorized, and written, social theorists and other scholars have overlooked what is perhaps most sociological about history.[3] Our aim is to identify the local technologies through which historical documents are generated and assessed, witnesses are interrogated, and provisional historical narratives are assembled, disassembled, and reassembled over the course of testimonial proceedings. In this way, we intend to show how the actual, practical work of making history can become an appreciable topic for sociology.

THE PRACTICAL TASK OF WRITING HISTORY

For members of the Iran-contra committee, the writing of history was first and foremost a practical problem. The committee's mandate was to produce a specific product: a chronology of dates, times, events, agents, and actions pertaining to American/Israeli covert arms sales to Iran and support of the counterrevolutionary forces in Central America. While the official Iran-contra chronology included in the committee's report shows little of the subtlety and sophistication of reports written by and for professional historians, it nevertheless displays ubiquitous features of conventional historical writing, and in this it shares with professional history many of the familiar themes and problems arising out of the attempt to render a collection of disparate, disorganized, and differently voiced historical documents into a singular, cogent, and univocal historical narrative.

By adopting the phrase "conventional historical writing," we do not mean to imply that all historical writing obeys these conventions, nor do we mean that such conventional features as we shall identify may serve as criteria for judging whether or not some piece of writing is, so to speak, historical. Rather, by conventional historical writing we mean to call attention to the routine, rather plain organization that forms the basis of most histories: an organization of dates, times, and ordinary methods of reasoning and writing about past events that is at best indifferent to debates and differences among professional historians. Consider, for example, the following passage from the committee's report concerning the difficulties that emerged during a covert shipment of U.S. Hawk missiles to Iran, which was mediated by Israel and involved landing and reloading in Portugal (country 15): "Informed by Secord of the difficulties in Country 15, North immediately asked CIA official Duane Clarridge to assist in obtaining clearances for the plane going there. Clarridge said Secord should contact the CIA Chief in Country 15, whose name North then relayed to Secord. At the same time, Clarridge sent 'flash' cables instructing the CIA Chief to call an official of Country 15 and his deputy to report immediately to the office for a 'special assignment.' "[4]

In contrast to any of the particular testimonies the report summarizes— e.g., testimony by North, Clarridge, or Secord—the narrative is written in an anonymous voice. It is stated as a factual account, without the disclaimers, qualifications, and partial recollections that are characteristic of particular witnesses' testimonies. It provides a linear chronology of events, and—unlike testimony—no explicit standpoint is mentioned from which the narrator came to see or know about the described events. Whether true or not, whether consensually validated or politically contentious, the text displays a factual style that subsumes particular witnesses' stories within a generalized, conventional history of the events in question.

The committee's work of writing history was not restricted to drafting a final report. On the contrary, the task of producing a conventional historical narrative was relevant throughout the committee's investigation, and it entered into the very organization and conduct of testimony. Over the course of North's testimony, questions were asked and answered, and documents were proffered, read, and discussed. These moves were made and challenged with an eye to the place occupied by that testimony in the accumulating record of the Iran-contra affair. In addition, fragments of that record were continually brought in play as previously certified story elements that were already in place. This use of agreed-on and relatively fixed points of reference over the course of testimony adumbrated a final version, or master narrative, even as the story remained to be written. As such, a detailed orientation to producing conventional history entered into the very constitution of the record on which the final version was to be based.

For the sake of clarity, we distinguish between two senses in which the testimony of Oliver North and other witnesses at the Iran-contra hearings might be considered historically significant. The first and perhaps most obvious is that the testimony was part of a series of events that were and continue to be popularly recognized as having historical import. That is, the interest evoked by the joint committee's work, and by the North testimony in particular, together with the celebration of these events in the press and in the popular imagination, provide a generic warrant for the attribution of historical significance to the North testimony and to the events in the past described by that testimony. The second and more radical sense in which the hearings have historical significance concerns the local emergence of a historical sensibility. In this sense, historical significance is a contingent yet relatively stable product of the work done by investigators charged with the responsibility of writing official history and of the testimony given by witnesses questioned on matters relevant to this historical task at hand. History, in this sense, is the outcome of embodied practices of signification, which practices, in turn, are inscribed in the public record no less than are the events themselves.

While the hearings were projected from the outset as historic events (events of major importance for U.S. history), just how they would prove to be historically significant remained to be extracted from their unfolding production. So, too, each and every detail of testimony was not historically significant simply because it was included within the organized proceedings of the Iran-contra hearings. Historical significance becomes visible as a practical accomplishment once we reject the idea that what the hearings would amount to as history was determined in advance of their actual conduct. However predictable or surprising, the historical character of these proceedings was (and continues to be) abstracted from the countless hours of testimony, the immense collection of documents, electronic mail messages, and tape recordings amassed by the committee. Were this not the case—were the record to stand as a morally untextured, neutral collection of facts—the business of the social historian would be limited to piecing together the evidence to show "what really happened." Although the committee's investigation took up such a mandate, it seems fair to say that the available details outstrip the understanding of any committee member, witness, or ex post facto historian of the events in question, so that what emerges as history is sensitive to demands of coherence and narrative style that are internal to the methods of archival organization and historical (re)collection.[5]

In sum, while it seems clear that historical significance was an a priori organizing feature for the conduct of the Iran-contra hearings and thus of the specific selections of testimony we shall consider, the manner of accomplishing the signification of history remained to be established within the ongoing production of the hearings as coherent, intelligible, investigative work. Our suggestion that the production of history involves practices for rendering the historical record "historical" is meant to indicate that such practices are already on the scene wherever and whenever a historical record is being assembled and ratified. Hence, the work of rendering history includes not only methods by which historical narratives are compiled and written, but, more importantly, methods by which a historical record is constituted in the first place.

PLAUSIBLE DENIABILITY AND THE PROBLEM
OF THE "HOSTILE NATIVE"

There is a poignant irony in using the Iran-contra hearings as an examplar of how histories are made and written. The successes of the witnesses who testified on behalf of the Reagan administration's actions and policies can be attributed in large part to their ability to preempt, defer, or in other ways foreclose attempts at assembling a definitive history of the events in question. The minority and supplemental opinions appended to the text of the committee's final report provide a striking testimonial to the failure of the investigation to produce a definitive history of the Iran-contra affair. The very presence of the minority report sustained the ambiguities, equivocalities, and dissent that pervaded the testimony, so that a distinctive feature of the would-be final report became its evident lack of finality. That "what really happened" in the Iran-contra affair was not decisively resolved; that it was undecidable in minute, at times, "tedious" detail;[6] and that this was the case despite the appearance of sincere efforts on the committee's part to retrieve "what really happened" from the rubble of testimony, is directly attributable to the conduct of the hearings themselves and to the novel character of the revelations they produced.

One such revelation was that the key witnesses (Oliver North and John Poindexter) had worked with the head of the CIA (William Casey) to fabricate false chronologies of the events and to destroy documents that might contradict those chronologies or implicate the president in potentially illegal activities. Over the course of the hearings it became increasingly clear that these fabrications and shreddings were done in anticipation of just the sort of official investigation being conducted by the joint congressional committees. Thus, it became increasingly clear that the documentary archive of the Iran-contra affair had, in many respects, been designed in anticipation of an official investigation, and designed in such a way as to be immune to its effects. As the joint committee report later acknowledged, "In light of the destruction of material evidence by Poindexter and North and the death of Casey, all of the facts may never be known. The Committees cannot even be sure whether they heard the whole truth or whether Casey's 'fall guy' plan was carried out in the public hearings."[7] Over the course of these hearings it became clear that the historical archive was itself a product of organizational work—of collecting, assembling, and deleting files, retrieving documents or shredding them, coding and recoding messages, and more. This circumstance suggests, in turn, the following as a general, rather diabolical property of the historical imagination: that it not only involves interpretations of evidence, but that the evidence itself is suffused with the workings of a historical sensibility.

In a related discussion, Garfinkel comments that a society's members act in various capacities as "practical historians" who reflexively orient to history while reproducing "it."[8] Taking up this theme, Sacks spells out some consequences of this reflexive orientation for historical and cultural investigations:

> In so far as you have dealt with a society that was aware of a history, that was oriented to a history, then you damn well have to consider that the things you found were put there for you, or for someone such as you, and could have been put there with various attitudes. For example, these things could have been put there as a way of suggesting the society was a social structure other than it really was . . . [i]t is in that kind of context that [Garfinkel] is not making a joke when he says that other societies may have been leaving things "jokingly" or "interestingly." The question is of developing resources for detecting that. We assume that we have an ancient world which was unsmiling when, of course, all the pictures of them indicate that they were constantly smiling.[9]

Although confronted with traces of a recent history of covert operations, the Iran-contra committee's "historic" undertaking was doubly problematic. Committee investigators assumed, and with good reason, that many of the evidentiary documents in their archive were constructed to make problematic the discovery of "the reasonably unknown ways in which a society might have operated to have produced those documents."[10] The committee was faced with the extremely likely possibility that the materials it collected as evidence of covert operations were planted, while other pertinent documents were methodically shredded, and, further, that this selective manipulation of documents was done in specific anticipation of their later discovery by just such a fact-finding body.

It is in this context that Sacks's question of "developing resources" for detecting the attitude in which documents and other artifacts were left behind finds analytic purchase. Committee investigators showed a keen interest in a collection of "PROFS notes" (electronic messages in the Professional Office network used by White House staff, which, it was claimed, were recovered after North and others had presumed they had been erased). They also treated testimony as an occasion where the spontaneous recollection of past events by differently motivated witnesses might reveal controversial matters that would otherwise have been hidden. This interest in generating residual and spontaneous fragments of evidence—in focusing on the accidents, lapses, and unrehearsed tellings of the historical natives—displays an orientation to the possibility that the archival evidence has been preinterpreted and worked over to produce and select those fragments *least* likely to have been left behind in the attitude of historical reflection.

"Plausible deniability" refers to a collection of techniques through which parties to an event anticipate the possible historical significance of that event. The policy was initially formulated for the CIA, although its official use was proscribed by Congress in the 1970s. It later became an unofficial rationale for the diverse covert operations run by the NSC staff and other shadowy groups. Plausibly deniable records and recording practices are designed to facilitate denials and to provide alternative rationales for activities and events that may later come under hostile scrutiny. The policy was cited, for example, by John Poindexter, when he took full responsibility for having authorized the diversion of profits from the Iranian arms sales to the contras. In his testimony before the committee, he asserted that he specifically withheld the authorizing documents from the president in order to give Reagan "deniability" in case the diversion should become public, and in this way the president was protected from the hostile scrutiny of the press and Congress. Although Poindexter certainly stretched the doctrine beyond its established legal connotations (which were, in any case, no longer operative), his use of it suggests a widespread practice through which officials compile and distribute organizational documents in anticipation of their later use as archival records within diverse, and potentially hostile, schemes of historical reckoning.[11] While respecting bureaucratic requirements for completing and preserving such records, officials construct a specifically vague archive that enables them to disclaim responsibility for activities that the self-same archive might later be used to reconstruct.

"Plausible deniability" also provides a witness with additional resources for neutralizing potentially hostile interrogation. Since the organizational circumstances under which documents are produced and collected can themselves be thematized as topics of investigation, witnesses can further destabilize the documentary record by formulating the possibility that the evidentiary documents at the interrogator's disposal were left behind under the auspices of a hidden ironic design. The suggestion that "original" documents may have been designed ironically furnishes what is at best an equivocal archive that, when uncharitable interpretations are raised, can readily be denied by suggesting alternative readings of the same evidence. Even though North and Poindexter explicitly admitted that much of the evidence the committee had at hand was composed to facilitate deniability, far from disambiguating the record, these admissions only deepened the committee's difficulties by raising the possibility that the admissions might themselves facilitate a strategic design.

What we identify as the problem of the "hostile native"[12] consists, first of all, in the possibility that certain of the documents used as resources for "fixing" a master narrative are subject to the historical reflections of parties to the events in question. Second, it consists in a circumstance, peculiar to testimonial discourse, where the same parties who designed the evidentiary documents are called on to help determine what those documents are about. This circumstance provides an opportunity for witnesses to address the attitude in which those documents were left behind, or, at the very least, to get on the record that the sense now being made of any particular document is somehow incongruent with that document's "original" sense.[13]

To the extent that writers of histories remain committed to the idea of

1. "Did I get 'em all?"

recovering singular and definitive versions of past events, and to the extent that they retain a conception of a body of historical fact that exists independent of the conditions under which facts are produced and the purposes to which they are put in situ, the presence of practical methods for prestructuring (and, in effect, prehistoricizing) historical evidence must be profoundly unsettling. Yet the suggestion here is that such practical-historical methods not only exist but are—in specific occupational settings, under specific circumstances—used shamelessly and as a matter of course. This is precisely the possibility raised by Oliver North when, having been asked what had happened to memoranda he had sent requesting presidential approval of his activities, he replied, "I think I shredded most of that," and then, with an absence of contrition that must have made even his most stalwart supporters on the committee shudder, he continued, "Did I get 'em all?"[14] (figure 1).

From this, it seems clear that the public spectacle of the Iran-contra affair instructs a cultural politics that challenges many of the working suppositions of Enlightenment historiography and its embodiment in the material practices of the modern liberal state. For this reason, these events are significant for recent debates about philosophical conceptions of the postmodern. Yet, even (or perhaps especially) in the context of a cultural politics of postmodernity, the lessons of Iran-contra have equivocal implications.

If we are correct, one of the central lessons of Iran-contra was that the documentary evidence of history comes to us, as it were, already warm, which means that history is, in a deep sense, up for grabs. As Horwitz has noted, the acceptance of the "nontransparency of evidence" is virtually axiomatic to arguments currently being advanced within postmodernist and New Historicist circles for an "anti-objectivist vision of historical knowledge."[15] Although the public avowals of truthfulness, and of a respect for truth, made by spokesmen for the Reagan administration did not express a postmodern vision of historical knowledge, these spokesmen evidently were adept at putting such a vision to practical use. The great irony is that critical, postmodern, and oppositional strategies are generally supposed to be congruent with a progressive cultural politics, and yet the most astute and well-trained practitioners of postmodern politics may well turn out to be affiliated with such groups as the NSC staff and the CIA. The antiobjectivist vision of historical knowledge was used at the Iran-contra hearings to construct an avowedly fragmentary, equivocal, and therefore fragile history, and to pass it off for what really happened in the Iran-contra affair.[16]

A strong sense remains in which the issues posed by the Iran-contra hearings have a merely secondary relation to scholarly debates concerning competing theories of historical knowledge. Even though, as Horwitz has shown, the hearings are materially relevant to these debates, it is important to recall that the public spectacle was not designed solely (or even primarily) for an audience of philosophers and literary critics. Moreover, the people involved most intimately with the production and conduct of the hearings were trained in areas of law, government, the military, newspaper reporting, and television production and were, for the most part, no longer haunting the halls of university departments. Although the hearings embodied many of the themes familiar to students of recent developments in the arts and humanities, they also instantiated orders of practical inquiry, social organization, and everyday work that are far removed from academic discussions. In short, the recognizable accents of realism and antirealism in the discourse at the hearings were less the expression of stable metaphysical positions than of rhetorical moves and countermoves in a particular, contingent historical and institutional setting.

MASTER NARRATIVES AND THE SOCIAL PRODUCTION OF HISTORY

The principal task of an historicist approach to social theory is to produce, criticize, and validate master narratives as the "motor forces of history."[17]

Such histories subsume the partial and contingent details of lived events within the explanatory matrix of an overarching historical purpose or scheme. In canonical form, the master narratives of social theory are written in a universal voice by authors who possess the professional credentials to write them. These features confer legitimacy and distinguish professional histories from more vulgar forms of situated stories, myths, and folk tales.[18]

Challenges to the traditional privilege enjoyed by the grand narratives of social theory are by now widespread and widely documented.[19] Critics of the classical picture argue that criteria of historical interpretation are neither stable nor universalistic, and that the facts of history depend heavily on the style of their narration. Hayden White, for example, argues that the distinction between factual histories and fictional narratives is parasitic upon canons of coherence and correspondence to which both forms of writing must inevitably appeal.

> Readers of histories and novels can hardly fail to be struck by their similarities . . . (v)iewed simply as verbal artifacts histories and novels are indistinguishable from one another . . . (e)very history must meet standards of coherence no less than those of correspondance if it is to pass as a plausible account of "the way things really were" . . . (a) mere list of confirmable singular existential statements does not add up to an account of reality if there is not some coherence, logical or aesthetic, connecting them one to another. So too every fiction must pass a test of correspondence (it must be "adequate" as an image of something beyond itself) if it is to lay claim to representing an insight into or illumination of the human experience of the world.[20]

By collapsing the distinction between fact and fiction, White is *not* recommending that the writing of history should come to a halt. Rather, he is arguing for a renewal of forms of historical analysis that address themselves to the stylistics of master narratives, and therein, to the practical methods by which the facts of history are constituted and assembled.

Within contemporary social theory, at least three general kinds of response to the perceived decline of master narratives have been at work. The first, which is most closely associated with Habermas's program of communicative ethics, attempts to salvage the project of universal history by situating the rational, utopian element of Enlightenment thought within the basic argumentative structures of everyday communication.[21] Habermas's central thesis is that human communication is intrinsically rational, that communicative rationality has an inescapably ethical component, and that by reconstructing the rational basis of speech, the basic terms of conduct that underlie processes of consensual will-formation can be specified and defended. Thus, Habermas's strategy is to reinterpret the decline of master narratives as an element within an even grander narrative and in this way to subsume the alleged "end of philosophy" within what he terms the "unfinished project of modernity." This strategy places Habermas squarely within the classic tradition of philosophy and social theory.[22]

A second response to the decline of master narratives is to argue that the period of Western history in which knowledge is validated by means of appeals to a transcendental narrative of rational thought and action is in fact something of a historical aberration now in the process of winding down. This line of argument is used by Rorty to pull the plug on the attempt by Habermas to resuscitate Enlightenment thought.[23] In Rorty's account, narrative knowledge is distributed, criticized, evaluated, and ratified in a manner independent of the metanarratives that form the currency of modernist philosophy and social theory. For Rorty, then, philosophical metanarratives are nothing more (or less) than the form that knowledge ordinarily takes within that singular form of discourse known as philosophy, a discursive field that, like any other, draws its sense and cogency from the "quiet agreement" of a community of copractitioners.

Rorty's achievement is to have placed philosophical metanarratives on humble footing. By conceiving philosophy as one among many practices for designing and disseminating narrative knowledge, he places the writing of history on mundane footing. For him, the recitation of history is up for grabs; it is the task of countless voices and narrational techniques. A problem with his position persists, however. Having dismantled transcendental philosophy, Rorty cannot as a good philosopher resist the temptation of putting something else in its place. While he rejects both the need for philosophy to operate as an independent arbiter of the "good" and the "just," he places his faith in the workings of the interpretive communities that produce the diverse and interwoven ordinary narratives of daily life. His famous reply to Habermas suggesting that philosophy should relax and "let ordinary narratives do their stuff" beautifully captures a theological moment at the center of his thought: we must place our faith in the intrinsic justness of quotidian social life to fill the ethical space left vacant by the decline of philosophical master narratives.[24]

In contrast to both Habermas and Rorty, Lyotard not only expresses a generalized "incredulity toward metanarratives"—a posture he takes to be definitive of postmodernism—but he extends that incredulity to the ordinary narratives (*petits récits*) that circulate throughout daily life.[25] As Arac has noted, "Lyotard does not trust the integrity of 'communities' any more than of 'totality.' "[26] In our view, the great merit of Lyotard's approach to narrative knowledge is that, unlike Habermas and Rorty, he expects little in the way of philosophical redemption or ethical guidance from the so-called ordinary structures of communication. For Lyotard, "grammar" is always a potentially equivocal and hostile force.

According to Lyotard, narrative knowledge is produced and circulated through the repetition of a story. The story is kept in play whenever a former addressee relays it to others. The story is validated not by reference to external standards, but by its ritual enactment and familiarity: "it certifies itself in the pragmatics of its own transmission without having recourse to argumentation and proof."[27] The grammatical constituents of narrative knowledge are thus proverbial and iterative utterances. Lyotard contrasts narrative knowledge to scientific knowledge, arguing that, at least in principle, scientific knowledge emphasizes the truth-value of denotative statements. Accordingly, scientific statements are set outside the commonplace expressions made by members of a historical community and are subject to critical testing by competent researchers, enabling a cumulative progression of new statements to be built on previously certified statements. Although modern science often purports to stand in judgment of commonplace maxims and homilies, Lyotard argues that the "language games" of science cannot legitimate themselves "scientifically." Instead, a metadiscourse of narrative knowledge—Lyotard's "grand narrative"—is required to confer legitimacy on a scientific program and its political-economic support system. Examples of such grand narratives include "the dialectics of Spirit, the hermeneutics of meaning, the emancipation of the rational or working subject, or the creation of wealth."[28]

Like many other panoramic treatments of history and society, Lyotard's assessment of the "postmodern condition" presents a typology that greatly exaggerates the differences between traditional mythology and modern rationality.[29] His picture of scientific knowledge, for instance, is indebted to the Vienna Circle's program for a unified science, even while it seeks to undermine the hegemony of science by emphasizing the incommensurable pragmatics of other species of knowledge. This is symptomatic of a contradiction that pervades Lyotard's theorizing. On the one hand, he wants to radicalize the "incredulity toward metanarratives" and turn it into a principle of philosophical analysis, while on the other, he relies upon a conventional philosophical tale in order to set up that principle's "truth value." By doing so, he turns the incredulity toward metanarratives into both a working method and a kind of "reflection of the age." In this way, as Jameson correctly observes, Lyotard's theory "becomes itself a symptom of the state it seeks to diagnose."[30]

A more substantive problem with Lyotard's notion of grand narrative is that it transforms an occasional distinction (that is, the distinction between telling stories and justifying them) into a generic contrast between two distinct narrational forms. Although this distinction allows him to isolate what is specifically modern about the contemporary era, thus setting out the condition that *post*modernity, by definition, supersedes, it makes it appear as though telling a story is an activity (or set of activities) separate from justifying the terms or methods by which that story is told. We wish to argue, by contrast, that a central feature of the social distribution of narrative knowledge is that telling stories is hopelessly intertwined with methods for establishing moral entitlements and justifications.

For all its difficulties, Lyotard's notion of grand narrative nonetheless suggests an original and interesting analytic postulate: that methods, grammars, and technologies for evidencing and justifying claims concerning historical knowledge are already present in, and constitutive of, the worldly events that professional historians describe. Further, it suggests that along with these has arisen an array of countermethods and locally operative "incredulities" for equivocating and undermining the "knowledge effects" of such historical methods and measures.[31] Accordingly, a way to redeem the claim that postmodern knowledge consists in an incredulity toward metanarratives is to attempt to locate particular sites where the plausibility, cogency, and durability of some metanarrative is specifically at issue, and to treat the contesting of that narrative as a resource for examining the practices of postmodernism in situ. Hence, our project attempts to take what is most plausible and suggestive in Lyotard's account of postmodern knowledge and to give it an ethnomethodological spin.

What Lyotard fails to consider is that the corpus of master narratives is more than a static body of origin myths, folk tales about a remote past, epic poems about heroes and demigods, proverbs, and rituals. It includes stories of the recent history of the tribe, including the conflicts, catastrophes, triumphs, and scandals recollected by storytellers and their hearers. Such stories are not merely idiosyncratic since they are told on behalf of a community (family, group, organization, or society). In addition, cultural narratives may be subject to dispute, and in some cases members may undertake investigations in which arguments are made and evidences proffered in the interest of establishing that a given story is not merely a version of what occurred, but is in fact an account of "just-what-happened."[32] While such arguments and investigations are rarely dignified with scientific status, it is important to notice that they nonetheless aim to establish singular "facts of the matter" and are routinely successful at doing so.

When we speak of "master narratives," therefore, we mean something different from "grand narratives" in Lyotard's sense. For us, a master narrative is a somewhat less grand account of a historical event; it is the plain and practical version (or limited range of versions) that is rapidly and progressively disseminated throughout a relevant community. Its key features are transmissibility and relative durability.[33] Examples from our own recent history include the Army-McCarthy hearings, the assassination of John F. Kennedy (or of his brother Robert), the Profumo affair in Great Britain, the Kent State massacre, the Watergate scandal, and the Vietnam War. Each of these was once a major news story; each was the subject for one or more official investigations; and each eventually became a widely familiar historical event, including a cast of characters, key actions occurring at particular locales on specific dates, and a complex organization of fateful occurrences and moral implications. Each of these stories can be elaborated in greater or lesser depth of detail, and each is said to signify a more general historical era or moral circumstance. Although points of doubt and disagreement may linger, sometimes to such an extent that questions once assumed to have been answered are reopened for further investigation, the basic terms of these events have nonetheless begun to settle in to history. These narratives are told and retold as relatively stable constituents of a history that anybody knows as a member of the relevant culture.

Master narratives are collaboratively fashioned. They have no single author but are the product of various positionings within a field of documents, testimonies, and descriptive possibilities. Authoritative contributors monitor this field for the writings and erasures that constitute the story's development into a relatively stable historical text. Authors assume partisan and nonpartisan identities; some are identified as key characters and eyewitnesses who testify about the event, while others purport to give nonpartisan reports, and still others write official histories based on authorized investigations. Few if any of these authors are trained historians, although their testimonies and reports often provide the raw archival data that are later consulted by professional historians. No single author has a free hand in compiling, ratifying, and certifying a master narrative, although some hands are freer than others. Both the temporality of an original event and a progression of accounts, investigations, and disputes about the event become part of a collective history.

Without exception, compilers of master narratives orient to the reality of an event. Their accounts explicitly aim to establish a real-worldly chronicle of actual persons, organizations, dates, actions, and motives. While they make free use of such literary figures as the hero, the femme fatale, the unwitting victim, the scapegoat, and the tragic coincidence, these writers seek to establish and maintain a singularly factual point of historical reference for narrative figures and tropes. Although their accounts are, at times, barely distinguishable from the docudramatic reenactments that often follow in the wake of a public scandal, the writers of master narratives exude a serious interest in getting to the bottom of the matter. In this aim, they display a tolerance for tedium and a faith in the power of positive inquiry that is most closely associated with the tenor and mood of the laboratory, the seminar, and other sites of scientific and academic investigation. In this way—and this point is absolutely crucial to our analysis—the earnestness and sincerity with which writers of master narratives pursue their task is integral to that task's adequate completion.

What Jean-François Lyotard and Oliver North have in common is a commitment to disrupting this picture of historical knowledge. While Lyotard's position is the more explicitly "theoretical" of the two, North, along with his colleagues and other experts within the intelligence community, remorselessly asserts the right to advance his local knowledge of events in opposition to the privilege accorded to the committee's master narrational task. In this sense, North's position is the more "applied" of the two, representing a material advance on mere theories of postmodernity. In short, while Lyotard and his colleagues have been occupied with the idea of postmodern culture, North and his associates have been putting it to work.

We should note, however, that Lyotard's conception of postmodernity also includes a practical moment. The "incredulity toward metanarratives" is more than just an attitude, it is also a resource underlying an entire form of life and critical practice. "Postmodern knowledge is not simply a tool of the authorities; it refines our sensitivity to differences and reinforces our ability to tolerate the incommensurable. Its principle is not the expert's homology, but the inventor's parology."[34] By identifying postmodern knowledge with a historical knowledge and material "sensitivity to differences," Lyotard means to identify tactical options (or "positions") that become available once the Enlightenment faith in positive inquiry, along with the consequent demand for self-justification, has been discharged. However, to the extent that these positions are defined solely by their mistrust of that earlier form of knowledge, they continue to revolve in its orbit. Incredulity is not what comes after, but is instead that which comes just after modernity, a kind of "pre-postmodernism" that stands in the breach between classical epistemology and the abyss of mirrors.

So far, we have been trying to build a case for the pertinence of the Iran-contra hearings to recent debates in philosophy and social theory and, in particular, to discussions concerning the nature and use of historical knowledge. We have argued that the notion of master narratives is central to these discussions, although perhaps not in the way many theorists seem to think. As an alternative to the predominant usage that identifies master narratives with the totalizing mythologies of philosophy and ideology, we have suggested a pragmatically respecified conception of master narratives that emphasizes the need for and use of a practical historical ground from which cogent narratives of past events can be assembled and ratified in situ. One benefit of this conception is that it calls attention to the actual workings of a historical record, a record neither groundless nor assured, but assembled in and through a determined struggle over history's accountabilities. The remainder of this chapter will be occupied with further specifying this conception of master narratives, with particular attention to the use of chronologies in the assembly of conventional historical accounts.

HOT AND COLD CHRONOLOGIES

Although master narratives (in the sense we use the term) have a characteristic plasticity, and are defeasible, they are not easily displaced, because they are built up through agreements among key constituencies and concordances among constituent records and testimonies. Their conventional status, recitation, and reiteration provide them with a variable degree of stability. During the Iran-contra hearings, much of the work of stabilizing (or "fixing") such narratives had to do with establishing dates in chronologies of events.

In his conclusion to *The Savage Mind,* Lévi-Strauss makes an elegant and powerful case for conceiving historical knowledge as a species of mythology.[35] He begins by arguing that history is distinguished from other forms of narrative by virtue of its dependence on dates. "Dates," he argues, "may not be the whole of history, nor what is most interesting about it, but they are its *sine qua non* . . ." (p. 258). If calendrical dates are the raw material of history, its basic form is chronology. The sense and significance of any particular date—its remarkableness, stability, and coherence as a historical object—depends on its positioning within some larger chronological order, as well as on its figural use as an element in that order. If, as Lévi-Strauss concludes, "[t]here is no history without dates," it also is true that there are no dates without history. That is, the work of assembling chronologies—what Lévi-Strauss refers to as the "code" of historical knowledge—is already available in and prefigured by the particular acts of dating.

As an illustration of this point, Lévi-Strauss distinguishes between what he calls "hot" and "cold" chronologies, or the "variable quantity of dates applied to periods of equal duration." Hot chronologies form a literary environment for "periods where in the eyes of the historian numerous events appear as differential elements," whereas cold chronologies cover those periods where, for the historian, "very little or nothing took place" (p. 259). The distinction marks the variable intensity of interest and activity with which historians approach what (in principle) are the innumerable facts and events of history.

A second thing Lévi-Strauss observes about the ordering of dates is that any particular date is always a member of some particular category of date as well, or as he puts it, "a date is a *member* of a class." So, for an example, for some purposes "November 22, 1963," will be a perfectly good way of dating J.F.K.'s assassination, but not for a coroner's inquest, which will likely require a recounting that follows an order of minutes, seconds, or even—in the case of J.F.K.'s assassination—fractions of seconds and frames of film. Likewise, for a historian of the 1960s, what is important about the assassination is that it happened relatively early in the decade, whereas a biographer might be specifically more concerned to record Kennedy's assassination in terms relative to his life (age, marital status, years as president, etc.). Hence, dates not only order events chronologically, but they order them categorically. Every particular date is also an index to a category or collection of dates, and these collections and category terms operate as methodic devices for assembling and organizing history. The upshot of these considerations is that the method for arriving at date references cannot be that of merely selecting from among an array of factually correct equivalents. On the contrary, the clarity, simplicity, and correctness of dating hinges on its providing an order of chronological reference suited to some present circumstance.[36] From this approach it follows that struggles over what constitutes a good or adequate date reference may be symptomatic of deeper disagreements concerning what constitutes the "present circumstance."

These reflections on chronologies not only evidence the different pressures exerted on the historical imagination by different periods or events, but they show the ways in which stable and coherent chronologies are the products of concrete historical work. As Hayden White observes, "not only are there 'hot' and 'cold' chronologies . . . more importantly, the dates themselves are grouped into 'classes of dates' which are constitutive of putative 'domains of history' that historians of a given age must confront as 'problems' to be solved. In short, appeal to the chronological sequence affords no relief from the charge that the coherency of the historical account is mythological in nature."[37]

For this reason, Lévi-Strauss's insistence on the mythological nature of historical accounts represents a fundamental challenge to any attempt at making a principled distinction between the "facts" of history and history's methods of assembly. This is not to say that no legitimate factual claims exist, or that history is without a basis. Rather, the central claim is that wherever, whenever, and in just those ways that factual claims are made and substantiated, they inevitably appeal to conventions of reading, writing, and reasoning about history that are not, in their own right, subject to the same criteria used for evaluating historical claims. Instead, it is the practical methods and technologies that constitute those criteria and, thus, that lend them their force.

A close connection exists between the idea that writing history is essentially writing myth and the idea that historians' practical methods can be studied for the ways in which fields of facts are rendered as story-able events. Following Frye's work on the stylistics of historical narrative, White summarizes his perspective as follows:

> it can be argued that interpretation in history consists of the provisions of a plot structure for a sequence of events so that their nature as a comprehensible process is revealed by their figuration as a *story of a particular kind.* What one historian may emplot as a tragedy, another may emplot as a comedy or romance. As thus envisaged, the "story" which the historian purports to "find" in the historical record is proleptic to the "plot" by which the events are finally revealed to figure a recognizable structure of relationships of a specifically mythic sort.[38]

The suggestion that the story being "found" through the work of history adumbrates its own plot structure (what White terms its "mode of emplotment")[39] is significant because it allows us to further specify how the facts of history intertwine with the methods of its assembly. Factual information (e.g., documents and other archival materials, oral histories, firsthand testimonies, etc.) is collected and assembled categorically, with an eye to its inclusion (or exclusion) within a developing narrative.

Consider, for instance, the following exchange between North and John Nields (counsel for the House majority), which is taken from the first day of North's testimony:

Nields: And in fact you, uh went out to the c.i.a. and spent uh virtually all the day Saturday there. (1.6)
North: What was that date? (3.2)
Nields: I believe it's the twenty-third.
(Nields): °November eighty-five,° (6.0)
Nields: ((throat clear)) You might want to check exhibit forty-six. (26.0)
North: °(let's see, that's the twenty-third,)° (3.5)
North: That is cor*rect.* ((throat clear))[40]

In this case, Nields's lead question, "And in fact you . . . uh went out to the c.i.a. and spent uh virtually all the day:: Saturday there," formulates the day in question as "Saturday" and hence, as one of the category "days of the week." Rather than simply confirming Nields's assertion of fact, North requests a reformulation of the day in terms of a specific calendrical date. This, in turn, occasions a search for the document upon which Nields's initial question was based. Having located the document, and having found his signature in a copy of the cia logbook for November 23, North then confirms that he indeed was there the entire day. Note, however, that while he has confirmed his presence at the cia, he has not acceded to the category structure "days of the week," even though it is, in a sense, factually correct that he spent "all the day Saturday there." The difference between the characterizations "all the day Saturday" and "November 23rd" consists in at least the following: whereas the name of the day can be located as part of the "events of the week" (and, perhaps, as "business that pressed on into the weekend"), the date in the month is a calendrical formulation that is detached from the familiar details of its spontaneous recollection within a narrative stream of witnessed events. If North accedes to the characterization "all the day Saturday," he accedes to the terms of a first-person narrative, and worse, to the plot structure of a story that he will be asked to tell.

From this example we can see how categorizations of dates and times adumbrate specific sorts of narratives. Further, the example shows how determinations of plot structure are bound up with the issue of gaining access to the recollections of a witness, and so, more generally, to questions concerning the conventional organization of memory. The following is a particularly clear illustration of how plot structure and category selection can be used to key into witnesses' recollections:

Nields: You were present, I take it, at a meeting on the twentieth of November in Admiral Poindexter's office.

North: Let me try to recall.

Nields: Thursday, early afternoon, the day before Director Casey was to testify before the House and Senate Intelligence Committee.

North: Yes, I was.[41]

Here, Nields's initial utterance refers to a meeting in terms of a calendrical date ("the 20th of November") and a specific location ("in Admiral Poindexter's office"). After North fails to confirm, Nields then reformulates the meeting in terms that locate it within the structure of the week ("Thursday, early afternoon") organized around a series of well-known events ("the day before Director Casey was to testify before the House and Senate Intelligence Committee"). This sequence inverts the epistemic trajectory of the previous example. Whereas in the earlier exchange the interrogator was forced to suspend the project of accessing the spontaneous recollection of a witness and to reformulate the event in terms amenable to documentary inspection—in this case, an event initially formulated in the language of documentary exhibits is then respecified in terms of a local narrative of familiar—perhaps even *unforgettable*—events. In this way, the "recollectable meeting" becomes an evident product of the course of interrogation.

Like the professional historians discussed by White, the different parties to the Iran-contra hearings had different, often conflicting interests in the developing story. Struggles between witnesses and investigators were not only about the presumed facts of the case, but they were about how those facts fit together (or could be fitted together) within a coherent narrative structure. In short, the generally agonistic character of the proceedings emerged out of the particulars of a struggle over emplotment. Specific testimonies and shards of documentary evidence were appropriated and put to use as elements within some developing story and, thus, were heard and routinely challenged not as isolated factual particulars, but as categorical descriptions embedded within a larger plot structure. Consequently, what we find on the videotaped record of the hearings is ultimately inseparable from previous contentions over what mode of emplotment should best "capture" the facts of the matter. The proper image, then, is not of the solitary author sitting down with the stable record of relevant events, dates, places, and personages involved, and from this record, deducing a singular chronology of events; instead, the image is of a multiplicity of contending and ever-shifting factions, each working to capture the facts within a plot structure most favorable to their interests. Even deeper, it is a record through which each faction tries to produce facts of particular kinds in anticipation of a later need to organize those facts in line with a specific mode of emplotment.

By focusing on the sorts of historical analyses that parties to the hearings were required to carry out over the course of the hearings, we can begin to glimpse a form of social inquiry based ultimately on investigations of historians' work. What remains to be considered is how the more specific theme of assembling and working with chronologies figured in the conduct of the committee's historical investigations.

TRUE AND FALSE CHRONOLOGIES

Published histories of the Iran-contra affair varied widely in depth and detail. At the short and shallow end was a two-page account of the "Road to Scandal" in *The Story of Lieutenant Colonel Oliver North,* by the editors of *U.S. News & World Report,* while at the deeper end was Theodore Draper's more scholarly account, *A Very Thin Line,* and in between were the official reports by the Tower commission and the Iran-contra committees. All of these histories employed chronologies organized in terms of a sequence of dates (between 1979 and 1987 in the case of the committees' report, or 1984 and 1987 in the case of the two-page potted summary by *U.S. News & World Report*). In all of the chronologies the "hottest," or most dense, documentation was for 1985 and 1986, with a particularly concentrated sequence devoted to November 1986, when news of "the scandal" first broke.

U.S. News & World Report

November 2. Hostage David Jacobsen released.

November 3. Beirut newspaper publishes first news about McFarlane's May 25 Tehran visit and arms-for-hostages deal. Reagan later denies story.

November 5–20. North helps draft misleading chronologies of Iran-Contra events.

November 21. Meese investigation begins. North tells secretary Fawn Hall to alter documents. Poindexter destroys 11-month-old presidential finding retroactively approving arms deal.

November 22. Justice Department investigators find North memo on Contra diversion. North shreds documents in presence of department investigators.

November 25. Poindexter is reassigned, North fired from NSC. Meese announces he has evidence of $10 to $30 million diversion to Contras from Iran deals. North and Hall smuggle documents out of North's office.

November 30. President calls North a "national hero."[42]

Report of the Congressional Committees

November 2. Jacobsen is released.

November 3. A Lebanese magazine, *Al-Shiraa,* discloses that the U.S. sent arms to Iran and that McFarlane visited Tehran.

November 5–6. Press accounts confirm the story, even as the White House issues a denial.

November 10. The President's senior advisors argue over how to respond. Reagan, according to notes taken at the session, agrees there is need for a public statement but tells his aides to "stay away from detail."

November 12–19. North and other White House officials prepare increasingly inaccurate chronologies of events in the Iran affair.

November 19. Reagan holds a press conference and makes major errors of fact. He insists, for example, that no other country was involved, even though Israel was shipping many of the weapons. He says 1,000 TOWs were sent when the number was actually 2,004. Minutes after the press conference ends, advisors correct the misstatement about Israel.

November 21. William J. Casey, the Director of Central Intelligence, appears before House and Senate Intelligence Committees after a major battle within the Administration over what he will say about the CIA's role in the November 1985 arms shipment. Attorney General Edwin Meese III says he is disturbed by confusion over the facts and suggests that the President have him conduct an inquiry. North is told that Justice Department officials will inspect his files the next day, and he begins shredding documents.

November 22. A Justice Department official, Bradford Reynolds, finds an April 1986 memo to the President that mentions the diversion of funds to the Contras.

November 23. North tells Meese there was a diversion of funds but misstates other crucial aspects of the deal.

November 24. Meese goes to the White House and tells the President of the diversion. White House Chief of Staff Donald T. Regan attends and his reaction to the news is "horror, horror, horror, horror."

November 25. Meese announces the diversion of money from the Iran arms sales to the Contras. Reagan announces Poindexter's resignation and North's dismissal.[43]

A Very Thin Line

November 2. American hostage, David Jacobsen, director of American University Hospital in Beirut, released.

November 3. Lebanese weekly *Al-Shiraa* publishes partially accurate exposé of U.S.-Iran dealings, including McFarlane's mission in May 1986.

November 4. Speaker Rafsanjani gives Iranian Parliament (Majlis) a partial, tendentious account of previous U.S.-Iran dealings.

November 8–10. North, Secord, Cave, and Hakim meet with Bahramani and Samii in Geneva.

November 10. President Reagan, Secretary of State Shultz, Secretary of Defense Weinberger, and other principals meet to discuss repercussions of *Al-Shiraa* revelations.

November 13. President Reagan makes television speech which unsuccessfully tries to explain dealings with Iran.

November 13. National Security Adviser Poindexter for the first time briefs congressional leaders.

November 14. Secretary of State Shultz makes first attempt to change President Reagan's Iran policy.

November 16. Secretary Shultz makes embarrassing appearance on *Face the Nation* television program.

November 18. Legal meeting called by White House counsel Peter Wallison, which first alarms Abraham D. Sofaer, State Department legal adviser.

November 19. Secretary Shultz privately tells President Reagan he has been misinformed.

November 19. President Reagan holds disastrous press conference.

November 20. Discussion in Poindexter's office on "chronology," implying systematic deception about November 1985 "horror story."

November 20. State Department legal advisor Sofaer suspects a "cover-up."

November 21. Attorney General Meese is commissioned "to develop a coherent overview of all the facts."

November 21. Poindexter destroys copy of Finding No. 1.

November 22. Attorney General Meese's aides, William Bradford Reynolds and John N. Richardson, Jr., discover "diversion memo" in Oliver North's office.

November 23. Meese interviews North, who confirms that "diversion" was in
   fact carried out.

November 24. Meese briefly informs Reagan of the diversion of funds from the
   Iran arms sales to the Nicaraguan contras.

November 25. Poindexter offers resignation. National Security Council and
   congressional leaders briefed.

November 25. Press conference in which Meese gives a distorted version of the
   "diversion" and threatens North with possible criminal charges.

November 26. President Reagan appoints Special Review Board (Tower Board)
   to conduct study of NSC staff.[44]

In each of these three cases the chronology was accompanied by a cast of
characters briefly identifying the persons named in the chronology. The
lists overlapped, although Draper's included more characters, while the
committee report and the *U.S. News & World Report* account gave slightly
more elaborate blurbs for each character. All three lists used similar formats in which the character's name was followed by a listing of his official
title(s) at the time of the Iran-contra affair, often including a brief summary
of his "involvement." The *U.S. News & World Report* account gave the
characters' ages, an indication of the relatively time-bound presentation of
its "news." John Poindexter, for example, was listed in the three chronologies, respectively, as follows:

> *U.S. News:* John Poindexter, 50, former national-security adviser. Said he
> authorized diversion of arms-sales proceeds to Contras, but did not tell Rea-
> gan. The Tower Commission claimed he "failed grievously" in duty to the
> boss. He says he did not tell the President about arms-sales diversion, ex-
> plaining that he wanted him to have "deniability."

> *Report of the Congressional Committees:* John M. Poindexter: The vice ad-
> miral who was National Security Adviser from December 1985 to November
> 1986. Allowed to resign after investigators learned of the diversion. Took full
> responsibility for authorizing the diversion of Iran arms sale proceeds to the
> Contras. Said he had not told the President about the diversion to protect
> Reagan from political embarrassment. Although praised throughout his
> Navy career as an officer who had a photographic memory, and a penchant
> for keeping superiors informed, he told the Iran Committees repeatedly that

he could not recall key events of his tenure and kept vital information from the President.

A Very Thin Line: Poindexter, John M.: Vice Admiral, U.S. Navy; Deputy National Security Adviser, 1983–85; National Security Adviser, 1986.

Although many interesting differences are apparent among these three chronologies and casts of characters, they do not directly contradict one another. The main differences have to do with the inclusion or noninclusion of details about characters, identities, responsibilities, and events. Each chronology is presented as an index for the more extensive stories told in each main text. The major parts of the committee report and Draper's book also proceed chronologically, providing discursive accounts that for the most part flesh out the skeletal chronological indices. With the aid of these indices, readers can infer some of the distinctive features of the particular stories told. For example, the *U.S. News & World Report* chronology includes an entry for November 30 that the other two chronologies do not. This entry—"President calls North a 'national hero' "—plays into the theme of North's heroism that preoccupies the particular text (a special issue of a popular conservative magazine, published at a time when "Ollie" was at the height of his fame). Or, in another case, Draper's chronology mentions the roles played by Shultz and Sofaer in pressing Reagan and Meese to begin an internal investigation of the scandal, whereas the other chronologies do not. Sofaer, the State Department legal adviser, had a significant role in Draper's account, but not in most other versions of the Iran-contra story. This different emphasis is also indexed by the relatively "hot" chronology Draper provides from November 14 through 21.

Although much more could be said about the particular differences among the chronologies, and about the story elements they prefigure, we should be careful not to ignore the tremendous, if rather bland, convergences among them. If one were so inclined, it would be possible to formulate a relatively uncontentious or bare-bones chronology that registers a minimal set of dates, events, and characters that none of the chroniclers would dispute. Taking some of their common elements, we have:

November 2. American hostage David Jacobsen released.
November 3. Lebanese weekly *Al-Shiraa* publishes exposé of U.S.-Iran dealings, including McFarlane's mission in May 1986.

November 12–19. North and other White House officials prepare false chronologies of events in the Iran affair for release to press and public.

November 21. Meese and other staff members from the office of the attorney general begin an investigation.

November 22–23. The "diversion memo" is found during the Meese investigation, and North is questioned about it.

November 25. Poindexter resigns, North is fired, and these events are made public.

While this chronology might be easily faulted for being sparse and uninteresting, it nevertheless indexes largely agreed-to landmarks in the history of the Iran-contra affair. Such a chronology does not, of course, reside outside history. Its specifications, like those of any other account, would be subject to revision and challenge in light of further revelations that might eventually show it to be erroneous, but it does begin to identify some of the referential specifics that frame the three chronologies as mildly different versions of the same story.

Although they differ in detail, all three chronologies presume an epistemic distinction between their accounts and the "false chronologies" constructed by North and others in mid-November 1986. The three "true" chronologies used a related set of predicates to describe the false accounts of the Iran-contra affair produced by North, Poindexter, Reagan, and others during that month, referring to "misleading chronologies," "increasingly inaccurate chronologies," "major errors of fact," and "systematic deception." According to the true chronologies, the false chronologies were constructed by North and others in November 1986. The more specific accounts (Draper's and the committees' report) identify inaccurate, misleading, or deceptive aspects of these false chronologies in descriptions of two arms shipments to Iran: an August–September 1985 TOW missile shipment of 504 from Israel to Iran, and a "horror story" (a characterization North offered during his testimony) involving a shipment of eighteen Hawk missiles in November 1985 (officially identified as "oil-drilling parts") from Israel, through Portugal, to Iran, using CIA proprietary airlines. The committee report describes the "most glaring misrepresentations" as follows:

The initial versions of the chronology, prepared by North on November 7 included fairly accurate references to those shipments. McFarlane then sent a PROF message to Poindexter on November 7 suggesting that "[i]t might be useful to review what the truth is. . . ." But McFarlane's version was not the "truth":

–He asserted that the August–September TOW shipments occurred when the Israelis "went ahead on their own" after McFarlane had disapproved; and

–He made no mention at all of the November 1985 Hawk shipment.[45]

Draper gives a more elaborate account of the false chronologies:

North, with the help of a few others, wrote and rewrote the chronology at least a dozen times between about November 5 and November 20. Records had been poorly kept. North himself did not know much about the early phase of the U.S.-Israel-Iran connection in 1985 and had to resort to McFarlane to fill in gaps. Above all, North tried to hide or distort some aspects of the story, as a result of which he repeatedly found himself in trouble.

One of the most troublesome subjects for North was the November 1985 "horror story." As North later explained, his version was largely false "because we were at that point in time making an effort to dissociate ourselves with the earlier Israeli shipments." In a chronology of November 17, he made it appear that the Israelis had been solely responsible for providing Iran with Hawk missiles in November 1985 and that the United States had disapproved of the Israeli action. This version was drastically altered in the last chronology of November 20, in which a number of new falsehoods were added.[46]

By citing later testimonies by North, Secord, McFarlane, and others, Draper is able to report admissions and descriptions of deliberate efforts to falsify the chronologies. According to these descriptions, the various drafts of the chronologies were attended by disputes and negotiations about how best to word them.

McFarlane later admitted that he had participated in an "exercise" to "gild the President's motives" and that he had concealed the fact that the U.S. government had approved of the Israeli shipments. McFarlane was apparently influenced by a "climate in which there was an obvious effort to, as I said, distance and to blur the President's role in the initial authorization, in both timing and substance." McFarlane later acknowledged that it had been "misleading, at least, and wrong, at worst, for me to overly gild the President's motives for his decisions in this, to portray them as mostly directed toward political outcomes," instead of toward the return of the hostages.

North also had some trouble fitting the CIA into the story. According to North, the CIA had given him a version which made it appear that it had had little to do with the Iran operation and that the NSC staff was largely or wholly responsible for it. North was disturbed, because it implied that he and the NSC staff had acted on their own and had to accept full responsibility for everything.[47]

As Draper summarizes them, the disputes over the chronologies covered particular words and phrases used to describe events. Regarding the November 1985 Hawk shipment, an initial CIA document included the sentence, "We in CIA did not find out that our airline had hauled Hawk missiles into Iran until mid-January when we were told by the Iranians."[48] Draper adds that "North was offended by the first three words" because they implied that others in the government (and specifically members of the NSC staff) were aware of what the planes contained. North succeeded in negotiating a change to "No one, in the U.S. G[overnment]."[49] North and Poindexter both admitted that they knew this wording was inaccurate. According to testimony at the hearings, despite North's and McFarlane's best efforts to "gild the president's motives" through the literary method of "constructive ambiguity," an array of evident inaccuracies and discrepancies became a source of intensive concern. British journalist Ann Wroe describes how officials from the CIA and the Israeli government advised that it would be better to deny the events and refuse to disclose the details than to release a document with discrepancies and inaccuracies, each detail of which "opened up a new nest of worms."[50]

Given the considerations raised by White and others regarding the formal similarities between fictional and nonfictional narratives, it seems worthwhile to take up the question of how, over the course of these and similar accounts of the Iran-contra affair, the false chronologies get picked up and discussed by the true chronologies, and so, how their falsity becomes an evident product of later historical work. Viewed retrospectively, there seems little reason to doubt that the chronologies assembled by North and his colleagues were, indeed, false. North and others later admitted that they intended to falsify the chronologies; they had an obvious interest in falsifying them; the serial changes in the chronologies give ample evidence of such intent and interest; and other witnesses testified that North attempted to enlist their support for writing chronologies they knew to be inaccurate at the time. We should remember, however (to paraphrase North), that it is "the very nature" of false chronologies to make fictionalized histories appear as fact, and thus, to make them unrecognizable as fiction. The identification of particular fictions is thus an investigative achievement that points to a more general difficulty of distinguishing true from false chronologies, a difficulty that, as we discussed, is often complicated by the archival work of the historical natives. The fact that some writers can be charged with, and will confess to, writing false chronologies does not allow us to say that the chronologies we accept as adequate are thereby true without exception. Moreover, between these binary possibilities is a broad discretionary zone in which chronologies can be written to be equivocal, undecidable, partial, minimally defensible, "gilded," speculative, or dubious, without thereby being impeachable.

In light of these possibilities, Draper's account of the writing of the false chronologies becomes exceedingly interesting, not so much because the chronologies were false, but because the disputes and negotiations over the writing and rewriting of the chronologies shows how the particular details of their composition emerged in the midst of interagency disputes, desperate attempts to maintain "damage control" over a story that was already becoming public, and related efforts to allocate and mitigate blame. North and his colleagues were described as authors who oriented to their historic task not as free agents, but as writers constrained in their work by what other writers and sources had already said and were likely to say in the future. Although they maintained a measure of authorial privilege, they were also attuned to the fact that the story was not theirs alone to tell. The writing was proleptic and defensive, constrained less by commonly known historical facts than by the as-yet undetermined details of a history that was about to break in the public media. The writers of the false chronologies thus aimed to seize a rare opportunity to make history by repeating select details of a yet to be realized historical narrative to which they would later be held accountable.

In a similar way, the interrogation of North becomes intelligible as an exercise in writing an "official history" in which the broad discretionary space between true and false chronologies becomes the subject of an interminable effort by committee investigators to pin down elusive details, as-

cribe diffuse responsibilities, and depoliticize their account of those details and responsibilities. This struggle occurs at the surface of the text,
where parties contest the particular words and phrases that specify the
relevant names and identities of characters, as well as the temporal frames
in which those characters acted, the institutional "contexts" that authorized and legitimated their actions, and the tacit understandings with
which those actions were carried out. In these respects, it is not far-fetched
to speak of the testimony at the hearings as a public contest over the writing
of history, word by word, line by line.

CONCLUSION

A basic premise of our study is that while social theorists have been busy
describing and arguing about what constitutes the general principles of
postmodern politics, key figures in the Iran-contra affair have been putting
those principles to work. It is in this sense that the Iran-contra hearings—
and the North testimony in particular—provide a perspicuous instance of
"applied deconstructionism."

As was mentioned at the outset, this study's principal aim is to explicate
those practical methods by which conventional historical accounts are
assembled and written. It should by now be clear, however, that our interest in these proceedings extends well beyond an analytic fascination with
the interactional organization of interrogation. Rather than employing the
texts of the Iran-contra affair solely as objects of rhetorical analysis, we aim
to use the televisual and literary record of those events to force an engagement between ethnomethodology and contemporary social theory. As a
move in that direction, this chapter attempted to clarify how ethnomethodological studies differ from classic sociological approaches to the question
of history, and thereby to clarify what we mean by the tendentious suggestion that "history" might yet become an appreciable topic for sociology.

3. THE CEREMONIAL

OF TRUTH

The Iran-contra hearings were staged as a ceremony, a solemn, highly public, and formal tribunal for exposing the truth about a scandal. That ceremony provided a forum for enacting a civic ritual through which public representatives would pass judgment on the legal and moral status of actions taken in "the highest office in the land."[1] Efforts were made to assure the appearance of a serious, thorough, and bipartisan inquiry that would "get to the bottom" of the scandal and demonstrate the government's ability to isolate and correct individual abuses of power. This, after all, had been the lesson that many commentators derived from the Watergate hearings, a series of tribunals culminating in the resignation of President Richard Nixon in 1974.[2] By the time Oliver North finished testifying, however, it was clear that the Iran-contra hearings had produced an entirely different "civics lesson" than had been foreshadowed by Watergate (figs. 2 and 3). The public reaction to his testimony, a response celebrated by the tabloid press and dubbed "Olliemania," cast North into the role of "the hero" that a disenchanted "America needs." From the vantage point of the celebrants, his heroic defense of secrecy, sovereignty, and adventurism neutralized the imperatives of system and accountability, and a politics of patriotism and nostalgia triumphed over the legal-rational authority of the bureaucratic state. Not everybody joined the celebration, but widespread suspicions about North's dissimulation and dissembling seemed unable to stem the publicity arising from his patriotic appeals to the sovereign authority of his "boss."[3]

The inversion of ceremonial intent that occurred during the hearings recalls themes from Michel Foucault's vivid depiction of the "spectacle of the scaffold." According to Foucault, the eighteenth-century punitive spectacle was a perspicuous display of the exercise of monarchical power in a "regime of truth" displaced by the modern regime of rational justice and disciplinary power. While our reading of the spectacle of the scaffold may confound selected aspects of Foucault's historicism, it provides an apt starting point for understanding the material instabilities of the ceremonial of truth at a modern public tribunal.

2. and 3. North and Sullivan
face Nields, the Joint
Committees, and the texts.

CONFESSIONAL TRUTH AND THE SPECTACLE
OF THE SCAFFOLD

In *Discipline and Punish,* Foucault charts the disappearance of what he
terms "the great spectacle of physical punishment" and its replacement by
the modern penal practices epitomized by the anonymous and totalizing
vision of Jeremy Bentham's panopticon: a design for prisons and workhouses in which a mass of inmates would be deployed before the gaze of an
unseen supervisor placed at the center of an inverted amphitheater. Foucault tells a dark, satiric story focused on the underbelly of justice at the tail
end of the ancien régime. Following an excruciatingly morbid account of
the extended and torturous execution of Damiens the regicide, Foucault
goes on to discuss the semiotics of ritualized torture in the service of confessional truth and regal authority.[4] Whether used to extract a confession in

a secretive inquisition, or for the production of a punitive spectacle, the body of the condemned was the point of articulation of a sovereign power.

Foucault's vivid examples not only illustrate the effects of sovereign power at its material points of articulation, but more importantly they demonstrate the instability and reversibility of those effects. The diary of Bouton, an officer who witnessed Damiens's execution, supplies Foucault with a grisly account of the "actualities" and "slippages" that destabilized the semiotic field of the early-modern spectacle: when the executioner lights the sulphur to burn Damiens's flesh, it does not burn properly; the pincers prove unwieldy and ineffective; the drawn and quartered body does not easily break and pull apart at the joints. The spectacle of sovereign authority is superseded by the image of a cruel, inefficient, and arbitrary force exercised against the criminal body. Foucault goes on to recount other stories of botched executions, rancorous and fickle crowds, and wretched criminals who became heroes and martyrs performing on the public stage afforded by the spectacle of the scaffold. These stories demonstrate how practical contingencies and unplanned outbursts often rendered the intended lesson of the public execution unstable and equivocal. The prearranged ritual through which the condemned were associated with their crimes, branded with the stigma of the misdeed, and enjoined to confess provided a set of props and signs that could be dissociated from the preordained demonstration of sovereign power and recombined spontaneously in the carnival atmosphere of the execution.[5]

> If the crowd gathered round the scaffold, it was not simply to witness the sufferings of the condemned man or to excite the anger of the executioner: it was also to hear an individual who had nothing more to lose curse the judges, the laws, the government and religion. The public execution allowed the luxury of these momentary saturnalia, when nothing remained to prohibit or to punish. . . . In these executions, which ought to show only the terrorizing power of the prince, there was a whole aspect of the carnival, in which rules were inverted, authority mocked and criminals transformed into heroes.[6]

In principle, the spectacular excess of punishment was the logical extension of the established methods for extracting a confessional truth from the body of the accused. The sovereign, or his agents, performed their investigations with a liberal use of instruments of torture to force the truth from the lips of a recalcitrant "patient." The interrogation was conducted in secret, out of the sight of the unstable crowds, so that the "truth" that was later exhibited in the punitive spectacle was a product of an unimpeachable sovereign prerogative. The accused's confession, when (re)enacted for the public in the *amende honorable,* underlined a truth that was independently derived.[7] The logic of the confession was organized to reiterate the "living truth" of a text that was written during a preliminary investigation conducted in secret by the sovereign's agents.

Foucault argues that Beccaria and other Enlightenment reformers criticized this mode of investigation primarily on logical rather than humanitarian grounds. The calculative reasoning of the utilitarian philosophers and moral managers led them to conclude that public executions and secret interrogations were relatively inefficient mechanisms for assuring public compliance with state justice. From their perspective, as Foucault reconstructs it, the problem with the forced confession was that the truth so revealed was equivocal; the guilty who resisted the pains of torture would obscure their guilt, while the weak might falsely confess to gain relief. Like the corporal spectacle of the public execution, the obscure discourse of the torture session was subject to disruptions and inefficiencies. Elizabeth Hanson describes the Elizabethan interrogation of Catholic "traitors" as a confrontation between, on one side, a confessional "truth" being promoted by the torturer's "inarticulate ministrations," and, on the other, the recitation of a counterdiscourse of heretical prayers and religious arguments by the prisoner. As long as this discursive opposition was sustained, the dialogue necessary for the production of the confession was deferred. Hanson notes:

> Here [the torturer] became inarticulate, dependent upon the rack, the manacles, and the "scavenger's daughter" to "command" the prisoner as the Queen could not, dependent upon the victim to supply him with information, and most importantly, dependent on the victim to speak in the discourse in which this information constitutes the "truth." . . . As long as the victim could refuse to speak in the torturer's terms, either by praying instead of answering, or by directly asserting the religious nature of the struggle ("the Queen could not command [him] to sinne"), he could protract the inarticulateness of the torturer, widening the gap between his enemy's discourse and the truth which both sides agreed that the victim possessed.[8]

Foucault argues that interrogation and punishment underwent a rapid series of transformations toward the end of the eighteenth century. Initially, crime became penetrated by Reason and a rational calculus, and punishment was to "fit" the crime, not only in the interests of justice, but as means of creating a vivid image, or "fable," that taught a moral lesson to an impressionable audience.[9] Consistent with the designs for asylums and workhouses, an ideal punitive city would display the compensatory labors and theatrical tragedies enacted by a panoply of criminal characters, analogous to the pathetic works and embodied sufferings of the souls depicted in Dante's *Inferno* and *Purgatorio.* The operative theory was to produce a "popular memory [that] will reproduce in rumor the austere discourse of the law."[10] Within a remarkably short time, a penal apparatus emerged that organized all of the contingencies and equivocalities of "truth's enactment" under a single plan—that of the prison and the disciplinary regime of the penitentiary. In the place of the populated and heterogeneous space of the public spectacle and the popular civics lesson, a cool, impersonal architecture of surveillance and control arose. Punishment became hidden within the penitentiary, while the previously secret inquisition became a public ceremony in which the accused was examined in the presence of an onlooking audience. Interrogation was thus made answerable to public standards of normality and rationality.

The modern ceremonial of truth thus represents an inversion of the spectacle of the scaffold. Where interrogation used to be shrouded in secrecy, it is now the focus of a public drama. Where punishment was once a public spectacle, it is now suffered off-camera after the dramatic verdict is reached.[11] What was hidden is now public, and what was public is now placed out of sight. An enlightened justice triumphs by replacing a regime of power/knowledge in which tribunals are held in secret and punishments are delivered in a most spectacular fashion, with the efficiency of a regime characterized by the "gentle" and ubiquitous rationality of discourse. This modern ceremonial of truth is thus underpinned by a massive program of discipline that seeps gradually and inexorably into the hidden recesses of practical moral life and brings the most obscure acts to light. Records are kept and used as modalities of action and examination, leaving behind "a whole meticulous archive constituted in terms of bodies and days" that situates the subject "in a network of writing."[12]

CONTEMPORARY INVERSIONS

In public tribunals like the Watergate and Iran-contra hearings, a spectacle is staged in which the sovereign (or chief executive) is made subject to the rigors of a public examination. This inversion of traditional lines of power and authority was underscored during the Watergate hearings when the president's efforts to invoke sovereign authority (executive privilege) were rebuked by the legislature and courts and were dismissed in the popular press as the desperate gestures of a bureaucratic official who had hoped to "rise above the law." Nixon's White House tapes became the key item of evidence. Through an ironic reversal, the president became the primary subject of his own system of surveillance. His profane utterances were recorded, transcribed, circulated, scrutinized, and found by many to be "egregiously crude, mean and mendacious."[13] The equipment he had installed, apparently with the intention of securing his place in history, had done its job. Nixon's fall became an allegory of the triumph of technological surveillance over a would-be sovereign who had hoped to control the machinery of history. A different outcome ensued in the case of the Iran-contra affair, in part because the administration managed to maintain sufficient control over the recording and dissemination of records. Unlike Nixon, Reagan was able to avoid getting snared by his staff's own intelligence-gathering apparatus. In both cases, however, a public tribunal became the focal point of a drama that threatened to undermine, reverse, or scramble the stable powers assigned to the executive and the legislature.

We believe that the "lesson" of Iran-contra has interesting, disturbing, and perhaps even liberating implications with respect to the efficient production of disciplinary truth attributed by Foucault to the modern examination. Such efficiency derives from the decentered operation, with its local exercise of discipline at the extremities of the body politic. There is no single focal point, and no discrete line of demarcation, either for the exercise of power or its disruption. When the examination of the record becomes a media spectacle and a carnival, with no single personage guaranteed the right to occupy center stage, transgressive effects may once again be potentiated.[14] As was gradually understood in the aftermath of Iran-contra, the committee's examination was rendered unstable and equivocal by the subjects under scrutiny. This relative failure complicates Foucault's emphasis on the anonymous efficiency of the intelligence-gathering, intelligence-producing, interrogative machinery of state. We are therefore led to question the clarity of the transition he proposes from a premodern regime of signs to a modern regime of electronic politics.

Like the spectacle of the scaffold, the Iran-contra hearings provided a public platform for launching discursive appeals and symbolic enactments that transgressed the anticipated design of the ceremony. Just as the punitive spectacle gave the body of the condemned an opportunity to consecrate its death in the final rebellion of a popular hero or suffering martyr, the nationally televised ceremonial of truth, arranged to get to the bottom of a political scandal, afforded North the opportunity to steal the scene and construct a televisual counternarrative in which he stood as a victim of unwarranted accusations, a tragic hero, and a potential martyr. Contrary to Foucault's picture of the modern carceral system of total surveillance deployed by a quiet, smooth-running bureaucratic machinery, North's gambit was to mobilize technologies of surveillance in the service of denigrating the "bureaucrats" in government. This openness to the contingencies of live performance was, in large measure, responsible for the high drama of the Iran-contra hearings.

Foucault's failure to take account of the contingencies, equivocalities, and everyday disruptions of the modern ceremonial of truth was not the result of some oversight on his part.[15] Rather, Foucault's histories were explicitly designed to startle our present-day sensibilities and disrupt our naturalized conceptions of madness, health, and justice. Moreover, he acknowledged that his later writings in part were made possible by an "insurrection of subjugated knowledges" that perhaps signaled disorganized sources of resistance at local outposts of the modern regime of truth.[16] Although certain popular "insurrections" occurring in the years after Foucault's death, such as "Olliemania," or the Los Angeles rioting in the aftermath of the 1992 Rodney King police trial, may not represent precisely what he had in mind, they do indicate that the hypermodern, televisually mediated ceremonial of truth may be subject to a revival of the dramatic disruptions potentiated by an earlier era's punitive spectacles. These events suggest that an alternative "history of the present" can be written, a history focused on the complex intermingling of modern technologies of surveillance and control with more ancient forms of rhetorical and performative practice.[17]

CEREMONY AND CIVIC RITUAL

The Iran-contra hearings explicitly were staged as a ceremony disseminated to a massive audience. The audience was in turn implicated in the
course of events through the "irradiative effects" of televisual ritual and
audience feedback.[18] The hearings were specifically designed as a tribunal,
but they also brought into play a number of other ceremonial and drama-
turgical precedents. Both North and his interlocutors made ad hoc use of
an open variety of discursive stratagems, rhetorical tropes, and ritual metaphors. "Ollie" himself became the major dramatic figure at the hearings.[19]
His and the other participants' memorable lines and poses were brought
into (and drawn out of) the production of the hearings as sound bites that
did not necessarily trace back to a coherent, determinate, and relatively
stable structure of discourse, such as an *énoncé* or a *mentalité* transcend-
ing the scene.[20] Instead, they were subject to occasional, strategic, and
sometimes playful uses and inflections. Just as selected elements of Foucault's spectacle of the scaffold seemed to assume a local and historically
displaced role at the hearings, various other binary oppositions, ritual formats, semantic inversions, and rhetorical appeals occasionally became
perspicuous in the testimony, but were subject to unexpected uses.[21]

In many respects the ceremonial aspects of the hearings were organized
along the lines of a courtroom trial in which witnesses are called to testify
and are examined and cross-examined by representatives of two adversarial parties. The familiar stylistics of courtroom drama pervaded the confrontation between interrogator and witness. The House and Senate majority counsels often assumed prosecutorial roles, and the key witnesses were
represented by lawyers. The press portrayed the event as though the Reagan administration itself was on trial, as indeed it was in many respects.
North particularly seemed to be on trial, and he and his lawyer, Sullivan,
occasionally complained that he was being subjected to a rump trial without the protections accorded to a defendant in a criminal or civil case.

The hearings were not just a trial, however. North and some of the other
witnesses faced the eventual possibility of a criminal trial, and accusations
and questions of responsibility were never entirely out of the picture, but
the committee did not have a mandate to pass judgment on criminal guilt
or innocence. The drama departed from that of a trial court in several other
respects. Although it resembled cross-examination, the structure of the

interrogation was not strictly governed by a body of courtroom rules and precedents. Unlike criminal trials, congressional tribunals are not bound by restrictions against hearsay testimony, and questioners are generally allowed broader discretion while exploring topics and inferences. On the other hand, witnesses also have certain privileges they do not enjoy in a trial court. They are not isolated in a dock facing the audience and at the side of the bench, and the ostensive purpose of the questioning is to obtain information rather than allocating blame for wrongdoing (although blaming often comes with the territory). The basic format of the hearings followed that of the Senate and House select committee hearings on Watergate, although in this case the House and Senate committees conducted joint (combined) hearings. The stated reason for using this approach was to avoid duplication and to reduce the attendant national agony of a prolonged investigation. After the fact, it seems that this procedure may have helped to maximize the dramatic effects of North's testimony by reducing the possibility of repeated interrogations in which his opponents would become better prepared for his stratagems.

Much of the drama at the hearings had less to do with the ceremonial structure of the courtroom than with the organization and themes of a nationally televised live event. As Wagner-Pacifici points out in her analysis of the "social drama" in Italian politics surrounding the 1978 kidnapping and murder of Aldo Moro, certain "aesthetic imperatives" apply to such events: "The major protagonists of a social drama are almost constantly surrounded by cameras and tape recorders, journalists and microphones, crowds and institutional settings. Too many stages are available for the protagonists not to feel that they are constantly 'making history.' Further, the ubiquity of mass media screens in our society have induced us to absorb the serial narrative mode—we are constantly being provided with acted-out scenarios."[22] At the Iran-contra hearings these elements were brought together in an explicit and intensified production in which witnesses were placed in front of banks of cameras to testify before a live national audience about an event that was marked for posterity.

As a show on daytime television, the hearings assimilated familiar dramatic figures and structures. Most obvious were the structures and personages of courtroom drama, but the occasion also enabled a histrionic witness like North to call on the rhetoric, classic poses, narrative figures, characters, and actors associated with sporting events, talk shows, war stories, and western movies. North's speeches, the poetics of his voice, his military uniform decorated with medals, and the physiognomic spectacle of his expressions as well as his bodily postures together worked to exploit the televisual medium to produce instantly recognized and celebrated dramatic effects. Following the first day of his testimony, North's performance was fueled by a veritable media explosion, an outburst of interest and coverage that built progressively over the next week. Before the end of his testimony, North proudly displayed a growing stack of supportive telegrams from the media audience as he responded to his interrogators' questions, and he and his allies on the committee were able to act with assurance of his celebrity, while pressing an ever more forceful counterattack against a cowed committee majority.

Of course, not everyone in the audience was thrilled with North's performance, but those who were angered by his testimony and dismayed by the popular reaction to it were unable to secure consensual support for their denunciations. Questions about North's credibility and the plausibility of his testimony were raised and addressed as part of an explicitly politicized scene in which the addressee never fully encompassed an undivided audience. Nevertheless, both parties in the interrogative drama treated the audience en masse as a unitary people. While speaking on behalf of "the American people," congressional interrogators were able to appeal only to a faction in an unstable and politically divided audience. The audience— or rather various representations of the audience—actively intervened in the staging of the spectacle, and the serious and nonpartisan pursuit of "disclosure and truth" was threatened at every turn by eruptions of politicized theater.[23]

In addition to calling on elements of the trial court and popular drama, the hearings were ubiquitously referenced to the more singular historical precedent of Watergate. "Irangate," as it was sometimes called, was widely billed by various pundits and media commentators as "another" Watergate. Like the nationally televised Watergate hearings in 1973 and 1974, the Iran-contra hearings promised to play a decisive and historic role, both as the source of an official history of the event, and as a public ceremony for coalescing and framing crises of authority and legitimation at the highest levels of state. Like Watergate, the affair was said to involve secret government operations, hidden sources of money, and shadowy characters. The transgressions of law and public trust seemed at least as serious, and there

were good reasons to expect that the outcome of the hearings would damage Reagan's presidency no less than Watergate had damaged Nixon's.[24]
Like Watergate, suspicions were voiced about a "cover-up" by the officials
who handled the scandal. Also like Watergate, a number of investigations
were undertaken, a special prosecutor was appointed, criminal charges
were laid, and broader issues of national security and executive privilege
were aired. And again like Watergate, a key witness who was implicated in
the scandal became the focus, and turning point, of the inquiry.[25] With
annoying regularity, the press cited the key question from Watergate: "How
much did the President know and when did he know it?" This question
was reiterated even while it was being called a distraction from other, more
pertinent issues.

> So as the network television cameras return to the Senate Office Building, a
> question from the days of Richard Nixon will again be relevant: "What did
> the president know, and when did he know it?"
>
> Because of President Reagan's emphatic denials that he knew of the diver-
> sion of Iran arms sales funds to the Nicaraguan contras, attention has been
> diverted from other important facets of the scandal. For example, Reagan's
> belated turnabout—acknowledging that he knew of the contra supply opera-
> tion and in fact it was his idea, despite congressional attempts to ban such
> aid—made only a tiny splash.[26]

Iran-contra did not simply resemble Watergate; it was grammatically,
politically, and organizationally linked to the earlier event. Although more
than a decade separated the two events, it is clear from the way in which
the Iran-contra hearings were set up and reported that committee members
and journalists treated Watergate as a vivid and immediate precedent. This
precedent did not determine what happened at the Iran-contra hearings;
instead, it afforded the participants in the later event an opportunity to
relive (and relieve) the lessons of Watergate and, therein, to revise the
institutional memory of that precedent-setting event. The "lessons of Watergate"—whatever they were, and however they were construed by the
different parties involved—were thus highly relevant to Iran-contra, not
only because they offered a measure of procedural guidance, but, more
important, because the more recent event provided an occasion for something different to happen this time around. This difference would eventually redefine the historical meaning of both Iran-contra *and* Watergate.

The lessons of Watergate also had rich and multifaceted relevance to how Iran-contra was described and produced. Congressional committees routinely conduct hearings, but only rarely are such hearings staged as public spectacles that mobilize the production and revision of popular histories.[27] Commentators often linked Iran-contra to a historical chain running backward to Watergate and more remotely to the Army-McCarthy hearings in 1954, a chain of historical scandals with a remarkably similar periodicity to the chain of cold war military actions running from the covert wars in Central America, back to the Vietnam War, and more remotely to the Korean War.[28] Although nationally televised congressional hearings are events of a different order than are wars, they are described in a popular discourse with similar kinds of references to a "national psyche" or as tests of a "national character" that leave traces in the collective conscience of "the American people" until the next such event comes along.

The theme of "another Watergate" was available in countless detailed ways, not only in what commentators said about the event, but in the silent framing of the hearings: the scheduling of telecasts, the placement of cameras, the sequencing of shots, and the deployment of bodies and gestures. As Jeffrey Alexander has put it, the Watergate hearings became a "liminal world":

> a world without history. Its characters did not have rememberable pasts. It was in a very real sense "out of time." The framing devices of the television medium contributed to the deracination that produced this phenomenological status. The in-camera editing, the repetition, juxtaposition, simplification, and other techniques that made the mythical story were invisible. Add to this "bracketed experience" the hushed voices of the announcers, the pomp and ceremony of the "event," and we have the recipe for constructing, within the medium of television, a sacred time and space.[29]

The recipe for (re)constructing Watergate was subject to highly singular uses, inversions, and inflections. For example, the camera shots of Betsy North seated in the gallery at the Iran-contra hearings as a silent backdrop to her husband's testimony recalled Maureen Dean, repeatedly shown by the roving eye of the cameras during John Dean's Watergate testimony. While the modestly dressed Betsy North was no double for the sleek and impassive porcelain figure of Maureen Dean, her demeanor made a conspicuous statement of rustic conservative virtue in light of the Watergate precedent.

Given the historical precedent of the Watergate hearings, it is worth considering not only the obvious similarities between these two events, but certain notable differences. In our view, both hearings thematized the "making of history" on a number of registers. Both were set up to address a major political scandal. Both provided highly visible public investigations designed to write the true story of the events in question, and both were staged as historic events in their own right. However, there were some major differences. Whereas the Watergate hearings, at least to a large faction of the viewing public, successfully reached a dramatic climax, the Iran-contra hearings failed to produce the same kind of allegorical resolution.[30] Historical and theoretical lessons can be drawn from this evident lack of moral closure.

A broadly held lesson of Watergate was that a series of executive excesses were reined in by a democratic exercise of legislative and judicial authority. Iran-contra, by contrast, yielded a far more equivocal story. Despite the fact that Watergate provided a performative template for the way in which the Iran-contra hearings were described and staged, the precedent did not govern the outcome. Indeed, as Iran-contra settled (however tenuously) into history, the contrasts with Watergate became ever more remarkable. No edifying civics lesson emerged from the hearings.[31] Although members of the committee majority invoked the transcendent authority of the American people over and against the authority of particular high government officials, they were unable to depoliticize the public treatment of the event. North and the other accused officials were able to sustain counternarratives of truth and rightness that divided the members of the investigating committee and enlisted the "will of the people" as a factious and equivocal voice.[32]

Nixon and his allies on the House and Senate committees also attempted to politicize the investigations of Watergate, but in that case Nixon's accusers were able to override executive privilege and develop enough bipartisan support for articles of impeachment that "The President," as he liked to be called, was forced from office. There are many possible reasons why this did not happen at the Iran-contra hearings. The Reagan administration successfully withheld and destroyed key documents without being held culpable; the administration's defenders on the Iran-contra committee gave more vigorous and bold defenses than did their counterparts on the Watergate committees; the mainstream media made less aggressive investigatory efforts; Reagan's meetings with the Soviet leader, Mikhail Gorbachev, and the impending "end of the cold war" distracted Congress, the press, and the public from the emerging scandal; public opinion at the time was generally more conservative than during Watergate; and, perhaps most important, the Watergate investigators successfully got hold of Nixon's White House tapes.[33] Whatever the ultimate explanation, it is clear that the Iran-contra committee's efforts came to a far less resolute end.

NORTH'S TESTIMONY:
THE PRODUCTION OF AN INVERSION

In news accounts of the Iran-contra hearings the watershed event was the testimony of Oliver North. He came into the hearings as the person suspected of being the main instigator of the arms trades and diversion of funds, or alternatively, as the official who would take the fall for higher-ups in the administration. By the end of his first day of testimony, however, he had established an altogether different persona. In the widely expressed opinions of many commentators, the character who emerged was an American hero. With a characteristic mixture of martial and filmic metaphors, *Newsweek* summarized the early part of North's testimony with the following lead paragraph:

> Lt. Col. Oliver L. North charged up Capitol Hill last week as the Rambo of diplomacy, a runaway swashbuckler who had run his own private foreign policy from the White House basement. But he captured the hill as Ollie: a new national folk hero who somehow embodied Jimmy Stewart, Gary Cooper and John Wayne in one bemedaled uniform. He touched off a tidal wave of telegrams, flowers and letters; "Give 'em hell, Ollie" bumper stickers, T-shirts and banners blossomed across the country. And the lawmakers who had prepared his solemn chastisement were instead deferring gently to his telegenic charm and Reaganesque views.[34]

A somewhat less enthusiastic account of North's transformation was given by journalist Daniel Schorr, who cited the Watergate hearings rather than popular cinema as the relevant media precedent:

Verdict by television can be a fickle thing. Before Senator Ervin's [Watergate] committee, [John] Dean was treated by Democrats as a conspirator and by Republicans as a traitor. Yet in five days at the witness table, with his wife, Maureen, seated behind him, exactly in camera range, Dean became a media celebrity. I hesitate to say "hero," but can recall that, as the hearings went on to other witnesses, CBS received dozens of calls from viewers demanding, in the words of one, to "bring back that nice John Dean and his lovely wife."

But, whatever had happened before in that national arena called the Caucus Room, there was nothing that remotely rivaled the "Ollie North phenomenon"—the wave of popular approval and adulation that he generated in his testimony in July 1987.[35]

Although many onlookers continued to denounce North as a cunning sociopath, over the course of his testimony North, his attorney, Brendan Sullivan, and a more diffuse "army" of emergent supporters successfully transformed the event from the interrogation of a prime suspect in a political scandal into the site of a raging political and moral debate through which "Ollie"—a new "American hero"—was canonized by the press.

"Olliemania" was touched off by North's first-day performance. Especially during the morning session on that day, he enunciated many of the memorable phrases that were to be quoted and replayed again and again in the popular media: "I came here to tell the truth—the good, the bad and the ugly"; "I don't like the insinuation that I'm up here having a convenient memory lapse"; and "My memory has been shredded." It was also during that first morning that North answered the key question the press had primed the audience to expect: "What did the President know about the diversion of the proceeds from the Iranian arms sales to the contras?" North backed the administration's claim that Reagan knew nothing about the "diversion," and he successfully countered the interrogator's rhetorical efforts to enlist "the American people" for a denunciation of administrative transgressions.[36] For anyone who entertained hopes that the hearings would bring about a bloodless coup against the Reagan administration, things went progressively downhill from that point on.

In this study we devote less attention to the spectacular highlights of North's testimony than to the matter of how they emerged from a more relentless discursive production. North's ringing speeches and memorable assertions were produced ostensibly as "answers to questions" in an interrogation. A close study of the opening moments of North's testimony will enable us to show how he and his attorney were able to secure "space" for bodily displays and rhetorical maneuvers that simultaneously exploited and transgressed the design of the interrogative examination. Before taking up issues concerning the details of testimony, however, it will be worth reviewing some of the negotiations that preceded North's appearance on-camera.

After being summoned to appear at the hearings, both North and Poindexter cited the Fifth Amendment against self-incrimination, and they refused to testify. Their refusals set up extended preliminary negotiations with the committee, and eventually they both were offered partial immunity from criminal liability in exchange for their testimony. This condition precluded any use of the record of their testimony for purposes of criminal investigations, with the exception of charges of perjury. North, Poindexter, and their attorneys also negotiated with the committee and the White House for the disclosure of the mass of evidential documents relevant to the committee's investigation. Related negotiations covered the duration of the hearings and the topics of the questioning, the disclosure of evidential documents, the order of appearance between North and Poindexter (North was to appear first), and the procedures for conducting the interrogation. North and Poindexter also negotiated what turned out to be a key advantage for producing testimony. Unlike the witnesses at the Watergate hearings, they were allowed to testify with their attorneys at their sides. During the hearings, North and his attorney, Brendan Sullivan, took conspicuous advantage of this arrangement with many sotto voce consultations while an interrogator's question awaited an answer. The committee also allowed North to testify without first giving his testimony in closed session before the public hearings. He met only briefly with committee representatives before testifying (figs. 4 and 5).

Meanwhile, the hearings began with testimony by Richard Secord, Eliot Abrams, Robert McFarlane, and North's secretary, Fawn Hall. Hall received the most media attention, partly because of what she had to say about the "shredding party" in North's office in November 1986 and partly because the cameras and commentaries played up her sexual attractiveness. As North's early July date with the committee approached, stories began circulating in the press characterizing him as a "loose cannon" whose zealous adventures had gotten out of hand. It was announced that

4. and 5. North confers with his attorney, Brendan Sullivan.

he intended to appear dressed in his marine lieutenant colonel's uniform, conspicuously bedecked with the insignia and medals commemorating his deeds in Vietnam and afterward. Some complaints were made about such dress because by wearing the uniform he appeared to represent a military establishment, despite the fact that the actions about which he was called to testify were conducted in a civilian capacity as a staff member of the National Security Council.[37] Numerous speculations were offered about his character and about whether he would "crack" under the questioning and implicate his superiors. At the time, many commentators assumed that he would stoically accept the fall guy role his superiors had appointed him to play. One of the committee members, Senator William Cohen of Maine, was even quoted as saying that North was likely to present himself "in a very low-key, very respectful, and not at all confrontational" manner.[38]

North began testifying on July 7, and he appeared for five more days. His testimony was televised live on all of the major networks. As with Watergate, the arena for the televisual spectacle had an inverted panoptic design. A gap separated the witness's table from the elevated tiers of congressmen and their staff. Committee interrogators sat directly across from the witness, and separate television cameras framed the witness and interrogator, while occasionally panning the committee and the gallery. For the most part, the televisual dialogue occurred as a confrontation between two separate and equivalent talking heads, each alternating on the screen as he spoke his turn, with occasional relief provided by other camera angles and split-screen displays of the interlocutors. The interrogation was the center of a spectacle, with two main speakers, flanked by their staff and allies, in a magnified and closely framed face-to-face encounter. The standard shot of North was aimed from the front right and below, so that he took on stature, accented by his military demeanor. The elevation of his image inverted the relationship between his body and the positioning of his interrogator, who was actually seated somewhat higher. This element of the televisual production was likely one of the many that helped enhance North's credibility for the television audience.

The pragmatic organization of the hearings left margins of free play in which the rules of the game and the criteria for their successful application were contested and modified from the outset of North's testimony. Through a relentless set of maneuvers, some of which were resisted by the committee majority, North and Sullivan were able to expand the initial tolerances of what the witness could say to the point that he eventually was able to extend his answers into uninterrupted speeches while at the same time denying that they were speeches. The pragmatic significance of these early concessions is nicely captured by Melvin Pollner's concept of "explicative transactions," which describes how participants in formal settings like courtrooms work to explicate and further establish a routine order of events. These are moments when participants invoke local precedents— what someone before them was able to do, or get away with—as grounds for their own actions and justifications.[39] For Pollner, explicative transactions represent liminal moments "in which meaning is deobjectivated" and "the constitutive power of the response comes to the foreground."[40] In our terms, such transactions are an occasion for an adept performance that recognizes and exploits the liminal moments of an event, trading off of threads of intelligibility to enroll an appreciative audience for the self-same performance. The opening session of North's interrogation by House majority counsel John Nields provided many such liminal moments in which the tenor of the hearings was shifted, sometimes loudly and dramatically, and sometimes gradually and imperceptibly, from an interrogation to a transparent political confrontation. This shift carried through the remaining five days of North's testimony and left an indelible trace on the "eventualization" of the Iran-contra hearings.

The televised portions of the session began with a series of ritual arguments that delayed the onset of the interrogation (the main event). Although the issue was already moot, some of the minority (Republican) members of the House and Senate committees challenged the select committee's technical authority to conduct the hearings. This question was quickly settled and was followed by a consideration of a request by North's attorney to waive a committee rule (5.3) prohibiting a witness from making "an opening statement." Senate committee chairman Inouye denied the request by citing the rule: "Any witness desiring to make an introductory statement shall file 20 copies of the statement with the chairman or chief clerk 48 hours in advance of the appearance."[41] Inouye added that the copies were filed "45 minutes ago" and stated authoritatively: "Unless the Committee determines otherwise, a witness who appears before the Committee under a grant of immunity shall not be permitted to make a statement or testify except to respond directly to questions posed by committee members or committee staff."[42] In accordance with the rule, Inouye proposed that the "opening" statement be given at the beginning of the session scheduled two days afterward, and Sullivan countered by pleading for the possibility of making the statement during the lunch break on the current (first) day of testimony. This too was denied. Sullivan went on to complain about the late date at which the committee had delivered a voluminous mass of records that, by agreement, were to be disclosed to the witness. He proffered a photograph showing North standing next to a stack of papers that reached well above his head, and he complained again about North's lack of sufficient time to familiarize himself with these records (figure 6).

No great imagination was required of viewers for them to recognize what was at stake in this wrangling. First, the request for an opening statement was an overt attempt to enable North to begin the hearings with a resounding defense of his (and his employer's) actions. For the duration of such a

6. Sullivan shows a photograph of North standing next to a stack of documents.

speech, he would be able to invert the interrogatory relation, to accuse his accusers and "set the record straight" before assuming a position as the subject of the committee's examination. Inouye's ruling threatened to defuse the sequential and pragmatic effects of such a speech by deferring it to a time, two days later, when the tenor of the hearings would be established and the television audience might not be so primed. Second, while it is highly unlikely that Sullivan entertained any hope (or desire) to postpone the hearings in order to give North more time to study the documents (many of which he had a hand in producing), the reference to the volume of documents created a pragmatic opening for a series of gestures through which North displayed his unfamiliarity with the documents and what they "said."[43]

It is notable that early in the interrogation, North and Sullivan nevertheless managed to create a space for many speeches and other editorializing maneuvers though ad hoc exploitations of opportunities that arose in the course of questions and answers. Although he was overtly constrained by the specifications of House rules, the game allowed enough free play for the witness to work the margins and occasionally break the frame of the interrogation. In subsequent chapters we shall elaborate the technical features of North's counterinterrogatory practices. For the present, we shall quickly go through the opening moments of North's testimony to identify some of the discursive maneuvers through which he began to mobilize a spectacular audience response. In our view, these discursive tactics operated in the dense details of the testimony, so that the memorable sound bites enunciated by North surfaced within a more relentless production.

After being given Inouye's directive to proceed with the questioning, House majority counsel John Nields opened a dialogue that was immediately forestalled by North's pro forma declaration of his Fifth Amendment right not to answer:

Nields: Colonel North, were you involved in the use of the proceeds of sales of weapons to Iran for the purpose of assisting the Contras in Nicaragua?
North: On the advice of counsel, I respectfully decline to answer the question based on my Constitutional Fifth Amendment rights.

The respective chairmen (Senate select committee chairman Inouye and House chairman Lee Hamilton) then each read directives by their own committees compelling North to testify and acknowledging his rights of immunity. Following these ritual readings, North's attorney summarized the conditions under which North would testify. Inouye acknowledged these conditions and then directed Nields to begin again with his questioning. The following exchange ensued:

Inouye: Mister Nields, proceed.
Nields: Colonel North, you were involved in two operations of this government of great significance to the people of this country, is that correct?
North: At least two. Yessir.

Note the contrast between the version of the question Nields asked earlier ("Colonel North, were you involved in the use of the proceeds of sales of weapons to Iran for the purpose of assisting the Contras in Nicaragua?") and the version with which he resumed ("Colonel North, you were involved in two operations of this government of great significance to the people of this country, is that correct?"). The earlier question names its recipient ("Colonel North") and then immediately moves to a syntactic formulation that establishes the ensuing utterance as a question ("were you involved . . ."). In contrast, Nields's second question, though beginning in the same way, gets formulated as an assertion ("you were involved . . .") which is then repackaged as a question through a tagging operation ("is that correct?"). Where the force of the earlier question is primarily interrogative, the later query can more readily be heard as the first move in an accusatorial line of questioning (see next chapter). Given that accusatorial questions strongly prefigure affirmative responses that will work to the detriment of the accused, this second question—hearable in one sense as a mere reformulation of the first—has the rhetorical effect of an accusatorial upgrade aimed at tightening the noose around the available responses open to the witness. To simply confirm this second question would be to comply with the terms of that accusation.

Both versions of the initial question are tied together by virtue of their sequential location, where the question asked on resumption raises the "same" question that already had been asked and not yet answered. Moreover, when phrased as an assertion, the terms of the initial question ("you [were] involved in the use of the proceeds of sales of weapons to Iran for the purpose of assisting the Contras in Nicaragua") suggest an answer (and an accusatory one) to the riddle posed by the second (What were the "two operations of this government of great significance to the people of this country" in which North was involved?). Unless the utterance "two operations . . . of great significance" to the American people is referentially connected to "the use of the proceeds of sales of weapons to Iran for the purpose of assisting the Contras in Nicaragua," it can reasonably be heard as equivocal, or as a characterization that asks the witness to guess what the questioner has in mind. In this case, North's response—"At least two"— exploits the former possibility. This response offers no explicit acknowledgment of the referential link between "two operations . . . of great significance" to the American people and "the use of the proceeds of sales of weapons to Iran for the purpose of assisting the Contras in Nicaragua." Instead, it gives an equivocal specification of the significance of North's activities and, ironically, a numerical minimization of that significance.

The rhetorical success of North's response—"At least two. Yessir."— derives from its treatment of Nields's second try at an initial question as though it was an isolated question about two of the many significant "involvements" North may have had. North compounds the irony with a disciplined pun on the terms through which he affirms the accusatory question with a "Yessir" that can suggest a military man's dutiful acceptance of a compliment for the things he had done "of great significance to the people of this country." In other words, North's response recontextualizes

Nields's accusatory utterance by suggesting a way it can be heard to praise North, not to damn him. As an "explicative transaction," this exchange sets the stage for the kinds of modulations, reversals, accusatorial dispersions (and aspersions), and categorical challenges that persist throughout the ensuing testimony. These moves can be appreciated by following the opening exchange beyond this initial sequence. The transcript begins again at Inouye's order to proceed:

Inouye: Mister Nields, proceed. (1.5)

Nields: Colonel North, you were involved in two:, (0.8) operations of this government of great significance to the people of this country, is that correct? (1.0)

North: At least two. Yessir.

Nields: And one of them involved the support of the contras during the time the Boland Amendment was in effect, (0.5) and another one involved the sale of arms to Iran. (2.0)

Nields: Is that correct? (0.8)

North: Yes, (ih) it also involved support for the democratic outcome in Nicaragua both before and *after* the Boland Amendment was in effect. (2.4)

Nields: And these operations were carried out in secret. (1.5)

North: We *ho*ped so.

Nields: They were *covert* operations.

North: Yes they were.

Nields: And covert operations are designed to be secrets, from our enemies. (1.0)

North: That is correct.

Nields: But these operations were designed to be secrets from the American people. (2.0)

North: Mister Nields, I'm- at a *loss* as to how we could announce it to the American people and not have the Soviets know about it. (1.5) An' I'm not trying to be *flip*pant, but I just don't see how you can possibly do it.

Nields: Uh- well, in fact Colonel North, you believed that the Soviets were a*wa*re of our sale of arms to Iran, weren't you. (2.5)

North: (Uh-) we came to a point in time when we were concerned about that.

Nields: But- but it was designed to be kept a secret from the American people. (3.0)

North: I- I think what- what is important, uh Mister Nields is that— (1.0) we somehow arrive at some kind of an understanding right here and now, as to what a covert operation is. If we could find a way to insulate with a bubble over (0.6) these *hear*ings that are being broadcast in Moscow, (0.4) uh- (0.2) a- and *talk* about covert operations to the American people without it getting into the hands of our adversaries, I'm sure we would *do* that. But we haven't found a way to do it.[44]

In this sequence North initially confirms a series of Nields's character-izations of his involvements and actions. North often expresses a slight and smart-alecky contentiousness in the way he delays and elaborates his an-swers, but he does not directly challenge the assertions and characteriza-tions presented in Nields's "questions" (which often are formed not as questions but as "statements" for confirmation). The confrontation be-comes more acute, however, when Nields asserts that "these operations were designed to be secrets from the American people," and North objects by saying that it would be impossible to preserve secrets from "our en-emies" if these were revealed to "the American people." Nields attempts to rebut this, and North then expands his argument into a dramatized bid to come to "an understanding . . . as to what a covert operation is." This utterance, which is (apparently) oriented to reaching an understanding, emerges from out of the interrogation and displays itself as a ringing asser-tion of the legitimacy of North's and the administration's covert actions. In effect, it is an ad hoc political speech that confronts the "opposing view" exhibited in and through the interrogator's questions.

Nields challenges North's last argument by attributing a quotation to North in which "the American people" figure altogether differently.

Nields: But you put it somewhat differently to the Iranians to who- with whom you were negotiating on the eighth and ninth of October in Frankfurt, Germany, didn't you. You said to them, [pause] that- [throat clear] "Secretary of Defense Weinberger, in our last session with the President said, 'I don't think we should send one more screw' "—talking about the Hawk parts— " 'until we have our Americans back from Beirut, because when the Ameri-can people find out that this has happened, they'll impeach you' "—referring to the President.[45]

Immediately after this statement, Sullivan raises the objection that this quotation was apparently taken from a transcript that North should be allowed to inspect before responding. Nields instructs Sullivan and North where to find the transcript in the notebooks they have on the table in front of them, and after much ado about their unfamiliarity with the exhibits, Sullivan and North locate the key passage. North then gives one of his more memorable speeches:

North: Mister Nields, this is apparently, uh- one of the uh- transcripts of tape recordings that *I* caused to be made of my discussions with the Iranians. I would like to note, that for *every* conversation, whenever it was possible, I asked for the assistance of our intelligence services, to trans- to tape record and transcribe every single session. So that, when I returned there would be no doubt as to what I said. I am the one who created these tapes, plus the seven hours of tape recordings that your committee found yesterday because I knew where they were, and I kept trying to alert you to them, and *I* am the one who created those tapes so there would *never* be any doubt in the minds of my superiors as to what I had said, or why I had said it. That is a *bald-faced lie* told to the Iranians. And I will tell you right now, I'd have offered the Iranians a free trip to *Dis*neyland if we could have gotten Americans home for it.[46]

Here we have yet another set of enemies ("the Iranians") who become the audience for a "bald-faced lie" in which North admits to having uttered the name of "the American people" in vain. The admitted lie is put in context by references to North's duty to his "superiors" and the noble aim of getting the "Americans" (hostages held in Lebanon) safely home. This passage is fascinating in a number of respects, but for the time being we will only note in passing that by admitting to a lie North negates what Nields says he (North) told the Iranians about what Weinberger told the president, namely, that "when the American people find out that this has happened, they'll impeach you." This statement, relayed through Nields's quotation of North quoting Weinberger, prophesizes an event that *now may come to pass,* and, more than that, it establishes foreknowledge of the dire consequences of actions that were taken and a motive for concealing those actions. The reflexive and projective implications of this statement are put out of play by North's admission of "a lie," an admission that breaks the chain of quotations and also protects itself from accusation by citing good patriotic reasons.

ENROLLING "THE AMERICAN PEOPLE" AND "THE TRUTH"

In his account of the ceremony of the public execution, Foucault asserts that "the main character was the people, whose real and immediate presence was required for the performance."[47] "The people" were also a real and immediate *virtual* presence at the Iran-contra hearings. The spectacle was televised live to a mass audience, and the drama that unfolded was obviously and explicitly oriented to the cameras. Moreover, "the American people" were repeatedly invoked both as the subject and addressee of the discursive exchange. Nields, the interrogating counsel for the House majority, and North, the interrogated witness, each tried to enlist "the American people" as an authority and recipient for their side of the story. In a vivid and immediate way, the interlocutors' discourse constituted the "struggle for the spiritual soul of the American republic" that Alexander attributes to the civic ritual of Watergate.[48] Two aspects of this struggle were especially prominent.

First, the interrogator and witness struggled to impose different pragmatic designs on the dialogical order. Nields tried to sustain an order of questions, each of which enjoined the witness to respond to the relevant point on the floor.[49] A monological "truth" was to be extracted through a contingent, utterance-by-utterance reconciliation of the interrogator's questions and the witness's responses. North, assisted by his attorney, opened up an alternative, schismatic possibility, which enabled him to expand his "answers" into speeches rebutting and denouncing the auspices of the examination itself.[50] As a result, the interrogation was transformed at several junctures into an occasion for a debate in which North made extended arguments (at times, speeches) opposing the moral and political tenor of the interrogator's questions.

Second, both the interrogator's questions and the witness's answers included explicit appeals to "the American people." They both proposed to speak in the name of "the American people," and they both attempted to ally their actions with a concern and respect for what "the American people want to know."[51] From the very outset of North's testimony, "the American people" became an explicit theme for a discursive confrontation that persisted throughout the ensuing days of the hearings. Consider once again the opening exchange, transcribed above.

From the outset, Nields's line of questions associates "the American people" with a concern for truthful and open communications by the government, and he suggests that North, and the administration that employed him, conducted a series of covert actions that were designed to be kept secret "from the American people." Here, Nields uses the category "the American people" to designate a more or less homogeneous population, a population distinct from the "enemies" of the people (in this case, communists and Iranian revolutionaries), and one that is categorically associated with a common right to hear "the truth." North counters this use of "the American people" by raising the specter of "the Soviets" and by insisting that it was impossible to insulate covert actions and communications from such "enemies" while disclosing them to "the American people." In his account, "the American people" are the beneficiaries of covert actions that oppose a common enemy, and this "people" cannot know, and would not want to know, the secrets entrusted to agents like North.

The confrontation evident in this exchange quickly came to a head when Nields interrogated North about the reports released to the press in the aftermath of the capture of Eugene Hassenfus in Nicaragua. Hassenfus, an American, survived the crash of an airplane that had been shot down and that evidently was running arms to the contras in Nicaragua at a time when Congress had proscribed U.S. military aid to the contras. The administration initially denied any involvement with Hassenfus or his operation.

Nields: In certain communist countries, the government's activities are kept
  secret from the people. But that's not the way we do things in America, is it?
  (2.2)
North: Counsel, I would to go back to what I said just a few moments ago. I
  think it is very important for the American people to understand, that this is
  a dangerous world, that we live at risk, and that this nation is at risk, in a
  dangerous world, (1.0) and that they (et-) they ought not to be led to believe
  as a consequence of these hearings, that this nation cannot or should not
  conduct covert operations. By their very nature, covert operations, or special
  activities, are a *lie*. (1.4) There is great deceit- deception, practiced in the
  conduct of covert operations. They are at essence, a lie. (1.0) We make every
  effort to deceive the enemy as to our intent, our conduct, and to deny the
  association of the United States with those activities. The intelligence committees hold hearings on all kinds of these activities, conducted by our
  intelligence services. The American people ought not to be led to believe by

the way you're asking that *question*, that we intentionally deceive the American people. (10.) Or had that intent to be*gin* with. The effort to conduct these covert operations was made in such a way that our adversaries would not have knowledge of them. Or that we could deny American association with them. Or the associated—the association of this government with those activities. And that is not wrong.

Nields: The American people were told by this government (1.4) that our government had nothing to do with the Hassenfus airplane. And that was false. And it is a principal purpose of these hearings to replace (1.0) secrecy and deception with disclosure and truth. And that's one of the reasons we have called you here sir. And one question the American people would like to know the answer to is what did the President know about the diversion of the proceeds of Iranian arms sales to the contras. Can you tell us what you know about that, sir. (0.6)

North: You just took a long leap from Mister Hassenfus's airplane.[52]

Note the way in which Nields initially invokes "certain communist countries" as a contrast to "the way we do things in America." The civics lesson is transparent: government lies and secrets are associated with "communism," so that North's justification of lies and secrets collapses. We become no different from communists if we oppose them with their own methods. North responds by upgrading the polemical defense of actions in "a dangerous world." With righteous and carefully measured tones he warns that "the American people" should not be misled about the good intentions of its (unofficial) secret agents. Nields also makes reference to "the American people" in his next utterance, again emphasizing that lies were told to them. From Nields's questions, the audience is able to infer that, since North and "this government" lied to "the American people" in the past, they (and specifically he) might lie at the present hearings. Nields associates the hearings with "the American people" and a mandate of "truth" and "disclosure." Like his Watergate predecessors, he attempts to align his position with evaluative standards that are "above" partisan politics— specifically, the democratic values of truth, openness, and public accountability—and he suggests that North and the administration transgressed those suprapolitical standards.[53]

The way Nields raises the "one question that the American people would like to know" pivots rather abruptly from the issue of government reports about the Hassenfus plane to the question that commentators had marked in advance as the key question in North's interrogation. This non-sequitur testifies to the primacy of the question, not merely as another question in a series, but as a nodal point in a set of associations and conventional historical references around which the emerging story of Iran-contra is supposed to crystallize. Technically speaking, the question is not topically disjunctive. Nields places it just after his references to "the American people" and the "principal purpose of the hearings to replace secrecy and deception with disclosure and truth," and he builds a transition to it by mentioning "one of the reasons" North was called to testify, and by prefacing the question with a phrase about what "the American people want to know." Nields builds more remote temporal associations when he enunciates part of "*the* question" memorialized from the Watergate hearings ("How much did the President know and when did he know it"). Nields has thus built a historical context for the question that aligns it with the interests of "the American people," highlights the significance of truthfulness, and recalls the precedent of Watergate. North's pun on Nields's "long leap from Mr. Hassenfus' airplane" makes light of Nields's entry into the climactic sequence of the interrogation, exposing the rather tenuous linkages the interrogator had built when leading up to the question.

North then launches into a long reply made famous through endless recitations of its constituent sound bites. He avows that, as far as he knows, the president knew nothing about the diversion of profits from the arms sales to the contras. The crescendo of this long speech is then supplied by a transparent allusion to a well-known tale of frontier justice and American heroism:

North: As I told this committee several days ago,[54] and if you will indulge me Counsel in a brief summary of what I said, (2.2) I never personally discussed the use of the residuals or profits from the sale of U.S. weapons to Iran (1.2) for the purpose of supporting the Nicaraguan resistance with the President. (1.0) I never raised it with *him* and he never raised it with me, during my entire tenure at the National Security Counsel staff. (1.4) Throughout the conduct of my entire tenure at the National Security Counsel, I assumed that the President was aware of what I was doing, and had through my superiors approved it. (1.0) I sought approval of my superiors for every one of my actions, and it is well documented. (2.0) I assumed (1.0) when I had approval to proceed from either (1.4) Judge Clark, Bud McFarlane, (1.0) or Admiral Poindexter, that they had indeed solicited and obtained the approval of the President. (2.0) To my recollection, Admiral Poindexter never told me that he met with the President on the issue of using residuals from the Iranian sales, to support the Nicaraguan resistance. Or that he discussed the residuals, or profits, for use by the Contras, with the President. Or that he got the President's specific approval. (1.0) Nor did he tell me that the President had approved such a transaction. (0.8) But again I wish to reiterate that throughout I believed that the President had indeed authorized such activity. (1.5) *No other person* (1.0) with whom I was in contact with during my tenure at the White House told me that he or she ever discussed the issue of the residuals or profits with the President. [North takes a deep breath and continues]: In late November, two other things occurred which relate to this issue. On or about Friday, November Twenty-first I asked Admiral Poindexter directly, *"Does the President know."* He told me he did not. And on November Twenty-fifth the day I was reassigned back to the United States Marine Corps for service, the President of the United States called me. (1.0) In the course of that call, the President said to me (1.0) words to the effect that "I just didn't know." (1.8) Those are the facts as I know them Mister Nields, I was glad that when you introduced this you said that you wanted to hear the truth. I came here to tell you the truth, the good, the bad, and the ugly. I'm here to tell it *all,* pleasant and unpleasant, and I'm here to accept responsibility for that which I did, I will not accept responsibility for that which I did not do.[55]

Immediately following this passage, committee chairman Inouye asked North, "Was that response from a written text?" North replied that he read it from notes that he had prepared for the session, but the implication was clear: this was, for all practical purposes, the kind of organized "statement" that North had been prohibited from giving at the outset of the hearings. He had managed to package it as an "answer to a question" that came off as an uninterrupted speech to the mass audience gathered around their television sets.

Consider for a moment some of the more literary features of this exchange and the way in which North's "answer" works to mobilize his audience and enlist "the American people" on his side of the argument, and against the committee majority.

(1) Nields has asked "*the* question" for which the audience has been prepared in advance by the commentators.

(2) This question is designed sequentially as a citation of "*the* question" from Watergate.

(3) "*The* question" follows rather abruptly after Nields's assertion of the committee's mandate—an assertion that linked the committee to "the American people" and identified its purpose with "truth" and "disclosure," in contrast to partisan interests in concealment (associated with "this government").

(4) North gives "*the* answer" that commentators before the hearings had said he would give (he asserts that as far as he knows, the president knew nothing about the "diversion" of profits from the arms sales).

(5) North forcefully expresses his intention to tell the truth in the present hearings.

(6) North cites the title of a Sergio Leone film, starring Clint Eastwood, *The Good, The Bad, and The Ugly* (1966), a well-known spaghetti western in which Eastwood (characteristically at that time) plays an ambiguous (anti)hero—an American cowboy who wanders through Mexico, carrying out violent assassinations against swarthy "bad guys." Eastwood retains his heroism in contrast to the unqualified evil of his foes. As in some other films starring Eastwood (e.g., *Dirty Harry* and its sequels), the hero violates legal and moral codes in the service of his violent efforts to eradicate unquestionable evil. Those who stand in his way in the service of legal and bureaucratic authority naively protect evil.[56] In this way, Eastwood's crusade against evil is enlisted by North on behalf of "the American people" and against deeply evil and swarthy foreigners in order to combat the historical precedent of Watergate; in doing so, North momentarily collapses the opposition between "secrecy and deception" and "truth and disclosure" presented by the interrogator.[57] Truth and disclosure become secondary concerns in the face of the unquestionable threats lodged in foreign lands. The question then becomes one of resolving just when, and in reference to which audiences, truth and disclosure are warranted. With enough force (and in light of the antibureaucratic themes so popular in the films of Clint Eastwood, Chuck Norris, and Sylvester Stallone) North now has the opportunity to implicate the committee majority as the cultural

enemy—as bureaucrats whose legalistic concern with truth and procedure naively puts them in league with foreign agents.

CONCLUSION

Foucault's "spectacle of the scaffold" provides a resonant image for describing how the "defendant" at the Iran-contra hearings was able to exploit the iterative, formal, and ritualistic elements of the ceremony to equivocate the sense and force of the accusatory narrative and thereby to enlist an audience for an emergent counternarrative of intrigue, honor, and military heroism. In significant respects this conception of the hearings runs against the grain of Foucault's analysis. After all, *Discipline and Punish* is about the disappearance of the contingencies, disruptions, and elements of carnival that subverted the "truths" of the premodern spectacle. It is a story about the rise of a penal architecture marked by the visual clarity and procedural discipline of a modern, utilitarian, and bureaucratic administration of justice. What the North testimony makes clear is that we have yet to enter an era in which truth's enactment is administered in advance. Nor have we necessarily entered, as Luhmann seems to think, a "transitional state" in which "society" is "still described naturalistically as a civil union, and social action moralistically as either good or bad."[58] Instead, even within the restricted limits of an interrogative discourse, the semantic and pragmatic "system" seems to permit a substantial degree of free play and moral equivocality, so that it becomes difficult in the end to specify what does or does not "fit" its preconditions.

It is commonplace among social constructionists to note that the sense and force of formal orders (rules, systems, etc.) is contingent upon the ways in which such orders are made relevant by actual courses of social activity. Testimonial discourse and the associated logical machinery for generating public admissions of guilt exemplify formal orders (as does Foucault's rendition of the architectural order of the panopticon and the modern penitentiary). Despite the material constraints and logico-moral compulsions that shape the disciplinary lattice of these formal orders, prisoners still escape, and the guilty still refuse to confess. As a matter of analytic principle, we are not interested in questions concerning the righteousness of such acts of resistance. Rather, we are interested in the resistances themselves, wherever and however they occur, without regard for the occupational, party, or any other categorical affiliations of their uses, except when such categories are directly relevant to the conduct of these acts. By focusing on the ways in which formal orders are contested, manipulated, and resisted, we aim to demonstrate both that formal orders are incapable of *determining* the actual course and outcomes of social activities and that they are nonetheless *practically* relevant to their conduct.

4. THE TRUTH-FINDING

ENGINE

> By virtue of the power structure immanent in it, the confessional
> discourse cannot come from above, as in the *ars erotica,* through the
> sovereign will of the master, but rather from below, as an obligatory act
> of speech which, under some imperious compulsion, breaks the bonds
> of discretion or forgetfulness.—Foucault[1]

Anyone who has undergone interrogation—whether by an angry parent or spouse or by a cross-examining attorney—can testify to a feeling of being caught up in a discursive machinery. The forceful press toward confessional disclosure can give even the most innocent subject the Chaplinesque sense of being swept up in an assembly line of questions and answers. Unlike the case of torture, however, no sovereign will is forcibly exerted on the victim's body. Instead, in the ideal case, the "gentle" devices of the examination compel the recalcitrant witness to yield in the face of logic, evidence, and reason.[2] By design, the rationality of interrogation is immanent, dialogical, and volitional, and it is thus more effective for exposing truth at a public tribunal than any instrument of torture. Like Socrates' interlocutors, witnesses are enjoined to adhere to elementary norms of consistency and coherence, while being led step-by-step to admit contradiction and yield to the interrogator's position. Harvey Sacks once remarked:

> it does seem to be the case, perhaps curiously so, that even when persons are
> under interrogation for possibly serious offenses, ones for which their lives
> may be at stake, confessions can be garnered by saying to them that what
> they said at one point is inconsistent with what they have said at another
> point. One might imagine them to say "How can it be inconsistent; I said
> both those things." . . . A preliminary investigation of the method of inter-
> rogation suggests that while exploration of what goes on in such situations is
> of great interest, it is by no means to be supposed that persons take lightly the
> reasonableness, consistency, clarity, and so on, of their answers, and may
> well be more concerned with preserving their claim to consistency than
> their claim to innocence.[3]

In the ideal case, such confessions are not compelled by a coercive threat or force applied by one party to the other. The witness is led to make damaging admissions and confessions on the basis of a logic embedded in the discourse of interrogation. Confessional truth, of course, is only one possible terminus. Witnesses have a chance to resist such compulsion, and they may complain, for instance, about being badgered by the cross-examiner. The possibility of obtaining rationally motivated admissions and confessions nevertheless is prominent as a source of tension in dramatic portrayals of interrogation, and in certain respects it animates the procedures of actual interrogative dialogue.

Especially when compared with the more polite forms of conversational exchange, interrogation is an intense, sustained, and often hostile type of dialogue in which one adversary attempts verbally to undress the other in an aggressive pursuit of confessional truth. Elements of theatricality are evident enough in the ordinary run of cases, so that the spectacle of interrogation easily lends itself to fictional appropriation. But like the simulated sexuality of pornography, the courtroom drama of theater, film, and television tends to elide the many resistances, complications, precautions, interludes, disappointments, and evasions encountered in actual encounters in favor of a relatively frictionless progression to the climactic moment.[4] The lawyer Perry Mason of the vintage American television series epitomizes the heroic interrogator who triumphantly extracts confessional truth from a hostile witness. In virtually every episode Perry defends someone who has been falsely charged with murder. He and his two assistants independently investigate the crime, and while doing so their on-camera actions let the audience in on the facts of the defendant's innocence. The real murderer is exposed when Perry's cross-examination extracts a confession of the dirty deed from an unexpected source, often a witness for the prosecution. The confession affirms a truth that was otherwise revealed through Perry's investigation. Following is a brief excerpt from the climax to an episode in which Perry interrogates a witness (Scranton) in a trial about the murder of a researcher (Lehigh) at a company (Trion). Perry is questioning Scranton about a report the murder victim had written exposing wrongdoings at the company.

Perry: Do I understand that you did not have a day-to-day knowledge of the
   information accumulated for that report?

Scranton: That's right. (1.5)

Perry: Then it must have been quite a surprise to you when you talked to Lehigh about it.

Scranton: But I never talked to Lehigh about it, Mister Mason. He was dead when we arrived at the laboratory.

Perry: I mean the first time you went to the lab, Doctor. (0.4) Before Mister Drake and I arrived.

Scranton: Well I *didn't.*

Perry: I think you *did,* Doctor Scranton. I think you found out how *thorough* Lehigh had been. I think you found out that your counterspy had even investigated *you.*

Scranton: *Mister Mason, we know who the spy is. What are you trying . . .*

Perry: I think the decedent showed you what he found in files A-100 and A-102. And I think he was ready to report to the board of directors that the very patents you had used to raise your financing for Trion were not yours to *pledge.* (1.8)

Scranton: No. (0.8) They weren't (1.0) But *Trion* was mine. (1.4) I built it from scratch. He had no reason to tear it down, I didn't ask much of him.

Perry: No, not much. (1.4) Only that he compromise his integrity as you'd compromised yours when you founded your company on an *out-and-out fraud.* (4.0)

((Dramatic music begins))

Scranton: He didn't understand. (2.0) He wouldn't listen, he was *rigid.* (0.4) Everything was black and white. (1.5) And when he refused the money I offered him, (1.6) I picked up the pipe to threaten him. I didn't intend . . . (3.0)

((Violins rising in background))

Scranton: I hit him. (0.8) *I hit him.* (0.8) *I did. I did. I hit him. I hit him.*

((Music reaches crescendo))

At the outset of this sequence Scranton strongly resists Perry's supposition that he had prior knowledge of Lehigh's report, but in the course of the exchange he is brought to a dramatic confession in which he breaks down in a cathartic admission of the truth. The confession is not coerced by means of an instrumental power, but it is yielded in the face of an imperative ground, in this case Perry's citation of the precise codes for two incriminating files that indicate a motive for the murder. Scranton never challenges the authenticity of these documents. He does not question Perry's access to these documents and entitlement to read them, and he accedes to Perry's interpretation of what they said. Scranton's last-ditch defense of his motive yields massively to the incriminating implications laid out in Perry's line of questions.

In such scenes, the interrogator's power is portrayed as a matter of rational compulsion. In Habermas's terms, the interrogator "raises a claim to power, to which the hearer, if he accepts it, yields."[5] The claim in this case is a citation of facts the witness seems unable to evade. Scranton's yielding is not simply a capitulation to the interrogator's will. Rather, it appears to be grounded in his acknowledgment of the intersubjective validity of the interrogator's position. In contrast, say, to the infamous Salem witch trials where victims were deprived of rational grounds for proving their innocence, this trial represents an "enlightened" ceremonial of truth and justice; the implied force of sanctions is legitimately brought to bear by means of the immanent truth of the interrogatory imperative.

As the televisual drama makes unambiguously clear, the success of the interrogation rests on a mutual acknowledgment of the validity claims raised in and through the adversarial dialogue. In this case, the confession of who did it resolves the initial discrepancy between Perry's and Scranton's positions, producing a "mutual understanding" that places Scranton on the receiving end of a "rationally motivated conviction." There is never any doubt about the referent here, since the program is designed to show the viewers a state of affairs that exists in a (fictional) objective world. The viewers are elevated to a kind of transcendental perspective from which they are able to see not only what the witness says on the stand but the scenes and flashbacks of events outside the courtroom. When Scranton confesses "I hit him," for instance, he affirms a fact otherwise presented in the filmic portrayal of scenes beyond the courtroom, although, in the interest of the drama, the full revelation of what actually transpired is deferred until the perpetrator's confession. This availability of an independent ground of investigation in the television drama stands in marked contrast to actual trials, where attorneys, juries, and judges are usually sequestered within the immediate scene of the courtroom, even though they do make extensive use of various orders of independent evidence to "test" the testimony they hear. In *Perry Mason,* there is no *Rashomon*-like (1951) suspension of what actually happened. On the contrary, the plot

revolves around the testimonial work of bringing initially discrepant stories into accord with an independently validated filmic reality.

Courtroom drama thus exemplifies an ideal conception of dialogue rich
with validity claims corresponding to a world that can be independently
examined. Again, borrowing Habermas's terminology, validity claims are
"redeemed" in reference to "convictions" so strong that witnesses grudgingly give in to the weight of the evidence and arguments against their
position. This drama of truth and justice allows for a clear and unambiguous recognition of the objective basis of the interrogator's validity claims.
One story, one real world, stands behind the collapse of the witness's discrepant version into a confessional acknowledgment of the facts. The interrogator's assertions confront the initially resistant witness with independently derived versions of "what you actually did," "what you actually
knew at the time," and even "what you now know to be the case." Unable
to evade the reasonableness of these claims and their rational linkage to a
conviction, the witness becomes a docile counterpart to the interrogator's
arguments. His point-by-point affirmation of elements of the adversary
story for all practical purposes certifies the inscription of the "agreed facts
of the case" on the public record. In brief, the dialogical exchange produces
a monological argument that is enunciated by one party and ratified by the
other. Ideally portrayed in this way, interrogation is a dialogue that immanently organizes its progression toward truth under the auspices of a
monologic, a logic suited to the production of arguments composed of
statements whose truth value and rational linkages can be assessed unequivocally. This monologic is more than a matter of formal logic, nar-
rowly speaking, since one of its crucial elements is the building of a singular story whose plausibility the witness seems unable or unwilling to
deny. As we can appreciate from the Perry Mason episode, the progression
toward the confession turns crucially on Perry's retelling of the story of
events leading up to the actual murder. He places Scranton in the scene
earlier than the witness had claimed, and he cites documentary evidence
that establishes a possible motive. Scranton fails to resist the persuasive
force of this evidence, and his subsequent defense of why "I did it" presupposes Perry's narrative as a scenic background. The confession thus
serves as both the completion and the certification of an emerging master
narrative of these events.[6]

Such portrayals of courtroom drama are, of course, the stuff of mythol-

ogy. The idea that an interrogative "machinery" exists that compels witnesses to confess a truth which is contrary to their own interests nonetheless has immense appeal outside popular fiction. The possibility that an
obligatory or binding force is situated within the sequential organization of
interrogation—that our communicative activities are, in this sense, orderly
and rational in fine detail—is fundamental to traditions of linguistic philosophy and legal theory. If only in the form of a vain hope, this possibility
inhabits efforts to ground normative accounts of human behavior in the
immanent intelligibility of speech. Such traditions aspire to wed models of
social structure with conceptions of logical determination.[7] Habermas, for
example, has attempted to found a political ethics on the emancipatory
potential latent in actual communicative action by forging decisive linkages between dialogical organization and truth-telling. Within modern legal theory, the compulsive pursuit of confessional truth also figures prominently in rationales for cross-examination, which according to Wigmore is
"the greatest legal engine ever invented for the discovery of truth."[8]

In a criminal trial a guilty plea effectively resolves a case. Similarly, in
a tort case a plaintiff who confesses to having made false claims, or a
defendant who admits the violations in question, effectively moves the
case toward an adverse resolution. There are, of course, exceptions (and
perhaps more than a few of them) when "forced" confessions are said
to occur—for example, in cases in which suspicion is present about the
person's sanity and motives, or disagreement over just what the charges
should be—but for the most part investigation of a crime ends at the point
of the guilty plea, and court procedures rapidly progress toward resolution.[9] Judges often treat a guilty plea as a sign not only of contrition, but of
the defendant's willingness to cooperate with the state's judicial apparatus. In other words, it is said to be a first step in the direction of reform,
warranting a more lenient sentence than when the defendant maintains a
plea of not guilty. Cross-examinations of witnesses other than the defendant also pursue a kind of confessional truth. Since it is assumed that
witnesses are generally interested in aiding their own side of the case,
damaging admissions and confessions take on significance as especially
strong corroboration of adversary claims. As noted, confessions in dramatic portrayals can take on a cathartic quality as the truth erupts from the
lips of the accused despite all efforts to conceal it. As Foucault points out
so incisively, in the modern world the confessional truth that emerges from

discursive examination is privileged over the tortured admission of guilt, *not* because of a humanistic distaste for the arts of torture, but out of a basic distrust in the sincerity of the coerced confession. In theory, confessional truth must therefore emerge freely, but in order for it to emerge, the confessional system requires a docile witness—a mythological character who is led by the force of an interrogation to admit what he or she least wants to—a character who is conspicuous both in histories of notable cross-examinations and popular courtroom drama.[10]

In the remainder of this chapter we describe the armature of the truth-finding engine of interrogation as a sequential machinery through which the co-participants restrict their actions to an orderly progression of questions and answers. We shall treat this engine and its mechanisms as the embodiment of a theoretical (and theatrical) hope that was integral to the conduct at the Iran-contra hearings. We then begin to delve into some of the methods used by a resourceful witness to resist and undermine the operations of this machine, a theme carried into later chapters.

THE TRUTH-FINDING ENGINE OF INTERROGATION

In theory, interrogation is a form of dialogue that instantiates the possibility of an immanent, logical analysis of its own contingent performance. Compared to the more free and open pragmatics of ordinary conversation, the speech-exchange system of interrogation is circumscribed by the court's mandate to pursue relevant matters of fact. Inherent in the conception of a legal engine designed for the discovery of truth is the idea that under the right conditions a sequence of questions can compel a reluctant witness to disclose the truth. Whereas for jurists, truth is the prime concern, from a conversation analytic standpoint[11] the most basic rule of interrogation is that the interrogator asks questions and the witness answers them. This banal characterization is not intended as a definition of what interrogation is, objectively speaking; rather, it provides an initial account of what participants and overhearers expect and demand of each other *while* they enact a progression of discursive moves at a tribunal. This does not mean that the parties to an interrogation simply produce an alternating string of questions and answers (they do many other things besides); rather, it means that they work with (and indeed play with and play off) a flexible set of discourse identities and entitlements associated with the rule. This basic rule forecasts nothing about the "rationality" inherent in a series of questions and answers, but we believe it can be extended to encompass a kind of teleological organization.

Like interviews and diagnostic exams, interrogations can be said to represent a relatively specialized adaptation of the ordinary conversational act of questioning, a domestication, as it were, of ordinary speech acts to the more restrictive organizational demands of interrogative fact-finding. Two gross features of such an adaptation can be noted: (1) a specification of the types of speech act that may properly be performed, and (2) a restriction on which of the participants may properly perform one or another of the paired components of a dialogical speech act. So, in court interrogation the examining counsel should properly ask relevant questions, while the witness should produce relevant answers to the questions asked.[12] This basic rule is supplemented by specific limitations on the forms that questions and answers can take, such as the formal restrictions against leading questions, irrelevant questions, and mentions of hearsay evidence. At the Iran-contra hearings such legal restrictions were largely relaxed (although they were not irrelevant), and were superseded by rules for congressional investigations.[13] These rules were designed to produce a public tribunal, where the televisually staged event would be transparent to an immense audience, without the characteristic tedium of more technical legal proceedings.[14] Nevertheless, the basic discursive protocols of direct and cross-examination were preserved during the hearings, as each witness was examined in turn by the joint committees' House and Senate minority and majority counsel.

It can be argued that the basic rule for "speech act types" and "speech act performers" is normative. This means more than that the rule is stated in explicit protocols.[15] It means that the rule is used: violations are sanctioned by complaints, objections, or other pragmatic moves to restore compliance.[16] So, for instance, when the witness does not answer the question on the floor, the interrogator may prompt the witness, or complain that the answer was absent or incomplete.[17] Similarly, a counsel who engages in activities besides questioning the witness may draw an objection from the opposing counsel. For example, at one point in the hearings, North's counsel, Brendan Sullivan, objected that Senator George Mitchell (a Democrat on the committee) was debating with North about a point of law:

Sullivan: . . . if I could suggest, sir, if you ask him what he did, what the facts were, and what his understanding was at the time, rather than get into a general debate about the—what the law is, it might be more helpful to the committee.[18]

According to the basic rule, in order to maintain the normative order of questioning, interrogators and witnesses must produce what they and relevant overhearers—judges, committee members, or opposing counsel—recognize as relevant "questions" and "answers." However, even though it can be formulated in a simple way, the rule that "the interrogator must ask relevant questions and the witness must answer them" presents a number of complications. Such complications implicate theories of speech and social action as well as the practical enactment of interrogative discourse.

A significant and influential literature within speech-act theory holds that a question is a special case of request, namely, a request for information.[19] In some variants, such as the "educators' question," the questioner has the answer in advance and is checking whether the answerer can produce it. It is a widely accepted fact that questions are often asked using utterances that do not take the form of requests, and, conversely, that utterances in the sentential form of questions often will be devoted to some other task besides questioning (for example, getting someone to pass the butter).[20] In practice, questioning and answering encompass a much broader range of actions than is recognized in formal accounts of speech acts. To a large extent, especially in the preliminary phases of interrogation, questioning is a matter of going over, for the record, what the witness presumably knows and may already have discussed. In contrast to the phases of examination in which the interrogator depends on the witness to disclose fresh information about the case (the prototypical elements explored with the questions: who, what, where, when, and why), long stretches of interrogation explore, refine, challenge, and recapitulate prior testimony. The participants in the dialogue often go over documentary evidence at a level of detail that may seem to members of a lay audience as a belabored pursuit of previously established elements of the record.[21] The witness is invited to collaborate in the retelling of the story and to respond to various lines of argument about its significance and implications. Consider, once again, the sequence at the outset of North's interrogation on the first morning of his testimony, which we discussed in the last chapter:

Inouye: Mister Nields, proceed. (1.5)

Nields: Colonel North, you were involved in two (0.8) operations of this government of great significance to the people of this country, is that correct? (1.0)

North: At least two. Yessir.

Nields: And one of them involved the support of the contras during the time the Boland Amendment was in effect, (0.5) and another one involved the sale of arms to Iran. (2.0)

Nields: Is that correct? (0.8)

North: Yes, i- it also involved support for the democratic outcome in Nicaragua both before and *after* the Boland Amendment was in effect. (2.4)

Nields: And these operations were carried out in secret. (1.5)

North: We *hoped* so.

Nields: They were *covert* operations.

North: Yes they were.

Nields: And covert operations are designed to be secrets from our enemies. (1.0)

North: That is correct.[22]

Were we to consider them in isolation from the rest of the dialogue, many of Nields's utterances in this excerpt would scarcely be recognizable as requests for information. Rather, they are phrased and intoned as declarative assertions that present North with matters of fact awaiting his confirmation. It would be incorrect, however, to treat this sequence as a violation of the basic rule for interrogation. The interrogation proceeds without objection from North or his counsel,[23] and in the published transcript of the Iran-contra hearings all of Nields's utterances in this sequence are punctuated by question marks.[24] It would seem, then, that despite the fact that Nields's utterances are put to North as declaratives, they are nonetheless understood in situ to be *doing* "questioning."[25] Accountable questioning thus appears to go on, regardless of any formal characterization of the constituent utterances as "statements" or "questions."

Although the formal characterization of utterances as questions is difficult enough, answers are even less easily defined. One reason for this difficulty in definition is that the identity of an utterance as an answer is contingent on its relevant relation to an earlier question.[26] Relevance is not a formal, syntactic matter. Whether or not an utterance that takes the form of an answer actually counts as a relevant and adequate answer is a local, sometimes contested, matter. Nevertheless, "questioning" and "answering" are relevant to the organization of testimony, even though no context-free analytic basis may exist for identifying the constituent utterances as unambiguous "questions" and "answers." This does not mean that formal, syntactic considerations were irrelevant. Occasionally, they became relevant, but more as local pragmatic resources than as criteria for establishing compliance to a rule. For example, later on North's first day of testimony, Nields leads him through a reading of Exhibit Two, a PROF note (an electronic message on the Professional Office network at the White House) sent by North to McFarlane. Nields refers to the date on Exhibit Two, and in the first line of the excerpt he asserts that this date is three days after that on another exhibit (Exhibit One) featured in his earlier interrogation of North:

Nields: And that's, three days after the date of the, (0.5) term- terms of reference on Exhibit One. (2.5)

Nields: You can check if you wish or you can take my word for it, it's dated April Four. (0.4)

North: Will you take my word.

((Background din; scattered laughter; pages turning)) (11.0)

(North): (Okay,) ((barely audible, said in conference with Sullivan)) (7.0)

(North): ((barely audible whispering with Sullivan)) (5.5)

Sullivan: Wha- What is your question, uh

Nields: I haven't asked a question yet, I'm simply: uh, (0.8) uh, (0.4) Well, the question is, isn't this three days after the date on the term of reference on Exhibit One?

North: Apparently it is. (1.8)

Nields: And this PROF message makes reference to Mister Ghorbanifar in the first li:ne? (2.0)

North: Yes it does.

Nields: And it makes reference to the fifteen million dollars (1.2) in line three.

North: That's correct.[27]

Here, we can see that the difference between the formal speech-act identity of an utterance as a "question" and its contextual adequacy as a device for doing questioning is locally exploited and managed. Typical of many interrogators, Nields begins not by requesting information but by informing

North of what Exhibit Two says. He gets no response from North, and he then invites him to confirm this information ("You can check [the date on Exhibit Two] if you wish, or you can take my word for it"). North takes the opportunity to deliver an ironic quip—"Will you take my word"—which alludes to the lack of reciprocity and mutual trust so integral to cross-examination. This draws some laughter from the audience. After an interval in which North's counsel and North silently read the document and whisper (off microphone) to each other, Sullivan addresses Nields with the question, "What is your question?" Nields begins by saying that he has not yet come to the "question," implying that what he has asserted to North about the references on Exhibits One and Two are preliminary or prefatory phases of a question he has yet to ask. This acknowledgment that he has not yet asked the question seems to put him into a bit of a bind in light of the rule that each of the interrogator's utterances should be questions, and he cuts himself off, and then reformulates his earlier declarative statement about the "terms of reference" on the document.[28]

By replacing the earlier preface ("And that's . . .") with "Well, my question is, isn't that . . . ," and using questioning intonation at the end of the utterance, Nields makes a conspicuous display of "doing a question," a display that among other things makes evident that for all practical purposes he had already done just that. This (merely) formal transformation brings the utterance into compliance with the requirement for interrogators to ask minimally recognizable questions (although this question seems built to be maximally recognizable). This reformulated question retains the sequential implication of the assertion already on the table. Whether phrased declaratively or as a syntactic question, the utterance awaits North's confirmation. The change is evidently cosmetic, merely a matter of form. Note also that this form of syntactic question is not retained much beyond the particular utterance. Shortly afterward, Nields reverts to declarative readings of documentary references ("And it makes reference to the fifteen million *do*llars . . ."). By reformulating the earlier assertion as a question, and thereby holding his (and North's) place in the unfolding interrogation, Nields has managed to defer asking the sort of question he initially admits not having yet asked ("I haven't asked a question yet . . .").

Nields's difficulties here point to a possible confusion between "question" as a form of sentence (for example, the sort of specimen that is presented and dissected in a grammar text) and "questioning" as an interrogator's relevant, legitimate activity. Sullivan's intervention in the above passage can be understood as a prod designed to get Nields to disclose the *point* of his citation and characterization of Exhibit One, which also invites the audience to construe the immediate interrogation as an irrelevant fishing expedition. Nields closes off any emergent dilemma by resorting to a grammatical transformation that enables him to resume his line of interrogation at the point it was interrupted, while conspicuously respecting the formal requirement to ask questions.

As noted, Nields initiates his interrogation of North with a series of "questions" that are often phrased and intoned as declarative assertions.[29] These assertions are not merely stated, but they are offered for the witness's confirmation. The interrogator overtly produces what Habermas, following Austin and Searle, terms "constative" speech acts—the sorts of true or false statements about the world that form the stock-in-trade of formal logic. The question-answer protocol of interrogation then requires, in turn, that the witness comment on the correctness of the assertion in reference to a worldly event. This format can also be used to package "normative" or even "expressive" speech acts whose contestable claims refer the witness to his or her own understanding of the events in question, to the "rightness" of those events, or to the activities of persons who worked to bring them about.

During these phases of interrogation the witness's participation consists minimally of a yes-no response to each of the interrogator's assertions in the series. The interrogation is carried forward by such responses, as becomes clear when the witness fails literally to state a "yes-no" answer. For example, consider the following excerpt from Vice Admiral John Poindexter's interrogation by Senate majority counsel Arthur Liman:

Liman: uh, would you uh (0.5) *tell* us Admiral, whether thee uhm- at this meeting there was a discussion again: (where there) was a discussion of thee Iran initiative. (1.5) ((Poindexter slowly nods his head 'in agreement'))
Liman: Is that so? You have to say "yes" or "no" in [order for it to [be picked=

                                               [[

Poindexter: [hhh   [Yes.
Liman: =up by the [stenographer.

                           [

Poindexter: [Yes there was.[30]

While Poindexter's head nod is easily recognized as an agreement to Liman's assertion, it provokes Liman's solicitation of a spoken yes or no for the sake of the record. The material record is far from incidental. Indeed, in many respects interrogatory dialogue subordinates itself to the accumulation of such a record.

Interrogators, of course, do more than invite the witness to answer yes or no. Often they use open-ended questions to solicit the witness's stories about the facts in question, or they invite the witness to react to previous testimony. When pressing a witness, however, an interrogator often tries to compel a binary choice between alternatives established by the question ("Answer me yes or no!"), thus facilitating the overhearing audience's task of assessing the testimony in binary terms (true/false; guilty/innocent). The practical imperative to choose operates as an interactively contingent variant of the classical law of the excluded middle, serving to link together successive utterances in a determinate way. Other binary options besides yes and no are often given, such as in the following sequence:

Nields: Was the one million dollars:: (0.4) to cover (0.5) *both* the transporting of arms from the U.S., (1.0) to Israel, and from Israel to Iran, or just one?

North: Well as I said just a moment ago, it was at least the latter (0.4) and may well have by this point in time included both. (0.6) I simply don't recall.[31]

As North's response illustrates, a witness presented with a binary choice can reinsert the middle or otherwise complicate matters by developing a response that commits to neither of the choices on the floor. North's phrase "at least the latter" leaves open the possibility that the alternative option might also apply, and by closing his utterance with "I simply don't recall" he professes to be unable to give a definite response.[32] Although a question may present a witness with a binary option, its very presence as a discursive object opens up other possibilities: the witness may object to the question or its presuppositions, ask for clarification, qualify the response with mitigating expressions and explanations, or develop a response to an aspect of the question other than what the interrogator intended.[33]

The interrogator's installation and enforcement of the excluded middle in order to establish determinate linkages between successive utterances in the dialogue require a witness who is a complicit, docile partner whose discourse is choreographed in relation to the design of a series of questions.[34] When the witness complies with the restrictive form of an interrogative utterance by giving a yes-no (or other binary) answer, the constituent communicative actions appear to progress toward a mutual understanding of sorts, an agreed-to version of the matters of fact in question. Although North was anything but docile, even his interrogation often took the form of a progression through a series of mutually agreeable accounts of the events in question. The more contentious exchanges emerged against a backdrop of more relentless, if less memorable, dialogue in which Nields would make an assertion and North would confirm or disconfirm:

Nields: They were *covert* operations.
North: Yes they were.

We can see here a kind of discursive building block. One participant (in this case, the interrogator) makes an assertion, and the other (the witness) produces a response that selects from the binary alternatives of yes or no. The interrogator's move succeeds—that is, it serves as a basis for carrying forward a step in an argument—only when the recipient takes such a yes or no position on the relevant validity claim.

Questions and answers are not simply strung together turn-by-turn. Like a bead on a string, each confirmed question makes reference to a larger structure within which its position and movement have a place. When a witness responds to a question, he is put in a position of accepting or rejecting the upshot of an entire series of an interrogator's assertions. Again, this stringing together of agreements requires a kind of collusion: a working together point-by-point through a chain of assertions and confirmations. It is only when North confirms his prior assertion that Nields moves on to his next assertion. This point-by-point cumulative production also enables North selectively to challenge the grounds of one or another assertion and to provide reasons for doing so:

Nields: And these operations were carried out in secret. (1.5)
North: We *ho*ped so.
Nields: They were *covert* operations.
North: Yes they were.
Nields: And covert operations are designed to be secrets, from our enemies.
    (1.0)

North: That is correct.

Nields: But these operations were designed to be secrets from the American people. (2.0)

North: Mister Nields, I'm- at a *loss* as to how we could announce it to the American people and not have the Soviets know about it. (1.5) An' I'm not trying to be *flip*pant, but I just don't see how you can possibly do it.

Nields: Uh- well, in fact Colonel North, you believed that the Soviets were aware of our sale of arms to Iran, weren't you. (2.5)

North: Uh- we came to a point in time when we were concerned about that.[35]

If we extract the first four of Nields's utterances from this dialogue, we see that they constitute a coherent chain of assertions and inferences:

And these operations were carried out in secret.

They were *covert* operations.

And covert operations are designed to be secrets, from our enemies.

But these operations were designed to be secrets from the American people.

This progression of assertions works to shape an argument that carries accusatory implications. The discursive constituents of this argument are questions, not in the sense that they request information from North, but in the way they hold North answerable to a problematic characterization of actions and motives. Nields asserts that the particular operations in question were "carried out in secret," so that they were an instance of the type "covert operations." He then presents a generic, and presumably legitimate, purpose for pursuing such operations: namely, to keep secrets "from our enemies." Finally, he contrasts this legitimate purpose of covert operations with the actual purpose of just these operations, using the implied opposition between "our enemies" and "the American people" to exhibit the illegitimacy of the latter in contrast to the former. This would-be argument is not asserted as a continuous monologue. Instead, it is laid out over the course of a series of utterances, the success of each step in the argument being contingent on North's confirmation of its particulars within the unfolding dialogue. While progressing from assertion to assertion in an attempt to build a robust chain of inferences, Nields evidently takes into account each of North's responses. His argument appears built along the lines of a "Socratic trap."[36] Had North unequivocally agreed to each of Nields's assertions, he would have been led into contradiction by avowing, successively, that "these operations" were covert operations, that covert operations are designed to be secret from "our enemies," but that "these operations" were designed to be secrets from "the American people." Contradictory implications would emerge from the series of affirmed assertions unless it was supposed that "our enemies" were indistinguishable from "the American people" (seemingly not a conclusion North would want to admit), or "these" operations were not (legitimate) "covert operations" (also not an agreeable conclusion).

The progress of the argument takes a different tack when North challenges certain presuppositions of the claim to rightness implicit in Nields's assertion, "But these operations were designed to be secrets from the American people."[37] North challenges the opposition between "secrets to our enemies" (in this context, the Soviets) and "secrets to the American people," by collapsing the distinction in the face of certain practicalities of running covert operations. Nields then counters by challenging the claim to "truthfulness" embedded in North's initial challenge, telling him that "in fact . . . [he] believed" that the Soviets already knew about the arms sales to Iran (thus negating the avowal that the overriding purpose of these operations was to keep secrets from "our enemies"). After a brief pause, North responds by confirming Nields's assertion while qualifying its argumentative force by using a temporal marker ("a point in time") to respecify as relatively indefinite the time when he and his cronies became "concerned" about the Soviets' knowledge of the arms sales.

This excerpt illustrates the different trajectories that can be occasioned when interrogators' assertions are accepted or challenged. It also demonstrates the possibility that a witness can give a reply that both confirms a prior assertion and qualifies the extent of confirmation (as in the ironic confirmation, "We hoped so."). This reply is interesting in its own right as an "answer" that both confirms and disconfirms a premise of the prior assertion. North confirms that as far as "we" were concerned, the operation was "secret," but in fact—as is abundantly clear from, among other things, the present hearings—they turned out not to be secret. While casting the question into an ironic frame, this utterance also adumbrates a potential counteraccusation. Where we can see Nields already working toward a focus on secrecy and deception as (in the present case) unwarranted modes for conducting foreign policy, North has already planted the seeds of a complaint regarding the betrayal of governmental secrets. (He will later suggest on several occasions that congressmen—including some members of the present committee—were known to leak state secrets to the press, thus jeopardizing covert operations like a bombing raid in 1986 on Libya.)

When the witness contests the interrogator's claims, the ensuing dialogue momentarily stalls the interrogator's monological line of argument. When North raises his objection about secrecy, for instance, Nields no longer builds on his earlier assertions, but instead he engages in a dispute over the terms of North's immediate objection. The dialogue thus enables a monological argument to proceed only for as long as the various discoverable claims it carries forward go unchallenged. Moreover, in line with a rationalist characterization of communicative action, both Nields and North "give grounds" or "reasons" when contesting each others' claims.

The interrogator takes the lead, at least at the outset of the dialogical dance, while the witness complies, resists, and deflects the line built up through the series of questions. The interrogator's control is produced, in part, by the way his questions tend maximally to state or prefigure a candidate answer ("And they were *covert* operations"). Whenever the witness simply confirms the answer contained in the question, it is as though he enunciated the terms supplied by the interrogator's question/answer. (This technique of putting words in the mouth of an interrogatee also is well known to newspaper reporters, and it sometimes occasions complaints by interviewees about their being misquoted.) By prefiguring the answer, the interrogator's declarative questions exhibit a strong "preference" for confirmation (see Methodological Appendix).[38] When the witness confirms, a mere token of confirmation ("yes" or "that's correct") suffices, although often it is followed by an elaboration, qualification, or explanation. On the other hand, when the witness challenges the trajectory prefigured by the question, he routinely does more than merely state a "no" position. The challenge is accompanied by reasons or objections that serve as grounds for diverting the interrogator's line of argument. In such circumstances, an interrogator may contest the objection or back off by rephrasing a question, for example, by replacing earlier terms of reference to which the witness has objected with formulations designed to solicit a kind of bottom-line agreement.[39] In other words, the interrogatory system exhibits a formal machinery that "prefers" agreement, while at the same time it provides the opportunity for reasoned challenges to the interrogator's questions. In Habermasian terms, it is a machinery that is weighted toward consensus, though, in providing room for reasoned disagreement, it aspires to a consensus achieved through rational means.

The "binding force" of interrogation is tied to the prospective teleological design of an interrogator's questions. Questions by interrogators solicit confirmation in order to link a series of assertions into a monological argument. (An orientation can thus be imputed to a sequence of questions, but its success is contingent on the witness's dialogically enacted agreement.) Each assertion can be rejected, but especially in a cross-examination taking a "no" position can place a witness in a dilemma. This dilemma arises from the following features of interrogation.[40]

(1) Counsel's questions are commonly built less as interrogatories than as assertions or descriptions. Rather than requesting that the witness provide some piece of information, they commonly inform the witness about a set of particulars to which the witness is being held "answerable."

(2) These assertions and descriptions are presented as formulations of facts—unqualified accounts of documented information and prior testimony (including previous statements by the current witness)—and inferences reasonably drawn or drawable from previously established or agreed-to facts.

(3) The sequential design of questioning provides the witness with an opportunity to confirm, challenge, or otherwise respond after each assertion or description. In this structurally minimal sense, such statements are also questions: they are designed as the first part of an adjacent pair of utterances produced by alternating speakers. The interrogator's question selects the witness as a next-speaker, a partner in a duet who is called on to say something in response, if only to confirm the validity claim(s) contained in the question.

(4) When asserted as factual descriptions or reasonable assertions, interrogators' questions strongly prefigure (or "prefer") witness confirmation. When a description or assertion is disconfirmed, the burden falls with the witness to provide a basis for that challenge. In other words, it takes much less discursive work to confirm than to dispute the interrogator's descriptions or assertions. By saying "yes" or "that is correct," the witness, for all practical purposes, confirms an earlier assertion or description. By contrast, saying "no" or "that is *not* the case" will likely occasion a direct challenge on the part of the interrogator unless (and often even when) that "no" position is elaborated by a further justification or counternarrative.

(5) Questions are designed, heard, and overheard as linked progressively and prospectively to an unfolding line of argument. That is, they are not treated as isolated utterances but as discursive building blocks. In cross-examination, the interrogator will often build a case that challenges the witness's previous claims, demands information that has not yet been disclosed, or in other ways impugns the witness's credibility and suggests alternative accounts.[41] These challenges are built into a developing argument in an adversarial dialogue, which eventually problematizes the witness's side of the case.[42] Questions are designed and heard as part of a developing series, which is presumed to have a point or to be leading somewhere, namely, to a challenge or accusation.

(6) Not only do interrogators and witnesses organize their actions in accordance with the above scheme; that they do so is accountable, and is an interactionally used feature of testimony. Insofar as questions evidently and projectably are part of interrogative sequences, so are answers responsive to the projectable point or accusatory implications of the developing line of questioning.

(7) The truth-finding engine of interrogation places the docile witness in a dilemma. If the interrogator is able to amass a coherent nexus of facts implicating the witness in a criminal act, the compliant witness is forced to collaborate in producing the evident basis for an eventual accusation. Once the accusation is made, a docile witness is placed in the untenable position of either (a) denying the accusation at the cost of contradicting previous affirmative testimony, or (b) accepting the accusation, and thus jeopardizing his own side of the case. In this sense, the mythical figure of the docile witness represents the optimal input for the truth-finding engine of interrogation.

A further aspect of the logic of the truth-finding engine is worthy of note. We argued above that a witness's confirmation affirms the validity claims offered in the interrogator's questions. For all practical purposes, the confirmed question becomes a documented "fact"—an item of record—on which further testimony can be based; or, in the case of a box or trap, it can become a device for leading the witness into self-contradiction.[43] In adversarial dialogue, questions often carry, or lead up to, accusations or impugnings of the addressee (or of the parties on whose behalf the addressee is testifying).[44] When the interrogator's question is heard as an accusation, confirmation by a witness is, for all practical purposes, tantamount to an admission of guilt.[45] One may therefore be led to wonder why a shrewd and strategically motivated witness would ever agree with the assertions of an adversary interrogator. However strongly they may prefer confirmation, interrogatives certainly enable a witness to take a negative position. Since disconfirmation can defer or deflect the interrogator's progression of arguments, one might figure that witnesses would take every opportunity to challenge an interrogator's premises. In theory, especially in light of the "deconstructive turn" in contemporary social theory, one might imagine that such subterfuge should not only be possible, it should be rather facile work, a matter of exploiting the theoretically guaranteed logical indeterminacy and interpretative flexibility of any discursive structure.

Although the rational-legal pragmatics of the truth-finding engine are indeed fragile, witnesses nevertheless can experience great difficulty taking advantage of transgressive possibilities that are most readily secured by those engaged in the detached and leisurely analysis of texts.[46] At least two sources of difficulty arise for the would-be "applied deconstructionist" seeking to counteract the operations of the truth-finding engine. The first arises from the temporality of interrogation. Not only does the dialogue unfold quickly, giving the witness little time out to devise the clever evasion or rebuttal, but it does so without allowing the witness an opportunity to inspect ex post facto where the line of questioning is heading.[47] For example, the witness may not yet know what documentary evidence the interrogator is ready to call into play. Second, once it has been allowed to develop, the interrogator's line of uncontested argument may make it difficult for the witness to deny (or, at least to deny plausibly) an accusation built on that discursive platform. This is especially the case when the interrogator's accusations base themselves on a master narrative that has been reiterated many times, not only by the current witness, but by many other parties to the construction of the historical event in question.

For the most part, North successfully overcame both of these difficulties. He and his attorney, Sullivan, proved to be unusually resourceful during the hearings, but more than that, their virtuoso performance was set up by the very construction of the historical archive about which North testified. The North team's success had much to do with his and his allies' retrospective-prospective management of documentary evidence—including the prospective design of plausibly deniable covert actions, the suppression and shredding of records, and the (apparently) well-rehearsed counternarratives North developed in his testimony—all of which created major difficulties for his interrogators. Rather than offering up a confessional truth, North sometimes projected an alternative terminus: "Again, I think we're going to end up agreeing to disagree."[48]

THE PRODUCTION OF A POLITICAL SPECTACLE UNDER THE RUBRIC OF INTERROGATION

Although interrogation, together with the various context-free specifications that have been assigned to that system, seemed immanent to the dialogue at the hearings, it would be more accurate to say that the question-answer system was an officially sanctioned but equivocally relevant discursive organization. Other, less officially approved and sometimes explicitly prohibited discursive moves often entered into the dialogue under the cover of interrogation. It was widely recognized and commented on throughout the hearings that North managed to make speeches, read statements, and engage in debates with the committee members and their counsel. Moreover, he managed to do so while "answering" the "questions" asked of him. Not only was it often difficult to say definitely whether North was speaking truthfully or not, it was similarly difficult to ascertain what sort of speaking he and his interlocutors were doing. No single, overriding system seemed relevant for characterizing the identity of the speakers and of what they were saying and doing.

In line with the classic problem of relevance for sociological descriptions,[49] an open-ended list of descriptive names and predicates can be assigned to the main character in the dialogues we have been examining:

> Oliver North, Ollie, lieutenant colonel, Vietnam veteran, white male, husband and father, American hero, pathological liar, author of best-selling book, NSC staff member, graduate of the U.S. Naval Academy, witness, etc.

All of the items on this list have been used on many occasions to describe North. For some purposes, and on some occasions, a subset of these identities can be treated as synonymous or interchangeable. This is not so, however, for names like "pathological liar" which express a hostile (or, perhaps, clinical) stance. Less contentiously, to call him a "witness" implies something about the relevant occasion. To address him as "Lieutenant Colonel" (rather than, say, "Ollie" or "North") implies something about the relevant relationships involved, the formality of the occasion, and the relevance of military identities. In social theory, relevance generally is established by invoking conceptions of role, identity, and context, but even here, the analyst often has recourse to an "etcetera clause," which acknowledges the potential open-endedness and slippage that attends any given characterization or list of characterizations.[50]

A similar point can be made about the abstract identities assigned to utterances. When characterizing North's utterances in our analyses, we employ descriptive terms such as: answer, story, narrative, avowal, recollection, speech, confirmation, ironic quip, utterance, statement, assertion, etc. For any utterance it is often possible to compound these terms into alternative characterizations and predicates, for example, "an answer to a question in which North recollects a story and avows not to recall particular aspects of the story." Further, categorical identities of a speaker and the speaker's actions often go together: a witness answers a question, a politician makes a speech, and so forth.[51]

Relevant characterizations of speakers and speech-act identities can prove to be contentious, both for analysts and participants. Is a particular sequence of utterances to be described by saying that "the male interrupts the female"? Or should it be, "the teacher corrects the student's answer," or "the adult cuts off the adolescent's utterance"? A distinctive analytical, occupational, and political economy can be implied by the particular selection of such descriptors.[52] In the case of an interrogation, it may seem uncontentious to say that the interrogator asks questions and the witness answers them, but at the hearings whether a question was being asked, had been asked before, was being answered, or had already been answered often proved to be a source of open discussion and conflict. Numerous complaints filled the airwaves:

"What is your question?"
"That wasn't the question."
"You're not answering the question."
"How many times must he answer that question?"

The very identity of "what the witness was doing" thus proved contentious. Just as equivocality and deniability applied to characterizations of past events, they also applied to characterizations of present events. While the parties to the hearings could claim at any point that they were asking

and answering questions in accord with the rules for a congressional hearing, they increasingly produced actions and sequences of actions that
might just as easily have been called speeches, debates, and sermons.
While the latter characterizations may have been relevant, they were also
deniable, as when North denied that he was reading a prepared statement
rather than answering questions, or when North and Sullivan denied that
he had not already answered a question on the floor, or when North objected to John Nields's characterization of his "speech" by insisting that he
had given an "answer" to a question. Not only were the identities of particular "speech acts" reflexively constituted and disputed, but many of the
disputes that broke out during the hearings retrospectively and prospectively implicated the relevant system of discursive rights instantiated at
the hearings. These covered the following and many other matters:

whether or not the witness could, or should, be able to give long answers
without being interrupted;

whether or not the interrogator had just interrupted, or was just now inter-
rupting, the witness's attempt to answer a question;

whether or not the pragmatic organization of the hearings was stacked
against the witness;

whether or not the witness should be able to read a written statement, prepared in advance, or to present a slide show used for political fund-raising
purposes; and

whether or not the witness was free to tell the truth in response to a question
on the floor about a potentially sensitive matter.

The committee cochairmen invoked procedural rules to resolve some of
these disputes, and they made rulings on others, but much of the wrangling
was not settled by discrete decisions or rulings. Instead, a more relentless,
utterance-by-utterance progression at the hearings built up and dismantled
various gestalt figures: question-on-the-floor and answer-to-the-question;
"my next question" as opposed to "the same question he had already answered"; an interruption of the witness's answer by the interrogator's next
question; and an equivocal answer-speech deniable as a speech. The hearings unfolded as an ad hoc production and performance in which various
pragmatic and semiotic configurations of what was going on were set up,
secured, presumed, implicated, contested, equivocated, associated, and
dissociated. The interrogator and witness evidently were not having an

ordinary conversation, they obviously engaged in rounds of close questioning, but their constituent actions were, at best, contentiously relevant as "questions" and "answers" in an interrogation. At times these actions came across as arguments exchanged in a debate, speeches playing to the viewing public, or soliloquies of political self-reflection.

Over the course of the six days of North's interrogation, the discursive system under which he and his committee interrogators were speaking gradually shifted in texture and tone, without entirely losing its recognizability as interrogation. Both North and his interlocutors professed at various times that they did not want to engage in "debate," but especially during the last days of his testimony, when the senators and congressmen on the committee took their separate turns at questioning, the dialogue often took the form of an open debate, or alternatively, of a forum for a series of political speeches. For example, consider the following dialogue with Sen. George Mitchell, a Democrat, on the last day of North's testimony:

Mitchell: Now, you said last week that you've obeyed the law. You haven't claimed, and I understand you don't now claim, that you are in any way above or exempt from the requirements of the law, is that correct?

North: That is correct, sir.

Mitchell: And you agree, don't you, that every American, whatever his or her position, must obey the law?

North: I do.

Mitchell: And that's true even if a person doesn't agree with a particular law?

North: Yes, sir.

Mitchell: Now, if the law is properly enacted and is constitutional but that law is [in] conflict with the President's policy, domestic or foreign, which is controlling, the law or the President's policy?

→ North: Well—(pause)—well, certainly, as I have indicated in my earlier testimony, the law is the law, and as you have also indicated in my testimony, I do not believe that any of us are above the law, and certainly in this case, while I am not a lawyer and—and do not profess to be able to play the various issues, pro and con, I continue to believe that the President's policy was within the law, that what we did was constitutional in its essence, that the President's decisions to continue to support the Nicaraguan democratic opposition in the way they were carried out from 1984 through my departure in 1986 fully fit within the structures of the particular statutory constraints that were contained in Boland. And so I don't see, Senator, that—that there is a distance at all between what was passed and what we did. Certainly there are folks who can argue the constitutionality of Boland, as to whether or not the Congress has the authority to tell a president that he can or cannot ask a head of state to send his agents, in this case myself, out to talk to foreign leaders. It is my understanding of the Constitution and the laws that there is no separation between what we did and the Boland constraints—

Mitchell: And—and—and—

North: —in my going out to talk with foreign heads of state or foreign leaders or to arrange for non-U.S. government monies to be used that met the rigorous constraints imposed by Boland.[53]

Although Mitchell begins this line of questioning in a way that we had earlier identified as typical of interrogation—he presents a series of characterizations for North's confirmation, which seems to be setting up a confessional acknowledgment of illegal conduct—the dialogue quickly evolves into a policy debate. The senator starts his questioning by soliciting North's agreement with a series of general assertions on behalf of North's earlier testimony. These initial assertions convey a general civics lesson about a citizen's responsibility under the rule of law. In language reminiscent of Jeffrey Alexander's account of the lesson of Watergate (see chapter 3), Mitchell invites North to agree that even "the President's policy" is not exempt from the rule of law.[54] At this point (marked by the marginal arrow in the transcript) North launches into a disagreement that extends his answer well beyond the frame of the question. He shifts the terms of the dialogue from matters of abstract principle to matters of application in the case at hand. He prefaces his utterance with the conventional pre-disagreement token, "Well," and he then confers with Sullivan before giving what might be called a speech. Initially, he refers back to his earlier testimony while professing a respect for the rule of law, and he then argues that he and the administration endeavored to adhere to the terms of the Boland amendment when they tried to support the contras during the period when that law was in force. Mitchell tries to cut him off, but North overrides this attempt and continues his monologue, contending that his and the administration's actions did not contravene the Boland amendment. North thus preemptively argues against an accusation that Mitchell has not yet made, namely, the accusation that North's and the administration's actions knowingly violated the law. North does not contest Mitchell's "value statements" about the rule of law; instead, he contests their singular application to the actions he describes. Although he defends the actions in question, he does so by giving an elaborate counternarrative packaged within the dialogical frame of an answer to a question. It is not as though the speech-exchange system here stops being an interrogation, but that it also becomes an occasion for a debate: a debate being a relatively symmetrical exchange of counterarguments, rather than an asymmetrical sequence of questions and answers. These arguments and counterarguments are advanced under the rubric of asking questions (often phrased as assertions) and answering them (often with long "answers").

The conventional design of interrogative "questions" and "answers" facilitates such transformation. This is because, as we have discussed: (1) interrogative questions often take the form of assertions presented to the witness for confirmation; (2) witnesses can (although they do not always) answer such questions as though they were phrased as syntactic yes-no questions; (3) sequences of such questions are used to build arguments; and (4) disconfirming answers generally adduce reasons or accounts addressed to the emerging arguments. In brief, interrogative sequences tend to lead up to arguments and counterarguments. To this list can be added that an interrogator's control over such exchanges depends crucially on foreclosing the witness's development of answers into arguments. This is done by commonplace interrogative devices of cutting off expansive answers, insisting that the witness "just answer the question," and enjoining the witness to "just answer yes or no." Toward the end of North's testimony, perhaps as a result of Sullivan's repeated objections about the interrogator's interruptions of North's answers, combined with North's much-publicized popularity and his vocal and energetic support from several of the Republicans on the committee, North's answers were allowed to expand with less and less resistance from his interrogators, so that he attained relatively equal footing with his interrogators in an adversary exchange.[55]

Debate was not the only option opened up by the interrogation. Especially under the friendlier questioning by North's committee supporters, North was given every opportunity to expand his answers into lengthy stories, speeches, and cooperative discussions, North remained on-camera for long intervals as he expounded upon his many tales of adventure, of dangerous enemies like archvillain Abu Nidal, and the rationales for his and the administration's actions. Toward the end of North's six-day drama, many of the committee members, Democrats as well as Republicans, prefaced their interrogations with solicitous remarks that praised and expressed support for him. For example, Representative Ed Jenkins, a Democrat, began with the following remark:

Jenkins: I know you have been [here] for a long, long time, and—I will try to keep my questions very, very short. Maybe I will not use the entire time [allotted to me]. Let me say in the beginning that with an issue like this I'm sure there will be many repetitive questions, and I want to apologize in advance because I know you will have answered some of them, but I want to get the picture in my mind so that I fully understand as best I can from your testimony as to what actually occurred. Before I ask you a question, as one Democrat as you probably know, I have always supported contra aid.

North: Yes sir. And I am sure that they are grateful for that. I am.[56]

Although Jenkins and others also raised concerns about North's and the administration's actions, they often participated with him in cooperative policy discussions about the legitimacy of covert operations and the means for assuring governmental oversight of those actions. The screws of the interrogative machinery were considerably loosened, to the point that it became undecidable whether interrogation was the most pertinent characterization of the speech-exchange spectacle.

Acting within a system of interrogation, which already included certain relaxations of the procedural rules for testifying in court, North, Sullivan, and their growing band of allies on and beyond the committee managed to produce relevant contexts of understanding of what was happening at the moment. This moment-to-moment production variously informed, ambiguated, and equivocated the spectacle of a witness answering questions in an interrogation. It is not enough to say that North and his team assigned or attached an alternative "definition of the situation" to the hearings. North and various Reagan administration spokespersons and supporters did indeed try to redefine the situation by saying, for example, that the hearings were a political dispute rather than an inquiry about administrative wrongdoings, but the discursive realization (and relativization) of the hearings was far more intricate, infrastructural, and material than any verbal attribution or definition could have been.

One of the more surreal incidents at the hearings involved a partly successful effort by a faction on the committee to allow North to give an anticommunist lecture and slide show as evidence of the "private" fundraising efforts he had assisted at a time when aid to the contras was prohibited by Congress. Several Republican members managed to persuade the committee majority to create a space for such a show on the last day of North's testimony. Earlier, he had testified about the slide shows he had presented to potential donors to the contra cause. The committee's cochairman, Inouye, and several other members initially resisted the motion. They argued that such a demonstration would be irrelevant, that it would not necessarily represent what North actually did at the fund-raising sessions in question, and that facilities for showing the slides could not be provided with the appropriate security arrangements. It was clear that what was at stake was the potential opportunity to put North on stage for giving a presentation tailor-made to attract support for his, and the administration's, Central American policies. Only in this case his fund-raising appeal as a salesman for anticommunism would be presented as a lengthy reenactment, displaced from one context to another and legitimated under the rubric of "giving evidence" at the present hearings. Eventually, chairman Inouye conceded under pressure from some of his vociferous colleagues to allow North to give his presentation, but without illuminating the slides. North then recited what he claimed to be his typical speech, while holding the slides aloft to the lights and describing them in words. This curious show tended to mute the rhetorical force of North's demonstration of the Nicaraguan threat, but it exemplified a lateral displacement and appropriation of North's audiovisual appeal as a fund-raiser from one discursive context to another.[57]

The discursive field of the hearings was shot through with "communicational ethics." Questions about truth, credibility, sincerity, and normative rightness made up the very animus of an interrogator's and witness's work before an audience of overhearers, and this implicated how they spoke as well as what they said. But as far as we can tell, these ethical questions did not trace back to a coherent, underlying foundation, whether conceived in terms of linguistic pragmatics or as more abstract cultural norms. Instead, virtually all of the abstract normative elements that might have counted as grounds for truth-telling, trust, and mutual understanding were contested and/or used as occasional points of leverage during the hearings.

It has been argued by some conversation analysts that "ordinary conversation" provides a kind of base system for various institutionalized alternatives (see Methodological Appendix). Accordingly, the transformation we have described between interrogation, debate, cooperative discussion, etc., would be seen to take place within an overarching system of talk-in-interaction that provided participants with a more flexible system of rights for designing turns and initiating adjacency pairs.[58] In this case, however, we consider that "conversation" is no less definitive a characterization of what North and his interlocutors were doing than were the other alternatives we have considered. Although we recognize the relevance of speech-exchange systems of various kinds for the local production of the discourse, we would argue that no single system provides a foundation; rather, available systems become serially, simultaneously, and contentiously relevant in and through the local production and local historicity of the event under analysis.

CONCLUSION

We noted at the outset of this chapter that a docile witness—like the hapless caricatures confronted by Perry Mason—confesses to the terms of the accusation out of an overriding respect for the logical properties of the interrogative argument and the body of facts adduced through it. In such an event, rational compulsion trumps self-interest. Although interrogation is not an ideal speech situation, the determinate operations of the truth-finding engine testify powerfully to the presence, mythical or otherwise, of a stable and rational grounding for testimonial discourse. The confessional reconciliation of adversarial positions affirms the force of good arguments over and against the accused's will to resist them. The force compelling the docile witness to confess is due less to some mystical urging toward rational consistency than to a practical inability to come up with reasonable stories other than those supplied by correct accusations. The discursive redemption of validity claims is at the heart of the matter; the operations of the truth-finding engine presume that a tissue of lies is difficult to construct, and once constructed, it is hard to sustain in the face of rigorous cross-examination. What remains to be examined is how a well-prepared and artful witness can resist the compelling force of the truth-finding engine without becoming ensnared by inconsistencies and contradictions.

The methods of this well-prepared witness include an array of discursive devices through which he challenges, qualifies, or fails to recall the descriptions, premises, or logical implications asserted by the interrogator, and, alternatively, answers precisely what is asked without saying anything more. Although North often gave ground on specific issues, and occasionally made conspicuous displays of contrition, he routinely managed to minimize his admissions while avoiding charges of evasion. In one sense, his ability to do so is hardly surprising. Jurists have often faulted the adequacy of cross-examination "as an instrument for ascertaining the facts of past history."[59] Thus, to say that rational interrogation is "the greatest legal engine ever invented for the discovery of truth," may tell us more about the crude state of legal technology than about the virtues of the particular engine. For our purposes, however, the occasional failures of the truth-finding engine are not only interesting because they provide a theoretical problem for jurisprudence and a tactical problem for interrogators, but also because they give us a glimpse of how interrogation is a reflexive production vulnerable to immanent modes of "practical deconstruction." Such deconstruction is not only a matter of contesting arguments and building counternarratives; it is a matter of dismantling selective elements of the discursive scaffolding of such arguments and narratives. As we have described it thus far, interrogation embodies a potent modernist mythology of sense and reason. The mythic nature of this engine inheres with the image of a consensually enacted and yet normatively constrained machinery geared to the disclosure of confessional truth, a dialogical exchange oriented to the production of a monological, factual story. The engine's counterpart, the "docile witness," is similarly a real mythical figure who, by testifying against his or her own interests, embodies the material connection between language, logic, and posttraditional legal rationality. But what happens to this engine when its fundamental elements—that is, the identities of "questions" and "answers," the rules for their use, and the rights, obligations, and validity claims associated with them—are themselves subject to challenge and equivocation? What happens when a witness's answer neither confirms nor disconfirms the question? What happens when the interrogator and the witness fail to agree that a question has been answered, or even that it has been asked? What happens when a witness, with the complicity of a portion of the overhearing audience, turns his "answers" into "speeches" that denounce and debate the political auspices of the tribunal? These actions not only transgress the terms under which we have thus far described interrogation, but they occasion doubts about what sort of discursive system is in place—that is, is it an interrogation, a political carnival, a debate, or what? And, accordingly, one can be led to wonder what sorts of normative standards, if any, are relevant and appropriate for understanding and assessing "what's going on" and "who's to blame."[60] In coming chapters we describe how the negative counterpart of the docile witness—a figure that might be dubbed a "hostile native"—provides a key point of leverage for a critique of the foundationalist mythologies associated with the truth-finding engine. With North as our applied deconstructionist, we shall examine the methods through which the truth-finding engine was set to idling.

5. STORIES AND MASTER

NARRATIVES

As noted in chapter 4, interrogators' questions often take the form of assertions for the witness to confirm, and question-answer sequences in testimony are used to build arguments turn-by-turn, point-by-point. Witnesses
are asked to corroborate a series of interrogative assertions, often at some
considerable expense to their own side of the case. In addition, they may be
instructed to respond directly to questions, or to limit themselves to yes or
no answers, thus allowing the interrogator unilaterally to articulate a line
of argument. To compound the pressure on the witness, the interrogator
springs each question at the first possible opportunity, before the witness
can elaborate an incipient answer beyond a simple yes or no or prepare to
defend against the next line of attack. If the witness hesitates slightly, he is
prompted, often with the suggestion that he is being less than forthright.
Any effort to object to the question, add an explanation, qualify, or otherwise extend the answer is nipped in the bud in a relentless interrogatory
pursuit.[1] Questioning is thus much more than a repeated use of a particular
speech act. It tends to impose a rhythm and pace, as well as a logical frame,
on the embodied flow of dialogue, which sets up, dramatizes, and soft-
pedals emergent truth effects.

Interrogation is central to the popular mythology of courtroom practice,
as it is the heart of the modern ceremonial of truth. We suggested that the
appeal of the public tribunal consists in its placing the body of the witness
at the center of an audiovisual field in which a discursive examination
takes place. This real-time struggle between witness and interrogator is
itself witnessed and assessed by a popular audience. The mythology has to
do with the very design of interrogation as a rationally compelling force for
disclosing a truth. From this point of view, the violent pressure that, in
earlier times, was applied to the flesh of the accused is transferred to the
discursive system of interrogation and is seen most directly in the expan-
sions and contractions of the space available to the witness in the embodied dialogue.

For these reasons, the practices of courtroom interrogation have often
been said to give inordinate control to interrogators, leading at times to the

abuse of browbeating, which Anthony Trollope, writing in 1858, likened to a form of torture.[2] The interrogator asks questions in rapid-fire series designed to fluster the witness and to dramatize the implausibility of the witness's counterclaims and refusals to answer. As with more gruesome carceral orders, confessional truth extracted by means of interrogation can be challenged as an artifact of the interrogator's manipulations.[3] A witness's attorney, for instance, is supposed to stand guard against the various forms of browbeating by raising objections against leading questions, rhetorical questions, untethered speculations, and other kinds of fishing expeditions. At the very least, such objections can disrupt the pace of interrogative pursuit. Even when an advocate fails to come to the rescue, witnesses are not entirely at the mercy of interrogators. The dialogical organization of testimony provides abundant opportunity for a witness to protest, counteract, evade, or otherwise thwart the trajectory of questioning. The fact that testimony is delivered before an overhearing audience provides the witness with the opportunity to enlist the audience's sympathy against an evidently brutish interrogator. In addition, witnesses often manage to append yes or no answers with explanations, qualifications, or extensions that texture their responses in ways that do more than simply comply with the interrogator's line of questioning. Indeed, the very point of calling a witness to testify in the first place would seem to be that they have something to say, something that is original, or that cannot be fully projected by the interrogator in advance of the actual testimony. In the modern ceremonial of truth, witnesses are called not only to confirm or disconfirm a series of facts that investigators already have in hand, but they are asked to elaborate, interpret, reveal, and react to evidence and to give their own versions of the events in question. In brief, witnesses are often asked to add their own stories to the record, not just to corroborate a series of already established details, and it is part of the legitimacy (and the point) of calling witnesses that they should have something informative to say.[4]

The witnesses and their attorneys at the Iran-contra hearings worked vigorously both behind the scenes and in the actual testimony to maximize their ability to testify within a relatively free dialogical space. As noted in chapter 3, the attorneys for North and Poindexter negotiated the right to testify under a partial immunity clause. This meant that none of the witness's testimony could be used as evidence against him in a criminal investigation on any charge other than perjury. North and his attorney, Brendan

Sullivan, also negotiated a right to appear side-by-side while North testi-fied—a setup that previous witnesses had not used and that had not been used at the Watergate hearings.[5] This arrangement allowed North and his lawyer to frequently engage in sotto voce exchanges before North answered particular questions. Sullivan's famous line, "I am not a potted plant!"— insisting on the attorney's right to intervene in the space between question and answer—was delivered in response to Nields's objection that questions were being addressed to Colonel North and not to his attorney. In the course of the hearings, Sullivan battled vociferously to grant his client the right to develop long answers, insisting at one point that "it's only fair that counsel let the witness finish his answer before interjecting another ques-tion."[6] Elsewhere, he pleaded for further "leeway" to allow his client to state his answers fully and without interruptions:

Sullivan: Please, Mr. Chairman. When a witness is struggling to appear before a group like this, and anticipates being questioned by thirty skilled ques-tioners, I think you have to give him some leeway in his responses. He's trying to explain. He's struggling to try to understand the questions and to explain the answers, and I don't think he should be cut off by counsel. Please sir.[7]

It is important to notice that by voicing these objections, Sullivan appeals to nontechnical standards of fairness and rightness in a transparent at-tempt to enlist the televisual audience in opposition to the committee's formal prerogatives. Such appeals were so successful that by the time Poin-dexter appeared before the committee a week later the committee inter-rogators showed a conspicuous willingness to grant the witness all the time he needed to complete his answers.[8] Far from being badgered by the interrogator, the witness secured a "right" to confer with his attorney be-fore answering, to defer responding while studying relevant documents, and to expand answers into extended narratives.

Even though it was eventually denied on technical grounds, Sullivan's motion that North be allowed to read a statement before starting his testi-mony became one of many negotiating tactics for granting North the infor-mal freedom to expand his answers into extended stories and speeches without interruption from interrogators or other committee members.[9] While North was enjoined to "respond directly to questions posed by committee members or committee staff," he and Sullivan established from the outset that North had something to say on his own accord, a statement that, by virtue of the very ruling aimed at its suppression, became a submerged oppositional text pressing to emerge from within the confined space allotted for North's answers. In this way, the course of interrogation became a stage for the piecemeal, improvisatory performance of a counternarrative to the committee's master narrational account. In sum, what North gained was the "right" to use the position of "answering questions" as a podium from which to make extended statements and speeches and to tell stories from his own point of view, while all the time claiming that what he was doing was nothing other than *answering questions.*

As we have emphasized throughout this study, the committee was charged with the responsibility of writing a master narrative that subsumed thousands of documents and hundreds of hours of testimony into a chronological account of a historical event. Since its authority rested on the successful display of a nonpartisan objectivity, the committee majority pursued a voice that was objective, bipartisan, and collaborative. To this end, witnesses like North were called on to recount details of particular meetings they attended and transactions in which they participated, to interpret documentary records they wrote or signed, and to give vivid recollections of what they experienced and understood in the various places, at the various times, in question. That is, they were called on to tell their own stories, and in this way, to contribute their first-person perspective to the building narrative of these events. It was presumed from the outset that North, Poindexter, and the other witnesses stood in a special relationship to these events (as eyewitnesses, participants, local experts, etc.), and therefore they were in a position to say things that might possibly contribute to the historical record. Such witnesses appeared under the presumption that they had special access to the events in question and that they therefore were uniquely entitled to testify about what they knew, recalled, or were otherwise prepared to say as participant-observers.

Such entitlements extend well beyond the narrow confines of congressional hearings. Ordinary conversational stories told among friends, family members, and coworkers are built around speakers' lived experiences. The moral entitlements to talk about one's own experience are so commonplace that a witness in court can try to presume a certain right to an unchallenged "my side telling," which has no explicit legal authorization, and without the need for further strategic appeal.[10] As we shall see, North's ability to use the moral entitlements that come with the territory of ordinary storytelling was a powerful resource for securing and maintaining a narrative position that counteracted his interrogators' control over the agenda and the pragmatic organization of the examination.

CONVENTIONAL HISTORIES AND
CONVERSATIONAL STORIES

The general outlines of the committee's investigative task should be familiar to any historian or social scientist. By interviewing a series of witnesses, assembling and colligating a body of documents, and compiling a comprehensive account of a historical event, the committee investigators aimed to transform the fragmentary, idiosyncratic, tendentious, and interested descriptions provided by witnesses and documents into an empirically based, disinterested account of the events in question. In their own way, the investigators were attuned to what C. Wright Mills called the "promise" of the sociological imagination: "to grasp history and biography and the relations between the two in society."[11] For them, however, the project of grasping history and biography was beset by the fact that witnesses were able to tell stories that subverted the very idea of a univocal history of events. Especially in North's case, the witnesses were able to enlist conspicuous support from key committee members as well as from significant parts of the media public. To understand the depth of such subversive possibilities, it is worth considering how a witness is able to develop stories that problematize conventional historical accounts.

Conventional histories are recited in an impersonal voice. Whether factual or mythical, they are stories of events, typically arrayed in chronological order, one event following from another. Such narratives often include quotations from testimonies and documents, and the narrator's voice often frames, interprets, and comments on the events and characters in the story. But rarely does the narrator assume the role of an actual participant in the story. Instead, the narrative is generated from the perspective of a "virtual participant"[12] who assumes the voice of a superwitness with no concrete position in the world described. This voice describes events and actions while taking account of the testimonies of more interested actors, and it attempts to rise above the limits imposed by partisan interests, hidden motives, organizational divisions of labor, social distributions of knowledge, and temporal and spatial localities.

The authority and legitimacy of conventional histories can, of course, be subject to challenge. In social theory, the positioning of the virtual participant has been subject to a range of epistemological and technical challenges relative to the disciplinary state of the art.[13] Despite efforts to impose limits on what counts as serious criticism, historians' and social scientists' narratives also remain vulnerable to popular sources of political suspicion and criticism. Official histories that describe an explicitly politicized field of action are especially vulnerable to vulgar incredulities toward master narratives. As mentioned in chapter 2, such incredulities formed a prominent theme during the Iran-contra hearings. The opportunity for witnesses to tell their own stories before the committee and the cameras enabled them to contest, deny, and equivocate selective details of the accumulating record on which the emerging master narrative was based. This possibility implied a source of authority that problematized the consensual grounds claimed by the committee investigators. Such authority, we shall argue, is based on some ordinary features of conversational storytelling.[14]

This point can be made clearer by considering some of the gross organizational differences between conventional historical narratives and witnesses' firsthand reports. Compare, for instance, the following excerpts from (1) a summary on the November 1985 Hawk missile shipment in a published version of the Iran-contra committee's final report, and (2) an interchange between Nields and North in which North is asked to give his version of "the story of the Hawk shipment" to Iran in November 1985.
(1) The Report

By the third week of November, the Israeli intermediaries and the Americans believed they had reached an agreement with [Iranian intermediary] Ghorbanifar on a plan that would gain release of all the hostages by Thanksgiving. The plan was, in essence, a straight swap: U.S.-made missiles in Israeli stocks would be sold to Iran in exchange for American hostages. As the exchange date approached, many details remained unresolved. They were only hammered out in separate and frantic long-distance negotiations among the Israeli intermediaries and Ghorbanifar, Ghorbanifar and his contacts in the Iranian Government, and the Israeli Government officials and NSC officials.[15]

(2) The testimony

Nields: Would you simply pick up the story of the Hawk shipment, starting with that call that you received from the Israeli official, and tell us in your own words what you remember, and we know that this is a more complicated story than the TOW shipment. And you can rely on me to ask you some questions after you have told your narrative.

North: All right sir. It is my recollection that on November 17th, I received a phone call in the evening from an Israeli official who was in New York indicating a problem. I then, I think while I was still on the line with him, got a call from Mr. McFarlane. My contemporaneous note at the time indicates that the two calls were, if nothing else, sequential.

Nields: I take it this was a call from Mr. Rabin?

North: It was.

Nields: And what was the problem?

North: Well, he did—at this point, he didn't go into it in any detail, that there was a problem with a shipment, a movement on the project that I knew about. I then got a call from Mr. McFarlane from Europe, telling me that Mr. Rabin would call. I told him I had already talked to Mr. Rabin. He said, "Look, just, you know, you go take care of that problem." This was a transatlantic open line telephone call as I remember it. And so my recollection is I flew up immediately to talk with Mr. Rabin. He then sent several of his Ministry of Defense representatives to talk with me. It was in that period of time that I became aware of what was really trying to be moved. Now I may have already known some of that from sensitive intelligence, but the full parameters of it were laid out for me by Mr. Rabin and his representatives.[16]

These excerpts from the report and the testimony both include narrative descriptions that present a temporal order of worldly events. There are, however, significant differences between them, differences that have to do with their distinctive interactional, narrational, and moral auspices. These include (1) the occasion for telling, or the way the testimony is solicited and recited as part of an immediate ("live") course of social activity; (2)

narrational positioning, or the way the narrator is positioned within the field of action described by the story; and (3) the entitlement to tell, or the way the narrator displays a moral right to tell the story from a particular point of view.

(1) The Occasion for Telling

The committee's report is a narrative of events in which the November Hawk shipment is summarily described in an impersonal voice. Although the report later elaborates some of the details of the shipment and in the process quotes selectively from testimonies and documents, its central effect is to situate the November Hawk shipment within an objective chronology of related events.

In contrast to the monological organization of the committee's report, North's account of the Hawk shipment can be characterized as a dialogically occasioned oral history. The occasion for telling is provided by House majority counsel Nields's utterance, "Would you simply pick up the story of the Hawk shipment, starting with that call that you received from the Israeli official, and tell us in your own words what you remember." The open-ended invitation to tell your story can be regarded as one of a family · of devices for soliciting testimony. While this solicitation would appear to open up a relatively free discursive space for witness's testimony, Nields's utterance also outlines what that testimony can be about and how it will be held accountable. In this way, we shall argue, the story solicitation adumbrates a course of inquiry in which witnesses' accounts will remain subordinate to the authority of the emerging master narrative.

As we discussed in chapter 4, interrogators often collaborate in the telling of the witness's story by making specific claims about what the witness already knows (e.g., Nields: "Uh- well, in fact Colonel North, you believed that the Soviets were aware of our sale of arms to Iran, weren't you.").[17] Interrogators also intervene in the course of a witness's stories to "check" or to "clarify" particular story elements (such as when Nields says, "I take it this was a call from Mr. Rabin?"). The task of clarifying witnesses' statements can also serve as an opportunity to summarize or amplify the upshot of what a witness is saying. During the North testimony, such clarifications were often stated as "incredulous hearings" that were then used to challenge the plausibility of the witness's account (Nields: "Is it your testimony that the documents that you shredded right after you found out that the Attorney General's people were coming in over the weekend to look at documents had nothing to do with the fact that his people were coming in to look at documents?").[18] The witness is likely to anticipate that the story invited by the open-ended story solicitation will be held accountable to the existing, accumulating record of the events it is supposed to describe. Indeed, the prospect that the story will be held accountable in this way is evident in the invitation itself. Nields's story solicitation includes a conspicuous display of foreknowledge regarding the events in question. He refers to an already familiar "call you received from the Israeli official," and mentions that "we know" this story "is more complicated" than a story about another missile transaction, "the TOW shipment." Nields adds that he will "ask . . . some questions" about the forthcoming story after North finishes telling it. In sum, when the interrogator invites the witness to tell his story, he makes it clear that he already has in hand a version of the events and their circumstances against which he can compare that story. In this sense, testimony is constructed to supplement the record by filling in details of a preexisting narrative. Consequently, testimony tends to produce confirmatory or disconfirmatory evidence rather than unanticipated revelations.

By asking North to "simply pick up" an established story as he remembers it, Nields invites him to describe a field of action from the position of someone who participated in and witnessed the activities that constitute that field. The invitation situates the witness within the story about to be told and explicitly requests a relational account that (1) elaborates on an event that is already familiar to the participants at the hearings, (2) recollects what the witness can say *now* about the past event, and (3) gives an account of North's connection to and understanding of the November Hawk shipment at the time in question. In contrast, the committee's report gives a comprehensive summary in which North's actions are a relatively minor part of a series of transactions between Iranian contacts, Israeli government agents, and NSC staffers. Although the report gives further details, these are arranged focally around the event, unlike North's narrative, which positions his own experience of the event at the center of the story. "Experience" here has no necessary relation to a concept of consciousness, and there is no sure way of checking that a narrative of experience will correspond to something actually perceived rather than a fictional event.[19]

That North's story is organized as a narrative of experience is neither unusual nor disruptive, as it is the very sort of story that Nields invites him to tell.

(2) Narrational Positioning

North's testimony "recollects" a set of contingent and relational details that are absent from the committee's report. According to Sacks, this is typical of conversational stories: "Stories are plainly ways of packaging experiences. And most characteristically stories report an experience in which the teller figures. And furthermore, in which the teller figures—for the story anyway—as its hero. Which doesn't mean that he does something heroic, but that the story is organized around the teller's experiences."[20] As an illustration, Sacks gives an example of a story told shortly after the assassination of Robert F. Kennedy: "Two ladies are talking on the phone and one of them, talking about the helicopter that carried Bobby Kennedy's body back to wherever they took it, says, 'You know, where the helicopter took off? That was the exact spot where our plane took off when we went to Hawaii.' To which the other responds, 'Oh for heaven sakes, weren't you lucky. If it had happened when you were going to take off, it would have ruined your trip.' "[21] He observes: "It's in that sort of way that an event which, in the 'objective reality' has the current teller figuring altogether incidentally, gets turned into an event in their lives specifically—or an almost-event in their lives specifically."[22] This narrational positioning is more than a matter of adding "personal" details to "the objective event itself." Rather, the very scene of the story is recentered on the speaker-character's life-world, a locus of action that would otherwise be "incidental" or completely insignificant in a public news report.[23] In the story related by Sacks, such incidental details of Robert F. Kennedy's assassination are made central, while the main historical event is relegated to the background. Although the response "it would have ruined your trip" may be a caricature of the kind of indifference to history that demonstrates a conspicuous lack of C. Wright Mills's "sociological imagination," there is nothing particularly unusual about the way the story is told and understood as a story for present company, a story "just for us."

Similarly, in the excerpt of testimony we have been considering, North appears as the hero or main character around which these events are organized, even though he describes his role in the November Hawk shipment as relatively indirect and insignificant. Alternatively, from the standpoint of the report's comprehensive summary of the objective event, the phone calls that North describes are incidental, or otherwise not worthy of mention. Not only does the report not mention these phone calls, it does not preserve the relational configuration of North's testimony. It simply says that a series of contacts took place. It does not elaborate how those contacts were witnessed by any of the various agents or officials.[24] This is not to say that the report was necessarily incomplete, that it deleted significant information, or that it gave a distorted account of the actual event, but rather that its organization differs from that of North's story and that this difference arises from a translation of situated stories into conventional historical accounts.

The difference between historical narrative and a narrative of experience should not be viewed as a difference between stronger (objective) and weaker (subjective) descriptions. The witnesses did not give comprehensive accounts of objective events apart from what they experienced. Gathering from Nields's invitation to "tell us in your own words what you remember," there was no expectation that North should do otherwise. In a courtroom, witnesses are entitled to say only what they experienced directly, as an event in their lives specifically, however incidental from the standpoint of a "virtual participant" in a narrative of events. Hearsay evidence was permitted by the House-Senate committee rules, but for the most part witnesses were entitled to tell their own stories of the events in question. This implicit ownership of an order of contextual details provides the storyteller with a conventional right to corroborate or contest details of an event that may already be known by other means. Moreover, a narrative of experience enables the storyteller to predicate relations to an event that transform its moral significance without contradicting the relevant terms of a conventional historical account.

(3) The Entitlement to Tell: A Binding Technique for Witnessed Events

A central and pervasive feature of stories told in conversation is that the topical arrangement of temporal, spatial, and other predicates establishes commonly recognizable social relations among the narrator, the occasion, the characters, and the scene described. Stories told in conversation tend to hang together, and the criteria by which their coherence is ordinarily seen and assessed are internal to the story structure. As Harvey Sacks described it in a brilliant series of lectures, conversational stories make use of narrative conventions that "bind together" characters, setting, events, and the narrator's experience in a context of relational details (see our Methodological Appendix).[25]

In this light, consider, once again, the excerpt from North's testimony cited above, and, in particular, the section where he describes a series of phone calls made on November 17, 1985:

Nields: And what was the problem?

North: Well, he did—at this point, he didn't go into it in any detail, that there was a problem with a shipment, a movement on the project that I knew about. I then got a call from Mr. McFarlane from Europe, telling me that Mr. Rabin would call. I told him I had already talked to Mr. Rabin. He said, "Look, just, you know, you go take care of that problem." This was a trans-Atlantic open line telephone call as I remember it. And so my recollection is I flew up immediately to talk with Mr. Rabin. He then sent several of his Ministry of Defense representatives to talk with me. It was in that period of time that I became aware of what was really trying to be moved. Now I may have already known some of that from sensitive intelligence, but the full parameters of it were laid out for me by Mr. Rabin and his representatives.[26]

North places himself as a character in the story, with a specific relation to the events described. He is situated deeply within the field of action as someone with unquestioned access to "sensitive intelligence," someone who receives phone calls and visits from representatives of the Israeli Ministry of Defense and who is instructed by McFarlane to "take care of that problem" (apparently, the problem of replenishing Israel for Hawk missiles to be delivered to Iran in an arms for hostages deal). Notice, however, that while North is central to his own story as a man of action, his knowledge and agency are made peripheral to the event. He appears mainly in the capacity of a mediator who relays messages and shuttles between the major characters (Rabin and McFarlane). Far from being a prime mover, he avows that he "became aware of what was really trying to be moved" (Hawk missiles) as a consequence of the series of phone calls with Rabin, and/or sensitive intelligence that, presumably, originated from the CIA.

The passive locution, "what was really trying to be moved" is interestingly noncommittal about who was trying to do the moving, but the story makes clear that whoever it was, it was not Oliver North. Accordingly, North-as-character emerges in the story as a joint operative who has limited access to and responsibility for the events that his actions help facilitate. This portrayal of his subordination is congruent with—although it does not necessarily imply—a "Nuremberg defense." It implies that his role in the Iran-contra affair was that of an NSC staff member who acted on the orders of higher officials.

A kind of displaced presence is built into this story, where the described events are centered on a moment and a viewpoint within the story.[27] The interrogator's mention of a "problem" and North's subsequent account of what transpired locate the scene from within which North-as-character becomes "aware" of a more extended set of actions involving other characters (i.e., "It was in that period of time that I became aware of what was really trying to be moved").[28] As he elaborates, such awareness goes well beyond what he immediately may have seen or heard, beyond even the relevant contents of his own state of mind, extending to a whole range of possible meetings, relationships, and modes of access to such things as "sensitive intelligence."

What is crucial here is that the narrative told in testimony makes no distinction between the story being told and the actual unfolding of the described events. Although recipients may recognize certain judgments and defensive moves being made by the narrator, these are not marked or denoted in so many words. The relevant identity of the narrator, the legitimacy of his actions, and the extent of his responsibility for those actions are made apparent by his selection and arrangement of terms describing the setting and series of events in the story. No separable moral claim is made. Rather, *a moral stance is built into the very description of the territory.*

FRAGILE STORIES AND THE REASONABILITY
OF TESTIMONY

We have argued that a witness's moral and narratological positioning in a story operates as a binding technique for bringing together the compositional details of witnessed events. We have also argued that this positioning is accomplished through the use of a constellation of local predicates that specify matters of entitlement, legitimacy, innocence, or guilt.[29] At the same time that the narrator's position within a story composes the witnessed event, it endows the story with moral significances. Put somewhat starkly: while the narrative of experience holds forth the promise of unique access to witnessed events, what it delivers is always a history with an attitude.

So far, we have been considering issues of story composition largely in terms of the internal coherence of story elements. Notice, however, that stories told in conversation are not composed by the speaker in advance of their telling; even if rehearsed in advance, they do not unfold monologically. Instead, they unfold dialogically and display an attention to the evaluations, expectations, and demands of the assembled listeners. This means that the moral and narratological positioning of the storyteller can be transformed or adjusted over the course of the story's telling to take account of the audience's reactions to the story being told. Consequently, stories are altered or adjusted in their course to suit the current audience and circumstances of the current telling.[30] The craft of storytelling consists in no small part in the teller's ability to size up audience response, so that by the end of the story the audience finds itself complicit with the teller's moral positioning.

In the case of the North testimony, the witness was constrained to tell stories elicited by potentially hostile interrogators. Moreover, the very way the story (about Rabin) was solicited signaled that the committee already had in hand documents, testimonies, or other pieces of independent evidence bearing on that story. When compared with stories told in conversation, the witness's control over the sense and trajectory of his own narratives was constrained by the formal organization of the hearings. Nevertheless, it was widely acknowledged that North was extremely successful at enlisting partisan support for his side of the story. His success resulted in no small measure from his ability to tell contentious (or fragile) stories that continually challenged the moral positioning of the listening audience. The dialogue at the hearings was not just between North and his interrogators; it included all the members of the committee, the press, and the massive audience of onlookers tuned into the proceedings. These diverse parties were carried along and represented by the moral texture of the witness's narrational positioning.

The compositional elements of a story—place-names, temporal formulations, character identities, perspectival indications—not only bind together a coherent narrative, but they can imply, or fail to imply, reasonability.[31] The teller of the story does not, however, own these implications. Given that the fragility of any story consists in its formal openness to criticism, it is always possible that a story might fail to gain the moral complicity it requires, that instead it might receive the criticism it invites. This possibility is perhaps most extreme under conditions of interrogation when a witness is brought to confess or to otherwise acknowledge critical implications that the interlocutor retrieves from the witness's own narratives.

In chapter 4 we argued that the truth-finding engine of interrogation relies on a distinctive mode of rational compulsion that can be used to leverage a witness's speech and induce him to confess to a truth that flies in the face of his own self-interest. In court hearings and in other settings where stories are morally evaluated and subject to challenge, reasonability is a primary resource for rendering judgments of guilt, innocence, and moral responsibility. Both teller and listeners rely on a presumptive background of recurrent events, standard routines, commonplace motives, and characterological types. Such background knowledge is not a static conceptual scheme or a communally owned and operated memory bank. Its deployment is highly specific, defeasible, and subject to local specification and challenge. It is used as an occasional feature of social practice and not as an omnirelevant cultural schema; it is tied to the singular constellations of events; and at times it can be idiosyncratic. A dramatic example is provided by Gluckman's study of Barotse law: "A learned but naive South African judge is reputed to have once refused to grant a divorce although a detective proved the wife had spent an afternoon in a hotel with a man. The judge stated baldly that he did not believe people had sexual relations in the daylight: hence the alleged lovers would not have committed adultery even if they spent an afternoon in a bedroom."[32]

Not only can a particular individual's presumptions about common knowledge turn out to be out of step with those of a larger community, but understandings that are apparently well-founded in a communal consensus can turn out to be prejudicial when a story is later corroborated by evidence of a highly improbable constellation of circumstances. Eggleston cites an example from Wigmore:

A woman living in Lancaster, on the hill that leads to the gaol, was considered to be suffering from hallucinations, because of her complaint that the head of her late husband (a negro) had rolled down the steps into her kitchen and had been retrieved by the devil wearing a black cloak. In fact, the devil was an eminent scientist, who had been making a study of the heads of criminals, and had, on the night in question, been carrying the head of a negro who had died at the gaol; he dropped the head in the street and it rolled down the steps of the old woman's house. As the removal of the head was not strictly lawful, he had wrapped his cloak round his face and calling out 'Where's my head? Give me my head!,' gone to retrieve it, confident that he would not be recognised. The old lady was right as to her basic facts, though wrong in her identification.[33]

Stories like this one demonstrate the fallibility of common knowledge and point up why it cannot always be trusted as a basis for making binding judgments. Nonetheless, it would be difficult to imagine how recipients of stories about events they did not witness themselves could otherwise assess the plausibility of those stories and the credibility of their tellers. For our purposes, it is sufficient to note that audiences *do* make judgments about the plausibility of events described in stories, and they do so on the basis of what typically occurs in "situations like that." Moreover, storytellers anticipate and count on the fact that their audience will make such judgments, and they design their stories accordingly.

THE CONTINGENT TRANSLATION OF STORIES INTO HISTORY

The committee and its staff were empowered to write an objective report of an event, whereas the witnesses they interrogated were able to invoke the authority of informed participants who observed particular details that were decisive for the composition of the event. The event itself necessarily was a synthetic construction . . . It was not "observable" from any single vantage point; it involved actions that were designed specifically not to be observable; and its constituent moments were dispersed temporally and spatially, produced by multiple agencies, and intermingled with diverse actions and agendas. The event itself was a montage of references, summaries, and inferences, pieced together from documents and testimonies. Although the Iran-contra affair was presumed to have narrative coherence, it nevertheless had to be assembled point-by-point by a potentially divided committee in front of a potentially volatile audience. Consequently, no guarantees were possible that the committee's history of the affair would take priority over a hostile witness's counternarratives.

It is worth examining point-by-point some of the efforts to translate the details of a witness's story into the specifications of a conventional history. This translational work can be seen to operate on precisely those terms of temporal, spatial, and characterological reference that bind the story together as a coherent narrative package. For this reason, witnesses are often able selectively to resist such translation by insisting on a storyteller's "rights" to situate his story in a singular recollection of a lived past. Consider, for instance, the following fragment taken from the first morning of North's testimony:

Nields: Colonel North, you shredded these documents on the Twenty-first of November, Nineteen-eighty-six, isn't that true? (1.2)

North: Try me again on the date. (1.0)

Nields: Friday, the Twenty-first of November, Nineteen-eighty-six. (1.8)

Nields: I started shredding documents as early as:: uh my return from Europe in October. (0.4)

North: I have absolutely no recollection (0.2) when those documents were des- were shredded. None whatsoever.=

Nields: =There's been testimony before the Committee that you engaged in shredding of documents on November the Twenty-first, Nineteen-eighty-six. ((Nields continues to pursue the question soon afterward))

North: [(as-)
        [
Nields: [Do you deny that?

North: I do *not* deny that I engaged in shredding on November Twenty-first. (1.2) I will also tell this Committee that I engaged in shredding (.) almost every day that I had a shredder. And that I put things in burn bags when I didn't. . . .

Nields: Colonel North, let me ask you this. There had been some uh- newspaper (0.4) publicity about the Iranian initiative, starting in early November, isn't that true? (1.0)

North: I don't recall specifically, uh (1.0) Counsel. (1.4)

Nields: You *do* recall that there was some (0.4) *publicity* don't you.

North: Oh absolutely, but I- I'm- you're (.) tryin' teh fix me with a date.[34]

In this excerpt, Nields is questioning North about some documents that, had North not destroyed them, would likely have been of great use to the committees' investigations. The very topic of the interrogation ("shredded documents") places questions of historical fact in a contingent relation to what the witness says about the existence and contents of particular documents. The interrogator's line of questioning locates the practical and moral significance of the shredded documents within a system of dates and historical references that suggest specific motives for their destruction. As a narrative of experience, the temporal and spatial predicates of Nields's account bind the narrator, characters, and actions into a coherent and unfolding scene. The binding force of the accusatory narrative operates on at least two fronts: the various references to dates, places, and activities hang together in a coherent narrative, while at the same time the references implicate and bind the teller to the scene as constituted by those particulars. Implications of innocence and guilt can turn on just how the narrator's voice responds to the force of the master narrative, and on how it reflexively places itself within a sequential assemblage of such terms. Although in the above sequence the task can be summarized by calling it a matter of building a chronology, the struggle between interrogator and witness is less a matter of agreeing on a correct correspondence between actions and dates than it is one of suggesting particular categorical identities and moral implications of those actions.

Nields's line of questioning presses North to provide a calendrical formulation that identifies when he shredded a particular set of documents (indeed, the initial question supplies a candidate date, "November 21"). North responds by professing not to recollect when the documents were shredded. As his subsequent elaboration makes clear, he is not claiming to have a faulty memory, nor is he denying outright that he shredded the documents on *some* date or that on November 21, 1986, he shredded *some* documents. Instead, he offers a biographical reference ("my return from Europe in October") as an approximate starting point for daily shredding, and later he adds that in any case he shredded documents "almost every day that I had a shredder." He thus embeds his failure to recall within the normal, usual, daily routine of shredding at his National Security Council office. He claims not so much that he fails to remember, as that what he is being asked to remember would have had no unusual or notable significance for anyone acquainted with his job and its daily run of activities. North apparently was enacting a concerted defensive strategy worked out in advance by his and his colleagues' legal advisors.[35] In this instance, the "precise" reference is significant since November 21 had previously been identified as the date on which North was informed by the attorney general's office about an impending investigation of his activities. If North were to admit to destroying key documents on that date, a strong presumption could be drawn about his particular motives for doing so. By refusing the kind of date the interrogator offers, North does more than give a mere approximation of when he shredded the key documents; he disavows the motivational horizons implied by the precisely dated juxtaposition of shredding, specific documents, and organizational activities. That is, he refuses a chronological binding technique for collecting his activities and their motivation.

In the subsequent exchange, Nields attempts to pursue a connection between North's confirmation of an undated temporal reference to "publicity" about the Iran-contra affair in "early November." Again, the line of questioning frames the shredding as a motivated reaction to impending public scrutiny of North's and his administrative colleagues' covert activities. North also disavows any specific recollection, and he explicitly objects to Nields' attempt to "fix" him "with a date." (This is one of a series of North's puns on the terms in Nields's questions; for Americans of North's generation 'fixing with a date' can mean setting someone up with a partner for a blind date.)

Both the interrogator's questions and the witness's disavowals make use of a pragmatic distinction between relatively precise and approximate chronological formulations. In the present case, however, these chronological measures are not selected for an overhearing analyst's disinterested assessment of the degree of correspondence between measures and events. Rather, the work of fixing North "with a date" is part and parcel of the committee's task of building a historical narrative of North's actions and their motivations. North's reference, "as early as:: uh my return from Europe in October" is not only an example of a relatively imprecise way of encoding an event, but it reconfigures the scene in which the event has significance. The temporal reference is not only vague, but it no longer is the same *kind* of reference as the dated reference proffered by the interrogator. As a consequence, the event (shredding *these* documents) is a different kind of event than the one implied by the more precise calendrical formulation. It now becomes another in a long series of days in which shredding documents was part of the routine course of affairs.

Whereas Nields's initial question highlights shredding as a motivationally significant part of the chronology of significant actions in November 1986, North performs a kind of gestalt switch by highlighting a particular event in his life (returning from Europe) against the backdrop of shredding-as-usual. An array of moral entitlements to perform the action described (shredding), and to recollect the particular action (shredding these documents) hinges on these different versions.

THE ATTORNEY GENERAL IN HIS ROLE
AS MR. MEESE

Although North often successfully problematized the conversion of testimony into evidence, his stories were far from invulnerable. In the following excerpt, occurring shortly after the sequence above, North deploys an odd reference to "Mr. Meese" that later draws questions from one of the committee members. Again, North is being questioned about the circumstances of his shredding of documents before an investigation by members of the Justice Department on November 21, 1986:

Nields: . . . Are you here telling the Committee that you don't remember whether on November 21st there was a document in your files reflecting Presidential approval of the diversion?

North: As a matter of fact, I'll tell you specifically that I thought they were all gone, because by the time I was told that some point early on November 21st that there would be an inquiry conducted by Mr. Meese, I assured Admiral Poindexter—incorrectly it seems—that all of those documents no longer existed. And so that is early on November 21st because I believe the decision to make an inquiry, to have the Attorney General or Mr. Meese in his role as friend of the President conduct a fact-finding excursion on what happened in September and November in 1985. I assured the Admiral, "Don't worry, it's all taken care of."[36]

North's story displays a transparently fragile design in its references to "Mr. Meese," "the Attorney General or Mr. Meese in his role as friend of the President," and a few moments later, "the Attorney General, in his role as Mr. Meese, and not the Attorney General."[37] When questioned later in the hearings by House committee member Peter Rodino on why he referred to "Mister Meese" as a "friend of the President," North gave the following account:

> North: Well, I'm not sure what—exactly what I meant in those terms. What I clearly intended to say was that no one told me then—it was not until four days later, on the 25th—that there was any criminal investigation or criminal concern in this whole issue. And my recollection is that the Admiral told me that morning, or that day at some point, that there was going to be a fact-finding inquiry conducted by Mr. Meese, not in his role as chief law enforcement officer or as Attorney General, but because he was close to the President; he was a person the President relied upon to be able to get to the bottom of all of this.[38]

When questioned further, North elaborated, "I mean what I'm saying to you Mr. Rodino, is that I characterized it after the fact as that kind of inquiry. At the point in time—I would guess, and I don't recall—." North cut off his answer at that point, and Rodino pursued the matter with further questions, which North answered by reiterating that at the time in question he "had absolutely no inkling of criminal investigations, criminal inquiry, criminal behavior, or anything criminal until the 25th of November."[39] North's story is fragile partly because such locutions as "the Attorney General, in his role as Mr. Meese, and not the Attorney General," simultaneously use and deny the relevant characterization "the Attorney General." It is as though North cannot avoid identifying Meese as "the Attorney General," even while he suggests an alternative identity. Where "the Attorney General" is an institutional title congruent with a story about an "inquiry," or "fact-finding excursion," on a date (November 21, 1986) associated with the public exposure of the Iran-contra scandal, North's strained suggestion that "the Attorney General" acted in "his role as Mr. Meese" tries to emplot a different sense to the event and the relevant identities: a "friend of the President" conducts an informal investigation of a problem that was not (or not yet) construed as a criminal matter. North tries to enhance the plausibility of this scenario by emphasizing that his reference to "Mr. Meese" is relative to what he recalls *now* about what he knew on November 21. He adds that his sense of the "fact-finding excursion" changed dramatically a few days later (November 25) when an official announcement was made that a criminal investigation would be initiated against him.[40] In light of the other identities and references included in the story, the defensive implications of North's characterization of Meese are self-undermining. North's story includes, and thereby acknowledges, the precedence of the relevant identity (attorney general) associated with actions that the story identifies as an "inquiry." "The Attorney General in his role as Mr. Meese" does invoke an alternative scenario, but its plausibility *by his own account* is unconventional ("Mr. Meese in his role as Attorney General" being the familiar way of speaking that North inverts). Where it might seem natural to inquire, like Rodino does, as to why North characterizes Meese in the way he does, it would seem odd or ignorant to ask under the circumstances, "When you refer to Mr. Meese as 'the attorney general' why do you use that term?" It is often said that it is difficult for a witness to construct a "tissue of lies" within the rapid-fire exchange of questions and answers of cross-examination. Here we can appreciate that, whether or not North is lying, his story metonymically retrieves a conventional tissue of references. He implicates typical identities, actions, and circumstances (an attorney general making an investigation in light of an impending scandal), even while his story builds an alternative scenario (Mr. Meese, friend of the President, conducting an informal "fact-finding excursion" to "get to the bottom" of a problem).[41]

CONCLUSION

We discussed several related features of testimonial stories that distinguish them from master narratives. These features have to do with the occasion of telling, the narrator's positioning in the story, the texture of relational details that compose a story, and the moral and characterological implications of those details. We argued that these compositional elements provide the story with a fragile design that can, in turn, be used to assess and influence audience judgments. The distributional property of stories—the differential right to tell "one's own" stories about events witnessed and suffered—is part and parcel of the way stories are packaged as narratives of experience rather than as narratives of events. Even when a testimonial story is about an objective event like a disaster, scandal, or other newsworthy matter, the event becomes specifically framed as an event in the narrator's life.

While the formal differences between narratives of events and narratives of experience may help us analyze the testimony at the hearings, a boundary between the two should not be too starkly drawn. As we shall see in the next two chapters, the dialogical production of the hearings involved an interplay between spoken "recollections" and documented "events" that is more complex than a mere confrontation between narrational forms. The fact that North was able to rely on the conventional entitlements of a narrative of experience only partially explains his success. What remains to be shown is how North and his defense team were able to mobilize such entitlements to build a counternarrative of righteousness and heroism in the face of a (potentially) hostile interrogation.

A key theme in this discussion are judgments about plausibility and credibility that are made by story recipients who did not experience the events described. Sacks makes a pertinent point when he notes that "recipients can apparently decide that a story was correctly told without having to go out to reobserve something the story reports, to see that that was the way to have observed it so as to tell the story that it contains."[42] The upshot of this remark is twofold. First, it makes note of the fact that persons commonly treat the ordering of events in a story as an adequate basis for evaluating its truth. Accordingly, the plausibility of conversational stories can be viewed as a routine product of conventional methods for reasoning about and understanding stories, and *not* of an "objective" or decontextualized correspondence between a report and some observable "actual events."[43]

The second, less obvious point is that witnessing is itself a socially organized activity. Conversational stories display a conventional texture and organization of events. Characteristically, that order is reported as the order of events themselves, not as an ex post facto product of the story's composition. This suggests the possibility that our experience of events is already shot through with an attention to their storyable features, and, thus, that the business of witnessing is inseparable from our use and mastery of orders of narrative composition. Stories are not just ways of *packaging* experiences; they are ways of *having* them as well. Moreover, stories not only describe or present experience, but they claim moral entitlement to tell the story and to be the sort of character portrayed in the story.

The display of a storyteller's entitlements is a central issue for witnesses in court cases and tribunals since they are enjoined to provide testimony that displays the witnessed character of their story. So, for example, the witness will say that certain things were seen and heard, and thus reportable as witnessed, in contrast to what may have been heard from others or inferred after the fact. It is precisely the witnessed character of testimony that provides the raw material for the court's investigations. It is not just that direct testimony tends to be granted a stronger evidential status than hearsay or speculation, but that the very structure of testimony—of stories told by a presumed participant/witness—provides the witness with an authoritative hold over the moral characterizations and positionings in his or her story. The problem for interrogators is how to hook a narrative onto the person in the dock;[44] in other words, how to constrain and counteract the witness's authority in the interest of building a master narrative in which the witness may become considerably less than a hero. This can be viewed as a special case of a confrontation between representatives of an "objective" inquiry and the intensely partisan inhabitants of a life-world that is rendered into the object of such inquiry, but in this case we can be led to appreciate how the inhabitants are far from powerless when testifying within the liminal space of a tribunal, a space in which biography and history, speeches and texts, and privacy and publicity confront each other in a vivid and potentially hostile forum.

Thinking back to "the sincere liar" discussed in chapter 1, we can begin to imagine how confabulators and pathological liars are able seemlessly to conflate fantastic stories with memories of lived experiences. This has to do with the way recollections are integrated with topical (and topological) designs that are inseparable from the way experiences themselves are packaged for later retelling. Sincerity comes into play, not only by virtue of the evidently unself-conscious way in which a fictional story is told, but also by virtue of the moral implications of the scene described and the entitlements claimed by telling it (entitlements that invite audience complicity). We shall develop these themes in the next chapter.

6. MEMORY IN TESTIMONY

"But you surely cannot deny that, for example, in remembering, an inner process takes place."— What gives the impression that we want to deny anything? When one says "Still, an inner process does take place here"— one wants to go on: "After all, you *see* it." And it is this inner process that one means by the word "remembering."— The impression that we wanted to deny something arises from our setting our faces against the picture of the 'inner process.' What we deny is that the picture of the inner process gives us the correct idea of the use of the word "to remember." We say that this picture with its ramifications stands in the way of our seeing the use of the word as it is.—Wittgenstein[1]

Throughout the hearings, the testimony was framed as "remembered," "recollected," or "recalled" matters of fact. It might even be said that the spectacle at the hearings took the form of an inverted "theater of memory." This analogy reverses the relational configuration of the medieval theater of memory, which Francis Yates describes as an amphitheater spread out before an orator, populated with statues whose dramatic expressions and grotesque postures act as mnemonic devices for recalling and emplotting the characters and tropes in a narrative.[2] In the spectacle of interrogation, by contrast, the witness is positioned at the center of an array of props and prompts, but instead of looking outward for iconic reminders placed at the periphery of the theater, he recollects "spontaneously," producing expressions and postures (sometimes of a grotesque sort) that are scrutinized from all sides by the eyes and cameras in the audience. His voice and face perform a theater of memory as he recollects, or professes not to remember, details from the past. Although this theatrical setup may accommodate performances that downgrade or even subvert the salience of accurate and forthright recollections, the interrogator and witness are nonetheless bound together in a drama through which the witness's memories are prompted, prodded, and examined. This dialogue also furnishes the visible and audible displays of credibility, sincerity, and spontaneity through which an audience can assess the witness's character.

Memory often is assumed to be a cognitive process that underlies what people say about the past. According to this view, testimony is the product of information-processing mechanisms located within the private recesses of a witness's brain. Many legal scholars, for example, treat testimony as an indirect and uncertain representation of what a witness actually remembers. Although it may seem natural enough to think about memory in this way, we shall argue that a close study of testimony can support an entirely different picture of information-processing. While testimony often focuses on a witness's recollections, and the public disclosure of information is very much at stake, it is crucial to understand that regardless of what goes on in a witness's mind his recollections are situated in a struggle over the production and control of the public record of an event. The public record comprises much more than an individual memory or even a collective memory of an event. It includes factual documents and testimonies that furnish the evidentiary sources for various stories and histories. These documents and testimonies, in turn, are imprinted with modes of individual recollection that call into play supraindividual intelligence agencies and their methods of information production and control. An initial appreciation of this point can be gained from the following report on a hapless witness's difficulties (the witness testified during the Scott inquiry, a British tribunal headed by Lord Justice Scott, which investigated allegations of government complicity in sales by British arms merchants to Iraq just prior to the Gulf war—a situation with an uncanny resemblance to the U.S. Iran-contra affair): "A grey-haired MOD [Ministry of Defence] civil servant, Alan Barrett, was having a miserable time on the witness stand, remembering and then forgetting Mrs. Thatcher's involvement in the flood of British arms to Iraq in the Eighties. Asked whether he had seen an MI6 intelligence report on Iraq's 'go-for-arms' strategy, Mr. Barrett replied, 'I am trying to think whether I was supposed to have seen it or not. I cannot recall.' Pushed further, he added: 'I am informed that I did not see it.' "[3] Barrett's references to what he was "supposed" to have seen and "informed" that he did not see are, to say the least, startling in the context of a public tribunal. It is startling that Barrett lets slip that his testimony about his own past experiences depends upon extrinsic organizational sources of information control. But while his explicit implication of such sources may be strange and self defeating, the existence of such methods of information control is not at all surprising.[4] It is not difficult to imagine that the recollections of a government official testifying at a tribunal are subject to a great deal of rehearsal and censorship. Such information control would originate, not with the operations of an information processor between the witness's ears, but with organizationally specific methods for producing, disseminating, concealing, and leaking state intelligence.

Because of the intensive scrutiny given to the pragmatic and epistemic implications of the way a witness recollects the past, tribunals like the Iran-contra hearings provide perspicuous instances of the social production of remembering and forgetting.[5] The joint committee's inquiry did not, of course, unfold as a cognitive-scientific investigation of memory. Rather, it was a public forum in which participants used, contested, and occasionally explicated a situated grammar of recall. These discursive struggles were highly instructive, both substantively and theoretically. They enable us to gain insight into the local production of history at the Iran-contra hearings, and they give us some critical purchase on prevalent conceptions of memory in the human sciences.

THE CONTRA MANTRA AND THE SITUATED
PRAGMATICS OF RECALL

In 1987 the magazine *Esquire* cited Poindexter, Secord, and Meese for "dubious achievement awards." These principals in the Iran-contra affair were sardonically honored for their incessant recitation of what the magazine called the *Contra Mantra*—"I don't recall" and similar phrases. According to the magazine's tally, Poindexter and the others made such avowals hundreds of times in their testimony before the joint congressional committees.[6] An examination of the transcript of Oliver North's testimony reveals that he too made relentless use of the following phrases:

"I don't recall";
"I don't recall at all";
"I can't recall a specific date";
"I guess- and I don't remember";
"I don't have a specific recall of that at this time point";
"I don't think so, I mean you may refresh my memory";

And finally,

"My memory has been shredded."

The dialogues in which these utterances occurred subjected the overhearing audience to an extended tutorial on the pragmatic uses of recall and nonrecall in testimony. Judging from newspaper editorials, poll results, television commentaries, political cartoons, and remarks by the principal participants in the hearings, it was obvious that avowals and disavowals of recall were heard not simply as reports on the state of the witnesses' memories, but as strategic moves in the game of testimony; moves that acted to qualify, withhold, or defer answers and to head off the pursuit of questions. Above all, these utterances were heard as methods for evading possible accusations, *including* the accusation of being evasive. Although it was easy to suspect that North, Poindexter, and the others were dissembling, the audience was not always clear at the time that they were doing so. Moreover, epistemic considerations—what the witnesses might actually have known, and whether or not they were telling the truth—were overshadowed by other aspects of their performances. Referring to North, Senators Mitchell and Cohen wrote in their reflections on the hearings that "the theater was far more compelling than our doubts" about the witness's truthfulness.[7]

Satirical treatments such as *Esquire*'s remind us that "I don't recall" is a familiar evasive maneuver which serves nicely to obstruct interrogators' lines of questioning when they seem to be heading in a direction that might compromise the witness's side of the case. A witness intending to conceal his knowledge of what he is asked can feign not to recall the matters in question rather than to fabricate an answer. The advantages of the technique were not lost on some of the more notable participants in historical tribunals. For example, according to a report on a conversation between former president Richard Nixon and Alexander Haig, which occurred in June 1973 as they plotted an administrative response to the Watergate investigations: "he and Nixon discussed how to respond to serious allegations being made by John Dean, the former White House counsel. According to a tape recording of the Nixon-Haig discussion that became public during the impeachment investigation, Haig advised Nixon to duck questions about the allegations by saying 'you just can't recall.' "[8] The psychologist Paul Ekman argues that when used disingenuously, nonrecall "is intermediate between concealment and falsification" because it exacts a lighter toll on the witness's efforts to resist the force of interrogation: "the liar avoids having to remember a false story; all that needs to be remembered is the untrue claim to a poor memory. And if the truth later comes out, the liar can always claim not to have lied about it, that it was just a memory problem."[9] The problem for an interrogator and an audience attempting to assess the truthfulness of what the witness says is that it can be difficult to decide whether "I don't recall" is being used evasively or not. Although a witness can be convicted for perjury if he or she falsely claims not to recall an event, it is exceedingly difficult to demonstrate such falsehoods beyond a reasonable doubt.[10]

So useful are avowals of nonrecall in an interrogatory context that they can become highly conventionalized replies to yes-no questions. An example can be found in an anecdote about Roger Braithwaite, a "shrewd jailhouse lawyer" in a maximum security prison. Braithwaite, described as "a gravel-voiced, gray-haired, forty-nine-year old armed robber who looked and spoke like a college professor," was a lay adviser who defended other inmates at disciplinary hearings. "If he went to court and the committee chairman denied his request to speak in his client's behalf, Braithwaite had other ways of communicating. He stroked his beard to tell a client to say 'yes,' he tugged his ear for 'no,' and drummed his fingers on the table for 'I don't remember.' "[11] When reduced to such a gestural code, "Yes," "No," and "I don't remember" become tokens in a primitive language game. We do not mean to attribute atavistic qualities to Braithwaite and his clients, but to speak of a recurrent practice that is usually far more complicated. Our analytic interest in such games is inspired by Wittgenstein's advice "to study the phenomena of language in primitive kinds of application in which one can command a clear view of the aim and functioning of the words."[12] Braithwaite's signal alerts us that "I don't remember" is not a report on a speaker's cognitive state any more than the terms yes and no act as reports on mental states of agreement or disagreement. Instead, they are expressions that perform those functions in an immediate social setting. One would not want to say that a prisoner caught in a tight spot in the interrogation who glances over at Braithwaite, sees him drumming his fingers, and then responds "I don't remember" is therefore unable to retrieve relevant contents from his mental faculty. Regardless of the truth or falsity of the prisoner's answer, Braithwaite's signal identifies "I don't remember" as a conventional token from a set of three responses to a yes-no question. As such, it is a distinct, problematic, and contextually useful alternative for answering such a query.[13]

It should be noted that the sorts of failures of recall we find so prevalent in testimony do not confirm any notion that the witness has forgotten the events in question. In such circumstances a witness's saying "I don't re-call" differs significantly from his saying "I forget" or "I forgot" (although it often does seem equivalent to "I don't remember"). As Jeff Coulter points out, avowals of forgetting make retrospective knowledge claims. Saying that one "forgot" something—for example, "I forgot that today is our anni-versary"—implies the existence of the object complement (the event, occa-sion, identity, or action in question).[14] *Something* had been forgotten, and one may admit to culpability for having forgotten it. Saying "I don't recall" or "I don't remember"—for example, "I don't recall that we've met"—may or may not imply the existence of an event in question; rather, a witness's use of the phrase can express a skeptical stance toward an event that he or she *would have* recalled had the event happened. Alternatively, the speaker can let the matter stand as an equivocal possibility, perhaps one to be resolved later.

The pragmatic uses of nonrecall have long been recognized by legal scholars. Wigmore, for instance, observes that a failure to recall poses a severe problem for an interrogator: "the unwilling witness often takes ref-uge in a failure to remember, and the astute liar is sometimes impregnable unless his flank can be exposed to an attack. . . ."[15] The problem for inter-rogators is that while "feigned lack of recollection" is a well-known eva-sive ploy, it cannot be assumed that all failures to recall are feigned. A witness's use of nonrecall presents a problem for jurists because it enables the witness to respond to a question without admitting or denying what the question suggests. "I don't recall" remains indifferent to the binary logic of yes-no questions, thus deflecting and diffusing the interrogatory pursuit of confessional truth. For instance, in a discussion of legal issues that arise when a witness professes not to recall matters about which he or she has earlier testified, Graham notes that such testimony does not contradict prior statements. "True loss of memory and a prior statement are not in-compatible; they do not evidence inconsistent belief, only a lack of cur-rent recollection. Moreover, if the witness lacks recollection, the rationale underlying the requirement of inconsistency is defeated. . . . The witness does not recall the event and therefore cannot testify concerning the truth or falsity of the prior statement."[16] Graham adds that when a witness fails to recall the events in question, "effective cross examination is not present. *There are not two versions of the event* to explore and the jury does not have the opportunity to observe the witness trying to explain away the inconsistency raised."[17] Unless it can be demonstrated that the witness's failures to recall are feigned, the testimony produces what Graham calls "the practical unavailability" of the witness.[18] The witness is unavailable in the sense that his responses to questions do not provide usable answers, and his speech interrupts the progressive development of an interrogative line. Although feigned lack of recall is often suspected, it rarely is demonstrated in court.

The following fragment gives explicit testimony to just this sense of "practical unavailability."

Nields: And I take it what you're saying now is that you- you had, with respect to that- the use of that million dollars for the contras, (0.2) you (0.4) you had not sought or received any approval from people higher in the U.S. Government. (3.5)

North: °(hmm:)° (2.0) I don't know that I did, I- I'm not saying I didn't. (1.2) uh, I think I may have apprised uh Admiral Poindexter at some point that I'd done that, (0.2) but I did not uh, (1.4) I do not have a specific recall of that at this time point, no.[19]

By saying "I don't know that I did . . . I'm not saying I didn't," North underlines that his lack of specific recall neither affirms nor denies his knowledge of the event in question. This expression links his apparent inability to recall with such an event's uncertain status. North thus avows that the event may have happened, but he provides no testimony to that effect. Logically speaking, this explicit lack of commitment to either binary alternative for answering the question tends to stall or neutralize the interrogative pursuit of confessional truth. In this case, we can see how North's avowed lack of specific recall problematizes the interrogatory work of building agreed-to chronologies of events. North's references to "at some point" and "at this time point" diffuse the temporal placement of his communication with Poindexter. With such references, North neither assigns unequivocal responsibility to his administrative superiors, nor does he assume responsibility for authorizing the diversion of proceeds from arms sales to the contras.

Recall and nonrecall are not mutually exclusive. When testifying, a witness often makes reference to limits, uncertainties, and indefinite horizons of what he does recall. For example, consider the following exchange, which concerns allegations about North's having transferred $1 million in profits from Iranian arms sales to a bank account of a dummy corporation (Lake Resources), monies which were then transferred to the U.S.-sponsored contra forces in Central America:

Nields: . . . was there any understanding or discussion (1.0) that a million dollars would be deposited in the Lake (0.4) Resources account (0.6) for the benefit of the contras?

North: Not at that point, no. I do'n- I don't- (0.4) *I do not recall,* (0.4) a specific discussion of that until (0.5) much later.[20]

North initially gives a negative response to Nields's question, and, after twice cutting himself off and starting again, he states forcefully that he does not recall a specific discussion until much later. The evident lack of fluency in his response may indicate that he is crafting a defensive reply to the question. It can indicate other things as well, however, and while North provides information relevant to the question, he frames this information in a *specifically indefinite* way. His response is not vague, as it introduces qualifying terms ("at that point," "a specific discussion") that restrict the terms supplied in Nields's question ("any understanding or discussion"). While North gives positive testimony about what he does recall (or, what he does not *not* recall), his formulation leaves open the possibility that the parties involved in the covert action had an understanding of what the $1 million was for before any specific discussion about it. But unless this possibility were explored and brought out in later testimony, it has no status on the record.

By neither confirming a plausible description that damages his case nor burdening himself with the task of contesting the description's plausibility, a witness who fails to recall may avoid the horns of the witness's dilemma. Interrogators are not left empty-handed, however, as the witness's professed lack of recall itself can be subject to judgments of plausibility. By juxtaposing the witness's nontestimony with a description of events that "one such as he" should certainly recall (or, in the case of an incriminating description, should certainly want to deny), an interrogator can suggest to an audience that the witness's professed inability to recall should be counted against his credibility. Even though a witness's audience may have no independent access to the events that the witness recalls or fails to recall, and though an audience may have no determinate criteria for deciding the plausibility of the testimony, its members can and typically do make judgments about the truthfulness of that testimony, and they do so without any need to peer into the witness's mind.

A lack of recourse to a witness's mind should not be viewed as an essential source of uncertainty that is compensated for by indirect inferences about memory. Instead, in certain respects what a particular witness *can* recall (credibly, plausibly, sensibly) is an irreducibly public matter. This description also applies to what a witness can *fail* to recall. As Ekman observes, a "memory failure is credible only in limited circumstances." He gives the example of a doctor, who when "asked if the tests were negative can't claim not to remember."[21] Although the doctor may very well have forgotten the test results, he "can't claim not to remember" them because it is a doctor's legal and professional responsibility under appropriate circumstances to produce records of such tests. To say that he forgot the results would not effectively excuse him from the responsibility to report the relevant information. Ekman gives a related example of a policeman asked by a suspect whether the room was bugged. Like the doctor, the policeman cannot claim a loss of memory. Although one can imagine that he might fail to remember whether the particular room was bugged, for him to admit such failure does not relieve him of responsibility for the relevant knowledge. (The policeman might disavow responsibility by saying that the room in question was under another policeman's jurisdiction, but this response differs from claiming a memory loss.) Even if true, such memory failure would come across as an evasion or, if not an evasion, as an admission of incompetence. The policeman cannot claim not to remember because members of his occupation are expected, as a matter of course, to collect and retain such information (in files if not in their heads).[22] This has less to do with psychology than with legal regulations and moral responsibilities that apply to particular occupational categories and their record-keeping practices. As Coulter puts it, "to have forgotten certain matters can lead to being held responsible not (merely) for a 'cognitive malfunction' but for a moral lapse. This intertwining of the 'psychological' and the normative is much neglected in extant memory models, but appears at once when materials taken from everyday life are examined."[23]

Because of the cognate vocabularies, it is easy to conflate conventional and legal responsibilities for collecting and reporting information with individual capacities to remember (the two, of course, do sometimes go together). Indeed, such confusion was encouraged by Iran-contra participants when they were asked to recall specific White House meetings in which participants planned and authorized the arms sales to Iran and the diversion of proceeds to the contras. President Reagan and others gave variants of what might be called the breakfast defense: "How would you be expected to know what you had for breakfast on a particular date six months ago?" Such a defense relies on a credulous audience to forget that the relevant mode of recollection for a bureaucratic official is to consult the files and retrieve the appropriate records. In this case, the plausibility of such a defense (in accordance with the policy of plausible deniability) was aided and abetted by the destruction of such files and records, which amounts to a particular kind of "forgetting." Moreover, it has been argued that a signal feature of the Iran-contra affair was that many members of Congress, substantial elements of the mainstream press, and much of the mass audience demonstrated a reluctance to challenge apparently absurd claims made, especially, by the president. This reluctance may be viewed as a variant of the phenomenon of the emperor's new clothes, in which the audience does not publicly acknowledge what it recognizes to be so out of deference to the sovereign official. In this case, such deference and complicity may have been combined with a forgiving acknowledgment of the sovereign's inability to maintain a coherent line of argument in defense of his actions.[24]

In less blatant ways than Reagan's breakfast defense, individualistic conceptions of memory were relevant to the rhetorical production and interpretation of testimony. Interrogators and their audiences selectively called judgments into play about what particular witnesses could or should have remembered and about the memorability of particular events for someone who lived through them. Such judgments involved variable degrees of abstraction from the case in hand, but they did not take the form of lay psychological theories in the sense of being general conceptual models of how the mind works. Instead, judgments about what should have been remembered, and by whom, were sensitive to contextual and rhetorical portrayals of events, scenes, agents, and actions.[25] In brief, such judgments were embedded in locally organized, and selectively contested, master narratives. For example, many popular accounts of Vice Admiral John Poindexter's testimony made much of the fact that he held a Ph.D. in nuclear physics and was reputed to have a photographic memory. During the hearings Poindexter's reputation worked against him, in contrast to Reagan, whose age, and rumored senility, more easily excused his poor recollections. Given the assumption that Poindexter was capable of recalling accurate images of his original experiences, his numerous failures to recall were treated by the media as all-too-convenient lapses that acted as a smokescreen to protect himself and the president he served from political (and potentially legal) damage.[26]

In the course of his testimony Poindexter also seemed to recognize that his various failures to recall might be viewed suspiciously. He occasionally emphasized that, while trying to recall particular incidents, he was constrained to report only what he remembered *precisely.* His interrogator (Arthur Liman in this instance) gave lip service to such apparently sincere efforts. For example, in response to a series of questions about a key meeting with Reagan, Poindexter replied:

Poindexter: I- uh I- I believe so, I- I can recall- and, and as I told you in the closed testimony, I- I want to obviously be very careful as to what I attribute to the President and what I don't. It's obviously an important issue, and so, unless I can remember something very specific, I'm reluctant to- to- uhm attribute things to the President, uh ih- either things he said or- or things I think he knows=
Liman: =And I think that's ess- And you know my view that I think it's essential that you- that it's only where you have an actual
      [recollection that you should uh- do that.
      [
Poindexter: [Right.[27]

One might imagine Poindexter here straining to describe the details of an image before his mind's eye, as though viewing it in poor light and trying extremely hard to describe only what he actually sees. Less charitably, he can be heard to be feigning, verbally obfuscating and dissembling. Considered as a performance, however, Poindexter's recollections and nonrecollections are precisely organized. He does not simply claim to forget relevant details, he fails to recall *with surgical precision,* as though he can make out the exact outlines of what he can or cannot remember. Moreover, this unusual precision seems to become a rationale for recalling only what he can "remember" exactly. Poindexter proposes, and Liman avers, that he should recall in testimony only those incidents where he can "remember something very specific." Accordingly, he can justify not recalling a meeting when he does not remember *exactly* who attended and what words were spoken. Even for someone with a prodigious memory, such standards most certainly would prescribe severe constraints over what can be remembered.

In this instance Poindexter appears to be "taking refuge in a failure to remember," but more than that, with Liman's assent, he is expanding that refuge by specifying an extremely narrow criterion for deciding what can or should be recalled. This criterion exploits a misleading picture of how avowals of recall and nonrecall are discursively organized. To understand how it might be misleading, consider Ulric Neisser's study of "John Dean's memory" in which Dean's testimony at the Watergate hearings is compared with the a record of the events that he purported to describe.[28] Neisser compared portions of Dean's testimony to transcripts of meetings in the Oval Office recorded on the White House tapes. The meetings occurred about nine months before Dean's testimony. Edited transcripts of the tapes were eventually released by the White House after bitter wrangling with the special prosecutor's office. By comparing transcripts of Dean's testimony at the Watergate hearings with the published transcripts of the White House tapes, Neisser devised a natural experiment regarding the correspondence between testimonial recall and "actual events." Although Dean avowed that his mind was not a tape recorder, his testimony was generally credited with being remarkably accurate. On the basis of his study, Neisser argues otherwise, concluding that, while Dean's memory was inaccurate, Dean himself was essentially truthful.[29] For instance, Neisser says that Dean's testimony about a meeting with Nixon and Haldeman on September 15, 1972, did not describe what took place in the actual meeting. Rather, Dean describes a "fantasy" of what "should have" occurred. According to Neisser, Dean put words into Nixon's mouth that were actually said at a different meeting, and he confabulated a version of how Nixon greeted him at the start of the meeting and praised him for the good work he was doing. "In summary, it is clear that Dean's account of the opening of the September 15 conversation is wrong both as to the words and their gist. . . . [In his testimony] Dean came across as a man who has a good memory for gist with an occasional literal word stuck in, like a raisin in a pudding. He was not such a man. He remembered how he had felt himself and what he had wanted, together with the general state of affairs . . ." (p. 13).

Despite the inaccuracies and self-serving features of Dean's testimony, Neisser asserts that Dean's recollections were faithful to the "tenor" of what happened if not to the "literal" words originally spoken, or even to the gist of what transpired. Neisser assigns the term "repisodic memories" to the kind of wrong-in-detail-but-essentially-correct recollections he finds in Dean's testimony: "Often their real basis is a set of repeated experiences, a sequence of related events that the single recollection merely typifies or represents. . . . [W]hat seems to be an episode actually *re*presents a *re*petition."[30]

Neisser presents a view of remembering that differs significantly from the traditional psychological and neurological view that "engrams" of memory are somehow stored on a neurological memory drum and then retrieved by mentally locating and reading back the trace of the original event.[31] He distinguishes between the truthfulness of a witness's account and the literal correspondence between the account and the details of the original event witnessed. His assessment of Dean's truthfulness included more than a literal comparison between the White House tapes and Dean's later testimony. It involved a holistic and forgiving assessment of the witness's ability to recover the past. Consequently, Neisser finds that the literal accuracy and the credibility of testimony are separable, in principle. Indeed, overly precise or literal testimony can raise suspicions. Judges sometimes rule that a witness's testimony is *too* detailed, or *too* consistent with independent records of the facts, and that it therefore has the appearance of being concocted or rehearsed, as opposed to being remembered.

Poindexter's efforts to testify only about what he can remember 'specifically' become interesting in light of Neisser's study. In a way, Poindexter exploits the very confusion between accuracy and truthfulness that Neisser tries to sort out. By equating accurate testimony with a faithful reproduction of the 'literal' details of the antecedent events, Poindexter entitles himself to exclude recollections that might otherwise be judged to be correct for the gist or tenor of what they describe. Consequently, the restricted criterion of memorability he adopts gives him definite rhetorical advantages for avoiding disclosure of details that are not already on record.

To fully appreciate the value of Neisser's study for comprehending the vicissitudes of memory in testimony, it is necessary to treat evaluations of a witness's recollections as a basic element in the interrogative production of history. Neisser, for his part, does not go this far. He neatly demonstrates the degrees of difference between Dean's Watergate testimony and the tape recordings of the meetings that Dean purported to describe, and Neisser also convincingly shows that such differences do not necessarily indicate the witness's intent to distort or conceal events from the past. However, Neisser clearly fails to demonstrate how he was able to decide that specific inaccuracies in Dean's testimony were excusable while his overall testimony was essentially truthful.[32] While Neisser's having the White House transcripts at hand might seem to furnish a great advantage for any effort to settle the matter, the issue is not so simple. Take, for instance, Neisser's determination that Dean's "repisodic memory" was truthful. Neisser makes clear that this truthfulness cannot be supported point-by-point, since the details of Dean's testimony are inaccurate, mixed-up, and organized in an "egocentric" way. Neisser's conclusions about Dean's memory thus depend on an overall assessment of the relation between the testimony and relevant events from the past. It is the product of judgments about Dean's and other speakers' intentions, judgments that require a grasp of the upshot of numerous conversations as well as an understanding of organizational routines and vernacular idioms used at the White House. The idea that witnessing (i.e., testifying about events in one's past) is a matter of representing what one actually experienced at a particular time and place is belied by the fact that Neisser has to turn away from the tapes he compares with Dean's testimony in order to assess the testimony's *essential accuracy*. His assessment is not empirically demonstrable in the same way that his findings of inaccuracy are disclosed through a comparison of relevant tape recordings. In addition, as Derek Edwards and Jonathan Potter point out, the "essential" truthfulness of Dean's testimony was itself contested during (and after) the Watergate hearings.[33] Defenders of the Nixon administration treated particular ambiguities and inaccuracies in Dean's testimony as evidences of his lack of credibility, whereas the majority on the House and Senate committees were more inclined to excuse such inaccuracies as expected lapses in credible testimony. Although Neisser decides in favor of Dean's credibility, he is unable to specify general criteria for doing so, and one can question whether his judgment qualitatively differs from the assessments made at the time by the Watergate committee members and media public. We are not suggesting that Neisser lapsed into forming a partisan opinion of Dean's testimony. Instead, we suggest that *he could not do otherwise* than take into account the sociopolitical horizons of Dean's truthfulness. Such an assessment required a wide-ranging review of the immediate and historical circumstances of Dean's testimony, and a judgment about a number of substantive matters that were contested at the time, as well as for years afterwards.[34] What is required is nothing less than a judgment of history, which is also a judgment *in* history.

CONDITIONAL RECALL

Judgments about a witness's recollections are inseparable from broader and often contentious moral and political considerations. Although questions about remembering and forgetting are often prominent in the production and assessment of testimony, they are rarely settled by comparing what the witness says to an independent representation of what actually happened.[35] Instead, a witness's spoken recollections typically reconstruct (or claim to reconstruct) what *did happen* by reference to what *could, would, or should have happened.*[36] Such conditional or modal expressions do not refer to memories in a concrete way, but in a broader sense they are relevant to how the past is reconstructed. By examining specific uses of such expressions in testimony, we can begin to see that the past is not something a witness has available in the form of a concrete representation of an event; describing the past implicates a range of claimable, assertable, and disclaimable rights and responsibilities associated with being a singular person.

North often described singular events in the past by referring to what he typically would have done or could have known at the time. Not only did such statements recall details by reference to context, but often they developed a particular sense of context, an implied background for what he was doing, what he may have known, and what sort of person he was "at the time" in question. Consider, for example:

Nields: Were you ever told that the president (0.4) had authorized the TOW::
    shipment to proceed? (0.2)
North: I was at some point, yes. (0.8)
Nields: To the best of yer recollection, whe:n? (2.0)
North: Well I kno::w I was told that in eighty-*six* as I was preparing the chro-

nologies, I was pro:bably told that in eighty- fi:ve or I would've asked (.)
more questions than I *did* about it. (1.4)
Nields: (W[ho)

⠀⠀⠀⠀⠀[

North:⠀⠀[I don't reca:ll it specifically.[37]

Here, North works backward from a known event ("I was told that in
eighty-six") to an earlier time ("eighty-five"), at which point, he now says,
his actions presupposed that he knew about the president's authorization
of the missile shipment. His recollection is organized by reference to what
he would have done if he had not known ("I was probably told that in
eighty-five or I would've asked more questions than I did about it"). By his
account, if he had not known in 1985 that the TOW missile sale to Iran had
been authorized by the president, he would have inquired about the warrant for executing the deal. The matter of fact—or in this case of probable
fact—is implicated by what he recalls not doing. In effect, he is claiming
that if he had not known at the time that the deal was authorized, he would
have asked more questions about it. Although the utterance takes the form
of a recollection, it is equally salient as a moral claim. North asserts that he
would have been disposed to act appropriately in the situation. He claims
not to be the sort of person who would act without first securing proper
authorization. His recollection is packaged together with a defense of the
moral status of the biography in which it is situated.

When making and assessing claims about the past, the witness and audience may draw methodological distinctions akin to those familiar to professional historians. For example, they may distinguish between what was significant and knowable to participants during the period investigated and
what is significant and knowable at the present time of the investigation.[38]
This distinction is prominent in the following question-answer sequence:

Nields: Were you a*ware* of any (0.5) relatively contemporaneous shipments of
Hawk missiles from the United States to Israel. (0.6)
North: I don't think so, I mean uh you may refresh my memory again but, I do
not know uh at this point in time that I knew that, no.[39]

A straight denial that he was "aware" of the transaction in question would,
of course, imply a degree of uninvolvement and an inability to testify about

what happened. By qualifying his answer by saying that "you may refresh my memory," North places the answer within a restrictive temporal and logical horizon. He marks it as an answer in and for the present, one that has no definite relation to an actual past. It is a holding action that can be retracted without cost of contradiction should it later prove inconsistent with other documents. In other words, North's answer both deals with the question at hand and defers to whatever Nields may later produce to challenge it. It is easy to interpret this as a strategic move, but whether or not it comes across as a deliberate stratagem depends on a judgment about whether North *would* recall that he was "aware" of the transaction in question. Memory is a key issue here, since North refers to the need to "refresh my memory" when deferring his answer. What is at issue is not a cognitive process describing how his memory actually operates. Instead, the issue is how he relies on his audience to accept what he *says* he remembers, forgets, remembers only in part, or remembers in light of later events as plausible, reasonable, and sincere claims. Memory is relevant, but only insofar as it is implicated through a mass of normative assumptions made by the speaker on behalf of his audience, and vice versa. Although this circumstance loosens the logical constraints imposed on the witness by a series of yes-no questions, an interrogator may still be able to press the witness by raising normative claims about what anybody (or anybody in a specific category, or in a situation identical with the one the witness is in) should or should not recall about his own past.

Modal formulations ("might have," "could have," "probably would have," "should have," "must have," etc.) do not necessarily weaken or mitigate the status of the facts that a witness is asked to recall. Instead, they can enable interrogators and witnesses to claim reasonable grounds for recovering a concrete past. Such expressions often do not respect the binary logic of yes-no statements strung together in syllogisms, as they admit an entire range of possible, probable, contestable, and incontestable inferences and conclusions. The credibility of a witness, and the plausibility of what he recalls, is thus tied to public criteria, arguments, and moral judgments.[40] These do not necessarily make up a stable and inflexible body of normative standards shared by members of a community because they are brought into play singularly, rhetorically, and contestably.

While there is no getting around the importance of what the witness says about the past, and about his knowledge of the past, it seems clear from these instances that a witness does not unilaterally control what can be said on behalf of his past or his knowledge. Although North and the other Iran-contra witnesses were resourceful, as the following excerpt shows they were not in full control of the entitlements to the details of their own pasts.[41] Note how Nields manages to frame North's (non)testimony by describing a scene that North surely would want to deny if he could.

Nields: Did you suggest to the Attorney General that maybe the diversion memorandum and the fact that there was a diversion need not ever come out?

North: Again, I don't recall that specific conversation at all, but I'm not saying it didn't happen.

Nields: You don't deny it?

North: No.

Nields: You don't deny suggesting to the Attorney General of the United States that he just figure out a way of keeping this diversion document secret?

North: I don't deny that I said it. I'm not saying I remember it either.[42]

As this exchange makes clear, North's avowal of nonrecall neither confirms nor denies that he invited Meese to suppress the "fact of the diversion." Nields does not simply let this stand unchallenged. He follows North's initial disavowal with requests for clarification which emphasize (1) that North's reply is not a denial, and (2) that his reply does not deny suggesting that the attorney general suppress evidence of (what turned out to be) scandalous administrative conduct. Nields dramatizes the second point by citing Meese's formal title as "the Attorney General of the United States," and then juxtaposes this with a colloquial restatement of North's position, "that he [Meese] just figure out a way. . . ." This formulation highlights the illegality of the described scene and takes an incredulous stance toward North's failure to deny that it happened. The reference to the attorney general places the described transaction under the jurisdiction of appointed government officials acting in their official capacities. This contrasts to the administration's claim that in November 1986, when Meese purportedly began his investigation of the Iran-contra diversion, he was acting in the capacity as "friend of the President" and not as "Attorney General."[43] By repeatedly soliciting North's confirmation that he does not deny what someone in his position certainly would want to deny, Nields shapes

North's nonresponse into an informal nolo contendere plea.[44] North conspicuously passes on the opportunity to contest Nields's version of the event, either by recollecting a different version, or (as he sometimes did) objecting that the question insinuated that he had done something that he would never be inclined to do. North persists in saying that he does not remember the incident, and by so doing he contributes nothing further to the story of the event beyond Nields's description of it. However, he comes close to making a damaging admission by not contesting the possibility that he would be inclined to suggest to Meese that he suppress the evidence.

From the exchange above we can appreciate how a witness's "practical unavailability" differs from his actual absence. The witness remains physically present, and the interrogator has the right to use further questions to prod him, to jog or refresh his memory, so that he becomes "available" once again for an overhearer's assessment of his credibility. The interrogator does not simply ask a single yes-no question, and he does not settle for whatever answer the witness gives. Instead, over the course of a series of questions and answers, the interrogator probes and pursues, and the witness iterates, qualifies, or circumscribes his initial avowals and disavowals. Rhetorical devices like those that Nields uses in this sequence dramatize the implausibility and incredibility of the witness's professed inability to recall. The effectiveness of these dialogical maneuvers does not depend on what in fact is in the witness's mind. Instead, the interrogator and witness engage in an agonistic struggle in the theater of memory, a struggle in which both parties try to invoke public standards of memorability, including what we have called master narratives, to specify convincingly for an audience what *could* make up the contents of the witness's past.

The relationship between plausibility and the production of history is complicated for at least two reasons. It is true that "probable" events have a good chance of being included in the historical record, but it is also the case that certain events (such as particular scientific discoveries) can sometimes gain plausibility by virtue of being so improbable that no one would have imagined them had they not occurred. A vivid instance is given by Garry Wills in an account of a 1986 summit meeting between Reagan and the Soviet leader Mikhail Gorbachev at Reykjavik, Iceland. According to Wills, at one point in the meeting Reagan apparently shocked the members of the team that accompanied him by promising to eliminate all U.S. nuclear weapons if the Soviets would do the same with theirs. In the immediate aftermath of the meeting, various administration spokespersons attempted a desperate exercise in spin control to deny that Reagan ever made such a promise. The accounts of what he had promised differed remarkably, but, as Wills notes, the very fact that it seems unthinkable that Reagan would make such an offer at the time contributed to its plausibility. "The evidence is that President Reagan offered to trade *all* of America's nuclear weapons for all those of Russia. We must accept this on the *lectio difficilior* principle that so odd a thing would not have occurred to anybody as an even remotely possible version of the event unless it had, improbably, happened." Wills goes on to argue, however, that while this unthinkable event was plausible by the very fact that no one would have imagined it could have occurred if it had not, this also made it easier to erase from the official story of the summit. "The effort at 'spin control' was successful, in the short run, because the unthinkability of the proposal made it relatively easy to deny. How *could* the President have tried to bargain away all nuclear weapons, the basis of our entire defense policy, and that of our allies, without even consulting those allies, or the Congress, or the Joint Chiefs of Staff?"[45]

THE POLITICS OF EXPERIENCE

What we are describing has puzzling implications for legal, literary, and social-scientific discussions of recall and remembering because it problematizes a natural tendency to treat what a witness says about the past as a report on an actual or imaginable prior experience (an already existent memory trace that predates and determines what a witness can recollect). From what we have argued, it would be absurd to think that it would be possible to consult a witness's memory image in order to judge whether his avowals of recall are truthful and sincere reports about the past. Far from suggesting that such judgments are impossible, however, the point is that lay and professional assessments of a witness's memory are made by reference to conventional views of what can or cannot be recollected. These judgments call into play defeasible and often politically contentious fantasies about what a witness can or should know and say about the past.

While interrogation is organized primarily as a dialogue in which the interrogator tries to persuade or cajole the witness into making admissions about his past, it is important to remember that the dialogue unfolds before an audience. Even if the interrogator fails to solicit confessions from the defendant, he can succeed in dramatizing the incredibility of the witness's apparent reluctance to acknowledge or recall what the line of questions suggests about his past. While invoking the presumed, and sometimes demonstrable, complicity of the audience, the interrogator pressures the witness to acknowledge or contest the interrogator's suggestions about what he must, should, or could have said, done, or known. In a courtroom hearing the contestants appeal to a judge or jury charged with resolving discrepancies in testimony and arriving at a singular verdict. By contrast, in a tribunal like the Iran-contra hearings, the dramatic interrogative en-counter provides especially fertile ground for the eruption of a politicized contest in which the contestants try to enlist the approval and support of different factions of a massive, overhearing audience. As discussed in chapter 2, this possibility was exploited from the outset of North's testi-mony. Consider again:

Nields: But these operations were designed to be secrets from the American people. (2.0)

North: Mister Nields, I'm at a loss as to how we could announce it to the American people and not have the Soviets know about it. (1.5) And I'm not trying to be *flip*pant, but I just don't see how you can possibly do it.

      . . . . .

Nields: But- but it was designed to be kept a secret from the American people. (3.0)

North: I- I think what- what is important, uh Mister- Nields is that- (1.0) we somehow arrive at some kind of an understanding right here and now, as to what a covert operation is. If we could find a way to insulate with a bubble over these hearings that are being broadcast in Moscow, uh- a- and talk about covert operations to the American people without it getting into the hands of our adversaries, I'm sure we would *do* that. But (we haven't) found a way to do it.[46]

In this excerpt North places a candidate historical "fact" in a counterfac-tual context, thus relativizing its meaning, its alleged historical status, and its apparent political implications. Where Nields suggests that particular covert actions were designed to deceive "the American people," North contests the suggestion by asserting that the particular operations could not have succeeded had they been done openly. Without denying the deceptive design of the "covert actions," North shifts the target of deception from "the American people" to "the Soviets." He does not deny that the administration withheld information from "the American people," but he uses the counterfactual conditional to reconfigure the context of the secrecy. He instructs his interlocutor (and especially the audience) on how to "understand" what a covert action is. He does so by laying out a fantastic image of a "bubble" to describe what the authors of the actions *would* do if they could. Interestingly, he slides from the discussion of "covert actions" into using the present hearings as an example of the kind of public discourse that cannot be "insulated" from Moscow, suggesting perhaps that the circumspection and deniability appropriate to covert actions should apply to the present hearings as well. By arguing that the authors of the covert actions in question would do what they obviously cannot do, North recontextualizes the moral and political implications of the design of the actions they did take. His mention of "the Soviets" in opposition to "the American people" is pregnant with political appeal to those who, like North, would be inclined to justify various transgressions of democratic ideals in the interest of combating a powerful foreign threat to those ideals.

CONCLUSION

The logical status of disavowals of recall ("I don't recall," "I don't remember," "I have no recollection of that," etc.) seems clear. Such utterances specifically obstruct an interrogator's attempt to exclude the middle when asking a yes or no question. However, as we have suggested, it is often difficult to show unequivocally (or even plausibly) that these utterances reflect a witness's intention to obstruct or evade the operations of the truth-finding engine. Avowals of nonrecall can, and often do, act to express a kind of innocence and righteousness.

Although a speaker may remain open to the possibility of being reminded of what he or she fails to recall, for the time being the witness can claim no definite responsibility for what is implied about the past. This slippage in the machinery of interrogation accounts for the usefulness of "I don't recall" for purposes of evasion, since the witness can later affirm without cost of contradiction what he does not acknowledge at the moment. As noted, however, this possibility does not necessarily give the witness a free hand, because he or she can still be held responsible for recalling what "anybody" (in a relevant category) *should* recall under the circumstances. An interrogator can tell a witness what *can* or *cannot* be said about the witness's own past, including his or her own past knowledge. Questions of power may certainly be involved, but a broader range of considerations also comes into play, which complicates any conclusion to the effect that the interrogator compels the witness against his or her own will to avow or disavow selected experiential claims.[47] Indeed, as mentioned in chapter 3, the modern tribunal is designed to avoid the appearance of a forced confession in favor of a public display of a confessional truth. We can now appreciate that the publicity of the tribunal is not only a matter of the public disclosure of the witness's secrets, but of the use of contestable public standards for assessing the moral status of the witness's acknowledgments, denials, and recollections.

Considered as a theater of memory, the tribunal is a discursive space in which the witness's private experience is articulated and scrutinized in terms of normative standards of what *can* be acknowledged or denied. Interrogators are not particularly interested in building elegant syllogisms, but, as discussed in chapter 4, they do try to build lines of argument from earlier testimony to pursue further disclosures and admissions. Interrogators do not simply lay out monologues for witnesses and overhearers to appreciate. Instead, they solicit witnesses' utterances and use them as interrogative stepping-stones for building arguments and contesting the witness's credibility. An avowal of nonrecall does not stop interrogation in its tracks since the examiner can always raise questions about the plausibility of the witness's failing to recall key events. As noted, interrogators also attempt to jog the witness's memory by citing prior testimonies and proffering written records. Such textual interventions into the dialogical production of testimony, together with the various modes of information control that went into the writing, shredding, and release of those records, raise another set of considerations about the successful erasure of history that transpired during the Iran-contra hearings.

7. THE DOCUMENTARY METHOD

OF INTERROGATION

That the investigator "does" a report is thereby made a matter for public record for the use of only partially identified other persons. . . . Not only for investigators, but on all sides there is the relevance of "What was really found out for-all-practical-purposes?" which consists unavoidably of how much can you find out, how much can you disclose, how much can you gloss, how much can you conceal, how much can you hold as none of the business of some important persons, investigators included.
—Garfinkel[1]

In previous chapters we examined fragments of testimony and sequences of interrogation. Written transcripts of the testimony provided the principal basis for our arguments about interrogation, stories, memory, and the social production of history. Just as the televisual spectacle of the hearings was predominantly framed as a verbal confrontation between witnesses and interrogators, so our analysis tended to place the unfolding dialogue at center stage. Such an intensive focus on transcribed testimony would be misleading if it encouraged us to forget that talk was but one discursive register in a dense intertextual field. That field included at least the following:

- –The televised hearings.
- –Recorded excerpts and written transcripts.
- –The committee's final report, including the minority report.
- –Media commentaries and other journalistic and scholarly reports.
- –Documents used as exhibits: PROFS Notes, North's notebook entries, CIA logs, White House records, transcripts of tape-recorded meetings, memos.
- –Representations, reproductions, and redacted (systematically censored) excerpts of particular documents and masses of documents reproduced in photographs, shown on camera, and exhibited in testimony.
- –A photograph of North standing next to a stack of paper, shown on camera by Sullivan to demonstrate the mass of committee documents.
- –A slide show presented by North, without a projector, for the ostensible

    purpose of demonstrating the presentation he showed to potential donors
    to the contra "cause."[2]

  –Telegrams sent to North and displayed by his side during the last few days
  of his testimony.

  –Poll results and testimonials presented by the media each day as the hearings proceeded.

Each of these registers employed distinctive communicative channels and
texts. Each brought into play distinct configurations of communicants,
audiences, and message contents; each was caught up in the interplay of
publicity, secrecy, and struggle over disclosure; and each required the elu-
cidation, translation, and colligation of information registered on different
surfaces. A less tangible record was also presumed and cited whenever
parties gave testimony and stated objections "for the record." These actions thus contributed to *the story* of the Iran-contra affair while being fully
understandable only in the context of that emergent narrative.

    In addition to the utterances and texts that explicitly contributed to
building the record, an indefinite body of records of great potential significance also existed. These records, which had been shredded, modified, or
withheld by officials and agencies of the executive branch, were concretely
absent from the hearings but highly relevant to the testimony. Committee
interrogators showed a keen interest throughout the hearings in decipher-
ing gaps in the documentary record, and they were similarly preoccupied
with actual and possible records and testimonies that had been composed
under the policy of plausible deniability. The various present, absent, and
potential elements of the intertextual field were not simply contained in a
determinate archive consulted by the investigators in preparation for the
hearings. In the course of the hearings these present and absent records
were mentioned, glossed, cited, quoted, read silently, and read out loud.
What the records "said" was contested, demanded, iterated, formulated,
juxtaposed, and speculatively addressed in a reflexive and generative operation.[3] Moreover, these reflexive, iterative, and citational moves were
thematized throughout the hearings, and in this way they entered into the
actual production of the public spectacle. In this chapter we shall identify
some ways in which the moment of testimony was situated within this
dense intertextual field.

SPEECH AND WRITING

Long portions of the hearings were consumed by on-camera readings and interpretations of documentary exhibits. Television commentators often characterized these episodes as boring and uneventful interludes in which the parties on-camera examined documentary exhibits and went over previous testimony. When the witnesses and interrogators spoke, they often were reading. At such times they visibly and audibly engaged in a study of documentary exhibits, which to the TV commentators made for a tedious spectacle of what they seemed to view as scholars at work (figs. 7 and 8). For lengthy intervals the dialogue between interrogator and witness consisted almost exclusively of collaborative readings and rereadings of a document, line-by-line, point-by-point. Even when they were not reading directly from documents, what the interlocutors said was never far removed from the massive pile of records. A distinction between reading and testifying nevertheless was significant in the production of the hearings. For instance, the following exchange ensued after one of North's impassioned speeches during his first day of testimony (which, like many of his speeches, was delivered as an "answer" to a question):

Chairman Inouye: Before proceeding, may I make an inquiry of the witness? Was that response from a written text?
North: Those are from notes that I made in preparation for this session, sir.
Chairman Inouye: It is not a verbatim written text?
North: No, sir, it is not.[4]

Although the testimony was conducted in and through a spoken dialogue, and although witnesses were invited to contribute spontaneously to it, the dialogue was always on the verge of breaking into writing. The distinction between speech and writing (or, more specifically, between answering a question and reading a statement) was relevant, sometimes as a normative concern, but in a continually shifting, nuanced, and contentious way.

One central organizational feature of the public testimony was that it was spoken "for the record." Indeed, it was recorded, transcribed, summarized, quoted, and recycled again and again in news reports, on video clips, and in various official or unofficial histories of these events (as it con-

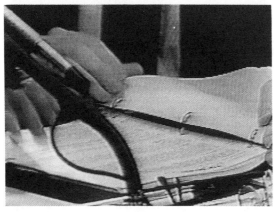

7. and 8. Scholars at work.

tinues to be cited and recycled here). Moreover, the interrogators and wit-nesses were surrounded by a desktop archive comprising several loose-leaf binders of committee exhibits and other writings prepared for the occa-sion, and a considerable amount of time was taken up by the interrogators' and witnesses' efforts to locate statements in their copies of this archive. The questions and answers were undoubtedly rehearsed many times over before the hearings, both by the committee staff and by the witness's legal team. As discussed in detail earlier, a witness's stories contended with the prospect of being translated into the terms of a conventional history, and his recollections about the past were significantly bound to the corrobora-tion and concordance provided by the documentary archive.

North and other committee witnesses also testified in closed session about matters that were held to be sensitive. These testimonies were akin to statements made to the press off the record, since they presumably informed the committee but were not incorporated verbatim into public accounts of the hearings. The distinction between what was on or off the record was interesting and subject to ironic use. For example, the names of several of the countries involved in the Iran-contra affair were marked during the hearings as officially unmentionable. A code of numbers (e.g., country 1 for Israel) was used by the interrogators and witnesses, but the witnesses often revealed the names of the countries, and television viewers were given keys to these names in captions and voice-over commentaries. The committee's final report also supplied readers with the relevant keys. Nevertheless, the code was maintained throughout the hearings as a thinly veiled diplomatic gesture.

The intertextual linkages that were so perspicuous during the hearings provide an interesting circumstance for reviewing a well-known dispute concerning the question of whether speech has primacy over writing. While the distinction between speech and writing was relevant, the interpenetration of speech and text at the hearings was so pervasive and multifaceted that it defies any attempt to impose a stable, a priori distinction between two discrete linguistic registers. With the vivid example of the Iran-contra hearings at hand, we can examine how the distinction between speech and writing, which has become such a preoccupation in academic scholarship and debate, was also a preoccupation, albeit in a more contingent and less scholarly way, for the interlocutors at the hearings. We shall argue that in the case before us an alternation from speech to text, and from text to speech, was something of a discursive armature in an interrogatory truth-finding engine. Moreover, the distinction itself became the site of ongoing resistance and dialogical struggle, as witnesses like North "deconstructed" efforts to instantiate clear-cut divisions between orders of linguistic register.

The discussion of the distinction between speech and writing is situated against the philosophical backdrop of the well-known debate between Jacques Derrida and John Searle.[5] In that debate Derrida argued that Searle (as representative of the analytic tradition in modern philosophy) subordinated writing to speech by insisting that linguistic intelligibility is located in authorship, authors' intentions, and stable contexts of usage. Derrida attempted to demonstrate that Searle unnecessarily privileged a narrow concept of "context" while shunting aside the possibilities for quoting, citing, or otherwise disengaging speech from its putatively "original" context and grafting it into an endless and uncontrollable play of transformative uses. Derrida's central point, then and now, is that a linguistic fragment or text does not lose its intelligibility when divorced from its "original" situation of authorship. Rather, it becomes an item in (and for) an indefinite series of original, yet intelligible, uses and readings. In this way Derrida argues that writing is autonomous from speech and that its intelligibility cannot be derived from the analysis of speech situations (ideal or otherwise). In his rejoinder to Derrida, Searle continued to insist on the primacy of discursive situations in which a speaker enunciates an utterance with serious intent or an author commits an idea to writing.

Without taking sides in the debate (and without going deeply into it), we figure that it alerts us to an interesting and taxing problem for participants at the Iran-contra hearings. While Derrida's commitment to the primacy of "writing" (construed very generally) and Searle's commitment to the primacy of "speech" (again construed very generally) provide polar positions for generating an energetic and fractious exchange of arguments, a different, occasionally fractious, dialogical exchange is generated in situ at the hearings in those places where the interlocutors endeavor to subordinate speech to writing and writing to speech. The elements of a speech situation that Searle insists are primordial—authorship, intention, context—are cited repeatedly by interrogators and witnesses to authorize and defend their accounts within the evidential horizons of documentary writings. At the same time, the authorless, context-free, and unintentional properties of such writings—exactly those features emphasized by Derrida—provide occasional (although defeasible) resources for interrogators and witnesses to use when placing their own utterances on the record. Where Derrida's account of the potentially limitless, open-ended displacement of the textual fragment suggests the radical indeterminacy of meaning—and, consequently, an inability to stabilize any single interpretation of a text by "fixing" it within an original situation, the very possibility of disengaging a text from the conditions of authorship and placing it within an intertextual field provides an interrogator with a weapon with which to extract confessional truths from the author of the self-same text. Such interrogative moves presume and seek to recover the elements of actual authorship and stable, generalizable contexts of action that Searle emphasizes. The analytical engine of the interrogation is thus set in motion and sustained by tension-laden alternating currents between writings and speakings, between documentary evidence and witnesses' testimonies, and between what is *on* the record and what is *becoming* the record.

As mentioned, the testimony at the Iran-contra hearings was an instance of speech generated within a dense literary field. The dialogues between interrogators and witnesses were officially set up as part of a fact-finding investigation in which the joint House and Senate committees were charged with producing a written report summarizing the hundreds of hours of testimony. The archive of notebooks surrounding the interrogators and witnesses were filled with copies of memos, printouts of electronic mail messages, telegrams, diary entries, letters, and transcripts of earlier testimonies. The records were used in the course of the testimony, and the testimony was spoken for the record. Written documents were sometimes read aloud, shown on camera, blown up on display panels, cited, and otherwise used as a basis for soliciting testimony and checking testimony against already established facts. Indeed, the sheer mass of the documents became a strategic issue when, at the outset of his testimony, North and his attorney, Brendan Sullivan, complained that they were given insufficient time to read and study the committee's records (see chapter 3).[6] This was initially proposed as a reason for postponing North's appearance. Two committee members, Sens. George Mitchell and William Cohen, later wrote that it was an especially cheeky maneuver, even for an attorney as bold as Sullivan.[7] They noted that Sullivan had initially stipulated the conditions for exchanging documents. After much debate, the committee acceded to the demand out of a fear that the hearings otherwise would be delayed inordinately. Although this motion for postponent was (predictably) denied, North repeatedly expressed unfamiliarity with many of the documents put before him. Even during those intervals when the notebooks remained closed, the fact that they were ready-to-hand pervaded the testimony. North often uttered expressions such as, "I don't think so, I mean you may refresh my memory again . . . ," suggesting the *possibility* that certain documents, some of which may have been unknown to him, might be called into play. The relevant archive was not a closed docket, its apparent influence extending well beyond the enumerated exhibits assembled in the notebooks. Missing (particularly shredded) documents were no less relevant than those that were present.

In the remainder of this chapter we shall deal with some of the practices used by interrogators and witnesses to juxtapose writings and spoken utterances. While the debate between Derrida and Searle provides a critical backdrop for the discussion, our intention is not to try to settle the debate by bringing empirical evidence to bear on the divergent positions, but to identify some of the many modes of juxtaposition and iteration that had a recurrent, generative role in the production of the hearings. These mundane modes of juxtaposition and iteration are far more diverse than could easily be conceptualized by a metaphysics of speech or writing. In our judgment, close examination enables one to form an understanding of practical efforts to subsume spoken testimony into a written report by, among other things, situating writings in speech.

THE DOCUMENTARY METHOD OF INTERROGATION

As emphasized in chapter 4, interrogation is designed as a truth-finding engine for compelling a witness to "spontaneously" reveal a confessional truth. Although interrogation retains some of the design of a conversational dialogue, it is a conversation far from a free and open exchange. Rather than viewing interrogation as derivative of a more primordial conversational structure, however, we prefer to treat it as a constituent of an investigation. As such, it is a dialogue whose generative details are relevant to, relevanced by, and inspectable as "evidence." Among other generative aspects of interrogation, the testimony links itself retrospectively to earlier testimony, and it is used prospectively to establish the evidential significance of later testimony. Accordingly, the production and corroboration of testimony at any given moment involve the reflexive iteration of prior testimony and the anticipation of later testimony. For example, questions to North were often citationally linked to earlier testimonies, and as is clear in the following instance, such citations were often designed to leverage confirmation.

Nields: There's been testimony before the Committee that you engaged in
    shredding of documents on November the 21st, 1986. Do you deny that?
North: I do not deny that I engaged in shredding on November 21st.[8]

At other times the interrogator would frame a question by asking the witness to "go over" an issue or phrase of a story the same witness had previously described. Sometimes the witness's earlier testimony would be quoted back to him or paraphrased, occasionally in the form of an incredulous reading. Such paraphrases rhetorically "clarified" the witness's position, challenging him either to confirm an evidently "extreme" statement that was likely to be difficult to defend, or to deny that he actually said (or meant) what the interrogator ascribed to him. Not surprisingly, witnesses often took the second option, using the present occasion to reformulate what they had been saying all along.

Nields: Is it your testimony that the documents that you shredded right after you found out that the Attorney General's people were coming in over the weekend to look at documents had nothing to do with the fact that his people were coming in to look at documents?

North: No, I'm not saying that.[9]

The citation of prior testimony in present testimony was one way in which speech was intertwined with text. Another, perhaps more obvious, way in which writing entered into the conduct of the hearings was through the introduction of documentary exhibits. The following exchange occurs in the course of a line of questions about North's having altered the chronologies describing a series of events connected with a 1985 covert arms transaction with Iran:

North: . . . No, the short answer is no. I think the chronologies had already started to be changed. I think my initial input from Mr. McFarlane predates this.

Nields: Well, let's check that against the record. I'd like you to turn to Exhibit 19. Do you have that in front of you?[10]

Note the complexity of the intertextual field made relevant through this exchange. At least three "chronologies" are at issue: one of them that North prepared, another that reflected McFarlane's input, and both of which are placed by North's testimony within a calendrical order of chronology construction. Another document (an item of evidence relevant to the question at hand, but not itself a chronology) is brought into play by Nields's reference to exhibit 19, which is drawn from a larger field that Nields calls "the record." Conventionally understood, this record is an accumulated corpus of case-specific evidence that provides a background—and a basis for checking—the immediate testimony.[11]

Documentary exhibits were cited, read, shown, and discussed with attention to a full range of their material and literary qualities:

- —their material existence and identity as papers, notebook entries, shredded documents,[12] and electronic messages.
- —Their surface qualities, including headings, indices, and places for check-marks and signatures.
- —What the documents "said" in so many words.
- —What the documents meant or implied.

To appreciate how these various references to, and readings of, documents came into play, we shall examine a continuous sequence of interrogation about exhibit Two. The interrogation occurred during the first morning of North's testimony. Exhibit Two was identified as a PROF message (an electronic message on the White House "Professional Office" computer network) from North to McFarlane on 4/7/86, at 23:18:58:

Met last week w/ Gorba to finalize arrangements for a mtg in Iran and release of hostages on or about 19 Apr. This was based on word that he had to deposit not less than $15M in appropriate acct. by close of banking tomorrow. Have talked at length w/ Nir who is handling him on thie [sic] bank xfer and Nir believes that Gorba may be having trouble closing the final arrangements back home. Per request of JMP have prepared a paper for our boss which lays out arrangements. Gorba indicated that yr counterpart in the T[ehran] mtg wd be Rafsanjani. If all this comes to pass it shd be one hell of a show. Meanwhile we have some evidence that Col Q [Qadhafi] is attempting to buy the hostages in order to stage a propaganda extravaganza. As far fetched as this may seen, CIA believes it is a distinct possibility. Bottom line: believe you shd avail yrself to this paper @ yr earliest convenience. Wd like to see you anyway. Am going home—if I remember the way.[13]

PROF notes were considered especially significant by the committee because, according to the testimony of witnesses from the NSC staff, North and his colleagues had erroneously assumed that when they "deleted" the messages, they erased them permanently. Backup copies of the "erased" messages were later recovered from the computer memory banks. Given the acknowledged efforts to produce numerous records under the policy of plausible deniability—anticipating and defending against investigations such as the one currently under way—these electronic communications were treated as spontaneous messages that expressed less guarded indications of the communicant's actual intentions. In other words, such communications were thought to disclose what the communicants systematically obscured when recording other messages "for posterity."[14] This treatment was in line with classic views of credibility, which ascribe special significance to signals, gestures, or indications that spontaneously escape a communicant's efforts to control a coherent "impression."[15]

A sequence of testimony regarding Exhibit Two began shortly after Nields had repeatedly interrogated North about another exhibit. Exhibit One was a draft copy of a memorandum sent by North to the president for approval. Among other things, it authorized the infamous "diversion" of Iranian arms sales profits to aid the contras. This document, which received a great deal of attention from the committee and the press, was held to have a similar evidential value to the PROFS notes. According to testimonies by North and other witnesses, Exhibit One was a draft copy of one of five or six memos that North sent through Poindexter "seeking Presidential approval" for the diversion of funds to the contras. According to the canonical history of the Iran-contra affair, this draft copy "emerged" from North's files on November 21 1986, during an internal investigation by the Justice Department. North testified that he shredded several other copies of this memo before the visit to his office by Justice Department members and that this particular draft copy (which, because it was a draft, had no indications of approval on it) had "escaped" his efforts to destroy evidence that would "damage" the president. (When pressed about whether this admission indicated an attempt to cover up scandalous evidence, North once again emphasized the damage to national security that would ensue from exposure of these actions to domestic and foreign enemies.) Again, the apparent slippage in the "intentional" design and erasure of documents under the policy of deniability lent this document particular authority and credibility. Nevertheless, in the end, it also proved especially suitable as evidence in North's defense by showing that the diversion was authorized from "above," but without specifying which official was responsible (Poindexter later took responsibility and absolved the president).

Prior to the sequence to be discussed, Nields already had asked North about the organizational circumstances of the diversion memorandum (Exhibit One), including the typical ways it would pass up the chain of command from North, through Poindexter, to Reagan. Much of the questioning concerned whether or not, and how, the president would have left traces of his authorization on the surface of the document. The draft copy was left blank where such authorization would have been recorded in the form of a check mark or signature.[16] In response to Nields's questions, North repeatedly failed to recall; after one such avowal of nonrecall, Nields asks him to "turn to" Exhibit Two. In the ensuing exchange, Nields instructs North on how to read a document that he (North) had written.

Nields: Well, in fact, isn't it true that it was Admiral *Poin*dexter that wanted you to send these memoranda up for the President to approve.

North: I- I don't recall Admiral Poindexter instructing me to do that, either.

(1)→ Nields: Well, would you turn to Exhibit Two? (9 seconds)

Nields: Do you have that in front of you? (3 seconds)

(2)→ North: I have a- uh- what appears to be a PROFS note from Admiral Poindexter.

Nields: And ah- below that (it's- is) a PROF note from, Oliver North.

North: Yes.

(3)→ Nields: And that's to Mr. McFarlane. (4 seconds)

North: I don't know how I can tell that, from what I'm looking at.

Nields: Well, if you look right above the reply denote of 4/7/86, it says, "To R-RCM."

North: Right.

Nields: And it's dated the 7th of April, 1986.

North: Right.

(4)→ Nields: And that's three days after the date of the, terms- terms of reference on Exhibit 1. You can check if you wish, or you can take my word for it. It's dated April 4th.

North: Will you take my word? ((looking up, grinning)) (26 Seconds; North and Sullivan examine notebook, whispering to each other)

Sullivan: What is your question, uh?

Nields: I haven't asked a question yet, I'm simply uh- uh, well, the question is, isn't this three days after the date on the term of reference on Exhibit 1?

North: Apparently it is.

(5)→ Nields: And this PROF message makes reference to Mr. Ghorbanifar in the first line?

North: Yes it does.

Nields: And it makes reference to the $15 million, in line 3.

North: That's correct.

(6)→ Nields: And then, in line 6, it reads, "Per request of JMP, have prepared a paper for our boss, which lays out arrangements."

North: That's what it says.

(7)→ Nields: And my question to you, sir, is, doesn't that mean that you are telling Mr. McFarlane, that Admiral Poindexter, that's JMP, isn't it?

North: Yes, it is.

Nields: Had asked that you prepare a paper for the President.

North: That's correct.

Nields: That's "our boss," isn't it?

North: He is, indeed.

(8)→ Nields: And uh "laying out the arrangements," and that refers, does it not, to the description of the transaction, uh, which is in Exhibit number one?

North: That's correct.

(9)→ Nields: So, far from telling you to stop sending memoranda up for the President's approval, Admiral Poindexter was specifically *asking* you to send memoranda up for the President's approval.

North: Well, uh, again, in this particular case, that's true, Mr. Nields, and I don't believe that I have said that Admiral Poindexter told me to stop. (2.5 seconds)

North: Did I?[17]

In this sequence, Exhibit Two becomes embedded within the ongoing testimony. It is displayed, selectively read, and progressively explicated. Over the course of the sequence, Nields leads North through a series of identifications, references, and explications. For all practical purposes, North's confirmations act to certify a set of agreed-to specifications. In other words, the locally organized series of these confirmations displays what the interlocutors will treat provisionally as undisputed facts about the document, its referential particulars, its meaning, and its implications for the inquiry at hand.

The sequence of questions and answers is organized in the manner described in chapter 4, with the interrogator presenting the witness with a series of "questions" in the form of assertions "asking" for confirmation. Only here, however, the questions and answers are organized with respect to a written exhibit, and the citation and reading of that document are crucially part of what might be called a "documentary method of interrogation." This is a variant of a familiar theme in Harold Garfinkel's ethnomethodological writings, which he calls the "documentary method of interpretation." "The method consists of treating an actual appearance as 'the document of,' as 'pointing to,' as 'standing on behalf of,' a presupposed underlying pattern. Not only is the underlying pattern derived from its individual documentary evidences, but the individual documentary evidences, in their turn, are interpreted on the basis of 'what is known' about the underlying pattern. Each is used to elaborate the other."[18] Our conception of the documentary method of interrogation points to somewhat different practice: an interrogatory method (or set of methods) in which material documents are used as resources for questioning a witness.

In the sequence above, Exhibit Two is brought into play just after North professes not to recall the fact that he is being asked to acknowledge ("that it was Admiral Poindexter that wanted you to send these memoranda up for the President to approve"). Nields offers to refresh North's recall by instructing him to "turn to Exhibit Two" (arrow at [1] above). He then undertakes a methodical examination of the document by initiating a dialogically organized series of assertions and confirmations. This collaborative reading of the document is part and parcel of the examination of North's present testimony. The sequence of interrogation leads the witness progressively into the document, starting with its mere presence as a textual exhibit, working through various identifications and indices, locating and reading a key passage, and finally explicating a locally relevant meaning of that passage.

At the line in the above transcript marked (1), Nields first mentions Exhibit Two just after North claims not to recall the organizational circumstances of sending the memo "up to the President to approve." Nields's citation of Exhibit Two, along with the instruction to "turn to" it as a material exhibit, clearly is responsive to North's failed recall. In line with standard legal procedures for refreshing a witness's recollection, Nields introduces the exhibit just after having elicited an expression of an exhausted memory. In conversation-analytic terms, the initiation of a move toward the document is sequentially relevanced by North's immediately prior avowal of nonrecall. It is offered as a repair or remedy for an apparently failed memory.[19]

Beginning at line (2), North acknowledges that he has found the material exhibit in the notebook in front of him, and he and Nields engage in a coordinated effort to "look" to find the particular PROF note that is about to feature in the interrogation. Note that time is taken (creating a substantial delay, during which North and Sullivan visibly search through the notebooks and studiously examine the pages). Not incidentally, it is an especially slow-paced and boring moment in the televised hearings—a spectacle of scholars at work. North's display of unfamiliarity with the document during the lengthy interlude in which he "studies" it as though for the first time visibly supports his and Sullivan's earlier claim that they had insufficient opportunity to examine the committee's records. This display also implicates the "failure to recall" that North professed, in effect, at the outset of this sequence, since this failure implicates more than an ability to remember off the top of his head.

At line (3), following Nields's instructions, North is now "on the same page" as his interrogator. At this point, Nields asks him to confirm the identity of the document, construed in classic semiotic terms as a message sent by him (North) to a receiver (McFarlane) at a particular time. North's account for this delayed confirmation—"I don't know how I can tell that, from what I'm looking at"—identifies the task at this point as a matter of converting the particulars on a surface that he is "looking at" to a recognizable and readable text. So, while he and Nields are accountably and materially on the same page, they have not yet aligned what they are supposed to be "looking at" on that page. This is less a matter of looking in a particular direction *at* something on the page than it is of identifying a heading that indexes what that page *is* as a communication. Consequently, while Nields and North formulate their task in classic terms (sender-message-receiver), they are concurrently engaged in a protosemiotic search that enables a joint reading of the same accountable document.

In the vicinity of line (4) the alignment continues between the interrogator and witness as the interrogator cites an identifying detail, and the witness confirms that he has found, and can confirm, that detail. At this point, Nields gives an intertextual reference by noting that the date on Exhibit Two is "three days after" the date on Exhibit One, then inviting North to "check" if he wants to or simply "take my word for it." North plays off of this last formulation, asking, while smiling, "Will you take my word?" and he and Sullivan opt to "check" by inspecting the document. A considerable delay occurs (26 seconds) while they do so, and within the context of this delay Sullivan bids to resume the interrogation by asking, "What is your question?" As discussed in chapter 4, Nields's response—where he cuts off an initial acknowledgment that he has not (yet) asked a question and then frames his prior assertion as a syntactic question—concedes locally (but only locally) to the rule for questions and answers in testimony. Moreover, North's ironic quip and Sullivan's question both use the occasion of "co-reading" as an organizational warrant for counteracting the interrogator's prerogatives and slowing the pace of his interrogative pursuit. Again, their visible "study" of the document—examining it as though they are reading it for the first time—together with North's many other displays of unfamiliarity, is congruent with their claim that they had been given insufficient time to study the committee's exhibits.

At line (5), Nields now recites a series of references in specific lines of the PROF document: to "Ghorbanifar" in the first line and to $15 million in the third line. These readings align the documentary references "Gorba" and "$15M" with the previously established identities of characters and transactions in an episode of the Iran arms sales story. In addition to soliciting North's confirmation of a referential translation from the documentary surface to the present telling of what the document "says," Nields progressively and publicly takes North through a particular passage within the body of the document. This co-reading alignment is "deepened," in the sense of progressively explicating an ever-more "meaningful" context of dates, intertextual linkages, familiar characters, and communicative actions, in order to set up a question that has not yet been asked. With each successive confirmation of these referential details, North agrees to follow Nields into the increasingly dense, vivid, and circumstantially rich texture of the scene of an event being indicated and implicated by the documentary particulars. Not only is North led progressively into the document, but he and the document are led inexorably into the story that the record metonymically indicates and implicates, a story that is being fleshed out for the television audience, which is becoming ever more familiar with who Ghorbanifar is, what happened in April 1986, and what was done with the $15 million.

At line (6), Nields begins to read aloud, leading North and the overhearing audience through the passage. North confirms, "That's what it says." The particular way he formulates this "confirmation" is interesting, and we can perhaps detect a hint of irony. Ironic or not, North's remark credits Nields with having correctly read a sentence from the document, and no more than that.[20]

At line (7), Nields formulates his "question." This order of "question" differs remarkably from the syntactic question that Nields asked earlier in this sequence in response to Sullivan's query, "What is your question?" Here, the question is connected retrospectively and prospectively to the ongoing dialogical search for an accountable meaning. Far from being the product of a subjective interpretation, such a meaning is designed to be publicly exhibited through a progressive co-reading of the document. Vernacularly understood, the question explicates a sense or upshot of what the entire line of questioning may be getting at. It includes an explication of what it is about this exhibit that *should be confirmed.* The phrase in Nields's utterance, "doesn't that mean," indexically invokes the line of text he had just read aloud ("line six" in Exhibit Two), and it adumbrates the meaning he goes on to state.[21] In the course of explicating this meaning he interrupts the question while embedding a further question within it about the reference "JMP." North confirms the reference, and Nields resumes the question about the "meaning" of the documentary passage, which North then confirms. Nields goes on to cite a further referential detail in the passage he had just read, a colloquial reference to "our boss" that he translates into the institutional title "the President." North seizes on this request for confirmation as an opportunity to give a slightly facetious display of loyalty and patriotism, "He is indeed [our boss]," pronounced slowly, full face to the cameras, almost salutingly, but with a wry smile. Again, while North has cooperated with Nields up to this point, by co-reading and jointly explicating Exhibit Two without contesting any of the interrogator's references and readings, he opportunistically uses the embodied, sequential delivery of the interrogation to sidetrack Nields's agenda with various minor editorial quips, expressions, qualifications, resistances, and posturings. If North's embodied delivery of "confirmations" was a written text, we might say that it contained parenthetical asides, underlinings, scare quotes, and footnotes (which, when inscribed on the audiovisual register of a talking head, might better be called headnotes and headquotes).

At line (8), Nields continues to propose meanings for particular references in the passage from Exhibit Two, which he had read earlier. Here, he focuses on the phrase "laying out arrangements," suggesting that it "refers" to "the description of the transaction" in Exhibit One. This citation suggests that a more elaborate description in Exhibit One should stand proxy for a colloquial reference used between two organizational insiders. The intertextual link establishes the significance of the colloquial reference in Exhibit Two, not only in relation to another document, but in reference to a previously established episode in the story of the Iran-contra affair.

At line (9), Nields states, as a concluding point to the foregoing series of questions about Exhibit Two, what he figures to have established about the meaning of the passage he had just read: "So far from telling you to stop sending memoranda up for the President's approval, Admiral Poindexter was specifically asking you to send memoranda up for the President's approval." This takes us full circle, back to the "fact" that North professed not to recall just before Nields turned to the exhibit: "isn't it true that it was Admiral Poindexter that wanted you to send these memoranda up for the President to approve?" (first line of the transcript above). The formulation does more than simply repeat the earlier question; it is phrased as a conclusion, logically derived from the preceding sequence of interrogation, a conclusion in which one premise is ruled out (that Poindexter had ordered North to "stop" sending such memoranda up for presidential approval) in favor of another (that Poindexter had ordered the memoranda). North confirms the conclusion, but he denies having "said" that Poindexter told him to "stop" sending memoranda. When Nields does not reply immediately, North prompts him with "Did I?" and again gets no reply.

This last interchange involves a fine example of interrogative gamesmanship. Indeed, North had never said that Poindexter told him to "stop sending memoranda up for the President's approval." At the outset of the sequence reproduced above, in the line prior to (1), North professes not to recall the "fact" that Poindexter "instructed" (note how this term replaces "wanted" from the question) him to send memoranda up to the president for approval. By refreshing North's recollection by leading him through a lengthy exegesis of Exhibit Two, Nields gets North to confirm the terms of the initial question. The alternative account that Nields proposes to reject—that Poindexter told North specifically to "stop sending the memoranda up for the President's approval"—seems to be generated by its contrast to the now confirmed "fact" that Poindexter did no such thing. But, since North only *professed* not to recall what Poindexter had "instructed him," he avoids any implication of self-contradiction by rejecting the imputation of having said what Nields suggests. This takes us back to the logical-grammatical status of nonrecall as neither confirmation nor denial (discussed at length in chapter 6). Nields appears to be fishing for a substantive account that can be contradicted with the agreed-to facts, but North does not take the bait.

The uses of documents to refresh or jog a witness's memory are familiar in discussions of legal testimony. Although documents are treated as possible remedies for a witness's avowed failures to recall, they do not provide unequivocal remedies because they also introduce further problems with the credibility and plausibility of "refreshed" recollections. As North demonstrated again and again, memoranda by themselves do not resolve the problems with a witness's failed memory. In addition, even when the upshot of these sequences was a confirmation of the interrogator's account of what the exhibit "said," the very out-loud and on-camera work of finding documents, looking at them, locating relevant selections, reading them, translating references, and explicating referential meanings provided opportunities for the witness and his lawyer to demonstrate and dramatize their resistance to the investigators' univocal narratives. Moreover, the laborious work of "going over" an exhibit to establish a minor point that the witness initially professed not to recall had definite pragmatic and dramatic consequences. At the least, such documentary work greatly extended the time it took to corroborate minor "facts," thus slowing the pace of interrogatory pursuit of a "spontaneous" and "confessional" truth. Moreover, the extended interludes created by the scholarly examination of documentary points considerably dampened the moment to moment drama of the spectacle. This weakness was indicated by instant analyses of television commentators and pundits, some of whom averred that particular phases of the hearings contained long and "tedious" questioning on "trivial" matters. It seemed to them that for long stretches the hearings were essentially eventless. Whenever North and Sullivan pored over the documents, the production of notable revelations and sound bytes was suspended in a studious silence. This is not to say that North and Sullivan were uninterested in the selective production of such revelations and sound bytes, but that a slower pace, with ample time out for "study" before answering the latest question on the floor, enabled them to have greater control over what would be revealed—and how. As it turned out, in light of the supposedly slow and tedious progress made during the first few days, the committee extended the scheduled number of days for North's testimony, but even then the sluggish pace could only help to minimize the production of storyable "revelations" in the testimony.

PLAUSIBLE DENIABILITY:
"MY MEMORY HAS BEEN SHREDDED"

Not only were particular documentary exhibits relevant to testimony, but entire masses of destroyed, doctored, withheld, and redacted documents were implicated. Although the committee managed to secure an immense mass of documents, the documents that were missing were even more notable. North's infamous "shredding" of an indefinite (but admittedly large) number of documents was a key theme in the questioning, as House majority counsel John Nields repeatedly and fruitlessly interrogated North about the contents of the shredded documents. Not surprisingly, North professed not to recall which documents he shredded at what time, and whether he shredded those particular documents because of their evidentiary value. But when Nields raised the obvious connection between missing documents and North's "memory," he was loudly rebuffed.[22] Several of North's "speeches" on the first morning of this testimony counteracted any suggestion of his culpability by giving a righteous and patriotic defense of "covert operations." In this counternarrative, the background against which secrecy, lies, and shredding were conducted was "a dangerous world" in which foreign and domestic enemies sought to undermine the interests of "the American people" (as discussed in chapter 3). Since a majority of the committee did not challenge the general right of the president to initiate covert activities (and only the more "progressive" elements of the press suggested that covert activities were antithetical to democracy), North's inclusion of particular actions under that heading enabled him to claim a righteous motive that seemingly was contested only on technical grounds.[23] The congressmen's main concern was whether the covert activities in which North and the NSC staff engaged had been properly authorized.

Regardless of what North's motives originally were for shredding documents, it was clear early in his testimony that his interrogators would learn little about what he shredded. During his first morning of testimony, North

enunciated one of his most often quoted sound bites, in which he pun-
ningly associated his failure to recall with the documents he had destroyed:

Nields: Sir, do you remember the question?
North: My memory has been shredded. If you would be so kind as to repeat the
    question.
Nields: You've testified that you shredded documents shortly after you heard
    from Director Casey that Furmark had said monies had been used from the
    Iranian arms sales for the benefit of the contras.
North: That is correct.
Nields: My question to you is—did you or did you not shred documents that
    reflected Presidential approval of the diversion?
North: I have absolutely no recollection of destroying any document which
    gave me an indication that the President had seen the document or that the
    President had specifically approved. I assumed that the three transactions
    which I supervised or managed or coordinated—whatever word you're com-
    fortable with, and I can accept all three—were approved by the President. I
    never recall seeing a single document which gave me a clear indication that
    the President had specifically approved this action.[24]

Shortly thereafter, his recall failed him when he was asked about the tie
between a date and the shredded documents.

Nields: So you shredded some documents because the Attorney General's
    people were coming in over the weekend?
North: I do not preclude that as part of what was shredded. I do not preclude
    that as being a possibility—not at all.[25]

Other documents that were not shredded were withheld from the committee by the White House, and many of those that were released contained blacked-out (or "redacted") passages "for national security" reasons. Some of North's notebooks were used a year later as evidence in his
criminal trial, but at the time of the hearings they had not been made
available to the committee, and a few committee members complained
about that inaccessibility. These struggles over documents indicate the
extent to which the parties to the Iran-contra hearings treated them as
crucial items. Put simply, they were treated as actual or potential con-

straints on what a witness could say—or not say—credibly. They were like-wise treated as resources for formulating interrogative questions, sources of leverage for probing a witness, testing his answers, and holding those answers *answerable*. And, it was acknowledged, the possibility that such documents might be used in this way was part of the very preparation of the documents.

Nields: Were you considering the issue of damage to the President when you were destroying documents from your files.

North: I was considering the issue of damage to the President when I was preparing documents. . . .[26]

North's response indicates that plausible deniability was not simply an interpretative policy that applied to the reading of documents, but it was inscribed in the very way specific notes and records were written and preserved. Interestingly, North is able to admit this much without reveal-ing just what might be meant by "damage to the President" or "domestic political damage." While admitting that a misleading documentary trail was laid, he maintained the equivocal posture which that trail permitted: "damage" need not imply evidence of impeachable transgressions; it can mean exposure of secrets to enemies and subversion of crucial diplomatic efforts.

GOING BACK OVER THE RECORD

The withholding and shredding of documents and the possible deniable preparation of the evidence released to the committee set up an especially difficult situation for converting testimony to history. For the most part, the committee interrogators aimed to use written documents as representa-tions of real-worldly events. The interrogators used such records to lever-age and corroborate testimony, but these fragmentary notes, memos, and other writings were "cut off from their anchoring source in a unique and present intention."[27] These circumstantial gaps in the record gave wit-nesses a relatively free hand to fill in the situational and intentional con-texts of those writings. North and the other 'hostile witnesses' were able to dissociate their testimony from particular texts by, among other things, exploiting undecidable features of the authorship, intention, and original

meaning of the "orphaned texts" brought into the interrogation. The committee's situation was not entirely hopeless, however, since it relied on the
possibility that particular documents and testimonies could be assessed
against a background of a totality of records and testimonies that was unlikely to have been assembled by means of a tight conspiratorial design.
Hence, the documentary method of interrogation involves colligating particular writings and testimonies against a background of a more general,
although still defeasible, "record" of events and episodes. The following
excerpt provides some appreciation of this process. The excerpt begins
immediately after a lengthy narrative by North on the November 1985
Hawk missile transaction.

Nields: I'd like to go back over some of the uh (3.5) issues arising out of this
   H:awk, ((throat clear)) transaction. The first one I'd like to address, uh Colonel North is- is the issue of money. (3.2) And uh, (2.0) I think the best place to
   begin is with uh, an item out of your notebook. . . .[28]

Nields's proposal to "go back over some . . . issues" is not just a matter of
elaborating upon already told details of a familiar episode. It also introduces a document (i.e., "an item out of your notebook") that shifts the
focus of the interrogation from North's testimony by itself to an independent document presumably of "the same story." After instructing North
(and his attorney) on where to locate a particular entry in this notebook,
Nields engages North in a co-reading of the document.

Nields: I'd like you to take a look at the middle of the page. It says (1.8)
   "Secord to call, a city in a foreign country,"
North: Yes (1.5)
Nields: Then underneath that it says, "Ben-Youssif start buy orders at four-
   teen million dollars or less,"
North: Right.=
Nields: =While we're on that, that's the uh, Ben-Youssif is the person at the
   Israeli purchasing office I take it?
North: He is.[29]

This sequential arrangement in which Nields reads a passage, explicates
the passage, and North confirms the readings presented to him continues.

Nields reads a passage, "Schwimmer to move one million dollars to Lake," and receives North's confirmation that "Lake" is "Lake Resources," a Panamanian-based company controlled by Secord that was used to supply the contras in Central America.[30] Nields then asks: "And what was Schwimmer to move a million dollars to Lake for?"

Nields's reading of the document locates and explicates a series of references ("Ben-Youssif," "Lake"), and presents these for North's confirmation. Note that Nields's explication of "Ben-Youssif" proposes a link between an institutional identity and "Israel," an already familiar party to the Iran-contra story. The identification of "Lake" with "Lake Resources," given the as yet unmentioned link between "Lake Resources" and the contra supply operation, sets up a line of questioning on a possible transfer of money from the Hawk transaction to the contras. Agreed-upon readings of the document thus exhibit a common sense of the document's historical significance, which can then be treated as a fact for the sake of further interrogation. The reading is thematic, under the topic of "money," since it begins with a mention of that topic and leads up to the question about the reference to "one million dollars."

Within the local production of the sequence, the document is granted a certain objective standing to the extent that its references to dates, amounts of money, persons, and institutional affiliations are cited by the interrogator and confirmed by the witness. As mentioned in chapter 4, conventional histories are assembled from such references. Yet the record does not speak for itself. The cryptic, and perhaps designedly equivocal, references in the record do not provide the committee with ready-made material to be woven into a chronology of the Iran-contra affair. North is consulted as an authoritative co-reader of the document in question and in this case as the author of the item in his notebook. While the document's conventional historical particulars provide a resource for the interrogation, the witness is able to secure entitlement to the experiences referenced by the document, and by so doing he is able to open up those references to alternative readings. However definite, the referential details of a document do not act as a foundation for the inquiry so much as they function as one set of resources among many to be used as part of the collective, and contentious, work of building an official history.

Nields's reading of the document closes with a question to North concerning what the $1 million was for. This question may be loaded in the sense that it is backed by as yet unmentioned documentary resources that can be invoked to challenge or confirm North's answer, but formally it gives North an opportunity to explicate an intention for the monetary figure, an intention whose place in the story of the Hawk transaction has yet to be established for the record.

Nields repeatedly pursues the question of what the $1 million was "for" in the face of various avowals by North not to recall the details of the transaction. After several such iterations, he refers to General Secord's earlier testimony as possibly in conflict with what North is able to recall "generally":

Nields: Now our records reflect that one million dollars was actually de*pos*-ited into Lake Resources on the *Twen*tieth of November. (3.8) Which is also earlier than Mister Secord testified was the first time when he had any obligations whatever with respect to transporting merchandise. And I need to *ask* you this question, it's an important question, (2.5) Was there any understanding or discussion that a million dollars would be deposited in the Lake *Re*sources account for the benefit of the Contras?[31]

At this point it becomes clear that the repetitive interrogation has not simply gone after more detail from North's immediately preceding account. Instead, Nields's recitation of the committee's records and his juxtaposition of North's present testimony with Secord's earlier statements enables him to suggest a narrative contrary to North's. This interrogatory narrative includes a set of references that were not mentioned in North's earlier accounts of the $1 million deal. Nields first cites "our records," as authority for inserting the $1 million deposit into a chronology of dates and events, and he argues that, according to Secord, the deposit was made before any "obligations" pertaining to the arms transaction. Nields then re-asks the question, explicitly framed as an "important question," and—for the first time—links that question to the determination of an alternative purpose for those funds: aiding the contras.

As a procedure for going back over prior testimony the documentary method of interrogation enables the interrogator to request clarifications and elaborations, and it also provides him an opportunity for challenging that testimony by citing recorded particulars that index a counterversion of the events in question. This method iterates a recognizable selection of previously used historical significations, enabling the interrogator to re-cast the pragmatic import of those terms, first, in light of the immediately preceding testimony, and, second, by juxtaposing it with other evidence. This method of interrogation also informs the witness about the evidenti-ary particulars to which his testimony is being held accountable.[32]

The witness is thus enjoined to collaborate in the telling of a story that extends and elaborates his previous version in unknown and potentially hazardous ways. We can also see that, to a considerable extent, the rela-tionship between the teller and the recipient of the story is inverted: the witness's entitlements to *his* narrative become circumscribed by his be-coming a recipient to a version purveyed by the interrogator and docu-mented by the witness's own writings. As noted, interrogation involves a kind of collusive relationship between interrogator and witness, but in this case it is complicated by a kind of collusion between the interrogator and the witness-as-writer of an evidentiary document, which puts pressure on the presently testifying witness to own up to or disavow authorship of the text the interrogator now controls. The question is, which of the two au-thors (the one whose text the interrogator reads or the one whose text the witness presents again) will establish the story line? This question has no set answer. Instead, the context of narrative elements that establish the story line is emplotted in a turn-by-turn exchange between interrogator and witness.

MINIMAL READINGS

Although documentary exhibits provide interrogators with leverage for prying admissions from an obstinate witness, the witness is far from de-fenseless. One way a witness can resist the evidentiary force of the docu-mentary method of interrogation is to treat an exhibit in Derridean fashion as a textual artifact divorced from anything specifically recalled about the original situation.[33] This divorce between text and authorial intention sets up the theoretical conception of a "social text" with its meaning deter-mined by the open-ended variety of situations in which a text may be read or used.[34] Here, we are suggesting something further, that when such texts are featured in an interactional struggle the social moorings of meaning are no less contingent than are the psychological moorings of authorship. Un-der such circumstances, textual exhibits enable readers, including in the

witness's case "the author himself," to position himself by means of the
text's authority and, in a sense, to efface his own "psychology" in favor of
the text's anonymous sensibility. Records were presented to North not only
to document facts known to the committee, but, in Nields's words, to "jog
his memory" of the actual events documented by the records in an indeterminate or fragmentary way. North's memory was rarely jogged, and on
several occasions he explicated the meaning of committee documents not
as transitive indices of his biographical experiences but as mere texts (or
merely legible texts) whose present meanings stood proxy for his recollections. He was able to do so plausibly (or at least contestably so) by treating
selected details of a record as trivial elements of a scene that were neither
memorable in themselves nor usable as recognitional keys to more memorable details. For example, in the course of an interrogation concerning CIA
involvement in one of the covert arms shipments to Iran, the following
exchange occurred:

Nields: . . . and the other thing that you did was to involve officials at the CIA.
(3.8)

(1)→ North: I think we did use communications support from the CIA, that's correct.=

(2)→ Nields: =Well you in fact uh- uh, you contacted uh Mister Clarridge didn't
you? (1.6)

(3)→ North: I ge- *yes* I did.

(4)→ Nields: And in fact you, uh went out to the CIA and spent uh virtually all the
day Saturday there. (1.6)

(5)→ North: What was that date? (3.2)

(6)→ Nields: I believe it's the twenty-third.
(Nields): °November eighty-five,° (6.0)
Nields: ((throat clear)) You might want to check exhibit forty-six. (26.0)
North: °(let's see, that's the twenty-third,)° (3.5)

(7)→ North: That is cor*rect*. ((throat clear))
Nields: You spent most of the day on the twenty-third at the CIA.
North: Yes.
Nields: And that was Mist- with Mister Clarridge. (2.4)

(8)→ North: Um, I'm sure that it was with Mister Clarridge, perhaps others, but he
certainly did clear me in, because his signature's right there.
Nields: And uh, indeed you re*turned* to the CIA the following day.

(9)→ North: On Sunday? (I'll) take your word for it. ((North looks through notebook))

(10)→ North: I *did*.[35]

In this instance, North responds to Nields's initial question with a spontaneous recollection, one given without the apparent aid of written notes
or records (arrow 1). (By such a characterization, we are not suggesting that
North had not, in fact, studied the relevant documents beforehand.) However, in the next turn (2), Nields locally exploits the terms of North's confirmation to build an interrogative statement of fact that challenges, and offers to correct, what North has just avowed ("Well you in fact . . . contacted
uh Mister Clarridge didn't you?"). North confirms in an interesting way (3):
"I ge- *yes* I did." We hear him to be cutting off the word "guess" and
replacing it with a more definite expression of confirmation. This in-
course adjustment from a conditional to a definite recollection seems designed to concede "spontaneously" to a documented fact that the interrogator has adumbrated. In a small way, North maintains his entitlement to
tell of his meeting with Clarridge while momentarily yielding to the terms
of Nields's question. Rather than withholding confirmation until the evidence is read, he embeds the "fact" within his biography as an acknowledged action ("I did"). Nields follows with further elaboration of the details of this "fact" (4), again phrased in the form of a declaration awaiting
confirmation; at this point, North yields entirely to the terms of a document
not yet exhibited. He asks, "What was that date?" (5). This position on his
part stands in marked contrast to the direct confirmation he had made
earlier, and it momentarily reverses the interrogative order. North is asking
Nields to give a calendrical formulation that specifies a set of details about
his (North's) past. Not only does this formulation (temporarily) reverse the
order of interrogative questioning and answering,[36] but, more important, it
shifts the locus of North's biography. Nields provides a tentative response
to North's request (6), and at this point he initiates a lengthy inspection of
an exhibit. North now orients to a documentary source, and he couches the
confirmation that he eventually produces ("That is correct." [7]) within
that document's reading. Despite his being a central character in the story
being told, he no longer relies on his unique biographical access. North's
unsettled "memory" finds a (potentially dangerous) resting place, and his

situation is reminiscent of Barthes's "vertigo" when faced with a photograph of himself in a situation he cannot remember:

> One day I received from a photographer a picture of myself which I could not
> remember being taken, for all my efforts; I inspected the tie, the sweater, to
> discover in what circumstances I had worn them; to no avail. And yet, *be-*
> *cause it was a photograph* I could not deny that I had been *there* (even if I did
> not know *where*). This distortion between certainty and oblivion gave me a
> kind of vertigo, something of a "detective" anguish (the theme of *Blow-Up*
> was not far off); I went to the photographer's show as to a police investiga-
> tion, to learn at last what I no longer knew about myself.[37]

While immersed in the details of his own past, a past no longer controlled
by his own recollections, North orients to the exhibit as an anonymous
reader. He does not, for instance, use it to touch off a vivid recollection of
his weekend at the CIA. Instead, his responses amount to a reading of the
surface features of the record. He confirms his meeting with Clarridge not
by recounting its details, but by citing the signature on the exhibit (8), and
he confirms what Nields asserts about his having returned to the CIA the
following day by orienting to the references on subsequent pages (9, 10).
Unlike the earlier "I did" (3), North's latest confirmation (10) is visibly and
sequentially embedded in an inspection of the record. It is expressed in no
less definite a way, however, and for all practical purposes it confirms the
"fact" that Nields had presented to him. The documentary locus of the
recollection, however, is far from irrelevant to the way the past is reconstructed from interrogation. To appreciate what such reconstruction can
involve, consider another instance when North reads a text where he is
accountably the author:

North: if my notes are accurate and I made that notation of the eighteenth
    on the eighteenth, the idea has at least occurred to *me* as early es the
    eighteenth. . . .[38]

Here, we see an autobiographical account ("the idea has at least occurred
to *me*") recollected not through the speaker's privileged access to events in
his own past, but through a reading of a text. Although the reader acknowledges that the text was written in his hand, authorship is irrelevant to the

reading he supplies. The "me" of November 18, 1985, is a referential figure in the text whose relationship to the speaker's biography is treated as the accountable "me," that is, a logically required figure derived from an examination of evidence at hand rather than situated in a personal reminiscence.

That a witness can address the interrogator's questions by reciting "what anybody can read off of the surface of a document" raises an interesting possibility that bears on the work of assembling conventional histories. The shift in position from author-character to documentary reader signals a reversal of the terms of conventional historical work. Here, the witness opts for the referential order of a historical record ("What was that date?"), rather than supplying a story organized around a storyteller's unique entitlements. While this referential congruence between conventional history and testimonial evidence eliminates problems of converting members' references into documentary references, it is bought at the price of gaining nothing unique or revelatory from the witness. Notice also that Nields's initial invocation of a specific time reference ("all the day Saturday") appeals to the terms of a participant's access to the event in question, namely, as an event lived through and thus memorable in terms of "a day within a week" or "the weekend." North's response ("What was that date?") does not follow Nields's lead; instead, it shifts attention away from a remembered weekend toward the documentary basis of Nields's reference. By merely restating what the committee members can already read from the record, North temporarily aligns himself with the terms of the committee's conventional historical mission, but at the same time his doing so disrupts their reflexive use of documents for eliciting historically useful testimony. In effect, by not supplementing the text with any recollections beyond what the interrogator already can read from it, North effectively recalls nothing and "becomes simply a conduit for the admission of stale evidence, whose reliability can never be tested . . . by cross-examination."[39]

Such readings do not demonstrate that the documents in question were originally written to facilitate plausible deniability. Rather, they leave the issue *specifically undecidable.* What they accomplish is to further maximize an epistemic divorce between documentary references and the witness's spontaneous, unrefreshed narratives. Although the witness confirms that the document's references are biographically relevant, they are assimilated to biography in only the most minimal and superficial fashion. In terms of the "hostile native"-archaeologist metaphor suggested in chapter 2, the native allows the archaeologist to piece together the fragmentary artifacts while disclaiming any special entitlement to an understanding more intimate than what can be merely deduced from the surface of those artifacts. At the same time, he holds his "native privilege" in reserve as a resource for selectively acknowledging or failing to acknowledge the biographical circumstances of the fragments unearthed at the investigatory site.

ASYMMETRIC READINGS

The procedures for co-reading evidentiary documents discussed earlier were important for establishing and publicly demonstrating what counted as recognizable identities, references, and facts. Facts, identities, references, and meanings were established for all practical purposes by fixing the particulars on the record in a collaborative and public reading. Typically, the interrogator led the way by characterizing the text, its authorship, the circumstances of its writing, its references, what it said, etc., and asking the witness to confirm those particulars and their sense. Although the initiative for such readings tended to reside with the interrogator, the confirmation of his readings required a reciprocal action by the witness, and the witness was able to, and often did, contest and modify the reading. In that sense, co-reading was symmetrical—openly and demonstrably enabled by both parties to the dialogue. Not all readings of documents in testimony, however, were a matter of reading aloud and reading together. Both parties to the interrogation expressed suspicions about the actual or possible documentary background of the spoken dialogues they were generating. Specifically, these suspicions concerned the use of prepared notes and undisclosed records as textual resources for questions and answers. In such circumstances, writings played a role other than as public evidence for corroborating or contradicting a witness's utterances. Instead, they were suspected to be, and investigated as, resources that violated the apparent spontaneity of the interrogative dialogue. A conspicuous instance of conflict over the asymmetric reading of documents occurred on the third day of North's testimony, shortly after Arthur Liman, counsel for the Senate majority, began his interrogation. Liman interrupted a line of questions to challenge North about a "book" he apparently was "looking at" (this challenge apparently is related to Inouye's question to North two days earlier [see transcript, p. 203] about whether he was reading from a "prepared text"):

(1)→ Liman: . . . On the 21st you did, in fact, discuss with Admiral Poindexter the problem of the diversion. Is that so? I'll tell you—you're looking at a book there. What is the book, sir?

(2)→ North: The book is made up of notes that I have made in trying to prepare with counsel for this hearing.

Liman: And—

North: It includes

(3)→ Sullivan: Don't tell him what it includes.

(4)→ Liman: Well, I think if a witness is looking at something that, I as counsel, am entitled to see what he's refreshing his recollection on.

Sullivan: I think you're wrong. That's a product of lawyers working with clients.

Liman: And you think that a witness is entitled to read something and that we're not entitled to see what he is reading?

(5)→ Sullivan: He is entitled to use his notes and to preserve the attorney/client privilege. Everything in that book is a product of the attorney/client and work product privilege, Mr. Liman. And you know that.

(6)→ Liman: Are you able to recall your conversation with Admiral Poindexter on the 21st about the diversion without looking at that book?

Sullivan: That's none of your business either. You just ask him the questions.

Soon afterward, Inouye scolded Sullivan for shouting and instructed North to answer the question. Sullivan again told North not to answer, and Liman then rephrased the question.

Liman: Lieutenant, do you recall testifying as recently as yesterday and the day before that on the 21st of November you told Admiral Poindexter that you had gotten rid of all the memos relating to the diversion.

(7)→ Sullivan: May we see the transcript that you're referring to. If you're trying to impeach him with yesterday's transcript, I want the page and line, please, Mr. Chairman. That's the only fair way to do it.

(8)→ Liman: Mr. Chairman, if he recalls, I'm entitled to have his answer.

Inouye: Please answer.[40]

Two related disputes occur during these hostile flurries, the first when Liman challenges North about a "book" he is "looking at" and Sullivan defends North's right to do so, the second, shortly thereafter, when Sullivan demands that Liman recite the transcript that he apparently is using as a basis for prompting North. In both cases, one party demands that the other read a document aloud, but in each case the epistemic significance and implications of the document differ radically.

At the beginning of the first excerpt (arrow 1), Liman mentions a meeting between North and Poindexter. He cuts himself off and observes that North is "looking at a book there," and he asks him to reveal what he is reading. North characterizes the book as "notes" prepared with his attorney (2). Sullivan cuts off North when he begins to say what the book "includes" (3). At this point, Liman argues that he is entitled to see "what he's refreshing his recollection on" (4), and Sullivan disputes this contention by saying that the notes are covered by the attorney-client privilege. Liman does not press the point, but he goes on to ask North to recall the discussion with Poindexter on November 21, "without looking at that book" (6). With this challenge, he attempts to isolate North's "recall" from the carefully designed defensive text prepared by the witness's legal staff, placing it in a free space and holding it accountable to the committee's documentary evidence. This challenge is akin to a schoolteacher's demand that students clear their desks of books and notes before taking a test designed to examine what the students know, or at least can write, as "free" individuals. In an inversion of Derrida's insistence that the intelligibility of a text may be cut loose from the circumstances of its authorship, Liman insists that a witness's speech can and should be cut loose from an anchoring source provided by a writing.[41] Instead, it should be anchored in a free subject, who responds unhesitatingly to the question on the floor and admits what he may not have been prepared in advance to say. In this case there is no absolute distinction between writing and speech. Instead, what we see is a pragmatic struggle to shift the witness's "memory" away from text and into the temporality of speech, all as moments in a dialogue. In this case, the maxim "the palest ink is clearer than the best memory"[42] takes on a peculiar sense; the very stability, iterability, and context independence of writing becomes suspicious because by answering from the book North defends against the possibility of making unguarded admissions and agreements that he may

regret. Moreover, since the line of questioning concerns what was shredded in anticipation of an investigation, the interrogator tries to prevail on
the witness to *say* what presumably is no longer documented and thus
cannot be leveraged by the documentary method of interrogation. In this
case, the free subject never emerges.

A related, though in some respects distinct, set of relevancies is raised by
Sullivan's objection when Liman mentions North's testimony at the hearings "yesterday and the day before." Sullivan demands that Liman recite
the lines of transcript that he apparently is using as a documentary basis for
his question (7). Liman does not comply with this objection. Instead, he
insists that he is "entitled" to have the witness's answer to what he "recalls" (8). Again, Liman attempts to isolate the witness's "unrefreshed"
recollection, but more than that he raises an ironic challenge to the way in
which North is answering. Before this sequence, Liman had asked North,
"You seem to be hesitating. Is there any doubt in your mind?" And Sullivan had replied, with a smile, "He's just looking for tricks, Mr. Liman."
By challenging North's deliberateness and then questioning his consultation of a "book," Liman not only attempts to shift North more thoroughly
into a spontaneous conversational exchange, but he is demonstrating for
the audience that the witness may be concocting answers strategically to
protect against "damaging" inferences and interrogative pursuits. Sullivan's rejoinder, "He's just looking for tricks," and his later demand that
Liman reveal the documentary basis for his question suggest a warrant for
the witness's hesitancy and strategic orientation; the interrogator is, after
all, a lawyer, and one known to be an especially astute cross-examiner, and
the witness must take care not to be caught out in contradicting a literal
reading of what he may have said earlier. Regardless of Sullivan's motive
for demanding that Liman read from the transcript, it is clear that he is
demanding a reciprocal reading of North's earlier testimony rather than a
fresh extension of that testimony prompted by mention of what he had said
before. Sullivan thus attempts to shift the focus of the interrogation to a
scholarly examination of "yesterday's testimony" in lieu of a fresh pursuit
"today" of what had been erased on or before November 21, 1986.

In sum, our analysis of this dialogic struggle, takes us through a thick
documentary field of juxtaposed moments: a "present testimony" framed
by a televised spectacle, a "book" of undisclosed notes somehow informing the testimony, a transcript of "yesterday's testimony," a described con-

versation between North and Poindexter "on November 21," and an indefinite collection of shredded documents relevant to North's and Poindexter's
conversation as well as to the present testimony. Each move in the present
testimony is a progression in and through this dense intertextual field, and
simultaneously each move works to establish the documentary significance and meaning of "the record" of the Iran-contra affair.

CONCLUSION

While retaining our focus on the spectacle of the televised interrogation of
a witness at a congressional hearing, we have suggested how the dialogical
interchange between interrogator and witness is situated within an intertextual field. It is fair to say that these textual "inscriptions" of testimony,
notes, and communications were crucial for linking the local site of interrogation to the temporally, spatially, and organizationally disparate sites
and actions that made up the historical conditions, topics, and consequences of the hearings.[43] "Inscription" offered no guarantees, however.
Our examination of particular interrogative attempts to forge linkages between documents and the immediate testimony indicates how such linkages were not predetermined by the existence of the records. In the case we
are examining, documents were "forged" with an explicit and admitted
purpose to anticipate and problematize the very sort of inquiry in which
they now served as evidence. Moreover, this forging of equivocal documents (and the accompanying shredding and redacting) was designed to be
"deniable" in detail, even when it was admitted in general. When these
features of documentary design are considered in light of the operations of
recall and the entitlements to experience that are warrantably, claimably,
and ordinarily featured in testimonies about the past, it becomes increasingly evident how the "ceremonial of truth" at the hearings became a re-
versible spectacle, a ceremony in which the resources of truth-finding
and truth-telling were turned into a machinery for producing an interminable and indeterminate spectacle of scholarship in which "nothing
much"—that is, a notable, reportable, accountable "nothing"—seemed to
take place.

CONCLUSION:

A CIVICS LESSON IN THE LOGIC

OF SLEAZE

As noted throughout these pages, a popular view of the 1987 Iran-contra hearings was that, in the end, nothing much seemed to have happened. In the years since then, this conclusion was underlined by the fact that no one was impeached, few criminal convictions occurred, and no significant government reforms were enacted. Despite occasional revelations coming out of the special prosecutor's criminal investigation, in the years after 1987, Iran-contra did not receive anything like the level of publicity that was given to North's testimony at the hearings.

Perhaps the basis for the conclusion that the Iran-contra hearings came to very little was that, despite some rather anxious moments, the two major figures in the executive branch survived the scandal. Although Ronald Reagan's popularity in the polls plummeted in the waning years of his presidency, after leaving office he faded from public view. Shortly after retiring, Reagan gave a rambling, tape-recorded deposition for the defense in John Poindexter's criminal trial, but this event was not shown on television and attracted limited public attention. He emerged briefly to give a speech at the 1992 Republican convention, which was warmly received by the audience. Late in 1994 he released a statement announcing that he had Alzheimer's disease. For cynical commentators this announcement seemed only fitting in light of his performance during the Iran-contra investigations, but it also contributed to a more general forgetting of questions about Reagan's culpability.

Former Vice President George Bush successfully fended off accusations that he had attended a number of briefings and planning sessions about the arms sales at the White House and that his staff was actively involved in North's and the CIA's Central America initiatives. To many commentators, Bush seemed disingenuous when he claimed that he had been out of the loop when the covert initiatives were under way, but efforts to confront him on the subject actually may have worked in his favor. During Bush's 1988 presidential campaign, CBS news anchor Dan Rather directly challenged his claims during a live TV interview, which erupted into a verbal fight after Bush objected to Rather's prosecutorial pursuit.[1] Bush apparently benefited from the confrontation, as Rather was given a large share of the blame for touching off an unseemly political dispute, while Bush's aggressive stance was cited as evidence that he was not the "wimp" that some opponents and political satirists suggested. The legacy of Iran-contra did not seem to haunt Bush during his successful campaign, nor did it seem to be a major reason for his defeat in 1992.

Iran-contra thus proved not to be "another Watergate." The reverse, in fact, seemed to occur as a spirit of forgetting retrospectively lightened the burden of history placed on the main Watergate culprits. Former President Richard Nixon certainly seemed to benefit from an official forgiveness and forgetting in the years after his resignation (occasional retrospectives on Watergate demonstrated that several of his former colleagues, including a few who served jail terms, also did reasonably well for themselves). Eulogies in the press and by key government officials after Nixon's death in 1994 abounded; even some members of Nixon's infamous enemies' list noted his image as a "statesman." Watergate was not entirely erased by such gestures of respect for the dead, however. As John Dean, who testified so crucially against Nixon, remarked, "Every historian who ever writes about Nixon will have to write that he was the first president who ever resigned. And then they are going to have to write why."[2] The publication of the diaries of former Nixon chief of staff H. R. Haldeman shortly after Nixon's death vividly reminded future historians that they will have at their disposal an immense, detailed archive of the daily affairs of the most heavily monitored president in U.S. history.[3]

The main characters in the Iran-contra affair did not emerge entirely unscathed either, but for the most part they avoided some of the more dire consequences that might have seemed in store for them when the scandal broke in 1986. Special prosecutor Lawrence Walsh's final report of his criminal investigation was released in 1994.[4] Walsh's investigation extended over seven years and cost millions of dollars. During the press conference accompanying the report's release, an embittered and weary Walsh reiterated a chronic theme when he complained of the White House's resistance to his requests for key documents. For the most part, the press reacted by concluding that the 2,500-page report contained few significant revelations.[5]

Walsh's report, and the earlier criminal trials of North and Poindexter, did not greatly modify the legacy of the hearings, even though they renewed questions about the former president's, vice president's, and several key cabinet officials' knowledge of the Iranian arms trades and the covert funding of the Central American counterrevolutionaries. Press coverage of the trials was far from sensational, and public interest in the news releases was short-lived and of little consequence for legislative initiatives. Prosecutors John Keker and Dan Webb reportedly cross-examined North, Poindexter, and other witnesses in an aggressive and effective way during their trials,[6] but the trials were not aired on television. North's subsequent conviction on three of twelve felony charges and Poindexter's conviction on five charges were overturned by a federal appeals court, mainly because of complications arising from the partial immunity clause that covered their testimony at the hearings.[7] Several other key figures, including Poindexter, McFarlane, Elliot Abrams (the former assistant secretary of state), Clair George (deputy director and chief of operations at the CIA), Alan Fiers (former head of the CIA's Central American Task Force), Duane Clarridge (former CIA chief of European operations), and Caspar Weinberger (former secretary of defense) were eventually indicted, most of them for lying to Congress as part of their participation in one or another aspect of the coverup. Of these, McFarlane, Abrams, George, and Fiers were found guilty, but President Bush pardoned them shortly before he left office. In an unusual move, Bush also pardoned Clarridge and Weinberger before their trials. Walsh did not react kindly to these pardons, as they closed off his last hope of cross-examining witnesses (including Bush himself) who might have revealed fresh information. Suspicions about Bush's motives were raised in the press, and it was suggested that the pardons would leave a stain on the history of his presidency.[8] This remained to be seen, as Bush and his one-term presidency rapidly faded from public concern.

Despite all of these evidences of collective forgetting, Iran-contra did leave behind some notable traces. The historical situation was nicely summarized by a former member of Walsh's investigative staff, who wrote, "if Iran-Contra never really took hold in this country, it never really disappeared, either, and as 1993 comes to an end it is reëmerging with a vengeance."[9] Although it seems that the individuals implicated in the Iran-contra affair got off lightly, and that the event itself seems largely forgotten, in another sense it has indeed reemerged with a vengeance. It would be impossible to isolate all of its political effects, but it seems clear that Iran-contra has assumed a place together with Watergate and other highly publicized hearings and televised trials in a unique corpus of precedent-setting cases. The elements of televised spectacle so perspicuous during the Iran-contra hearings—especially the dramatic interrogation of the key witness—increasingly have become part of an entertainment package through which U.S. politics and civics are conducted. As we write, an investigation is under way of President Clinton's financial dealings while he served as governor of Arkansas. The very name of it—"Whitewater" (after the locale of a failed Arkansas savings and loan bank featured in the story)—connotes "another Watergate." Although the financial deals involved in this case were alleged to have occurred before Clinton became president, the scandal and its investigation are framed explicitly by reference to Watergate and Iran-contra. Clinton's administration is charged with a cover-up of damaging information, and his defenders countercharge that zealots in the opposition party have manufactured a scandal in the hopes of deposing a president they were unable to defeat in an election. Congressional Republicans have been accused of carrying forward a vendetta to get the Democrats for having used committee hearings during the Reagan and Bush administrations to weaken the presidency and oppose presidential nominations to the Supreme Court. As those before him had done, Clinton appointed a special prosecutor, and congressional hearings were undertaken. As was the case with Watergate and Iran-contra, participants in the investigation moved to establish nonpartisan auspices in the face of obvious party alignments, although Whitewater involved a novel twist when a panel of federal judges, headed by the same Reagan appointee who had written the majority opinion for the appeals court decision that overturned Oliver North's criminal convictions, ruled that the special prosecutor appointed by Clinton should resign. In the interest of objectivity, the panel appointed a judge who had served as solicitor general under former President Bush.[10]

Clinton also has been named in a sexual harassment lawsuit filed by an Arkansas woman, Paula Jones, who claimed that when Clinton was governor of Arkansas, he had shown his penis to her as a way of expressing an overt invitation that she refused to accept. Jones alleged that she could prove the truth of her accusation by identifying the offending member, but thus far no such crucial test has been scheduled. Such an exposure of the most private of presidential parts would perhaps provide the ultimate profanation of the Chief Executive, producing a high point (and perhaps a death blow) in the history of phallocentrism. Nevertheless, Jones's lawsuit created consternation among many of the feminists who earlier championed Anita Hill for testifying openly about her alleged sexual harassment by Clarence Thomas. Hill testified on nationwide television during the Senate confirmation hearings on Thomas's Supreme Court nomination, and at the time Thomas's supporters objected bitterly that Hill had been recruited by his liberal opponents. In the present case, Clinton supporters objected that Jones had been propped up by some of the same right-wing politicians who cried foul during Hill's testimony and that the Jones lawsuit was concocted in a transparent attempt to embarrass, distract, and weaken the president. Even if in these particular cases the investigators may be justified on other grounds, it is difficult not to conclude that charges of scandal, and public investigations of them, have proved to be potent political tools.

Aside from congressional tribunals, televisual spectacles of criminal hearings have also proved to be a robust source of entertainment, although "entertainment" does not adequately characterize the depth of public interest in highly publicized soap opera trials increasingly covered live on television. Several trials aired on a program called *Court TV* have become extremely popular in the United States, so much so that commentators speculated that the public obsession with the murder trial of actor and former football star O. J. Simpson would distract many citizens from other political and national events (including the 1994 elections) and perhaps even lower the nation's economic productivity. In this case, the spectacle was heightened by the celebrity status of the defendant, as well as by the trial's occurrence at a time when public interest in "real" courtroom drama had been raised to a high pitch. Simpson's celebrity lawyers showed themselves adept at mobilizing popular media attention as part of the defense. Not only did they build their case on legal precedent, but they called into play the images and figures of racial injustice made prominent during the trial of white Los Angeles police officers accused of beating a black man, Rodney King (an event recorded by a bystander's videotape camera and replayed countless times on television). The not guilty verdict in the King trial touched off major disturbances in Los Angeles.[11] Simpson's legal staff hired an investigator who was prominent during the King trial, made allegations that one of the Los Angeles Police Department detectives who testified for the prosecution had acted out of racist motives, and in many other ways played off of media attention and the televisual precedents of *Court TV.*

In brief, the U.S. public has witnessed an intensifying series of spectacular trials and tribunals in the aftermath of Iran-contra: the Robert Bork and Clarence Thomas confirmation hearings for U.S. Supreme Court appointees, the Rodney King trials, Whitewater, the Simpson case, and others. Each of these encapsulated a civics lesson (and/or antilesson) about legal philosophy, gender relations, sexual impropriety, racial injustice, wealth, and political power, and all of them together have become a substantive, and increasingly routine, part of the political and cultural landscape. This trend might be described in Weberian fashion as "the routinization of scandal" in U.S. politics, although the phenomenon is by no means limited to the United States. A massive scandal in Italy, dubbed *Tangentopoli* (bribe city), has so far resulted in the arrest and detention of dozens of leading government and corporate officials and continues to haunt Italian politics. In Britain, where the tabloid press routinely celebrates government sex scandals and royal family soap operas an inquiry—in many respects reminiscent of the Iran-contra hearings, but without the publicity and live telecasts—has investigated secret government decisions contravening official policy that allowed private arms sales to Iraq during the Thatcher administration.[12] The mobilization and management of publicity during such trials and tribunals has created special problems, such as (especially in the United States) how to select jurors who have not formed opinions about a widely publicized event, how to manage increasing demands for electronic recording and dissemination of previously closed events, and how to maintain the appearance of nonpartisanship in an event that has unmistakable political overtones.

The most persistent reminder of Iran-contra has been the rise of Oliver North as a contracultural figure in U.S. politics. Not only did he emerge relatively unscathed from the investigations of Iran-contra, but to a large extent he converted his troubles before Congress and the special prosecutor into further evidence of a heroic defiance of bureaucratic authority.

With the aid of hindsight, it can be said that North launched a political movement on July 7, 1987, when he first appeared on-camera during the Iran-contra hearings. It was at that time that his telegenic presence, rhetorical opposition to his congressional interrogators, and populist appeals were broadcast with stunning clarity. After the hearings, North's effort to raise funds for his defense against Walsh's criminal investigation was highly successful. His talents as a fund-raiser already had been recognized before the scandal broke, when he was recruited to work with a "private" fund-raising group set up by the White House to circumvent congressional restrictions on aid to the contras. The hearings became a platform for demonstrating his rhetorical abilities, and he went on to become a leading fund-raiser for right-wing political causes. His campaigns in the late 1980s and early 1990s on behalf of the North Legal Defense Fund, his Family Safety Trust, and the Freedom Alliance (a fund-raising group that enlisted him) raised some $9 million, more than enough for his legal and security purposes. Financial contributions came mainly in relatively small amounts from individuals, rather than in large allotments from political organizations and major corporations. North also amassed a small personal fortune from the sales of his best-selling autobiography, *Under Fire,* and from the fees he commanded on the lecture circuit.

And in 1994, Oliver North, the (anti)hero of Iran-contra, secured the Republican nomination to campaign for a U.S. Senate seat in Virginia. The subsequent election race, with North running in a field of several candidates, including the sex-scandal-ridden Democratic incumbent, was one of the most expensive and well-publicized in U.S. history. North was his party's nominee for the Senate seat, despite the fact that former President Reagan, several Iran-contra principals, Virginia Senator John Warner, and many other prominent Republicans endorsed alternative candidates and cast aspersions on his honesty and trustworthiness.[13] Nevertheless, after his nomination, Republican leaders officially endorsed his candidacy rather than divide the party. In the end, North lost the election after having led in the polls up until the final few weeks of the campaign. Poll results and retrospective commentaries indicated that doubts about his character and honesty were among the most frequently given reasons for voting against him, despite his and his campaign's efforts to counteract such charges and accuse his opponents of lying about his record.

Despite his election loss, North is likely to remain prominent in U.S.

politics. His charisma, of course, is far from universally appreciated. Some journalists and spokespersons for the political left describe him in vitriolic terms.[14] More moderate pundits and spokespersons also have weighed in against him by voicing doubts about his truthfulness and fears about the divisive effect of speeches in which he denounced the federal government and national press establishment.[15] In an especially cruel blow to this man of arms, a Virginia judge denied his application for renewal of a gun license on the ground that the criminal convictions for obstructing congressional investigations (despite the fact that they were overturned) showed that he was a person of bad character. North's supporters were characterized by the mainstream press as a constituency of Christian fundamentalists and other "far-right" elements of the U.S. citizenry. However, many people who assumed that North had lied, or even that he was a pathological liar, nonetheless considered him a hero. The two attributions—liar and hero—were not incompatible. Indeed, in North's case, a definite method seemed to be part of his myth. Heroes in myth and drama, and sometimes in nonfiction, often secure their heroic status by deceiving enemies.[16] As we noted in our analysis of North's testimony at the hearings, the audience did not judge the credibility of his testimony on the basis of the truth or falsity of particular statements. Instead, the key issue became whether Congress (and especially its "liberal establishment") should be considered as in league with the nation's enemies. It came down to a question, "Who would you trust with the truth?"

THE LOGIC OF SLEAZE

House majority counsel John Nields announced early on in his questioning of North that the "principal purpose of the hearings" was to "replace secrecy and deception with disclosure and truth." It soon became clear that any possibility of attaining that purpose required the collaborative production of a dialogue that would enable an unambiguous resolution of those differences. At every turn, the effort required a bipartisan effort to respect suprapolitical and impersonal standards of truth-telling and disclosure: a recognition of legal authorization, a disclosure of required information, and a judgment of how relevant laws and policies applied to the case even when such judgment might be damaging to partisan interests. Ideally, the proper conduct of the investigation would exemplify the proper conduct of government. Like the Watergate hearings, the investigation would be a civics lesson in which bipartisan cooperation would triumph over secret agendas and unlicensed operations; it would be an occasion for affirming the maxim that "trust was the essential ingredient, the lubricant that made possible the workings of a democracy."[17]

Numerous commentators derived the historical lesson from the Watergate hearings that "the system worked" to cleanse itself of individual misconduct. The rule of law was reaffirmed in the face of abuses of power.[18] A counternarrative to the liberal evocation of constitutionality also was sustained, which held that Nixon's political enemies, after having lost decisively in the 1972 presidential election, found an alternative method for deposing the chief executive.[19] Although both of these narratives were salient during and after the Iran-contra hearings, in our view the relevant lesson of the hearings became something else altogether. During the hearings, liberal evocations of truth and trust were opposed point-by-point by counternarratives of "present danger" and equivocal denials grounded in missing or inconclusive documents. No clear bipartisan resolution occurred. Instead, many partisan squabbles ensued.

For those who adhered to the liberal-constitutionalist stance so clearly invoked by spokesmen for the committee majority at the outset of North's interrogation, the hearings unfolded as an increasingly disturbing spectacle. Many onlookers and commentators remained convinced that a scandalous truth had been obscured and covered up by a barrage of slick maneuvers performed by sleazy characters in the administration before a somnambulent and complicit audience. Unable to obtain significant convictions or legislative changes, indignant opponents could only denounce the administration as a disreputable operation.

The increasingly common charge of sleaze in higher government and business circles implies any of a number of misdeeds, corrupt operations, and modes of dishonesty. The term can refer to clear-cut violations, but often it implies a more diffuse taint, or sometimes an entire climate of corruption. The particular meaning of sleaze we find most pertinent is relatively restricted: as an informal matter of inference or rumor, a person or group is known to have behaved in a dubious fashion, but no official proof obtains. Sometimes, as in the cases of former presidents Ronald Reagan and George Bush, the determination by official inquiries that there is no *proof* that the administrative conduct in question violated any laws is cited by the accused parties and their allies as confirmation that the charges are groundless and ideologically motivated (a tactic sometimes called "reverse McCarthyism"). In Oliver North's case, the fact that he was convicted of criminal charges and then acquitted on appeal supplied both his detractors and supporters with ammunition. His opponents were able to cite the convictions as evidence of his bad character, while he and his supporters could cite the fact that he was exonerated after long and expensive investigations by his enemies. In this case, and many others, the charges and countercharges resolve in terms of a "friend-enemy grouping," which divides roughly along conventional party lines. (It should be noted, however, that denunciations of North by prominent Republicans were treated as especially telling testimony against him.)

Sleaze has certain obvious disadvantages as a theoretical term. It is an epithet, a charge, an attribution that often remains at the level of "mere suspicion"—a matter of opinion. To claim that an act or person is sleazy often is to take up a position in an ongoing controversy that has little prospect of definitive resolution. It is a fine term in a heated discussion among colleagues and co-conspirators, but it is question-begging when employed on occasions in which legal and formal standards of proof and decorum apply. At a more subtle level, similar objections can be made about more respectable theoretical attributions of motive or power. In either case, however, the theorist's problem is a member's resource, and social theorists' inability to agree on or otherwise to stabilize uses of terminology is symptomatic less of the poverty of social science than of substantive properties of the social world. Like many of the general issues discussed in preceding chapters, the concept of sleaze, if we can be permitted to dignify this term with the status of a concept, points to substantive sources of frustration and uncertainty in the conduct of the hearings. Accordingly, it is possible to describe the practical circumstances and institutional conditions that support charges of sleaze.

Charges of sleaze were most readily aimed at figures like Edwin Meese, even though the accusations slid off their target. Meese, the nation's chief law enforcement officer under Reagan, managed to get through his Senate confirmation hearings despite suspicions that he cashed in on government connections while serving as one of Reagan's advisers when Reagan was governor of California. In the aftermath of the Iran-contra affair, despite suspicions about Meese's role in a cover-up, special prosecutor Walsh decided that insufficient evidence had been gathered to indict him. Charges of sleaze feed upon such combinations of continuing suspicion and legal (or quasilegal) irresolution. Meese's televisual appearance also provided sleaze with a virtual physiognomy. Compared to the crisp and angular North, with his military uniform and upright bearing, Meese presented a more rounded and jowly figure, combined with a less resolute voice. We are reminded, at a much milder level, of Barthes's description of Thauvin, an aging professional wrestler cast in the role of the villain, who "displays in his flesh the characters of baseness" and whose appearance in the ring encourages the crowd to "be frenetically embroiled in an idea of Thauvin which will conform entirely with this physical origin: his actions will perfectly correspond to the essential viscosity of his personage."[20] In Meese's case, physiognomy was accented by a name that seemed to combine the very sound of sleaze with a poetic pluralization of mouse. The consonantal slide across the first phoneme of the word sleaze onomatopoetically suggests a viscosity that enables slippage between the binary poles of decisive factual or moral resolution. It takes its place among a family of words connoting slippery slopes, slithery and slimy characters, slick operators, and moral slouches.

Sleaze is more than a negative attribute of particular persons, bodies, and actions, however. It can be described at a more systematic level as a lubricant that flows through the cracks of legal-rational authority. In theoretical terms, it can be given a functional role analogous to that of trust. In classic sociological theory, trust fills in the essential gaps between stable normative order and situated conduct; it licenses interpretations of, and discretionary departures from, the letter of the law in the pursuit of equity and civility.[21] Unlike the classic role of trust in the collaborative spectacle of truth, sleaze enables actors to exploit equivocality and indeterminacy when asked to comply with the binary terms of moral regulations. Where trust is cited as the quintessential mode of precontractual solidarity, sleaze refers us to inadmissible machinations that make the system work through secret deals, official lies, and transgressive alliances. Trust and sleaze parallel each other so precisely that the very assertion "Trust me!" invokes the one, while provoking suspicions of the other. However, the charge of sleaze signals more than an absence or violation of trust. Its constitutive role can be likened to that of the disciplinary power which Foucault locates at the extremities of modern institutions of legal and rational authority.[22] Like a

Foucauldian "regime of truth," a *regime of sleaze* is constituted at a level of fine detail by actions and transactions occurring at countless locales. In a regime of truth, disciplinary coercions transform what once was unorganized into overtly visible and manageable machine-readable data and extend centers of power/knowledge into the fine details of intimate conduct. Sleaze works in a more obscure fashion as a lubricant that enables slippage and reduction of friction at points of contact within the interior channels of the machinery of state.

Sleaze is the attribute of a specific (or "definite") indefiniteness. By definition, it denotes a material network that is slight, flimsy, or insubstantial, but which nonetheless hangs together like a cloth of tawdry materials with a loose and careless weave. In contrast to a fabric of trust, which binds together a consensual social order, or a network of power that enables the determinate projection of coercive surveillance, sleaze proves to be flimsier and more readily degraded by exposure to light. In the case before us, sleaze refers to characters and actions that lack "analyticity." Because they resist or elude efforts at establishing their stable and discretely bounded "positions," such characters and actions resist demonstrable resolution into right or wrong, true or false, good or bad, and related binary oppositions. In the socio-legal field, an accusation of sleaze is not easily translated into official sanctions against the subject of the accusation. To charge an official with sleaze is to express suspicions that may well turn out to resist more demanding methods of proof. The very procedural definiteness of legal determination provides sleaze with an institutional habitat, an unresolved position between the stock polarities of yes or no judgments. The sleazy character takes refuge in this shadowy space between strong suspicions and formal convictions by denying accusations until proven in a more exacting forum and by then interpreting the lack of such proof as personal (or administrative) vindication. Sleaze protects itself less by weaving a tissue of lies than by holding together a thin, flimsy, but legally defensible fabric of possibilities of doubtful—but *only* doubtful—veracity. When no smoking gun emerges, the figure accused of misdeeds can counterattack, throwing the charges back at the opponent as an indication of irrational hostility and political intent.

Sleaze is a modern expression for denouncing an abusive casuistry.[23] While charges of sleaze may be difficult to pin down with hard or direct evidence, thus remaining chronically contentious, irresolute, and subject to rival opinions, they are no less characteristic of a contemporary political/legal discourse than are more determinate charges. Accusations and modes of combating them slide past each other, while they reflexively reinforce an embedded logic of sleaze.

PRE-POSTMODERN POLITICS

Although far from novel, the logic of sleaze may be especially salient in a pre-postmodern era characterized by a desperate adherence to modernist conceptions of truth and rationality, and to the institutions that enforce them, while at the same time bearing witness to their disruption and decay. According to Yaron Ezrahi, this condition occurs at the tail end of a transition from the monarchical spectacle through a modern era of technologically mediated virtual participation:

> the increasingly pronounced distrust of the possibility of fixed neutral points of view, the resubjectivization of the "attestive individual gaze," the increasingly acknowledged contributions of observers to "making" what they see, and the repoliticization of the Enlightenment synthesis which underlie the modern enactment of democratic politics. Postmodernism in this context is largely the spread of reflexive orientations which acknowledge the self-denying theatricality of democratic politics as an exchange of fictions of the politically real between virtually self-exposing political performers and their virtual critical witnesses.[24]

The postmodern spread of "reflexive orientations" in contemporary televisual politics is often epitomized with the example of the actor-president Reagan. The actor, assisted by a huge team of speechwriters, advertising experts, and press agents, performs on stage and is described by the press as a strategic performer.[25] Far from negating the effects of such strategies, however, the publicity redefines the terms under which effectiveness is judged. Cynically understood, political actors are judged on the engrossing and inspiring qualities of their performances and not on whether the things they say are true, realistic, or acceptable as policy. So, for example, prior to North's initial appearance before the cameras at the hearings, press commentators had been given advance notice of how he would answer the "key question" about presidential knowledge, and they revealed this answer to the audience. The drama shifted away from the question of what North would say to that of how he would perform his scripted testimony. Would he be convincing? Might he slip up? This sort of focus on performance has become a regular feature of political coverage. Shortly before presidential candidate George Bush began his speech at the 1988 Republican convention, TV commentators who had read an advance copy of the speech speculated on-camera about whether Bush would "appear presidential" when delivering it, and afterward the commentators dispassionately referred to the efforts of spin doctors to manage the audience response. The commentators explicitly referred to the speech writers who had composed the text and described how particular sound bites had been prepared to be extracted for use by the media. The transparency of stage management and strategy did not negate the effect of the speech; rather, it was part and parcel of how a recital by a would-be president was assessed.

An emphasis on performance, impression management, and theatrical politics is far from novel. Consider such examples as Julius Caesar's battle stories in which he features as a hero of mythic proportions, the presidential campaign of William Henry Harrison (a patrician general nicknamed "Tippecanoe" after a 1811 battle, who was portrayed by his staff as a log cabin president), or Prime Minister Winston Churchill's wartime use of actors to record his speeches for radio broadcasts.[26] In these cases a notable difference exists between the impression created for the public and the concealed facts of the matter later revealed by historians. This difference collapses, or at least becomes more complicated, in cases of reflexive media portrayals, where performances and strategies are transparently portrayed as such. No longer does a naive audience credulously trust a performance. Instead, the believability of the performance as a characteristic performance, not its representational truth, becomes the relevant evaluative criterion.

Familiar postmodernist themes can be invoked regarding the indistinguishability of fact and fiction, the stress on immediacy rather than consistency between present and past, and the rise of hybrid forms of docudrama, infotainment, and stage-managed politics. In this context, the familiar forms of critical explanation that cite media complicity and public credulousness are always ready to hand, as are the more totalizing pictures of a culture of simulation and spectacle.[27] One is tempted to conclude that truth is no longer part of the picture, and that the ancient binaries associated with accuracy, sincerity, and deception have collapsed. On the basis of this study we are reluctant to settle for such a totalizing picture. Consider, for example, a prototypical case in which a political candidate promises overtly and without qualification that there will be "no new taxes" if he is elected. Commentators may point out that the candidate is in no position to promise such a thing, and this may be well understood by most members of the audience. Nevertheless, if the opposing candidate remains silent, or makes a more qualified promise of the same sort (e.g., "I'll try as best I can to keep tax increases to a minimum."), it should be easy to judge which of the two candidates is performatively committed to resisting the inevitable pressures to raise taxes. The unqualified promise may surely turn out to be representationally false; yet it remains pragmatically indicative. The more honest promise in the interactional context will be heard as expressing relatively weak commitment.[28] Consequently, the promise may be assessed on a sliding scale of intensity, rather than being taken as a prediction of what the candidate will in fact do. Even so, the binary opposition—new taxes/no new taxes—is not entirely out of play. The candidate runs the risk of being contradicted later, as George Bush was when he agreed to a tax increase after silently mouthing his famous pledge not to do so during the 1988 campaign, and the opposition can be counted on to be ready to point out such contradictions. The risk may be worth taking, however, given confidence that an alleged contradiction can be mitigated or neutralized by citing unanticipated contingencies, so that the public, if the economic circumstances look favorable to the pledge at the time, will not care greatly. In this case, the logic of sleaze is not simply a corruption of the binary relation implied by the promise, but it has to do with the overt use of a binary function to express a degree of commitment along a sliding scale (or, as the case may be, a slippery slope). As a result, political actors can speak like absolutists while conducting their affairs as practical relativists (or, in some circumstances, applied deconstructionists).

THE TRANSPARENCY OF STRATEGIES

One of the more curious aspects of the Iran-contra affair was that some of the witnesses, and particularly North, described a series of strategic actions—including an entire fall-guy plan—that involved the concoction of a version of the scandal that would implicate North and Poindexter while permitting the president to disclaim knowledge of the most damaging actions. In accounts of strategic interaction and game theory, the masking of strategy is ordinarily felt to be essential to success.[29] A chess or poker player who reveals his or her strategy greatly weakens its effectiveness. In this case, the transparency of strategies did not negate their effects, but, rather, appeared to enhance their chance for success. This apparent paradox can be understood by examining the partial way in which strategies were revealed.

The revelation of strategy was partial and was yielded in the face of pressures not to get caught in a cover-up. North and Poindexter did not entirely reveal their hands at the hearings, and what they did disclose was cast into relief against a shredded background. Moreover, North denied vociferously that he was dissembling at the hearings and carrying forward the fall-guy plan, and Poindexter did the same, although in a less histrionic way. North would not say what he had shredded, despite persistent questioning on the subject, and he refused to acknowledge that he destroyed potentially significant evidence. He gave various reasons for shredding, suggesting it was a regular part of the day's work or an effort to avoid political damage (but not criminal liability) to the administration. However motivated, the shredding certainly set up North's and his colleagues' inability to recall just what was in the shredded documents. The claim that "the President did not know" about the diversion of funds to the contras thus retained an element of plausibility, even though it remained suspect. In the immediate context, it was not enough to figure that Reagan *must have* known. Rather, such knowledge required demonstration—an admission or documented evidence—that he signed his name or otherwise authorized the diversion. The single surviving copy of such an authorizing document—a facsimile without a signature or presidential mark—did not demonstrate such knowledge. Moreover, Poindexter testified that he did not explicitly solicit Reagan's approval, and he said actions were taken in this manner to preserve the president's deniability. According to this version, the president's denial of knowledge was sincere, as he did not literally authorize the diversion. He could be (and was officially) accused of a lax "management style," but not of a more direct involvement in events that might have led to impeachment proceedings or criminal indictments.

The plausibility of such denials is enhanced by a well-known organizational phenomenon. Subordinates often anticipate what the boss would want them to do without his directly ordering them to do it. Given the popular version of North as an overenthusiastic soldier, and of Reagan as a distracted, not fully involved executive, the idea that North routinely ran ahead of his orders seemed plausible enough. But, again, the possibility was alive at the hearings that this account itself was available as part of a defensive strategy. The difficulty here was that no clear-cut demarcation could be sustained among the authorization of deeds, the deeds themselves, and the testimonies about them. As North and Poindexter openly testified, their deeds were designed to facilitate denials of their authorization in later testimonies about such deeds. This was, in fact, *precisely how* they were authorized, and not by default of executive management.

Questions of authorization, responsibility, and deniability often come down to the exact words used in the immediate circumstances. Take the historical account of the murder of Thomas à Becket by four knights serving King Henry II.[30] King Henry is alleged to have said, in exasperation over Archbishop Becket's continued resistance to his designs on the church, "Will no one rid me of this turbulent priest?" The four knights took this complaint for an order and rode to Canterbury where they felled Becket. King Henry reacted to the subsequent outrage by walking barefoot through Canterbury and being flogged by monks as penance for the deed, but his repentance, while acknowledging some responsibility, left the king's original intention open to question. He did not give a formal order, nor is it obvious that the utterance should be assigned the illocutionary effect of an order, at least not when treated as an isolated statement.[31] Similarly, according to North's testimony, Reagan told him to be sure to keep the contras together "body and soul" at a time when congressional aid had been cut off. Given the absent records, and the indistinct recollections of what Reagan may otherwise have said or implied, it was possible to deny that Reagan intentionally *authorized* the particular actions that North and Poindexter undertook. At the same time, Poindexter and North were able to defend their actions as carrying out what they understood the president intended.

POSTMODERNITY AS TOPIC AND RESOURCE

A fundamental ambivalence associated with postmodern theory has to do with a portrayal of the unchecked hegemony of Western rationality permeating and reconstructing the capillary orders of discourse, body, sexuality, and civility, coupled with a tendentious celebration of the breakdown of those orders. It seems unclear whether this situation is one of desperation, immense freedom, or both. The result is a social theory that moves by fits and starts, sliding between the alternatives of radical antimetaphysics and the celebration of the schizophrenic multivocality of competing metaphysical systems (ontologies, epistemologies, and their associated systems of identity).[32]

As Habermas has argued, the postmodern denunciation of Enlightenment metanarratives has tended to foster a sometimes stifling political ambivalence: when presented in the form of post-Marxist critiques of modernity and capitalism, such denunciations often trade on established distinctions, egalitarian conceptions of rights, classic notions of ideology, and grand narratives regarding, for instance, the nature of the (post)modern condition. At the same time, the self-absorbed and self-deconstructive tendency that is prominent in postmodernist writing threatens to dissolve the political force of those distinctions, conceptions, and narratives.[33] The complaint, once lodged against the medieval casuists, also finds purchase here: that the writers' enthusiasm for subtlety and complexity loses sight of a more reasonable "moral balance."[34] Habermas's interrogation of postmodernity attempts to force a confrontation between contradictory theoretical and practical tendencies in the hope of eliciting a confession of normative values, his argument being that the denunciatory force of postmodern criticism presupposes an adherence to the Enlightenment values incorporated into and explicated by his own theory of communicative ethics. Our strategy in this book has been to examine the details of an actually existing interrogative dialogue that was designed to force a circumscribed, practical variant of the confrontation that Habermas has in mind for philosophy. Our conclusion, to quote Derrida out of context, is that this confrontation "never quite takes place."[35]

The truth-finding engine of interrogation incorporates certain Habermasian features. Its communicative enactment presupposes a consensus between the adversary interlocutors on standards of truth, truthfulness, rightness, and intelligibility. The docile witness's adherence to these standards provides the motive force of the engine, as the witness is compelled by an immanent aversion to self-contradiction to testify against his or her own particular interests. The machinery operates through mutual adherence to a reticulum of reasonable presumptions about events, actions, and motives in a common life-world and a knowledge and respect for relevant social norms. For Habermas, the postmodernist interlocutor proves to be an especially tough nut to crack. This interlocutor relentlessly refuses to acknowledge the analytic fissures and logical joints that enable "truth," "rightness," and "sincerity" to be separated from their opposites and pursued interrogatively. Habermas's intention is to force the interlocutor to acknowledge that postmodernist theories evade the values implicated in the theorist's conduct. North's interrogators faced a related challenge: to force him to acknowledge that he and his administrative colleagues had evaded or violated commonly recognized laws and normative standards. In North's case, the subject of the accusation was charged with a practical rather than a theoretical evasion of common values.

What we have described in this book thus might be viewed as a confrontation between a representative of Enlightenment values (the committee interrogators) and a cynical representative of a postmodern attitude (North), who cloaks that attitude with evocations of those same Enlightenment values. Cast in this way, the dialogues at the hearings instantiate a mythical confrontation between the standard-bearers of two opposing armies, one outfitted with a modernist rhetoric and the other with postmodern armaments. We recognize the perversity of this picture. North and his allies overtly express reverence for truth and traditional morality and accuse their opponents of corruption. Photographs circulated by North's press agents show him at his Virginia home, accompanied by his "best friend" Betsy and his well-groomed kids. North portrays himself as a traditional Christian family man standing up against domestic and foreign threats to "our American way of life." We cannot imagine that North regards himself as a modernist, let alone a postmodernist, nor that the many enthusiasts of postmodern literary and social theory would want to claim him as one of their own. It also may seem ludicrous, in an era of public cynicism about congressional ethics and truthfulness, to cast the congressional representatives on the committee as legitimate representatives of Enlightenment truth. Indeed, as was demonstrated over the course of the hearings, the committee members—and in particular, those who spoke against North and the Reagan administration—were unable to take for granted that they spoke on behalf of "the American people" and were unable to make a compelling case for a suprapolitical consensus that denounced the actions of North and his colleagues.[36] The confrontation between North and the committee might best be characterized as a dialogue where one party attempted to invoke a transcendent truth and rule of law and to speak on behalf of a people, while the other party relentlessly attacked the determinateness, definiteness, and suprapolitical "representativeness" of the committee's linkages to a public and a set of universal standards. Consequently, a pure confrontation between defenders of Enlightenment truth and justice and a postmodern hero who problematizes the binary oppositions of Enlightenment logic and ethics never quite took place.

At the beginning of this study we described North as an "applied deconstructionist." We are now in a position to say something more about what we mean by that characterization. In the context of shredded records of the past, North occupied a relatively free space for creating an uncorroborated narrative. He was in a position to express the relevant postmodernist themes—collapsing fiction and biography, producing flexible interpretations—without announcing them. Viewed in this way, North's postmodernism inverts the tendency that Habermas critiques. The challenge for Habermas is to demonstrate that the postmodernist writer presupposes the very value categories that in theory (but only in theory) are problematized by deconstructionist criticism.

> The variations of a critique of reason with reckless disregard for its own foundations are . . . guided by normative intuitions that go beyond what they can accommodate in terms of the indirectly affirmed "other of reason." Whether modernity is described as a constellation of life that is reified and used, or as one that is technologically manipulated, or as one that is totalitarian, rife with power, homogenized, imprisoned—the denunciations are constantly inspired by a special sensitivity for complex injuries and subtle violations.[37]

To the extent that Habermas succeeds in demonstrating this claim by reading the works of Foucault, Derrida, and others, he reveals that the argumentative infrastructure of their anti-Enlightenment tracts presupposes the very rational and ethical standards their overt theoretical pronouncements disown. The problem for Habermas is to explicate how the texts in question tacitly acknowledge those standards. North's interrogators faced a different challenge. Getting him to acknowledge adherence to traditional standards of truth-telling and legal-ethical conduct was easy. The problem was to get him to talk and write in such a way as to allow those standards to take the measure of his conduct. As we have elaborated, his answers to questions often provided narratives that problematized the application of logical and ethical distinctions. With massive help from his support staff, select members of the committee, and television, radio, and newspaper audiences, North demonstrated discursive methods for undermining and politicizing the objective, dispassionate, and impartial auspices of the committee's investigation. Like a good postmodernist critic, he did not simply impute an ideology to his interlocutors; he enabled an audience to see how their discourse was always already political. He showed great facility at disclosing the partisan political agenda lurking beneath the committee's apparent objective orientation, and he relentlessly produced counternarratives that problematized the unequivocal statements of historical fact presented to him. He dissociated authorship from texts, even when those texts were written and signed by his own hand, and his recollections provided a tutorial on the social construction of "memory." He questioned the linguistic reference and determinacy of legal statutes (particularly the Boland amendment's prohibitions of contra aid), and he proved to be a hero in the media space of daytime television. Perhaps the most telling blow that North struck against his liberal interlocutors was in getting them to acknowledge the relativity of truth by reference to the political utility of deception. In their report the committee majority asserted that the uncontrolled privatization of covert actions (i.e., the conduct of state-sponsored deception outside normal bureaucratic channels) was the danger at hand, but they did not denounce the political sanctioning of deceptiveness itself.[38] The debate between North and his interrogators thus centered on which agencies could practice covert operations and under what forms of government supervision. More contentiously, the debate concerned the question of access to those secrets and deceptions. North suggested, sometimes directly and sometimes implicitly, that in the present circumstance Congress could not be trusted to know about the covert activities sponsored by the executive branch. He argued (and this was contested) that congressional opponents of administrative initiatives were liable to leak damaging information about covert operations to the press. It seems, then, that both parties to the debate willingly accepted the notion that so long as covert operations were conducted through approved channels there would be legitimate sanction for withholding information and disseminating disinformation to a large public. The question at issue, as North articulated it, was whether the Congress was explicitly, or by default naively, in league with America's enemies.

POWER IN CONTEXT

It can be argued that the political divisiveness that characterized the Iran-contra hearings was a predictable consequence of the historical and political context. One could readily suspect that the committee's irresoluteness in getting to the bottom of the Iran-contra affair was a consequence of powerful economic and media interests, together with a collusive aversion to instability by entrenched factions from both parties.[39] However, this did not seem to be a foregone conclusion at the time of the hearings, and in any event we think it is worth examining how an interrogative machinery that was overtly designed to produce confessional truth was transformed into a forum for a political debate. Aside from any substantive historical effects, the testimony provides a vivid tutorial on the production of historical undecidability. The various testimonial methods of recalling, co-reading, and counternarrating discussed in these pages demonstrate how a witness was able to resist and displace the force of interrogation.

What we have found from paying detailed attention to the observable production of the Iran-contra hearings is not only that a series of tacit agreements conspired to enable viewers to "overlook the observable," but that a series of subtle and pragmatic shifts took place in the production of the observable scene in which testimonial narratives and counternarratives were read, iterated, and evaluated. Under the auspices of a ceremonial of truth, the witness was held answerable to a monological "record" that was recited by the interrogators, whereas in the freer spaces of debates with his political opponents and collaborative exchanges with his allies on the committee, North's utterances became part of a political spectacle in which contending parties battled over the relative powers of the executive and legislative branches. The transformation between, and the more constant equivocality of, these two ways of conceptualizing the spectacle was achieved intensively and in detail through some of the discursive practices we have identified:

—The (re)writing, redaction, withholding, and shredding of documentary evidence to enhance equivocality and deniability.

—The refusal to testify in closed session before the hearings, combined with North's and Poindexter's Fifth Amendment pleas.

—The request for (and occasional yielding of) time slots during the hearings where North could present prepared monological "statements" in addition to answering questions put to him by the committee.

—The claim at the outset of the hearings that the committee had given North and his legal representatives insufficient time to study the surviving documents that the committee had in hand.

—The extensive use of avowals of nonrecall to sever the present testimony from a recollectable past.

—The use of qualifiers, mitigating phrases, and other descriptive formats that problematize the yes or no definiteness of "answers to questions."

—The incessant demands by North and his counsel that he be allowed to finish long "answers" without being "interrupted" by his interrogators.

—The demand for time, on-camera, to "study" the documentary exhibits used to "refresh" the witness's recall, and the derivation of testimony from the "mere reading" of those texts.

—The packaging of counternarratives and speeches into turns for "answering questions."

—The successful efforts by North's allies on the committee and in the government to dramatize the interrogation as a partisan political inquisition.

All of these detailed practices can be given a strategic cast by describing them as deliberate maneuvers that reflected the overall purpose of limiting the disclosure of damaging evidence. However compelling it might be to interpret them in that way, to say that a concerted strategy lay behind the methods of testimony and preparation of records, etc., would be to ignore the systematic *denial* of such a strategy that was so prominent throughout. Repeatedly, when North and his allies were accused of establishing duplicitous rationales for their activities—"forgetting" key facts, not revealing what was written on shredded documents, and turning the hearings into a political carnival—they denied such intentions and maintained that their actions were governed by normal, reasonable, and (often minimally) legitimate purposes. For us to say unequivocally that North and his allies acted in an insincerely strategic way would be to take a position in a dispute rather than to describe its discursive outlines. Since a denial of strategy (or, relatedly, a selective admission of strategy) is embedded in the very constitution of the testimonial record, we have tried to indicate how that record provided a basis for abundant suspicions that never fully got to the bottom of the affair.

Although North was, and still is, a fascinating character, we do not want to inflate the importance of his individual presence. To a large extent, the furor surrounding his testimony at the hearings had to do only partly with the sorts of discursive maneuvers we have described. Much of what we have said about the organization of questions and answers, disavowals of recall, the documentary method of interrogation, and lies and truth-telling could have been exemplified with excerpts from other witnesses' testimonies, as well as with excerpts from more ordinary tribunals and trials.[40] It is not so much that North accomplished uniquely brilliant moves in testimony; his actions were mainly notable because of the publicity to which they were subjected and the significance assigned to them. We should not conclude that North and his Reagan administration colleagues survived the congressional investigation *because* of their conduct at the hearings. It is not as though specific discursive practices were the primary *cause* of a historical outcome. Particular speeches, televisual poses, etc., were perspicuous moments in a historic spectacle, but they were no less embedded in history than were many other aspects of the hearings.

A final word about "context" is in order. There is no question that North and the other Reagan administration witnesses had access to expensive lawyers, staff resources, political and media support, mechanisms of information control, and other sources of power and influence that are denied to the vast majority of defendants in more ordinary trials. The committee also had considerable legal and administrative resources at its disposal so that the struggle we have described, while being witnessed by the masses, occurred largely among members of an elite. These and many other matters would have to be taken into account by any effort to explain the historical outcome by reference to a calculus of forces existing in advance of it. We have not tried to produce such an explanation. Instead, we endeavored to describe occasions in the testimony where context (earlier testimony, an archive of records, an emerging historical narrative, the immediate circumstance of the testimony) served as both a topic and a resource. We have not described *the* context as a totality (How could we?), nor have we interpreted particular moments in testimony by citing a stable set of contextual factors. Instead, we described discursive moves that situated themselves in the context of prior moves, while themselves contributing to the contextual configuration. To disavow explanation by reference to a priori "factors" does not deny their relevance as resources. North's expensive support team, the agencies with which he worked, the audiences he managed to enroll with his denunciations of Congress and evocations of popular film heroes certainly would not be available to any hapless witness. But these and many other things were sources of leverage that North and his interlocutors used in context. North appropriated resources, such as a pile of supportive telegrams, that were not available a priori, and he and Sullivan also rhetorically ascribed superior power and immense resources to their opponents (even the question of whether, and to what extent, the hearings were a face-off between opponents was a contentious matter). As we view the situation, the particular interactional consequences and public media effects did not simply flow from a static configuration of power.

Consequently, we have not had much use for conceptions of power that invest particular persons, positions, or organizations with an inherent force or ability to exact compliance and to influence institutional processes. Other forms of power may seem more salient. Ever since Foucault "discovered" the constitutive modalities of disciplinary knowledge, it has become customary to link all forms of established knowledge with networks of power, uneasily coexisting with residues of the older sovereign forms. One might say that the inverted panopticon of a televised tribunal provides a machinery for constituting sovereigns of the screen, personifications of political enunciation whose vivid centrality no longer is guaranteed by inheritance, election, or military coup. The throne is attained through the mobilization of cameras and audiences, and it is lost when the fickle cameras wander elsewhere. Another salient form of power might also be identified: the power to resist. This differs from the repressive power from which Foucault distinguishes the "positive" and "creative" force of disciplinary bio-power, insofar as the power to resist is a matter of "ensuring that nothing happens."[41] As we have tried to demonstrate in the case of the Iran-contra affair, such nullity was a contingent achievement that encompassed an entire series of activities that denied their own accountability as methods for concocting, leaking, shredding, and forgetting history. But to give the name "power" to all of these activities does little to affect the story we have told, and the use of that concept makes it only too easy to assume that an underlying currency or homogeneous "force" is responsible for historical outcomes, typically understood only through the wisdom of hindsight. The multivocal and polylithic operation we have described proceeds according to different laws.

North's testimony, together with the "populist" movement that embraced him as its hero, brought into vivid relief an unmistakably historical phenomenon. This does not mean, however, that North made history all by himself, or that he impressed his own personal meaning upon it. If it can be said that "North is a compass point" whose performative message is "more real than the reality the committee sought to uncover, more seductive than anything the polymorphous, acephalous Committee could reconstruct,"[42] then, as we read this compass, it points clearly to the widely recognized cynicism that inhabits and surrounds contemporary politics. But to leave it at that—to treat the conduct and outcome of the hearings as emblematic of the "condition of our age"—would be to miss the point of focusing on the local organization of discourse at the hearings. It is all too easy to invest the present period with themes that happen to be in vogue among scholars today. Nothing we have examined leads us to suppose that the civics (non-)lesson produced by the hearings was a foregone conclusion, or a necessary product of an emerging historical discourse. Rather than encouraging cynical resignation, we figure that a more explicit acknowledgment of the discursive and political infrastructure of the modern ceremonial of truth enables the articulation and criticism of modes of action that were, in this case, clumsily and ineffectively pursued in the name of legal-rational truth and justice.

METHODOLOGICAL

APPENDIX: POSTANALYTIC

ETHNOMETHODOLOGY

Ethnomethodology is an approach to the study of practical action and practical reasoning that was founded by Harold Garfinkel,[1] who came up with the term in the 1950s when he was engaged in a study of jury deliberations. A jury room had been bugged for purposes of research, and a number of prominent social scientists began to investigate the tapes to find out how the jurors conducted their deliberations. Garfinkel noticed that the jurors themselves addressed a number of methodological issues in the course of their deliberations. He also observed that they did not pretend to act as though they were scientists or professional lawyers, but that they nevertheless concerned themselves with making adequate interpretations of the evidence, making use of precedent, rendering judgments on the credibility of witnesses, and putting together plausible reconstructions of events outside the courtroom. As he put it,

> you have this interesting acceptance, so to speak, of these magnificent methodological things, if you permit me to talk that way, like "fact" and "fancy" and "opinion" and "my opinion" and "your opinion" and "what we're entitled to say" and "what the evidence shows" and "what can be demonstrated" and "what actually he said" as compared with "what only you think he said" or "what he seemed to have said." You have these notions of evidence and demonstration and of matters of relevance, of true and false, of public and private, of methodic procedure, and the rest. At the same time the whole thing was handled by all those concerned as part of the same setting in which they were used by the members, by these jurors, to get the work of deliberations done. That work for them was deadly serious.[2]

As the term ethnomethodology suggests, it is an approach to the study of the "folk methods" through which social actions are produced and made intelligible. As the above passage indicates, Garfinkel was especially interested in methods connected with detecting facts and interpreting evidence:

for telling the truth and telling whether a truth has been told; for assessing evidence at hand; for judging the plausibility of a story and the credibility of its teller; and for assigning identities to persons, places, and times. Many of the problems addressed by such methods are familiar to professional academic researchers. Commonly a distinction between "folk" (or "lay") procedures and professional (or "scientific") procedures places professional in a superior epistemic position, but Garfinkel took the distinction in a different direction. While acknowledging that folk methods may be local and ad hoc, he viewed them as stable features of social settings where, for better or worse, practical judgments are made, actions taken, and their consequences realized. In addition, though they may have no privileged claim to establishing transcendental truths, folk methods will often serve as practically adequate for discerning and establishing "the truth of the matter" in situ. In their own ways these methods instantiate the familiar distinctions (truth/falsity, fact/opinion, knowing/believing, etc.) and practically resolve the vexed problems of epistemology.

Although the jurors studied by Garfinkel did not use approved methods of social science or legal scholarship, he reasoned that this omission did not necessarily indicate irrationality, error, ignorance, or bias. In his view, transcendent standards of precision, validity, and reliability did not, and could not, apply to the local situations in which jury deliberations and other ordinary practical actions are conducted. Consequently, he recommended that sociologists should suspend their professional concerns with methodology, while seeking to investigate the ethnomethodologies used in countless other settings of conduct. Even though ordinary methods may seem to be loose, biased, or otherwise faulty ways of conducting inquiries, they are substantively part of the way routine social scenes are assembled. Participants in all sorts of lay and professional activities have an interest in getting facts straight, distinguishing truths from lies, finding out how one or another organization really works, etc. To say that their methods are unscientific does not address their constitutive relationship to the social settings in which they take place. Garfinkel was not suggesting that commonsense methods are generally adequate for social-scientific purposes, or that we have no right to criticize particular instances of them; rather, he was recommending that we investigate the constitutive relationship between commonsense methods and the stable social phenomena they produce and implicate.

The epistemic stance taken by ethnomethodologists is neither normative nor denunciatory. Unlike many social-science inquirers, ethnomethodologists do not draw an ironic contrast between folk and scientific methods of inquiry. They do not view folk methods as degraded, partial, or ideologically biased versions of scientific methods. Instead, following a policy articulated by Garfinkel and his student and colleague, Harvey Sacks, ethnomethodologists remain "indifferent" to established theoretical contrasts between scientific and commonsense methods. They endeavor instead to discover how folk methods (and among them, the day-to-day practices in science, law, and other professional settings) are produced and made intelligible in their own right.[3] Indifference is a difficult and dangerous practice in contemporary social science because it rules out virtually all of the analytic moves through which social scientists set up programmatic distinctions between surface (evident, overtly expressed) structures and beliefs and the underlying realities that cause or motivate them. Such distinctions are associated with a number of thematic contrasts. These include the programmatic contrasts between instrumental and substantive rationality, between the surface structure of discourse and the (ideological or grammatical) deep structure, between manifest and latent functions, and between agents' professed values and their actual interests. Such contrasts between commonsense reasoning and analytic methods have indispensable methodological value for both positivistic styles of research and anti-positivistic critical inquiries.[4] While it is easy to denounce one or another "privileged" analytical standpoint, it is far more difficult to avoid reserving similar privileges for one's own investigations.

Aside from the methodological difficulties involved in following through on the policy of indifference, social-science audiences commonly express disappointment with "mere descriptions" that do not explain the case under study through reference to the underlying or contextual structures of power and meaning specified by selected social, cultural, literary, and political theories. Related disappointments pertain to the general absence of a normative stance in ethnomethodological studies. In response to such forceful demands, we should keep in mind that ethnomethodology is not, and never will be, a universally practiced social-science method. Scholars with other ambitions are free to embrace alternative approaches, of which there are many. Ethnomethodology's ascetic disavowal of familiar interpretative models is logically necessary for setting up investigations of a substantive field of language use and practical action that remains largely unstudied. This field is composed of intelligible actions performed on singular occasions. We commonly hear that science is adequate only for purposes of specifying general, underlying regularities and not for understanding or predicting singular events. This view considers singular events, complicated by uncontrolled sources of variability, as too messy for science. In the human sciences this picture of knowledge often leads us to suppose that the origins of social order are invisible, unconsciously assimilated, misrecognized, and/or confusedly known to the cohorts of lay and professional practitioners whose work produces them. Ethnomethodology takes a different tack, which is neither to invent yet another version of scientific sociology nor to abandon the effort to investigate a real-worldly society. An inkling of ethnomethodology's conception of order is communicated with phrases like "order at all points,"[5] the observation that everywhere we turn in our familiar social landscape we find intelligible and recognizable actions, events, gestures, utterances. Relatedly, Garfinkel and Sacks announce the possibility of investigating "demonstrably rational properties of indexical expressions,"[6] context-bound linguistic expressions, which according to their view are sensible in context, and studiably so. While this conception permits the detailed description of phenomena of order—the competencies exhibited to members, for members, and by members (members being masters of the relevant language games), as part of the local production of recognizable actions—it leaves no room for the special epistemic privileges often assigned to the use of social-science methods and theories. This disavowal not only covers the programs in sociology that attempt to emulate one or another version of natural science, but it implicates many cultural or interpretative schemes and theories.

ETHNOMETHODOLOGY AND CULTURAL ANALYSIS

Our discussions in this text of themes such as ritual, spectacle, and ceremony, as well as our use of Foucault to set the agenda for chapter 3, range far afield from ethnomethodology. These themes are more familiar to students of semiotics, structural and poststructural anthropology, cultural criticism, discourse analysis, and symbolic interactionist sociology. But while we acknowledge a debt to those areas of scholarship, we are not conducting an interpretative or (post)structuralist analysis of our materials. For one thing, we have not set out to interpret the videotaped "surface" of the testimony by reference to one or another abstract cultural framework or code. Instead, we describe how a whole array of possible legal, cultural, and discursive resources were available, and were in fact used, by the parties to the hearings. These resources included various binary oppositions, linguistic categories, procedural rules and protocols, references to cherished constitutional rights and ethical values, invocations of national interest, and popular media themes. Sometimes these were brought into play predictably—and with obvious reference to earlier historical events and political themes—but what interests us most is how the instantiation of such cultural resources took place as part of a *dialogical* production. Consequently, we intend to describe the singular, interactional encoding and *resistance to encoding,* performed at the surface of a media text by a witness and his interrogators. Some readers nonetheless may figure that we must be interpreting the videotext of the hearings by reference to a tacit theory, even if we deny doing so. Indeed, it has been our experience that many colleagues have been willing to offer us the theory we need, or to tell us that we already are using such a theory in an ad hoc way. By politely refusing such offers, we are not denying that we must interpret the videotapes and written texts that make up our materials; we are, instead, denying that it is necessary to organize such an interpretation around a core theory or cognitive model.

The question is not of getting a more accurate or complete picture of the event. We are prepared to acknowledge that, for example, Victor Turner's framework for describing historical crises nicely encapsulates the stages of the Iran-contra drama: (1) a breach of a relationship occurred that was regarded as crucial by the relevant group (the arms trades and diversion of profits carried out without informing Congress), which (2) provoked a rapidly mounting crisis in which a latent cleavage in the society became salient (conservatives vs. liberals); (3) legal and ritual means were then used to redress the crisis and seek reconciliation (the hearings and other investigations), and (4) when these proved unsuccessful, a schism was opened up along the preexisting lines of cleavage (separate final reports were written, and a political movement coalesced around the heroic figure of North).[7] Turner's conceptions of liminality (unanchored, transitional phases) and of symbolic inversion also suggest relevant features of the spectacle we are describing. From time to time we invoke these terms, but not in order to put a determinate theory in place. While we agree that Turner's analytic frameworks and themes do indeed provide cogent headings, outlines, indexes, and vocabularies, we see little reason to endow them with an invariant or determinate status, for example, as "root paradigms in people's heads that become objectivated models for future behavior in the history of collectivities."[8] Instead, we tend to view them as no more and no less than formats and figures of speech that can be useful for social scientists as well as for the people studied.

Perhaps we can clarify this point with the image of a gestalt shift between figure and background. Instead of treating moment-to-moment dialogue (or practical action more generally) as an unstable flux organized around context-free structural axes and paradigms, we tend to view such dialogue as an intelligible production involving more than one party, using various stable elements of language in unique combinations as part of a meaningful scene. This is not a one-sided emphasis on *parole* at the expense of *langue,* because it refuses from the outset to separate the two dimensions. The difference, on the one hand, is between starting out by isolating and defining the structures and elements of meaning, and, on the other, beginning in the midst of the action and describing how speakers in an ongoing exchange commit themselves to doing (and meaning) something through what they say.[9] Although both starting points, in principle, can get at the intertwining of linguistic forms and situated usage, they lead to very different understandings of the role of formal structures in communicative actions.

A comparison might help here. In a lengthy article that advances a general model of "the discourse of American civil society," Alexander and Smith discuss the Iran-contra hearings as one of a series of historical examples to which their model applies.[10] The model makes up the analytic theme and central figure in their text. They present it in the form of a series of three lists describing the discursive structure of "actors," "social relations," and "social institutions." In each list, one column contains several adjectives making up a "democratic code," while the adjacent column includes an equal number of contrasting adjectives in a "counterdemocratic code." For example, under social relations the democratic code contains such terms as "open," "trusting," "critical," and "truthful," whereas the counterdemocratic code contains "secret," "suspicious," "deferential," and "deceitful."[11] After discussing the advantages of this scheme over alternative models of culture in social theory, Alexander and Smith demonstrate how it applies to a series of nineteenth- and twentieth-century political crises in the United States. After discussing a few examples, including the Teapot Dome and Watergate scandals, they lead into the section on Iran-contra with a brief narrative describing the event.

> In late 1986 information emerged that a small team in the Reagan administration, spearheaded by Lieutenant-Colonel Oliver North, had sold arms to Iran in return for which Iran was to use its influence to obtain the release of American hostages held by various Islamic groups in the Middle-East. As a further twist in the tale, the money raised from the sale was used to support a secret operation in Central America backing the anti-communist "Contra" guerrillas in Nicaragua. Once the action came to light, a process of generalization rapidly occurred in which the motivations, relationships, and institutions of North and his association became the subject of intense public scrutiny.[12]

This concise summary closely follows the outlines of the conventional history of the affair elaborated in our Introduction; but whereas Alexander and Smith are interested in a "process of generalization," we are interested in the local discursive methods for reciting, confirming, and disputing the "facts of history" included in the conventional historical account. Alexander and Smith go on to quote a series of excerpts from some of the lengthier monologues presented at the hearings by Cochairman Lee Hamilton and Representative Carl Stokes (both Democrats on the committee) and Oliver North. These excerpts demonstrate that Hamilton and Stokes aligned their speeches with the democratic code, while selecting from the menu of items in the counterdemocratic code when denouncing North's actions, whereas North selected from the democratic side of the ledger when arguing that "his own motivations were, in fact, compatible with the discourse of liberty."[13] The codes stood fast, while the interlocutors struggled to identify themselves, and not their opponents, with the democratic side.

We see no reason to doubt that the items on Alexander and Smith's list make up something like what C. Wright Mills called a "vocabulary of motives,"[14] only in the case we are describing the terms were also used as references to nonindividual purposes and evaluative standards that have a prominent place in the U.S. Constitution. We seriously doubt that Alexander and Smith's list is as potent a cultural object as they seem to suggest, but we grant that it is akin to a dictionary or index of rhetorically effective themes for demonstrating patriotism and for making denunciations and for defending against them. No doubt when this index is used to scan the record of testimony at the hearings, many concordances turn up. Such an analysis can be likened to plucking adjectival raisins from a lingual pudding. The gestalt switch we propose focuses on the pudding (the dialogical matrix), while presuming that the raisins (for example, references to truthfulness, secrecy and "the American people") were drawn from a cupboard in which they were placed alongside an immense variety of other vocabularies, binaries, idioms, and sequential machineries. (And in this case, the cupboard was swarming with cockroaches.) In chapter 3, for example, the topic we try to keep in view is the dialogical production of a spectacle composed of a whole array of pragmatic moves, posturings, citations, and other verbal devices or ingredients.

Because of our refusal to assign priority to the semiotic axes, ritual phases, cultural schemes, and nominal elements of one or another abstract model, some readers may be inclined to liken us to empiricists, reductionists, naive realists, or behaviorists. Worse, insofar as such models are often linked to particular historical, ethnic, class, and gendered epistemologies and identities, it may seem as though we are ignoring the context of the events we discuss. How can we pretend to be so innocent of epistemological and moral presuppositions? Can we be unaware, as everyone should know in this day and age, that a text cannot be understood without reference to the historical, political, social, class, economic, technological, and gendered circumstances of its production?[15] We can only answer yes, we are aware of such sophisticated understandings of text and discourse, just as Wittgenstein was aware of their precursors when he divorced his conception of philosophy from the prevailing "craving for generality" of his day:

Our craving for generality has another main source: our preoccupation with the method of science. I mean the method of reducing the explanation of natural phenomena to the smallest possible number of primitive natural laws; and, in mathematics, of unifying the treatment of different topics by using a generalization. Philosophers constantly see the method of science before their eyes, and are irresistibly tempted to ask and answer questions in the way science does. This tendency is the real source of metaphysics, and leads the philosopher into complete darkness. I want to say here that it can never be our job to reduce anything to anything, or to explain anything. Philosophy really *is* "purely descriptive."[16]

Certainly, many writers today who favor interpretative and symbolic theories of culture and text do not set out to follow the method of science (though more than a few remain preoccupied with it). Nevertheless, the analytic tendencies to search after an underlying unification of diverse phenomena, and to relate the surface of a given text to a simple cultural code, set of binary axes, scheme of stages, and/or specification of contextually relevant social identities, were never more prevalent than they are today in explicitly antipositivistic interpretative programs.

Wittgenstein's renunciation of the craving for generality in favor of description may seem quaint in light of prevailing tendencies to consider "pure description" as an epistemological impossibility, and it may recall the sorts of avowals of neutral, value-free description so often criticized these days for disguising an author's normative slant and deleting the contingencies involved in the construction of such descriptions. Again, it may seem that from Wittgenstein we have adopted an unsophisticated conception of discourse that has been surpassed by more recent developments in literary and cultural studies. Note, however, that Wittgenstein is not endowing description with a special epistemological status; indeed, he is arguing against the craving for generality, which he describes as a "contemptuous attitude towards the particular case."[17] Such a contemptuous attitude denigrates mere description for its failure to subordinate the concrete details of a case to a theoretically specified foundation, ideology, or generalized discourse. For Wittgenstein, descriptions of singular activities are valuable precisely because they cast into relief diverse, unexpected, yet intelligible organizations of language use.

Several familiar problems are associated with efforts to identify deeper, or at least simpler, structures of thought or action "reflected" in particular instances of conduct. These include the inseparability of the point of view of the historian or social scientist from the substantive configuration of values, meanings, discourses, or social contexts assigned to a case.[18] Different observers, armed with different theoretical and cultural expectancies, are likely to impute different presuppositions to the actors and to emphasize different contexts of their action, to the point of calling into question whether they are describing the same case at all.[19] In other words, actual cases exhibit a surplus of detail that permits the ascription of an open variety of sometimes incompatible analytical categories. As we construe it, however, the problem is not epistemological. As stated, we are not saying that it is impossible, or somehow incorrect, to interpret the record of testimony in terms of Turner's, Alexander and Smith's, or any other model of narrative stages or schema of binary themes. Indeed, far from being impossible, it seems all too easy to accomplish such methods for "detailing generalities," which as Garfinkel describes them are a matter of "designing a formal scheme of types, giving their formal definitions an interpreted significance with which to develop and explain the orderly properties of the types as ideals, and then assigning the properties of the ideals to observable actions as their described properties of social order."[20] The problem is that when a simple structure is given priority over the more complicated and seemingly amorphous relevancies of actual usage, everyday actions can seem to become the somewhat muffled expressions of a "cultural dope," which as Garfinkel describes it is a puppet or dummy moved by a theoretically specified arrangement of external forces and internal mechanisms.[21] As Alfred Schutz pointed out, the problem is not that such simplifications create a partial picture of social reality, but that they stand in the way of understanding the local and interactional production of an infrastructure of activities glossed over by a given model.[22] Linguistic and cultural codes and paradigms certainly do provide resources for producing and understanding conduct, but given the variety of available codes, the open-ended configuration of elements in any given paradigm, and the necessity for ad hoc uses of language within the exigencies of an actual situation, any effort to specify a closed scheme of elements prior to an occasion of its use begs the question of how the parties to the occasion establish the relevance, and implement the use, of just that scheme. To speak of a dialectic between theory and practice is insufficient, because the various discursive and conceptual resources that *might* be invoked on an occasion are not necessarily bound together in a binary table inscribed in an abstract space remote from the action.[23] Instead, even when they are finite and formally encoded, systems of laws and rules are continually reworked and inflected by reference to the occasions on which they are used. In effect, they become open-ended constituents of a practice.

ETHNOMETHODOLOGICAL RESPECIFICATION

Ethnomethodology's orientation to singular details is often misunderstood as an epistemological perspective that credits the existence of local, micro, or immediately visible events and actions, while denying the existence of larger, or more abstract, social and cultural phenomena (e.g., power, the state, demographic trends, structures of inequality, systems of meaning, etc.). Such thinking mistakes an investigative orientation to a phenomenal field—held to be real, intelligible, studiable and largely unstudied in the human sciences—with a metaphysical stance to the effect that anything beyond the limits of that field is a doubtful construction. Such a view is belied by the overt and repeated insistence by ethnomethodologists that ordinary language concepts and commonsense knowledge for the most part are not lesser forms of knowledge requiring scientific validation.[24] Vernacular conceptions of power, knowledge, meaning, historical context, and so forth, are ubiquitous. In a study like this one, we could not avoid using them if we tried, even while selectively taking up specific themes related to history, biography, and memory, to explicate a circumstantially specific understanding of their meaning and relevance. This approach differs from the aims of a causal explanation *and* from an attempt to formulate general schemes of "meaning" that define an epoch. It also implies nothing *in general* about the validity of any unexplicated conceptions used in this study or any other.[25] Garfinkel gives a rationale for this sort of project when he describes ethnomethodology as a way to "respecify" the "classic" themes in the human sciences. These themes include a long list of vernacular terms identified with basic social science concepts, including order, reason, meaning, method, and structure. Rather than endowing them with transcendent status as problems or principles, Garfinkel proposes that they are unexplicated terms for social phenomena that can be investigated in the local-historical circumstances of their production. This perspective differs from any attempt to fix a more comprehensive or adequate definition of these concepts than has been done thus far in the traditions of scholarly inquiry, since it involves more of a reorientation to a different field from which one derives the insights and pleasures of scholarship. In outline, an ethnomethodological respecification includes the following steps:

(1) Take a "methodological" distinction, problem, or concept (for instance, the difference between fact and opinion, the distinction between intended action and unintended behavior, the relationship between what someone says and what they "really mean," the question of whether professed reasons should be accepted as adequate explanations).

(2) Treat the "problem" as a matter of routine, local relevance for a particular kind of practical inquiry (such as jury deliberations).

(3) Describe the way members make use of the distinction or concept, and how they handle any problems associated with its use, and show how this use is embedded in routine courses of action (jury deliberations and their outcomes, coroner's investigations into the causes of death, suicide prevention center personnel's methods for discerning the difference between a serious and a crank call, etc.).[26]

In the present study we have taken up several familiar topics in the human sciences—history, spectacle, narrative, memory, intertextuality, and truth—and have explicated them in a study of a particular case. Although we examine extant theoretical writings on these matters, we are not applying a given theory to the analysis of the case. Instead, we describe how the parties to the hearings made use of, for example, memory as an accountable theme for claiming, disclaiming, imputing, resisting, or discounting particular relationships between biography and history. We are not proposing an inquiry free of presuppositions; instead, we are disclaiming that our inquiry is theory-laden in the sense of being framed by a professionally fashioned nexus of definitions, propositions, and a priori expectancies.[27] The promise of such an approach is to gain a more differentiated appreciation of the phenomena in question (and of their situated uses and fates) than we would gain if we were to address them as "concepts on holiday." This sort of inquiry is not intended to satisfy certain popular academic demands for explanations, critiques of power, and systematic theories, and we doubt that many of our colleagues in the human sciences would want to follow the sort of path we have taken. We do believe, however, that ethnomethodology is not a blind, empirical endeavor and that its mode of research does bear on some of the more ubiquitous conceptual usages in the human sciences.

CONVERSATION ANALYSIS

Ethnomethodologists have conducted rigorous descriptive studies of the local production of discourse and other modes of practical action in a range of settings.[28] This action-centered approach can take different methodological forms, such as ethnographic observations at the site of an activity, intensive studies of tape-recorded discourse and practical action, and textual demonstrations of particular modes of practical action and practical reasoning. At present, the most sustained line of research has concerned the sequential organization of conversational discourse. Over the past thirty years, conversation analysts have investigated audio- and video-tapes of naturally occurring social interaction, and their research has produced a sizable body of detailed studies.[29] To a large extent, conversation analysis (as this offshoot of ethnomethodology has come to be called) has developed independently of Garfinkel's initiatives. Many conversation analysts have gravitated toward an almost formalistic way of describing systems and machineries" of talk-in-interaction, which at times seem to endow the talk they describe with an autonomy and agency of its own.[30] Although our study tries to avoid any suggestion of empirical or ethical foundationalism, our investigations, transcriptions, and analysis of testimony rely heavily on conversation-analytic studies of interrogation, storytelling, disputation, and witnessing.[31] For readers who are unfamiliar with this approach, we will briefly outline three of the general organizational features identified by conversation analysts that inform our analysis: adjacency pairs, the preference system, and storytelling.[32] Other pertinent organizational phenomena are introduced throughout this book in relation to particular issues and examples.

Adjacency Pairs

This type of conversational device is composed of paired acts produced by different speakers. A simple case is the exchange of a greeting and return greeting:

A: Hello.
B: Hello.

Other adjacency pairs include summons-answer, question-answer, and invitation-acceptance/decline. In terms of the adjacency pair formulation, an initial greeting is a first pair-part, while a responsive greeting is a second pair-part. One way of selecting a particular person as next-speaker, then, is to produce the first part of an adjacency pair, and to do so in a way that targets that particular person as the recipient of that particular utterance.

The two pair-parts that compose the adjacency pair are linked together through a relation of conditional relevance. This linkage is more than a matter of latching together objects (analogous to amino acids chained together in a protein molecule), as the linkage implicates the conversational participants' prospective and retrospective production and calibration of joint understandings, materialized through what each of them says and says in return. The utterance of a first pair-part—an utterance recognizable in context as an initial part of a type of adjacency pair—establishes criteria for what general kind of action shapes a relevant response (for instance, a recognizable question sets up the relevance of an answer, a greeting sets up the relevance of a return greeting, etc.). Though a response to a first pair-part does not necessarily produce reciprocal constraints on the first speaker, it may do so. When more than two speakers are present, an answer does not typically select the person who asked the immediately preceding question to be the next speaker, nor does the answer necessarily constrain what the next speaker will say in the way that a question would do. The nonreciprocal character of these constraints becomes important when we consider speech-exchange systems such as interviews and interrogations where one party typically asks questions and the other typically answers.

Preference Organization

The relationship between first and second pair-parts goes beyond a brute categorical association between, for example, questions and answers. For some adjacency pairs preferences are clear for one or another of the alternative actions relevant to a specific position in an order of turns. In the case of invitations, for example, where an invitation forms a first pair-part, a relevant second pair-part would be either an acceptance or rejection of the invitation contained in the first part of the pair. According to conversation-analytic research, under certain conditions a preference becomes apparent when an invitation receives an acceptance (and not a rejection) in subsequent turns. The preference for acceptance of the offer contained in an invitation is, it is argued, a structural feature of talk made visible by the fact that invitations are often designed to be insulated against rejections, whereas responses to invitations are often designed to avoid being viewed as overt rejections even when they are, in effect, just that.[33] So, for instance, regarding the preference for agreement, Sacks remarks of the following excerpt that "you can see that this response is not only formed up so that the disagreement is made as weak as possible, it is held off for a great part of the turn."[34]

A: Yuh comin' down early?
B: Well, I got a lot of things to do before gettin' cleared up tomorrow. I don't know. I w ... probably won't be too early.

Other types of speech activity also exhibit "preferences" for one or another alternative mode of uptake. In the case of questions designed to take yes or no answers, Sacks proposes the following rule: "if a question is built in such a way as to exhibit a preference as between yes or no, or yes-or-no-like responses, then the answerers will tend to pick that choice, or a choice of that sort will be preferred by answerers, or should be preferred by answerers."[35] Not only do answers "in agreement" with questions predominate, "agreeing" and "disagreeing" (or nonagreeing) answers are designed and placed differently in the organization of question/answer sequences. In summary, "preference for agreement" subsumes the following organizational features.

(1) Answers that agree are placed contiguously to questions; that is, at a first opportunity, at the beginning of an answer.
(2) Answers that do not agree are variously deferred and are often prefaced by qualifying phrases or weak agreements.
(3) Answerers shape their answers to display agreement to a question's "preference":
    A: How about friends. Have you friends?
    B: I have friends. So called friends. I had friends. Let me put it that way.[36]
    Rather than saying, for instance, "No, I don't have friends anymore.," the answerer starts with a conventional expression of agreement that he then

undermines with a succession of contrary assertions. While the disagreement is evident, it is displayed with a far more elaborate organization than is commonly the case for agreements.

(4) Questioners shape (or revise) their questions to prefer agreement. This revision can be indicated by modifications of initial questions in the face of a recipient's expressions of disagreement or delayed responses.[37]

A: Can you *walk?*

    (0.4)

A: Would it be too hard for yuh?

B: Oh darling I don't know. Uh it's bleeding a little, I just took the bandage off yesterday . . .

(5) In more extended sequences, participants often back off initial positions and attempt to remedy disagreement by either reaching an understanding or compromising.[38] In the following sequence, for instance, note the reformulation that Steven's hair receives in pursuit of a basis for agreement:[39]

Linda: Well *Ste*ven's hair's the same color as Craig's,

Joan: Is it?=

Linda: =((falsetto)) Yeah=

Joan: =*I* thought Craig's was lighter.=

Linda: =*No*, I don't think so Craig's [hair isn:'t

                                    [

Joan: [(*Oh.*)

    (.)

Linda: Just about th' same color. [*It* might be a *tee*ny bit,

                                   [

Joan: [*Yea*:ah,

Joan: tch Ye[ah

              [

Linda: [But,

Linda: Just maybe streaks,

Joan: Oh(yeah)

"Preference" is analytically separate from any personal preferences imputed to individual speakers. Indeed, when acting in accord with the interactional preference system, persons may end up doing, or obliging themselves to do, things that they personally would prefer not to do. The

existence of preference systems does not mean that speakers cannot disagree, reject invitations, disobey orders, and the like. Although it might be
true that in American middle-class culture, people try not to express direct
disagreement with one another, they nevertheless *do* manage to disagree,
and when they do so, they tend to frame their disagreements in accordance
with the specifications of the preference for agreement. By producing delayed, weak, or mitigated tokens of agreement, speakers manage to express
disagreement and to preface moves into more open arguments. Hence,
even where the preference for agreement is apparently shattered, it remains the gateway through which a transition to open disagreement is first
defined and managed.[40]

Stories

Numerous conversation-analytic studies have examined stories in conversation and their constituent structures. Our account of conversational storytelling draws on a series of lectures by Harvey Sacks. The lectures were
tape-recorded and transcribed, and for some twenty years were circulated
in mimeographed form.[41] Both our account and Sacks's are heavily indebted to Harold Garfinkel's ethnomethodological writings and lectures.[42]
Several conversation-analytic studies focus on how stories are introduced
into conversational dialogue and are sensitive to the local sequential context.[43] In the present study we focus more on issues of narrative design,
moral entitlement, and the social distribution of stories; these are themes
that also were central to Sacks's work on stories, but they have been given
less attention within conversation analysis.

One of the key themes Sacks identifies when discussing narrative organization is how the storyteller "figures" in the scene described in the story.
The storyteller's presence in the story goes well beyond specific mentions
of ego and of subjective meaning. For example, the selection of predicates
to describe and juxtapose scenic details, the temporal ordering and sequencing of narrative phases, and the grammatical tense of the story all
serve to establish the teller's place within events and to provide grounds
for inferences regarding what happened and what its significance might
be. Storytellers commonly deploy spatial and temporal predicates that are
relative to the teller's and audience's past and present relations to the

events in the story. Instead of calendrical dates, proper names for persons, and geographical place-names, storytellers will often use "member-relevant" terms such as home, the office, downtown, across the street, at this point, and here, terms that presuppose the target audience's familiarity with the speaker, the unfolding scene in the story, and various common locales and occasions.⁴⁴ Consider the following story of an event that took place in the vicinity of a department store ("Cromwell's").⁴⁵ Ellen and Jean both work at Cromwell's, and Ellen has called Jean to tell her about an incident she had seen that afternoon:

Ellen: Well I just thought I'd re-*b*etter report to you what's happened at *C*romwell's toda:*y*=

Jean: =What in the world's ha:ppened. [hhh

                [

Ellen: [Did you have the day o:ff?

Jean: Ya:h?

   (0.3)

Ellen: Well I: got out to my car at fi:ve thirty I: drove arou:nd and of course I had to go by the front of the sto:re,=

Jean: =Yea*h*?=

Ellen: And there were *t*wo (0.2) police cars across the street and leh-e *c*olored lady wanted to go in the main entrance there where the *si*:lver is and all the [( )], (things).

Jean: [Yeah,]

   (0.4)

Ellen: A:nd, they wouldn't let her go i:n, and he, had a gu::*n,*

   (0.2)

Ellen: He was *h*olding a *g*un in his hand a great big lo:ng gu::*n?*

Jean: Yea:h?

Ellen: And then *o*ver on the *oth*er si:de, I mean to the *r*ight.of there, where the (0.2) em*p*loyees come ou:t, there was a *who*:le, *oh*:: must have been ten uh *e*ight or ten employees standing there, because must have been a:, it *s*eemed like they had every entrance *b*a:rred.

I don't know *w*hat was goin[g *on*

        [

Jean: [*Oh* my *G*o:d,

Ellen's "report of what happened" is set up by reference to a time ("five-thirty")[46] and a route she took by the store, which she characterizes as the normal route ("of course, I had to go by the front . . ."). These unremarkable features of her daily routine become notable by reference to the spectacle she locates at "the main entrance." Note the constellation of predicates: "two police cars across the street" the occupants of which apparently were restraining "a colored lady" who "wanted to go in . . . where the silver is." These "member-relevant" descriptions of places and characters hang together in a quasi-causal texture that describes the unfolding of events as an incident seen at a glance, one that involved typical characters (police, colored lady), doing typical things, in a commonly known public area. Without saying it in so many words, Ellen's story implies that the police restrained a suspect (or otherwise implicated party) in the vicinity of "the silver."[47] The context of the story's typified features and identities enables the pronominal references to "he" and a "gun in his hand" to be associated with the earlier mention of "police cars." The partitioning of the spatial field and the characters within it continues as Ellen mentions the "other side" where a group of "employees" are identified. This locates the employees (both spatially and morally) at a distance from the drama unfolding between the "police" and "the colored lady."

A storyteller ordinarily is granted a certain right of ownership over details of his or her own story, and the plausibility and coherence of such a story necessarily turn on the teller's claims to have experienced the events being told. How the teller experienced the events—as a storyable matter—has to do with the teller's unique access or "entitlements" to those events. This relation between experience and storyability runs deeper than the question of how stories draw on a fund of experiences; it also has to do with an attunement *in the course of an experience* to the possibility of later telling a story about that experience.[48] Witnessing and storyability are, in this sense, methodologically interwoven. Given the centrality of teller-as-character in conversational stories, a certain right or "entitlement to tell" comes with having lived or suffered through a storyable event. This right can extend to next of kin and other intimates, but unlike the entitlement to relay jokes and news stories, this right does not travel freely throughout a community. It is not so much that a speaker would be punished for telling someone else's story, but that such telling might strike others as boring or unmotivated; that is, the question would arise, "Why are *you* telling us this?" The entitlement to tell is less a matter of a speaker's a priori right of ownership to a story's events than of the temporal and sequential details internal to the story as it is told. The orders of times, places, actions, and identities within the story imply a reciprocal position from which the teller experienced, witnessed, heard about, acted within, inferred, or evaluated the scene. This positioning conveys a variable sense of distance or intimacy between the scenic particulars within the frame of the story and the narrator's relation to them. The unfolding story thus establishes how the speaker came to be in a position to know what she is talking about, and moreover, how the teller happened to care about or otherwise concern herself with the event. In other words, a story's order of details simultaneously displays the teller's local identity as hero, next of kin to key characters, mere bystander, etc., and it establishes how it is that the teller is entitled to tell just that story. Moreover, by virtue of telling the story, the narrator claims a right to have seen and talked about the events in it; a right to say something interesting, relevant, and appropriate to the immediate recipient(s); and a right to have been so positioned in the social world as to talk about the events reported. Strange as it may sound, one must establish a right to have seen something and to have seen it *that* way (as storyable). As Sacks observes in a discussion of the conversation between Ellen and Jean, an entirely different configuration of identities and rights can be imagined.

A rather different sort of thing, but again having to do with the status of the thing she sees, is [the matter of] *which* particular scene [Ellen] has seen is relevant to [the possibility] that she could have paused to watch it and could have reported it. That is, it's not that we have a scene seen and described independently of the actual scene. It's by virtue of the fact that it takes place in a public street, involving officials seeable as such at first glance, seeable as doing their business, that [Ellen] could pause to watch and then report it, as compared to the bunches of scenes that, catching out of the corner of one's eye, one knows that he shouldn't be watching. It's none of your business, you shouldn't be watching, you shouldn't have seen it. To have captured it in your eye is to already have embarrassed yourself, and you'd better not tell anyone you saw it because they might well say "Why the hell were you looking?" or "What kind of person would notice that?" "Why are you so fascinated by that sort of thing?" etc. So one of the things that the features of the scene described in the report tells the hearer is that what was seen was something that the person who saw it had rights to see. It's not that she saw a scene and described a scene, but that the described scene carries with it the legitimacy of her having seen it.[49]

A related issue that Sacks discusses is the matter of *fragile* stories.[50] A fragile story makes potentially contestable assumptions or takes potentially controversial moral positions about the events or persons it describes. Such assumptions and positions may be taken by the audience to be unproblematic, or they may be taken up as items for subsequent criticism or argument. When a story element is produced as fragile, a positive audience reaction can be taken as a sign of the audience's complicity with the terms of the story. This quiet agreement can, in turn, provide an assumptive basis for extending the narrative in a particular direction. A speaker can thus test an audience, and by doing so, he can embed his moral complicity within the further development of the story.[51] From the perspective of the narrator, the fragility of the story consists in the fact that the judgments made might easily be reapplied to a story's teller as a way of impugning the propriety of those judgments or the character of the teller. Discussing a story where the teller uses his position as a character in the story to criticize other characters, Sacks remarks: "Where, while any story might be heard in a way that leads to a questioning or a doubting of the version the teller gives, this one has discoverably formal sources for its possible fragility. Saying it in a sentence for now, they have to do with that the stories involve a character who happens to be the teller here, doubting motives, reasons, things of that order, of another character, where the doubting that's been introduced could, readily in this case, be applied to the teller-character's report of his own behavior."[52] Whether or not a possibly contentious item receives the sort of criticism it invites can thus serve as a resource for a story's teller to discern the extent to which listeners are willing to go along with the implications of the story while it is being told. Telling a fragile story can work nicely to inform the teller about recipients' attitudes toward the story by providing a marked opportunity for recipients to voice specific criticisms concerning the terms of the story and/or its sense. Where opportunities for criticism are provided but not taken up, teller may rely (at least provisionally) on the acquiescence of recipients to the terms and sense of the story told thus far as a basis for continuing that telling.

Since stories provide resources not only for understanding what happened but also for assessing a teller's positioning within those events, the teller is able to (and typically does) tell stories in such a way as to place herself as a central character and in a favorable light. In other words, people tell stories in such ways as to control inferences about the moral character of the teller-as-character's actions in the story.[53] By remaining silent where an opportunity for relevant criticism has been provided, recipients can "conspire" with the teller to protect the story from inferences that would undermine the heroic portrayal of the teller-as-character's position. Whereas doubts about and disparaging of the motives and moral qualities of other characters in the story may be expressed, the focus of the story (where its fragility succeeds) is never turned to the possibility that the motives for telling the story in such a fashion can similarly be placed in doubt. The theme of fragile stories is relevant to our analysis of the North testimony (especially in chapter 5) insofar as it sheds light on one of the basic methods by which a listening audience can be enlisted in support of a morally contentious narrative.

INSTITUTIONAL TALK AND COMMUNICATIVE ETHICS

Many studies of social interaction in institutional settings (classrooms, testing situations, doctors' offices, service organizations, courtrooms, etc.) have made use of conversation analysis (as well as discourse-analytic variants and hybrids).[54] A sizable number of these studies examine courtroom, or courtroom-like, conduct, describing how ordinary sequential procedures and commonsense methods of reasoning serve as resources for courtroom proceedings.[55] They do not claim that testimony is nothing more than an occasion for conducting highly regimented conversations. Instead, they argue that insofar as interrogations are conducted in a natural language, and insofar as they include parties (such as witnesses, juries, or television audiences) who are specifically identified as *ordinary* members of the society, interrogations are subject to nonspecialized analyses of their organization.

Often, conversation-analytic studies treat ordinary conversation between peers as a normative backdrop for analyzing and evaluating what happens in particular instances and collections of instances, of organizationally situated action. A point of departure for many studies is the claim that mundane conversation occupies a central position (a foundation, baseline, or substrate) within an entire ecology of systems of talk-in-interaction. As Sacks, Schegloff, and Jefferson describe it, conversational turn-taking is an "economy," organized by a "machinery" whose operations are general in scope, subsuming all forms of interaction in which talk is ordered by turns, and in which one party speaks at a time. According to their model, conversation is organized in a much more fluid, and less "prespecified" way, than other systems of talk: rights to talk or remain silent, the content of what a speaker can say, the length of time the speakers can talk, all are not determined in advance for conversation, but instead are allowed to vary, and are managed locally. These facts distinguish conversations from meetings, debates, interrogations, and other formal or institutionalized speech situations.[56] Conversation thus takes on a kind of foundational status.

> It appears likely that conversation should be considered the basic form of speech-exchange system, with other systems on the array representing a variety of transformations of conversation's turn-taking system, to achieve other types of turn-taking systems. In this light, debate or ceremony would not be an independent polar type, but rather the most extreme transformation of conversation—most extreme in fully fixing the most important (and perhaps nearly all) of the parameters which conversation allows to vary.[57]

This foundational conception of conversation is normatively charged, and some interpreters have derived from it a principled ethical stance to the effect that coparticipants in conversation assume of themselves, assume of each other, and assume of each on behalf of the other a set of rights to act freely and responsibly in an open system.[58] This conception of conversational free exchange has been used as a normative standard in microanalyses and critiques of power in doctors' offices, classrooms, and other institutions, and in exchanges between men and women. Power in such instances takes hold through institutionalized asymmetries in participants' rights to speak, finish what they start to say, initiate topics, and perform speech acts of various kinds.[59] So, for example, a doctor, educator, or interrogator assumes a right (and an obligation) to initiate and sustain lines of questioning and is in a position to challenge or assess the answers given by the patient, student, or witness. In such circumstances, when a patient, student, or witness exercises conversationally legitimate options to give as well as receive orders, for example, initiate as well as respond to inquiries, or make as well as accept assessments, such moves may transgress asymmetric rights to employ specific turn types and to assume specific conversational prerogatives. Depending on the circumstances, such moves may come across as offenses, jokes, wisecracks, or momentary times out from a restricted system of institutional talk.[60] When described as a base system transformed into more restricted configurations in various institutional settings, the machinery of conversation seems ideally suited for integration within programs, such as Habermas's, that aim to specify a pragmatic ethics of human communication.[61]

There are obvious attractions to an attempt to analyze and evaluate specific systems and occasions of discourse by reference to a "naturally organized" system for establishing protoethical rights and obligations to speak and listen. Among these attractions is the possibility of reconciling ethnomethodology's micro researches with more general social-theoretic models and normative programs. For the most part, conversation analysts describe pragmatic norms other than those associated with truth-telling, but their conception of conversation as a relatively unforced exchange of utterances has some surface affinity with Habermas's idealized conception of undistorted communication enabling the expression of truth. The bridging idea is the association between unconstrained "free" action and truth-telling. This association also happens to be prominent in modern conceptions of jurisprudence and science, as exemplified by restrictions against forced testimony in court and arguments supportive of the autonomy of scientific investigation from religious or political interference. Conversely, someone whose rights to speak are restricted in an asymmetrical way—for example, an employee conversing with a boss—is not free to speak a truth that may jeopardize the employee's position.

Interrogation in courts and tribunals becomes especially interesting in this regard. Although explicitly oriented to truth, interrogation involves a differential assignment of question and answer turns to the two principal participants in the dialogue. This, along with the various interrogative strategems designed to force confessional truth from a witness's lips, produces anything but the pragmatic conditions for a free exchange. To figure that interrogation is a method of domination may therefore seem reasonable.[62] Although more gentle than torture, the intrinsic mechanisms of interrogation problematize the admissions and confessions that they are designed to bring into the open insofar as these arise from an asymmetrical distortion or constraint upon the witness's conversational prerogatives. But, in our view, the idea that interrogation is a method of domination assumes too determinate a picture of testimony. Guided by the startling empowerment, at the time, of North by the very interrogative machinery that one might have thought was weighted in favor of his interrogators on the joint House-Senate committees, we can begin to grasp how North and his allies did not simply seize hold of a pre-given system of discursive levers; they did not simply reverse the force of an interrogative machinery and turn it against its operators. Instead, the actions of North and his colleagues selectively, collusively, and unobtrusively *relativized* the operative speech-exchange system(s) in which, and through which, they acted.

Our treatment of the hearings as a spectacle runs somewhat contrary to a research policy employed effectively in conversation analysis, which is to decompose events endowed with spectacular public significance into their mundane conversational constituents. Schegloff, for example, argues in favor of giving priority to the analysis of general features of talk-in-interaction before proceeding to more spectacular or "unique" occasions: "before addressing what is unique, analysis must specify what is the generic domain within which that uniqueness is located."[63] This is good advice in light of the fact that it is all too easy to allow a notable case involving famous people and "significant" events to bear the burden of interest in a study. The problem with this advice is that "the generic domain" of mundane talk-in-interaction is inexhaustible. One could spend a lifetime working out the relations between a set of unique materials under analysis and the generic domain of mundane conversation. While such an effort might certainly contribute to the conversation-analytic corpus of findings, it is not so clear that it would enable a singular understanding of the case under examination. The generic domain of conversation is not the only relevant backdrop against which singular events take on their specificity and sensibility. While a spectacular case, when construed as an occasion of talk at work, may recall general properties identified by conversation analysts, such properties may be irrelevant to a consideration of the spectacle as such. Recognizable constituents of the event, such as a speaker's presence on television, his wearing of a uniform, his being surrounded by cameras, and his speaking on behalf of a government, do not become materially irrelevant simply because the talk largely is composed of generic procedures that can be found elsewhere. While studies of such spectacles may not discover any "new" forms of talk to be added to the conversation-analytic corpus, other things may be more perspicuous.

Although we *do* think it is pertinent to take account of what conversation analysts have said about talk and bodily actions in various settings, our policy is to treat the hearings less as an occasion of "talk" than as a variegated production within which talk was situated (whether mundane or not in its analytical details). The key point for considering the relevance of conversation or any other determinate system of speech exchange (including the abstract construct, "talk-in-interaction") is that we see no reason to figure that *any single* context-free system should necessarily hold fast as a foundation, as a base system establishing the rules, when we play our various language games. In the instances we have examined throughout this book it should be clear that alternative normative systems, including alternative systems of talk, implicating alternative conceptions of what was right and appropriate for the witness to say and do (or to have said or have done in the past), became contentiously relevant as background conditions for legitimating the moves made by the participants. While describing such maneuverings, we are not proposing to retreat to a value-neutral position—a "view from nowhere." Instead, we are attempting to explicate our materials in a way that grants foundational status to no single system or theory of communicative action. If this means that, by default, we remain held in the grip of unacknowledged normative presuppositions, so be it. Our descriptive language is ordinary, and, as such, it bears countless implications that we cannot hope to specify or control. Our descriptions are assailable, defeasible accounts, uncommitted to any single analytical model of conversational pragmatics or communicative ethics. Our ethnomethodological approach therefore is postanalytical in the sense that we presume that, and selectively describe how, the sources of intelligible action and defensible judgment are not contained within even the most elaborate system of prescriptions and specifications.

NOTES

INTRODUCTION

1. Michael Schudson, *Watergate in American Memory: How We Remember, Forget, and Reconstruct the Past* (New York: Basic Books, 1992). Schudson (p. 20) also speaks of a conventionally accepted basic narrative that provides a "bare bones chronology of 'Watergate.'"

2. McFarlane was national security adviser from October 1983 until December 1985, at which time Poindexter assumed the position.

3. Ronald Reagan, nationally televised speech, March 4, 1987, responding to criticisms stated in the report of the presidentially appointed special review board. For a published version of the report, see John Tower, Edmund Muskie, and Brent Scowcroft, *The Tower Commission Report: The Full Text of the President's Special Review Board* (New York: Times Books, 1987).

4. Although the reference to a "civics lesson" is borrowed from Foucault (*Discipline and Punish: The Birth of the Prison,* trans. Alan Sheridan [New York: Vintage Books, 1979], p. 112), one need not be a Foucaultian to appreciate the point. In a newspaper article on the criminal trial of John Poindexter, North's boss at the National Security Council, the article describes the prosecutor's opening presentation to the jury: "[Dan K.] Webb, 44, a boyish-looking Chicago prosecutor with flat Midwestern vowels and a common-man manner, offered the jurors *a tightly organized history and civics lesson* for about an hour and three quarters, interwoven with accusations of lies, obfuscation and conspiracy on the part of the defendant." Ethan Bronner, "Poindexter's Iran-contra trial opens," *Boston Globe,* March 9, 1990, p. 10. Emphasis added.

5. *Joint Hearings Before the Senate Select Committee on Secret Military Assistance to Iran and the Nicaraguan Opposition and the House Select Committee to Investigate Covert Arms Transactions with Iran,* 100th Congress, 1st Session, H961-34, Testimony of Oliver L. North, part 1 (Washington, D.C.: U.S. Government Printing Office, 1988), p. 10. Hereafter cited as *Joint Hearings,* North.

6. North: "I came here to tell you the truth—the good, the bad, and the ugly." Ibid.

7. See Schudson, *Watergate in American Memory,* chap. 9, "Memory ignited: The metaphor of Watergate in Iran-contra," pp. 165–84; Ann Wroe, *Lives, Lies, and the Iran-Contra Affair* (New York: I. B. Tauris, 1991).

8. Social constructionist perspectives can be found in virtually every social science. For a selection of studies in the field of "social problems" research, see Gale Miller and James Holstein (eds.), *Reconsidering Social Constructionism* (Hawthorne, N.J.: Aldine, 1993). Representative collections of constructivist and related studies are presented in Karin Knorr Cetina and Michael Mulkay (eds.), *Science*

Observed: Perspectives on the Social Study of Science (Beverly Hills, Calif.: Sage, 1983), and Andrew Pickering (ed.), *Science as Practice and Culture* (Chicago: University of Chicago Press, 1991). For a review and critique of constructionist approaches, see Michael Lynch, *Scientific Practice and Ordinary Action: Ethnomethodology and Social Studies of Science* (Cambridge: Cambridge University Press, 1993).

9. This relativist view is criticized by Peter Berger and Thomas Luckmann, *The Social Construction of Reality* (New York: Anchor Books, 1966).

10. Stanley Fish, *Doing What Comes Naturally: Change, Rhetoric, and the Practice of Theory in Literary and Legal Studies* (Durham, N.C.: Duke University Press, 1989), p. 225.

11. Ibid., p. 226.

12. For a more complete working out of this position, see David Bogen and Michael Lynch, "Do we need a general theory of social problems?," in Miller and Holstein, *Reconsidering Social Constructionism,* pp. 213–37. See also Graham Button, "The curious case of the vanishing technology," in Graham Button (ed.), *Technology in Working Order: Studies of Work, Interaction, and Technology* (London and New York: Routledge, 1993), pp. 10–28.

13. An official history of the Iran-contra affair is presented in Daniel K. Inouye and Lee H. Hamilton, *Report of the Congressional Committees Investigating the Iran-Contra Affair* (Washington, D.C.: U.S. Government Printing Office, 1987); abridged ed., ed. Joel Brinkley and Stephen Engleberg (New York: Times Books, 1988). This document also includes a minority report that elaborates a reconstruction of the key events and a set of recommendations more supportive of the administration's side. A later report, based on the independent counsel's investigations of criminal charges, includes sections on "basic facts" and "underlying facts." Lawrence E. Walsh, *Final Report of the Independent Counsel for Iran/Contra Matters—United States Court of Appeals for the District of Columbia Circuit* (Washington, D.C.: U.S. Government Printing Office, 1994); abridged ed. (New York: Times Books, 1994). Other reports and chronologies include Tower et al., *The Tower Commission Report;* William S. Cohen and George J. Mitchell, *Men of Zeal: A Candid Inside Story of the Iran-Contra Hearings* (New York: Viking, 1988); Scott Armstrong (executive ed.), *The Chronology,* a report by the National Security Archive (New York: Warner Books, 1987); and Theodore Draper, *A Very Thin Line: The Iran-Contra Affairs* (New York: Hill and Wang, 1991).

14. For a discussion of "production" as compared with prevailing conceptions of "social construction," see Garfinkel's remarks in Benetta Jules-Rosette, "Conversation avec Harold Garfinkel," *Sociétés: Revue des Sciences Humaines et Socioloes* 1 (1985): 35–39.

15. The conception of "ethnomethodological respecification" is discussed in the Methodological Appendix. See Harold Garfinkel, "Respecification: Evidence for

locally produced, naturally accountable phenomena of order, logic, reason, meaning, method, etc. in and as of the essential haecceity of immortal ordinary society (I)—an announcement of studies," in *Ethnomethodology and the Human Sciences,* ed. G. Button (Cambridge: Cambridge University Press), pp. 10–19.

16. This argument for recasting the concerns of contemporary philosophy in pragmatic terms is elaborated in David Bogen and Michael Lynch, "Taking account of the hostile native: Plausible deniability and the production of conventional history in the Iran-contra hearings," *Social Problems* 36 (1989): 197–224.

17. For a debate about sociological treatments of deconstruction as a way of describing substantive arguments in law and science, see Stephen Fuchs and Steven Ward, "What is deconstruction, and where and when does it take place? Making facts in science, building cases in law," *American Sociological Review* 59 (1994): 481–500; and Ben Agger, "Derrida for sociology? A comment on Fuchs and Ward," *American Sociological Review* 59 (1994): 501–5.

18. Constructionist approaches in the social sciences antedate a more recent infusion of deconstructionist influence from literary theory. For the most part, however, social scientists who have embraced deconstructionism treat it as an extension of social constructionism. See, for example, the selections in a special section on "Writing the social text," *Sociological Theory* (1990): 188–245. For a critical response, see Michael Lynch and David Bogen, "In defense of dada-driven analysis," *Sociological Theory* 9 (1991): 269–76.

19. Symbolic interactionism is the most well-established approach in American sociology that has embraced broadly deconstructionist themes and initiatives. Symbolic interactionism originated early in the twentieth century with Herbert Blumer's systematization of a coherent sociological perspective from George Herbert Mead's philosophical writings and lectures at the University of Chicago. In this spinoff from American pragmatism, a dualistic "self" (consisting of an acting agent bound together with a societally attuned reactive subject) communicates and interprets the actions of other "selves" by means of symbolic expressions. G. H. Mead, *Mind, Self, and Society* (Chicago: University of Chicago Press, 1934); H. Blumer, *Symbolic Interactionism: Perspective and Method* (Englewood Cliffs, N.J.: Prentice-Hall, 1969).

20. See, for example, Michael J. Shapiro, *The Politics of Representation: Writing Practices in Biography, Photography, and Policy Analysis* (Madison: University of Wisconsin Press, 1988).

21. Jacques Derrida, "Signature, event, context," *Glyph* 1 (1977): 172–97.

22. The idea that deconstruction describes an embedded property of action in a coherent field studied by sociologists is explored in an ethnographic study of scientific work. Bruno Latour and Steve Woolgar, *Laboratory Life: The Social Construction of Scientific Facts* (London: Sage, 1979; rev. ed., Princeton, N.J.: Princeton University Press, 1986).

23. For an illuminating account of the history and contemporary implications of case-specific practical reasoning (or casuistry), see Albert Jonsen and Stephen Toulmin, *The Abuse of Casuistry: A History of Moral Reasoning* (Berkeley: University of California Press, 1988).

24. See Wes Sharrock and Bob Anderson, "Epistemology: Professional scepticism," pp. 51–76 in Button, *Ethnomethodology and the Human Sciences,* pp. 51–76.

25. Foucault, *Discipline and Punish,* p. 47.

1. THE SINCERE LIAR

1. Niklas Luhmann, "Politicians, honesty and the higher immorality of politics," *Theory, Culture & Society* 11 (1994): 27.

2. Lawrence E. Walsh, *Final Report of the Independent Counsel for Iran/Contra Matters—United States Court of Appeals for the District of Columbia Circuit,* 3 vols. (Washington, D.C.: U.S. Government Printing Office, 1994).

3. See Peter Winch, "Nature and convention," chap. 3 of *Ethics and Action* (London: Routledge and Kegan Paul, 1972), p. 62.

4. See Sissela Bok, *Lying: Moral Choice in Public and Private Life* (New York: Random House, 1979). Bok's definition is corroborated in the more playful and nuanced treatment of lying in J. A. Barnes, *A Pack of Lies: Towards a Sociology of Lying* (Cambridge: Cambridge University Press, 1994), p. 11. Barnes also mentions that lies, lying, and deception are "slippery" concepts which defy tight definition. The two elements of lying are implied in special prosecutor Lawrence Walsh's statement that he decided not to prosecute former Secretary of State George Shultz for lying in his testimony at the hearings "because there was a reasonable doubt that Shultz's testimony was willfully false at the time it was delivered." Quoted in Theodore Draper, "Walsh's last stand," *New York Review of Books* (March 3, 1994), p. 28.

5. Barnes observes in *A Pack of Lies* that in many circumstances, such as in politics, participants are wise to expect the opposite. It is frequently said that judges and lawyers assume that witnesses lie with such great regularity that charges of perjury tend to arise only for special reasons. Also see Marcus Stone, *Cross-Examination in Criminal Trials,* 2d ed. (London: Buttersworth, 1995), p. 48.

6. Paul Ekman, *Telling Lies: Clues to Deceit in the Marketplace, Politics, and Marriage* (New York: Norton, 1985), p. 25.

7. John Locke, *Essay Concerning Human Understanding,* 2 vols., ed. A. C. Fraser (New York: Dover, 1959 [1690]), bk. IV, ch. 15, sec. 5. An elaboration on these "prudential maxims" and their relevance to the moral/epistemic judgments of seventeenth-century English natural philosophers is presented in Steven Shapin, *A Social History of Truth: Civility and Science in Seventeenth-Century England* (Chi-

cago: University of Chicago Press, 1994). On the role of these maxims in law and natural philosophy, see Barbara Shapiro, " 'To a moral certainty': Theories of knowledge and Anglo-American juries, 1600–1850," *Hastings Law Journal* 38 (1986): 153–93.

8. North was convicted on three charges on May 6, 1989: aiding and abetting an obstruction of congressional inquiries in November 1986, destroying and falsifying official NSC documents, and receiving an illegal gratuity (a security fence). The charges referred to actions before the hearings, and not to his testimony during them. See Walsh, *Final Report*, p. 120.

9. Theodore Draper, *A Very Thin Line: The Iran-Contra Affairs* (New York: Hill and Wang, 1991), p. 516.

10. Ben Bradlee Jr., *Guts and Glory: The Rise and Fall of Oliver North* (New York: Donald I. Fine, 1988), p. 544.

11. Ibid., p. 547.

12. Constantine C. Menges, "The sad, strange mind of Col. North: An NSC colleague explains why Ollie met his Waterloo," *Washington Post,* Nov. 27, 1988, p. D4. Haynes Johnson attributes a similar judgment of North to Arthur Liman, chief counsel to the Senate select committee: "Liman had seen many people like North. They could not distinguish easily between fantasy and fact." Johnson, *Sleepwalking Through History: America in the Reagan Years* (New York: Anchor Books, 1991), p. 354.

13. Michael Rogin. *"Ronald Reagan," The Movie: And Other Episodes in Political Demonology* (Berkeley: University of California Press, 1987), chap. 1.

14. Quoted in anonymous editorial, "Liar-hero of the American right," *Observer* (London), June 12, 1994, p. 23.

15. For grand-theoretical treatments of the role of trust in modern society, see Niklas Luhmann, *Trust and Power: Two Works* (Chichester, Sussex: John Wiley, 1979); Anthony Giddens, *The Consequences of Modernity* (Stanford, Calif.: Stanford University Press, 1989); Bernard Barber, *The Logic and Limits of Trust* (New Brunswick, N.J.: Rutgers University Press, 1983). A more pervasive role for trust is demonstrated in Harold Garfinkel, "A conception of, and experiments with, 'trust' as a condition of stable concerted actions," in *Motivation and Social Interaction,* ed. O. J. Harvey (New York: Ronald Press, 1963), pp. 187–238. A concise review of historical and contemporary philosophical writings on the importance of trust for maintaining social order is presented in Shapin, *Social History of Truth,* pp. 8–15. For a critical discussion of assumptions about public cynicism and apathy in the era of televisual politics, see Robin Erica Wagner-Pacifici, *The Moro Morality Play: Terrorism as Social Drama* (Chicago: University of Chicago Press, 1986), pp. 290–94.

16. *Newsweek,* July 20, 1987. The question: "Is North telling the whole truth, is he holding back certain information to protect himself, or is he holding back certain

information to protect others?" The responses: "Whole truth," 19 percent; "Protecting himself," 23 percent; "Protecting others," 53 percent.

17. Editors of *U.S. News and World Report, The Story of Lieutenant Colonel Oliver North* (Washington, D.C., 1987), p. 30.

18. "Liar-hero of the American right," p. 23.

19. Michel Foucault, *Power/Knowledge: Selected Interviews and Other Writings, 1972–1977* (New York: Pantheon, 1980), p. 90.

20. Saul Kripke, "Outline of a theory of truth," *Journal of Philosophy* 72 (1975): 690.

21. While noting that little sociological research on lying and deception has been produced, Barnes (*A Pack of Lies*, p. 5) briefly mentions the immense philosophical literature on the Liar Paradox. He is correct in saying that for the most part the logicians' interests are irrelevant to a sociological conception of lying, but as we shall argue, variants of the paradox may be pertinent in other ways.

22. A. Stroll, "Is everyday language inconsistent?" *Mind* 63 (1954): 219–25. For a critical discussion of Stroll's argument, see Harvey Sacks, *Lectures on Conversation,* ed. G. Jefferson (Oxford: Basil Blackwell, 1992), 1: 693–700. Also see David Bogen, "Beyond the 'limits' of Mundane Reason," *Human Studies* 13 (1990): 411ff.

23. For a related discussion of a vernacular use of "everyone," see Harvey Sacks, "Everyone has to lie," in *Sociocultural Dimensions of Language Use,* ed. M. Sanches and B. G. Blount (New York: Academic Press, 1975), pp. 57–79.

24. Robert L. Martin attributes to Tarski the position that natural languages are unsuitable for strict logical analysis: "anyone who thinks that truth is expressed or is expressible in natural language is committed thereby to a contradiction, and so is proved wrong." "Introduction," Martin (ed.) *Recent Essays on Truth and the Liar Paradox* (New York: Oxford University Press, 1984), p. 5.

25. This sequence is discussed at greater length in chapters 3 and 4.

26. July 7, 1987, morning session, ML/DB transcript.

27. Johnson, *Sleepwalking Through History,* p. 349.

28. See Cohen and Mitchell, *Men of Zeal,* pp. 184ff.

29. Bok, *Lying,* p. 142.

30. Ibid., p. 146.

31. Ibid., p. 149.

32. Seven years after the hearings, North went further in denouncing the Congress when, as a candidate for the U.S. Senate and employing language reminiscent of Nixon's vice president, Spiro Agnew, he drove a rhetorical wedge between "the people" and "the permanent political potentates of pork" in the federal government. See "Liar-hero of the American right," p. 23.

33. Stephen Turner points out that "[t]he 'concept of the political' was defined for [Carl] Schmitt by the *possibility* of a struggle metastasizing into a struggle of the most extreme kind, a 'friend-enemy grouping' that manifests itself in war or revolu-

tion." Turner, "Depoliticizing power," *Social Studies of Science* 19 (1989): 555. Reference to Carl Schmitt, *Political Theology: Four Chapters on the Concept of Sovereignty,* trans. George Schwab (Cambridge, Mass.: MIT Press, 1985), pp. 25–30.

34. The idea of "warding off inferences" is developed in Sacks, *Lectures on Conversation,* p. 457.

35. July 9, 1987, morning session, ML/DB transcript.

36. This textual format was characteristic of the period of 'high casuistry,' especially in the sixteenth century. See Albert Jonson and Stephen Toulmin, *The Abuse of Casuistry: A History of Moral Reasoning* (Berkeley: University of California Press, 1988), p. 143.

37. North finished off a long speech on the first morning of his testimony by asserting: "Those are the facts, as I know them, Mr. Nields. I was glad that when you introduced this, you said that you wanted to hear the truth. I came here to tell you the truth—the good, the bad, and the ugly. I am here to tell it all, pleasant and unpleasant, and I am here to accept responsibility for that which I did. I will not accept responsibility for that which I did not do." This passage is discussed in greater detail in chapter 3.

38. Shapin (*Social History of Truth,* p. 111) describes the grave significance of accusations of lying among "gentlemen" in early modern England and other parts of Western Europe. Truth-telling was such a valued quality in "gentle" society that a direct accusation of lying was likely to elicit a challenge to a duel. According to a seventeenth-century English courtesy text quoted by Shapin, the phrasing of accusations about truth-telling was all-important if a gentleman wished to avoid the *mentita,* or "giving the lie"—the accusation of lying—which under particular circumstances was guaranteed to force a challenge to a duel: "If I say vnto another man, *Thou saiest not true,* thereby I reproue him, and consequentlie offer iniurie: but if I say, *That which thou saiest is not true,* that speach is not iniurious, and may be without burthen of him vnto whom it is spoken." William Segar, *The Booke of Honor and Armes* (1590), facsimile reproduction (Delmar, N.Y.: Scholars' Facsimiles & Reprints, 1975), pp. 5–11.

39. Bok, *Lying,* p. 175.

40. Sacks, *Lectures on Conversation,* p. 506. See chapter 5 for further discussion of Sacks's notion of "fragile story," a story in which the teller is featured as a character and where other characters' motives, reasons, and actions are portrayed in a doubtful or negative light.

41. Ibid., p. 313. Also see Roy P. McDermott and Henry Tylbor, "On the necessity of collusion in conversation," *Text* 3 (1983): 277–97.

42. Ekman, *Telling Lies.*

43. William Healy and Mary Tenney Healy, *Pathological Lying, Accusation, and Swindling: A Study in Forensic Psychology* (Boston: Little, Brown, 1926), p. 26.

44. Ibid., p. 44.

45. Anna Stemmermann, *Beiträge und Kasuistik der Pseudologia Phantastica* (Berlin: George Reimer, 1906), cited in Healy and Healy, *Pathological Lying,* pp. 27–28.

46. Shapin, *Social History of Truth,* p. 96. Reference to Henry Mason, *The New Art of Lying, Covered by Jesuits under the Vaile of Equivocation* (London, 1624).

47. See Yaron Ezrahi, "Technology and the civil epistemology of democracy," *Inquiry* 35 (1993): 1–13. Ezrahi draws on and develops a political application of the concept "virtual witnessing," developed in the social history of science by Steven Shapin and Simon Schaffer, *Leviathan and the Air Pump* (Princeton, N.J.: Princeton University Press, 1985).

48. R. D. Hare, A. E. Forth, and S. D. Hart, "The psychopath as a prototype for pathological lying and deception," in *Credibility Assessment,* ed. John C. Yuille (Dordrecht: Kluwer Academic Publishers, 1989), p. 35. Although Hare, Forth, and Hart speak of "the psychopath" here, we read this term to apply to a broader variety of confabulators, regardless of diagnosis.

49. Erving Goffman, "The insanity of place," in *Relations in Public* (New York: Harper and Row, 1971), pp. 335–90.

50. Oliver Sacks, *The Man Who Mistook His Wife for a Hat and Other Clinical Tales* (New York: Perennial Library, 1987), p. 111.

51. Ibid.

52. Garfinkel's well-known experiments using mock-ups of counseling sessions and job interviews with rigged answers provide further indications of how a restricted setup can enable wildly implausible performances to come off as believable. See Harold Garfinkel, *Studies in Ethnomethodology* (Englewood Cliffs, N.J.: Prentice-Hall, 1967), pp. 58ff.

53. Jürgen Habermas, *Theory of Communicative Action* (Boston: Beacon Press, 1984), 1:105.

54. The design of the "truth-finding engine" of interrogation is discussed in chapter 4.

55. See Shapin, *Social History of Truth,* pp. 79ff.

56. The distinction between expressions "given" and "given off" in social interaction is developed in Erving Goffman, *The Presentation of Self in Everyday Life* (New York: Doubleday, 1959), pp. 2ff.

57. See William O'Barr (ed.), *Linguistic Evidence: Language, Power, and Strategy in the Courtroom* (New York: Academic Press, 1982); William Labov, *Sociolinguistic Patterns* (Philadelphia: University of Pennsylvania Press, 1972); S. M. A. Lloyd-Bostock and B. R. Clifford (eds.), *Evaluating Witness Evidence: Recent Psychological Research and New Perspectives* (New York: John Wiley, 1977); B. Pryor and R. W. Buchanan, "The effect of a defendant's demeanor on jury perceptions of credibility and guilt," *Journal of Communications* 34 (1984): 92–99; W. L. Bennett, "Storytelling in criminal trials—a model of social judgment," *Quarterly Journal of*

Speech 64 (1978): 1–22; Augustine Brannigan and Michael Lynch, "On bearing false witness: Perjury and credibility as interactional accomplishments," *Journal of Contemporary Ethnography* 16 (1987): 115–46.

58. Paul Ekman, "Why lies fail," in Yuille, *Credibility Assessment*, pp. 71–82.

59. Ekman, "Why lies fail," p. 76.

60. Charles Goodwin, "Forgetfulness as an interactive resource," *Social Psychology Quarterly* 50 (1987): 117.

61. Ekman, "Why lies fail," p. 73. Stone, *Cross-Examination in Criminal Trials*, p. 51, underlines this point by saying that psychological "technique or test" cannot appreciably assist "common-sense" judgments about lying in the interrogative situation and that insight about lying "certainly cannot be derived from so-called body language." Stone argues that the psychologist might learn more about lying from a skilled cross-examiner than vice versa. In our view, sociologists are in no better position, and we have endeavored to treat the interactional exposure of "lying" as a practical phenomenon rather than a problem to be solved through application of a social science method.

62. John C. Yuille, editor's introduction, in Yuille, *Credibility Assessment*, p. 4.

63. See Joan Didion, "Insider baseball," *New York Review of Books*, Oct. 27, 1988, p. 24.

64. Jeffrey Alexander, "Culture and political crisis: 'Watergate' and Durkheimian sociology," in J. C. Alexander (ed.), *Durkheimian Sociology: Cultural Studies* (Cambridge: Cambridge University Press, 1989), p. 200.

65. *New Yorker*, July 20, 1987, "Notes and Comment," pp. 19–20.

66. "It was a remarkable show, better than the soaps, many thought, and it was all live on television. . . ." Johnson, *Sleepwalking Through History*, p. 361.

67. See Theodore Draper, "Rewriting the Iran-contra story," *New York Review of Books*, Jan. 19, 1989, p. 38. Draper characterizes letters reported by Senators Cohen and Mitchell, *Men of Zeal*. Like Liman, Cohen was a target of anti-Semitic letters, although he is not Jewish.

68. See Mark Crispin Miller, "Deride and conquer," in Todd Gitlin (ed.), *Watching Television* (New York: Pantheon, 1986), pp. 183–228.

69. *New Yorker*, July 20, 1987, pp. 19–20.

70. See D. R. Watson, "Some features of the elicitation of confessions in murder investigations," in *Interaction Competence*, ed. George Psathas (Washington D.C.: International Institute for Ethnomethodology and Conversation Analysis and University Press of America, 1990), pp. 263–95.

71. Johnson, *Sleepwalking Through History*, p. 363. This is also discussed in Mitchell and Cohen, *Men of Zeal*, p. 75.

72. Johnson, *Sleepwalking Through History*, pp. 364–65.

73. For further discussion of opening moves in the testimony, see chapter 3.

74. July 9, 1987, morning session, *Joint Hearings*, North, pt. 1, p. 190.

75. In his diagnosis of what went wrong for the committee's interrogators, Draper ("Rewriting the Iran-contra story," p. 38) placed the onus on Liman and Nields: "They too often behaved as if they were less interested in eliciting information from witnesses than in arguing with and getting the better of them." Given the dialogical setting, and North's, Secord's and other witness's formulations of "answers" to present counterarguments and counternarratives to those supplied in the interrogator's "questions" (see chap. 4), it is difficult to assign unilateral blame for the conversion of "information seeking" to "argument."

76. Alexander and Smith document that both North and spokesmen for the committee majority enlisted a "democratic code" of values while ascribing a "counter-democratic code" to their opposite numbers. It seems that both sides struggled over the possibility of such documentation and over the relative symmetry or asymmetry of its distribution, so that the issue was less a matter of "coding," as Alexander and Smith would have it, than of a production and a struggle over the terms of the production. Jeffrey C. Alexander and Philip Smith, "The discourse of American civil society: A new proposal for cultural studies," *Theory and Society* 22 (1993): 188–92.

77. Ibid., 104.

78. See Daniel K. Inouye and Lee H. Hamilton, *Report of the Congressional Committees Investigating the Iran-Contra Affair* (Washington, D.C.: U.S. Government Printing Office, 1988); p. 375ff. on "covert action in a democratic society." Committee members Cohen and Mitchell (*Men of Zeal*, p. 167) write that "no member of the Committee favored a prohibition. We all recognized that there are some circumstances in which the United States must conduct such operations. The problem is that covert operations, by their very nature, conflict with democratic values."

2. THE PRODUCTION OF HISTORY

1. Friedrich Nietzsche, *The Use and Abuse of History,* trans. A. Collins (Indianapolis, Ind.: Bobbs-Merrill, 1949), pp. 8–9.

2. Howard Horwitz, "'I can't remember': Skepticism, synthetic histories, critical action," *South Atlantic Quarterly* 87 (1988): 788.

3. Similar arguments are made, although for different programmatic purposes, in Robin Erica Wagner-Pacifici, *The Moro Morality Play: Terrorism as Social Drama* (Chicago: University of Chicago Press, 1986), and Mitchell Dean, *Critical and Effective Histories: Foucault's Methods and Historical Sociology* (London: Routledge, 1994).

4. Daniel K. Inouye and Lee H. Hamilton, *Report of the Congressional Committees Investigating the Iran-Contra Affair,* with *Supplemental, Minority, and Additional Views* (Washington, D.C.: U.S. Government Printing Office, 1987), pp. 180–81.

5. See Dorothy Smith, "The social construction of documentary reality," *Sociological Inquiry* 44 (1974): 257–68.

6. At the end of the morning session on North's first day of testifying (June 7, 1987), television commentators mentioned the "tedium" that attended the repeated interrogation on apparently minor documentary matters.

7. *Report of the Congressional Committees Investigating the Iran-Contra Affair, with Supplemental, Minority and Additional Views,* p. 11 (cited in Horwitz, "I can't remember," pp. 813–14 n. 2).

8. Richard J. Hill and Kathleen Stones Crittenden (eds.), *Proceedings of the Purdue Symposium in Ethnomethodology,* Institute Monograph Series, no. 1 (Purdue, Ind.: Institute for the Study of Social Change and the Department of Sociology, Purdue University, 1968), p. 158.

9. Ibid.

10. This is a paraphrase of Garfinkel, in ibid., p. 152.

11. Although we are focusing on the more overt and sensational case of documentary practice within the intelligence community and high-level governmental agencies, ethnomethodological studies of organizational behavior suggest that this kind of "practical-historical orientation" is a routine feature of organizational life. See, esp., Harold Garfinkel and Egon Bittner, "'Good' organizational reasons for 'bad' clinic records," in Garfinkel (ed.), *Studies in Ethnomethodology* (Englewood Cliffs, N.J.: Prentice-Hall, 1967), pp. 186–207.

12. See David Bogen and Michael Lynch, "Taking account of the hostile native: Plausible deniability and the production of conventional history at the Iran-contra hearings," *Social Problems* 36 (1988): 197–224.

13. Doug Benson and Paul Drew provide an analogous example of a tribunal where witnesses are called to account for the sense of their own documentary reports of an event. See Benson and Drew, "'Was there firing in Sandy Row that night?': Some features of the organisation of disputes about recorded facts," *Sociological Inquiry* 48 (1978): 89–100.

14. Testimony of Oliver North, morning session, July 7, 1987, *Joint Hearings, North,* pt. 1, p. 14.

15. See, for instance, the essays by Stephen Greenblatt et al. in H. Aram Veeser (ed.), *The New Historicism* (London and New York: Routledge, 1989).

16. This achievement leads Horwitz to a similar conclusion that "[f]oregrounding the oppositional possibilities of a hermeneutics of suspicion does not eliminate but rather neglects the problems of relativism." Horwitz, "I can't remember," p. 794.

17. Georg Lukács, *History and Class Consciousness,* trans. Rodney Livingstone (London: Merlin Press, 1971), pp. 46–47.

18. The linkage between theoretical attempts to transcend commonsense knowl-

edge of social structure and the tie to "sociology's endless project" is articulated in Harold Garfinkel, and Harvey Sacks, "On formal structures of practical actions," in *Theoretical Sociology: Perspectives and Development*, ed. J. C. McKinney and E. A. Tiryakian (New York: Appleton-Century-Crofts, 1970), pp. 337–66.

19. As Stanley Fish has noted, the "anti-foundationalist" sentiment that lies behind such challenges has a broad and established basis in philosophy, literary studies, history of art, legal theory and the social sciences. As Fish concludes: "Obviously it is not an isolated argument; in fact, today one could say that it is the *going* argument." Stanley Fish, "Anti-foundationalism, theory hope, and the teaching of composition," in *Doing What Comes Naturally: Change, Rhetoric, and the Practice of Theory in Literary and Legal Studies* (Durham, N.C.: Duke University Press, 1989), p. 345.

20. Hayden White, "The fictions of factual representation," in *The Literature of Fact: Selected Papers from the English Institute*, ed. Angus Fletcher (New York: Columbia University Press, 1976), pp. 22–23. Reprinted in Hayden White, *Tropics of Discourse* (Baltimore: Johns Hopkins University Press, 1978). For a related use of White's conception of history in a study of the production of an event, see Wagner-Pacifici, *Moro Morality Play*, pp. 2ff.

21. The most succinct overview of this element in Jürgen Habermas's work can be found in Habermas, "A reply to my critics," in *Habermas: Critical Debates*, ed. John B. Thompson and David Held (Cambridge, Mass.: MIT Press, 1982), pp. 219–83. See also Karl-Otto Apel, *Understanding and Explanation: A Transcendental-Pragmatic Perspective*, trans. Georgia Warnke (Cambridge, Mass.: MIT Press, 1984).

22. See, for instance, Lukács, *History and Class Consciousness:* "dialectics insists on the concrete unity of the whole" (p. 6). On the "totalizing" impulse behind Habermas's conception of "cognitive interests," see Peter Winch, "Apel's 'Transcendental Pragmatics,'" in S. C. Brown (ed.), *Philosophical Disputes in the Social Sciences* (Atlantic Highlands, N.J.: Humanities Press, 1979), pp. 51–73.

23. See Richard Rorty, "Habermas and Lyotard on postmodernity," in *Habermas and Modernity*, ed. Richard J. Bernstein (Cambridge, Mass.: MIT Press, 1985).

24. Ibid., p. 164.

25. Jean-François Lyotard, *The Postmodern Condition: A Report on Knowledge*, trans. Geoff Bennington and Brian Massumi (Minneapolis: University of Minnesota Press, 1984).

26. Jonathon Arac, "Introduction," in Arac (ed.), *Postmodernism and Politics* (Minneapolis: University of Minnesota Press, 1986), p. xiii. The depth of Lyotard's skepticism is best communicated by Arac's translation of the concepts of "*grand récits*" and "*petits récits*" as "tall tales" and "white lies."

27. Lyotard, *Postmodern Condition*, p. 27.

28. Arac, "Introduction," *Postmodernism and Politics*, p. xxiii.

29. For a sustained effort to collapse the categorical divisions between premod-

ern, modern, and postmodern epochs in social theory, see Bruno Latour, *We Have Never Been Modern,* trans. Catherine Porter (Cambridge, Mass.: Harvard University Press, 1993).

30. Fredric Jameson, "Foreword," in Lyotard, *Postmodern Condition,* p. xi.

31. The notion of "knowledge effects" is borrowed from Althusser: "The *mechanism* I propose to elucidate is the mechanism which produces this *knowledge effect* in those very special products we call *knowledges.*" Louis Althusser and Etienne Balibar, *Reading "Capital",* trans. Ben Brewster (London: Verso, 1979), p. 62. Although we find much in this notion that is suggestive, we are less taken by his subsequent distinction between "scientific" and "ideological" knowledge effects, by which he means to distinguish (roughly) between knowledge that is true and knowledge that is not.

32. On the use of the distinction between interpretive and perceptual claims in everyday and psychiatric discourse, see Jeff Coulter, "Perceptual accounts and interpretive asymmetries," *Sociology* 9 (1975): 385–96. See also Melvin Pollner, " 'The very coinage of your brain': The anatomy of reality disjunctures," *Philosophy of the Social Sciences* 5 (1975): 411–30.

33. In a related discussion, Bruno Latour uses the expression "immutable mobiles" to emphasize the combination of transmissibility and durability that is sustained when documents are circulated within a communal network. See Latour, "Drawing things together," in *Representation in Scientific Practice,* ed. Michael Lynch and Steve Woolgar (Cambridge, Mass.: MIT Press, 1990), pp. 19–68.

34. Lyotard, *Postmodern Condition,* p. xxv.

35. Claude Lévi-Strauss, *The Savage Mind* (Chicago: University of Chicago Press, 1966), pp. 258–62.

36. For a more detailed discussion, see David Bogen, "Linguistic forms and social obligations: A critique of the doctrine of literal expression in Searle," *Journal for the Theory of Social Behavior* 21 (1991): 31–62.

37. Hayden White, *Tropics of Discourse* (Baltimore: Johns Hopkins University Press, 1978), p. 56.

38. Ibid., p. 58. See also Northrop Frye, *Anatomy of Criticism: Four Essays* (Princeton, N.J.: Princeton University Press, 1957).

39. The seminal discussions of this notion can be found in Hayden White, *Metahistory* (Baltimore: Johns Hopkins University Press, 1973), pp. 5–11, and in his "The interpretation of history," in *Tropics of Discourse,* pp. 51–80.

40. July 7, 1987, afternoon session, ML/DB transcript.

41. *Joint Hearings,* North, pt. 1, p. 37.

42. Editors of *U.S. News & World Report, The Story of Lieutenant Colonel Oliver North* (Washington, D.C.: U.S. News & World Report, 1987), p. 47.

43. Inouye and Hamilton, *Report on Iran-Contra Affair* (abridged, 1988), pp. xxiii–xxiv.

44. Theodore Draper, *A Very Thin Line: The Iran-Contra Affairs* (New York: Hill and Wang, 1991), pp. 609–10.

45. Inouye and Hamilton, *Report on Iran-Contra Affair* (unabridged, 1987), p. 299.

46. Draper, *A Very Thin Line,* p. 486. For a fascinating story of the negotiations that took place during the construction of the false chronologies, see Ann Wroe, *Lives, Lies, and the Iran-Contra Affair* (New York: I. B. Tauris, 1991), pp. 272–79. Wroe (pp. 272–73) describes the intensive efforts through which the chronology writers disclosed as few operational details as possible and put a diplomatic cast on the details they did include. Robert Earl, an assistant of North's, used the words "constructive ambiguity" to describe these literary methods during his testimony, and his interrogator, Arthur Liman, acknowledged that it was "a terrific phrase." We also think so. Also interesting, for our purposes, was the expression used to describe the last version of the document North and his colleagues constructed. According to Wroe (p. 278), this was called the "historical" chronology.

47. Ibid., p. 487.

48. Ibid., p. 488, quoting from testimony at joint hearings, pt. 3, p. 213.

49. Ibid.

50. Wroe, *Lives, Lies, and the Iran-Contra Affair,* p. 279.

3. THE CEREMONIAL OF TRUTH

1. The concept of "civic ritual" and the prevalence of democratic values in the hearings is discussed by Jeffrey C. Alexander and Philip Smith, "The discourse of American civil society: A new proposal for cultural studies," *Theory and Society* 22 (1993): 151–207. Also see Philip Smith, "Codes and conduct: Towards a theory of war as ritual," *Theory and Society* 20 (1991): 103–38.

2. This "liberal-constitutional" view was one of the more robust legacies of Watergate, according to Michael Schudson's account of the "collective memory" of the event, and it also seems to have framed Jeffrey Alexander's reconstruction of Watergate. Another common view was that Watergate was a political attack on the president by his enemies and rivals. The balance between these and other less popular views shifted during the Watergate hearings, and popular opinion seems to have been sensitive to later events like Iran-contra and Nixon's gradual rehabilitation in mainstream politics by the time he died. Michael Schudson, *Watergate in American Memory* (New York: Basic Books, 1992), pp. 24–27; Jeffrey Alexander, "Culture and political crisis: 'Watergate' and Durkheimian sociology," in Alexander (ed.), *Durkheimian Sociology: Cultural Studies* (Cambridge: Cambridge University Press, 1989), and Alexander, "Three models of culture and society relations: Toward an analysis of Watergate," *Sociological Theory* 2 (1984): 290–314.

3. By "televisual tradition," we mean the nostalgic longing for patriotism, family,

and the pioneer tradition epitomized by cowboy movies, World War II films, family sitcoms, and other reruns of a filmic past. See Michael Rogin, *"Ronald Reagan," the Movie: And Other Episodes in Political Demonology* (Berkeley: University of California Press, 1987).

4. Michel Foucault, *Discipline and Punish: The Birth of the Prison* (New York: Random House, 1979), p. 3.

5. In a study of a more recent era of criminal justice, Haines argues that "flawed executions," where the ceremonial integrity of the execution breaks down and offends against public sensibilities of justice and propriety, provide instances of "suddenly realized grievances" coalescing movements against the death penalty. Herb Haines, "Flawed executions, the anti-death penalty movement, and the politics of capital punishment," *Social Problems* 39 (1992): 125–38. Also see Stephen Trombley, *The Execution Protocol: Inside America's Capital Punishment Industry* (New York: Crown, 1992).

6. Foucault, *Discipline and Punish*, pp. 60–61.

7. Ibid., p. 37.

8. Elizabeth Hanson, "Torture and truth in Renaissance England," *Representations* 34 (Spring 1991): 61.

9. Foucault, *Discipline and Punish*, p. 113.

10. Ibid.

11. It is interesting in this light to consider the (counter-)historical implications of contemporary movements in the United States to promote the use of corporal and capital punishment and to publicly broadcast executions.

12. Foucault, *Discipline and Punish*, p. 189.

13. "Alive on Tape," anon. editorial, *Nation* July 1, 1991, pp. 3–4.

14. Ann Wroe (*Lives, Lies, and the Iran-Contra Affair* [New York: I. B. Tauris, 1991]) lucidly describes comedic and cinematic elements of the covert actions and media spectacle. She notes that a key aspect of "Olliemania" was its transient entertainment value. A similar thing can be said about *Court TV;* although the murder trials of the Menendez brothers and O. J. Simpson are deadly serious matters, the public spectacles attending the telecasts were rife with playful, vulgar, and commercial elements of unreality and absurdity. Also see Peter Stallybrass and Allon White, *The Politics and Poetics of Transgression* (London: Methuen, 1986) for a more general discussion.

15. Foucault acknowledges that the Benthamite machinery did not function in accordance with the ideal plan, but he argues that prisoners' rebellions and resistances indicate that this machinery was more than a utopian idea. "Questions of method: An interview with Michel Foucault," *Ideology and Consciousness* 8 (Spring 1981): 10.

16. Michel Foucault, "Two lectures," in *Power/Knowledge: Selected Interviews and Other Writings, 1972–1977*, ed. Colin Gordon (New York: Pantheon, 1980), p. 81.

17. See Bruno Latour, *We Have Never been Modern* (Cambridge, Mass.: Harvard University Press, 1993).

18. The idea of an "irradiative effect" derives from Marc Guillaume, "The metamorphoses of epidemia," *Zone* 1/2 (1986): 58–69.

19. The semiotics of "North" are playfully described in James Der Derian, "Arms, hostages, and the importance of shredding in earnest: Reading the national security culture (II)," *Social Text* 22 (1989): 79–91.

20. See Methodological Appendix for an elaboration of this point.

21. Victor Turner observes that "scattered ideas" from theoretical systems may be relevant when "taken out of systematic contexts" and used by anthropologists to "illuminate social reality." Turner, *Dramas, Fields, and Metaphors: Symbolic Action in Human Society* (Ithaca, N.Y.: Cornell University Press, 1974). Here we are suggesting something else, that narrative themes and semiotic oppositions are occasionally part of the ordinary production of the event we are studying, but that these do not trace back to a coherent theoretical source (see Methodological Appendix).

22. Robin Erica Wagner-Pacifici, *The Moro Morality Play: Terrorism as Social Drama* (Chicago: University of Chicago Press, 1986), p. 231.

23. The themes of transgression and political carnival are explored in Stallybrass and White, *Politics and Poetics of Transgression.*

24. Schudson (*Watergate in American Memory,* pp. 165ff.) describes a number of substantive aspects of how the "collective memory" of Watergate influenced the reactions by the public and press to the incipient Iran-contra scandal. He also observes how members of Reagan's administration tried to "pre-empt" the likelihood that their actions would be viewed under the rubric of "another Watergate." Not only was "Watergate" a set of literary themes and topics, but its precedent was institutionalized in legal restrictions placed on covert actions and methods for evading those restrictions.

25. Although the Army-McCarthy hearings were not often mentioned as a precedent for Iran-contra, Daniel Schorr noted that North's and Dean's pivotal roles were preceded by that of the army's chief counsel, Joseph N. Welch, who told Senator Joseph McCarthy, "while America watched, 'Senator, I think I never really gauged your cruelly or your recklessness.' " Schorr, "Introduction," *Taking the Stand* (New York: Times Books, 1987), p. vi.

26. Thomas Palmer, "Some of the questions North will face," *Boston Globe,* July 7, 1991, p. 12.

27. The subject of popular history is rich and deep. Our treatment will touch only upon those themes that are most pertinent to the conduct of the Iran-contra hearings. Aside from the substantive and procedural relevancies that we have emphasized here, Watergate may have been widely recognized as a precedent because of the way popular histories are periodized by decades (1950s, 1960s, etc.), with landmark events marking their beginnings and ends (so that the 1960s began not in 1960,

but with the civil rights movement a few years earlier, and ended with the resolution of Watergate in 1974). See Fredric Jameson, "Periodizing the 60's," in *The 60's Without Apology,* ed. Sohnya Sayres et al. (Minneapolis: University of Minnesota Press, 1984), pp. 178–209; and Fred Davis, "Decade labeling: The play of collective memory and narrative plot," *Symbolic Interaction* 7 (1984): 15–24.

28. Alexander and Smith ("Discourse of American civil society") link Iran-contra and Watergate to a series of scandals and crises, including the impeachment of President Andrew Johnson and Teapot Dome. Popular commentators tended to focus on more recent events occurring within the lifetime of televisual politics.

29. Alexander, "Culture and political crisis," p. 200.

30. Wagner-Pacifici (*Moro Morality Play,* p. 204) states that "Every social drama has its final act. And it is in this act that the final unmasking occurs. (The 'truth' of this unmasking may, of course, never be universally accepted.)" No such "final unmasking" has occurred with Iran-contra, despite a series of investigations spanning a seven-year period, and the "drama" subsided soon after North and Poindexter testified.

31. A reviewer of an earlier draft of this chapter commented that many Americans who supported North, and saw the hearings as a trial, celebrated "the fact that North 'got off' " and thus "would have restored their faith in the system." We do not believe this is the case. During his testimony, and in his later fund-raising campaigns, North enlisted support *against* "the system" represented by Congress and the government "bureaucracy." Even when seeking to join "the system" as a U.S. senator, his speeches rhetorically appealed to those who were turned off by government.

32. Alexander and Smith ("Discourse of American civil society," pp. 190–91) give a brief account of how North and other Iran-contra principals, like their Watergate counterparts, rhetorically enlisted an array of values associated with a "democratic code" and set in opposition to a parallel "counter-democratic code." As we discuss in our Methodological Appendix, Alexander and Smith's account demonstrates how both sides interpretatively aligned their speeches with democratic themes and defended against antidemocratic implications, but it does not (and apparently is not intended to) delve into the dialogical interplay of utterances invoking these and other binaries, lists, stock lines, and more quotidian grammatical devices.

33. Twenty years after Nixon's resignation, John Dean reminisced: "It was my word against the president, his chief of staff, his top adviser, his former attorney general. I thought, this is not going to be a pleasant experience because people may say you're the liar. Until the tapes came out, there was a high possibility that would have been the way it came down." Judy Keen, "Watergate whistle blower talks about it 20 years later," *USA Today,* international ed. Aug. 8, 1994, p. 4A.

34. Larry Martz, *Newsweek,* July 20, 1987, p. 12.

35. Schorr, *Taking the Stand,* p. vi.

36. The sociopolitics of enrollment is articulated with exemplary clarity by Michel Callon and Bruno Latour, "Unscrewing the big Leviathan: How actors macrostructure reality and how sociologists help them," in *Advances in Social Theory and Methodology: Toward an Integration of Micro- and Macro-Sociologies,* ed. K. D. Knorr Cetina and A. V. Cicourel (London: Routledge and Kegan Paul, 1981), pp. 277–303.

37. The National Security Council was established during the Truman administration as an advisory body composed of key members of the presidential cabinet, but it gradually became an adjunct foreign policy agency under the direct control of the president, largely displacing the role of the secretary of state. NSC "staff" members thus differed from the nominal members of the NSC (the vice president, secretary of defense, and secretary of state), who often had little to do with the operations conducted under the rubric of the NSC. See Theodore Draper, *A Very Thin Line: The Iran-Contra Affairs* (New York: Hill and Wang, 1991), pp. 5ff.

38. Quoted in Adam Pertman, "Today, it's North's turn to testify," *Boston Globe,* July 7, 1987, p. 12.

39. Melvin Pollner, "Explicative transactions: Making and managing meaning in traffic court," in *Everyday Language: Studies in Ethnomethodology,* ed. G. Psathas (New York: Irvington Press, 1979), p. 228. In the traffic court hearings described by Pollner, earlier cases were used as local grounds for "explicating" the organizational routines of courtroom practice and for attempting—whether successfully or not—to hold the traffic court answerable to those standards.

40. Ibid., p. 229.

41. Daniel Inouye in *Taking the Stand: The Testimony of Lieutenant Colonel Oliver North* (New York: Pocket Books, 1987), pp. 3–4.

42. Ibid., p. 4.

43. We discuss this matter further in chaps. 5 and 6.

44. Morning session, July 7, 87, ML/DB transcript.

45. Ibid.

46. Ibid.

47. Foucault, *Discipline and Punish,* p. 57.

48. Alexander, "Culture and political crisis."

49. For a rich unpacking of the spatial-temporal organization of "floor," see Douglas Macbeth, "Classroom 'floors': Material organizations as a course of affairs," *Qualitative Sociology* 15 (1992): 123–50.

50. In a brief pre-ethnomethodological paper, Harold Garfinkel describes the use (and potential reversibility) of denunciations in "degradation ceremonies." Garfinkel, "Conditions of successful degradation ceremonies," *American Journal of Sociology* 61 (1956): 420–24.

51. Here we are borrowing some terms from the "actor-network" approach to studies of scientific and technological innovation developed by Callon and Latour,

"Unscrewing the big Leviathan." Although their theory is somewhat overbuilt for our purposes, it provides a way to speak about the discursive machinations through which "actors" (in this case "the American people") simultaneously become a "real and immediate presence" and a referential subject of a text. Accordingly, there is no contradiction in saying that "the American people" are the "live audience" for the participants' persuasive maneuvers and a nominal figure in their rhetorical appeals.

52. Morning session, July 7, 1987, ML/DB transcript.

53. See Alexander and Smith, "Discourse of American civil society," p. 191.

54. North met with the committee before the televised sessions, and although he did not review much of what he would testify, he provided the committee with a summary of how he would answer the "key question" about the president's involvement. Consequently, his answer at the hearings was no surprise, either to the members of the committee or the commentators from the press who prepared the audience for what North would say. For instance, on the morning before North's appearance the *Boston Globe* (July 7, 1987, p. 1) stated: "Assuming North does not implicate President Reagan in any wrongdoing, and lawmakers stressed that they had no evidence he would, no one has more to gain or lose from his performance than North himself." The dramatic structure of the testimony therefore had less to do with what it revealed and more to do with the way it mobilized the audience to join sides in a well-rehearsed dispute.

55. Morning session, July 7, 1987, ML/DB transcript.

56. Eastwood and his movies were the source of an even more memorable quotation, this time enunciated by Reagan, as a warning to Congress in the event it should give him an opportunity to veto a proposed tax increase: "Go ahead. Make my day." Rogin, *"Ronald Reagan," the Movie*, p. 7.

57. See Alexander and Smith, "Discourse of American civil society," p. 191; and Der Derian, "Arms, hostages, shredding."

58. Niklas Luhmann, "Politicians, honesty and the higher immorality of politics," *Theory, Culture & Society* 11 (1994): 28.

4. THE TRUTH-FINDING ENGINE

1. Michel Foucault, *The History of Sexuality* (New York: Pantheon, 1978), 1:62.

2. The Foucaultian contrast with torture should not mislead us into thinking that interrogations are like seminar discussions. For a more graphic portrayal, see D. R. Watson, "Some features of the elicitation of confessions in murder investigations," in *Interaction Competence,* ed. George Psathas (Washington, D.C.: International Institute for Ethnomethodology and Conversation Analysis and University Press of America, 1990), pp. 263–95.

3. Harvey Sacks, "Notes on police assessment of moral character," in *Studies in Social Interaction,* ed. David Sudnow (New York: Free Press, 1972), p. 444. Cited in

Melvin Pollner, *Mundane Reason* (Cambridge: Cambridge University Press, 1987), pp. 19–20.

4. See Erving Goffman, *Gender Advertisements* (Cambridge, Mass.: Harvard University Press, 1979), for an argument in favor of using "fictional" materials for purposes of social analysis.

5. Jürgen Habermas, *The Theory of Communicative Action,* trans. Thomas McCarthy (Boston: Beacon Press, 1984), 1: 300. For an empirical study that attempts with some success to integrate Habermasian distinctions with an analysis of actual discourse, see John Forrester, "Critical ethnography: On fieldwork in a Habermasian way," in M. Alvesson and H. Wilmott (eds.), *Critical Management Studies* (London: Sage, 1992), pp. 46–65.

6. The role of stories in the dialogical production of master narratives is discussed in greater detail in chap. 4.

7. These assumptions are related to what Stanley Fish calls "theory hope" in modern philosophy. Fish, *Doing What Comes Naturally: Change, Rhetoric, and the Practice of Theory in Literary and Legal Studies* (Durham, N.C.: Duke University Press, 1989), pp. 342ff. In this case, however, what is hoped for is an analytical structure that can be attributed to the inherent operations in a domain of civil society, i.e., "free" or "natural" communication. We also want to emphasize that the "hope" for a determinate model of discourse is not simply an academic predilection, but something embedded in the ceremony of the public tribunal.

8. John Henry Wigmore, *Wigmore's Code of the Rules of Evidence in Trials of Law,* 3d ed. (Boston: Little Brown, 1940), p. 29, sec. 1043.

9. Although it is generally believed that what a person says against his or her own interests is likely to be truthful (Mike Hepworth and Bryan S. Turner, *Confession: Studies in Deviance and Religion* [London: Routledge and Kegan Paul, 1982], p. 85), some legal scholars say that "forced" confessions and other false confessions occur much more frequently than is usually assumed. See Lawrence S. Wrightsman and Saul M. Kassin, *Confessions in the Courtroom* (Newbury Park, Calif.: Sage, 1993). For a history of the concept of confessions in English jurisprudence, see Peter Mirfield, *Confessions* (London: Sweet and Maxwell, 1985).

10. See Edward Wilfred Fordham, "The Tichburne case," in *Notable Cross-Examinations,* (London: Constable, 1951), pp. 11ff.

11. See Methodological Appendix.

12. See John Heritage and David Greatbatch, "On the institutional character of institutional talk: The case of news interview interaction," in *Talk and Social Structure,* ed. Deirdre Boden and Don Zimmerman (Berkeley: University of California Press, 1991), p. 98.

13. In their "inside story" of the Iran-contra hearings, Senators William Cohen and George Mitchell discuss some of the differences between a trial court and a congressional hearing; they also speculate about whether these differences worked

to North's advantage. Cohen and Mitchell, *Men of Zeal: A Candid Inside Story of the Iran-Contra Hearings,* (New York: Viking, 1988), pp. 160–61.

14. J. M. Atkinson and Paul Drew, *Order in Court: The Organisation of Verbal Interaction in Judicial Settings* (London: Macmillan, 1979), p. 106, point out that the lack of legal technicalities in a government tribunal carries attendant risks for witnesses who are thus not afforded certain routine legal protections.

15. At the outset of the North testimony, for instance, the select committee chairman, Senator Inouye, cited the House and Senate select committee rules to prohibit North from beginning his testimony with a prepared statement: "Unless the Committee determines otherwise, a witness who appears before the Committee under a grant of immunity shall not be permitted to make a statement or testify except to respond directly to questions posed by committee members or committee staff" (*Joint Hearings,* North, pt. 1, p. 3). See Atkinson and Drew, *Order in Court,* on the accused's right to withhold answers and the inferences that are drawn from the exercise of this right.

16. Official transcripts of tribunals and court hearings tend to respect this rule by appending whatever counsel says with a question mark, and whatever the witness says with a period. The transcriber's rule seems to be: if an utterance can be heard as a question, hear it as a question. Moreover, some court transcripts use the symbols "Q" and "A" to denote the exchange of turns between counsel and witness during direct and cross-examination.

17. Certain exceptions are allowed, such as questions for clarification by the witness or objections by the witness's counsel, but these are inserted within the overall frame of questions and answers.

18. *Joint Hearings,* North, pt. 2, p. 38.

19. See J. R. Searle, *Speech Acts: An Essay in the Philosophy of Language* (Cambridge: Cambridge University Press, 1969), p. 69; and K. Bach and R. M. Harnish, *Linguistic Communication and Speech Acts* (Cambridge, Mass.: MIT Press, 1979), p. 48.

20. See Searle on "Indirect speech-acts," *Speech Acts.*

21. Case-hardened attorneys often are said to hate surprises, and often lines of questioning that seem to be exploring unknown territory have been rehearsed in advance in private session. This was the case with the interrogation of many Iran-contra witnesses, but only to a limited degree with North. See Seymour Wishman, *Anatomy of a Jury: The System on Trial* (New York: Times Books, 1986).

22. Morning session, July 7, 1987, ML/DB transcript. Many interrogations begin with a recapitulation of previously established matters. Later in the hearings, the opening question asked by Arthur Liman, counsel for the Senate majority, provided an interesting variant: "Colonel, is it fair to say that November 25, 1986, was one of the worst days in your life?" This question relies on North to recognize the date, and the presumed significance of the date, as the day when Reagan announced at a press

conference that North had been fired. North responded by turning to Sullivan for a lengthy, whispered consultation.

23. Objections did sometimes arise concerning, for example, whether a question was being asked, whether the question on the floor had been answered, etc., but these objections had little to do with the general linguistic form of the utterances in dispute.

24. *Joint Hearings,* North, pt. 1, pp. 8–9.

25. Atkinson and Drew, *Order in Court,* pp. 49ff. note that questions and answers can be used to package a variety of specific actions like challenges, accusations, denials, justifications, and rebuttals. Nevertheless, they insist that the basic rule for interrogation operates as long as a "minimal" characterization of the utterances as questions and answers can be sustained.

26. Harvey Sacks, *Lectures on Conversation* (Oxford: Basil Blackwell, 1992), 2: 427.

27. Morning session, July 7, 1992, ML/DB transcript.

28. According to studies of news interviews, interviewers typically begin a sequence of questions with prefatory remarks to establish background, and, before speaking, interviewees normally wait until a question has been asked. Interrogators, on the other hand, do not lay out preliminaries as one uninterrupted bloc, and they wait for the witness to confirm point-by-point as a formal way of establishing "agreed facts of the case" for the record. For an interesting counterexample, see Steven Clayman and Jack Whalen, "When the medium becomes the message: The case of the Rather-Bush encounter," *Research on Language and Social Interaction* 22 (1988–89): 241–72; and Emanuel A. Schegloff, "From interview to confrontation: Observations of the Bush/Rather encounter," *Research on Language and Social Interaction* 22 (1988–89): 215–40.

29. This was not the only procedure for conducting interrogation. As discussed in chapter 5, a witness can be asked simply to recite a story about the events in question. Nevertheless, coherent lines of interrogation often employed the device of asserting questions for confirmation.

30. Afternoon session, July 19, 1987, ML/DB transcript.

31. Afternoon session, July 7, 1987, ML/DB transcript.

32. Avowals of nonrecall are discussed at length in chap. 6.

33. See Alec McHoul, "Why there are no guarantees for interrogators," *Journal of Pragmatics* 11 (1987): 455–71.

34. See Ray McDermott and Henry Tylbor, "On the necessity of collusion in conversation," *Text* 3 (1983): 277–97.

35. Morning session, July 7, 1987, ML/DB transcript.

36. See Dusan Bjelic, "On the social origin of logic," unpublished Ph.D. dissertation, Boston University, 1989, chap. 2.

37. Readers may note that these "empirical" assertions cannot be unambiguously

classified in accordance with the formal categories of speech acts and validity claims. North criticizes Nields's assertion, "But these operations were designed to be secrets from the American people," not only by attacking the "rightness" of its presuppositions about the norms under which the operations were governed, but by challenging the motivation it ascribes to the corporate designers of covert actions and the characterization of the objective events in question.

38. This is a strong variant of the type of question discussed by Pomerantz under the heading of questions that supply information about answers. Anita Pomerantz, "Offering a candidate answer: An information-seeking strategy," *Communication Monographs* 55 (1988): 360–73.

39. For a discussion of a "maximal property" of agreements, see Paul Drew, "Contested evidence in courtroom cross-examination: The case of a trial for rape," in *Talk at Work: Interaction in Institutional Settings,* ed. Paul Drew and John Heritage (Cambridge: Cambridge University Press, 1992), pp. 470–520.

40. These points summarize the discussion of the "witness's dilemma" in Augustine Brannigan and Michael Lynch, "On bearing false witness: Perjury and credibility as interactional accomplishments," *Journal of Contemporary Ethnography* 16 (1987): 127ff. Also see Drew, "Contested evidence," and Atkinson and Drew, *Order in Court.*

41. A common technique for mounting such challenges is for the interrogator to begin by laying out common ground, previously established through earlier testimony and documentary evidence. Nields (*Joint Hearings,* North, pt. 1, p. 25) asserts: "Well, let me put it to you this way, I take it that we're on common ground that the President signed a finding in January of 1986, authorizing the sale of arms to Iran?" In this case, he is responding to North's nonconfirmation of earlier questions, as though he is resecuring a confirmed position from which to reopen the problematic question. The phrase "I take it that" is often used by interrogators when proposing to go over an already established point or to formulate the witness's position.

42. In examinations-in-chief, the progression also tends to lead the witness to points supportive of the interrogator's "side," although the questioning is rarely a site of struggle or resistance (although it can be one).

43. For an illuminating primer on methods of cross-examination for leading forensic chemists to admit a lack of knowledge about the techniques they practice, see J. S. Oteri, M. G. Weinberg, and M.S. Pinales, "Cross examination of chemists in drug cases," in *Science in Context: Readings in the Sociology of Science,* ed. Barry Barnes and David Edge (Milton Keynes, U.K.: Open University Press, 1982), pp. 250–59.

44. See Atkinson and Drew, *Order in Court.* In this case the witness is treated less as a target of possible accusations than as a source who may reveal information damaging to higher-ups in the administration that employed him.

45. In ibid., Atkinson and Drew speak of a "preference" for denial of accusation.

46. See McHoul, "Why there are no guarantees," for a discussion of transgressive possibilities.

47. Activities in real time occur "first time through," with a local historical trajectory that is essentially unavailable to the retrospective standpoint of the historian who knows how it turned out in the end. For a discussion of the "first time through theme," see Harold Garfinkel, Michael Lynch, and Eric Livingston, "The work of a discovering science construed with materials from the optically discovered pulsar," *Philosophy of the Social Sciences* 11 (1981): 131–58.

48. North to Senator Mitchell, in *Joint Hearings,* North, pt. 2, p. 39. For a comprehensive account of the well-rehearsed strategies of North and his colleagues for answering questions and minimizing the disclosure of damaging information, see Ann Wroe, *Lives, Lies, and the Iran-Contra Affair* (New York: I. B. Tauris, 1991), pp. 248–66.

49. See Alfred Schutz, "Concept and theory formation in the social sciences," in Schutz, *Collected Papers* (The Hague: Martinus Nijhoff, 1962), 1: 48–66; and Harvey Sacks, "Sociological description," *Berkeley Journal of Sociology* 8 (1963): 1–16.

50. Harold Garfinkel, *Studies in Ethnomethodology* (Englewood Cliffs, N.J.: Prentice-Hall, 1967), p. 21; Sacks, "Sociological description."

51. See Lena Jayyusi, *Categorization and the Moral Order* (London: Routledge and Kegan Paul, 1984); and Harvey Sacks, "An initial investigation of the usability of conversational data for doing sociology," in *Studies in Social Interaction,* ed. David Sudnow (New York: Free Press, 1972), pp. 31–74.

52. See E. A. Schegloff's criticism of conversation-analytic research by Zimmerman and West in which "interruptions" in conversation are used as an index of power in conversation. Schegloff, "Between micro and macro: Contexts and other connections," in *The Micro-Macro Link,* ed. J. Alexander et al. (Berkeley: University of California Press, 1987), pp. 207–34; and Don H. Zimmerman and Candace West, "Sex roles, interruptions and silences in conversation," in *Language and Sex: Differences and Dominance,* ed. B. Thorne and N. Henley (Rowley, Mass.: Newbury House, 1975), pp. 105–29.

53. Morning session, July 13, 1987, in *Joint Hearings,* North, pt. 2, pp. 31–32. For Mitchell's own account of his interrogation of North, see Cohen and Mitchell, *Men of Zeal,* pp. 147–82.

54. Jeffrey Alexander, "Culture and political crisis: 'Watergate' and Durkheimian sociology," in Alexander (ed.), *Durkheimian Sociology: Cultural Studies* (Cambridge: Cambridge University Press, 1989).

55. In addition to *answering* his interrogators' questions, North assumed a "right" to *answer to* accusatory implications of those questions. The equivocality between answering a question and disputing the terms of the question was nicely exhibited in the Bush/Rather interview before the 1988 elections, in which Bush insisted on "answering" a question that had not been asked. See Clayman and Whalen, "When the medium becomes the message."

56. Afternoon session, July 10, 1987, in *Joint Hearings,* North, pt. 2, p. 1.

57. This sense of "displacement" and (re)contextual iteration is elucidated in Jacques Derrida, "Signature, event, context," *Glyph* 1 (1977): 172–97.

58. See, for example, Don H. Zimmerman, "On conversation: The conversation analytic perspective," *Communication Yearbook* 11 (1988): 424ff.

59. Barbara Wootton, *Crime and Criminal Law: Reflections of a Magistrate and Social Scientist* (London: Stevens, 1963), pp. 33–34.

60. See Lawrence Nichols, "Whistleblower or renegade: Definitional contests in an official inquiry," *Symbolic Interaction* 12 (1991).

5. STORIES AND MASTER NARRATIVES

1. An advantage for the interrogator who cuts off a witness in this way is facilitated by a commonplace device for disagreeing in conversation, the use of a "Yes, but . . ." format. Answerers who disagree commonly preface their disagreement with a token of agreement. See Harvey Sacks, "On the preference for agreement and contiguity in sequences in conversation," in *Talk and Social Organization,* ed. G. Button and J. R. E. Lee (Clevedon: Multilingual Matters, 1987), pp. 54–69. An alert interrogator can shape the immediate sense of an answer by quickly breaking in after the yes component, thereby cutting off the qualification or disagreement that was likely to follow.

2. Anthony Trollope, *The Three Clerks* (1858), chap. 11; cited in C. P. Harvey, *The Advocates' Devil* (London: Stevens and Sons, 1958), p. 141.

3. A memorable example is supplied by Dickens's apocryphal report on the trial of "Bardell against Pickwick," in which Mr. Skimpin questions Mr. Winkle regarding the regularity of his contact with the plaintiff, Mrs. Bardell: "On this question there arose the edifying browbeating customary on such points. First of all, Mr. Winkle said it was quite impossible for him to say how many times he had seen Mrs. Bardell. Then he was asked if he had seen her twenty times, to which he replied, 'Certainly—more than that.' Then he was asked whether he hadn't seen her a hundred times—and so forth; the satisfactory conclusion which was arrived at, at last, being, that he had better take care of himself and mind what he was about. The witness having been by these means reduced to the requisite ebb of nervous perplexity, the examination was continued. . . . *The Pickwick Papers* (London: Penguin, 1972 [1836–37]), pp. 567–68; quoted in Harvey, *The Advocates Devil,* p. 140.

4. The search for "fresh" testimony is constrained by interrogators' general preference to know in advance what a witness is prepared to say in response to a line of questions. The aim is to control the display of testimony in such a way that the audience will hear it as coming spontaneously from the witness. Trial lawyers often rehearse their examinations of the witness they call in order to avoid surprises—

unanticipated answers that strengthen the opponent's case. In addition, when cross-examining the other party's witnesses they attempt to avoid surprises by withholding questions that may elicit damaging information. They do not always succeed, however. Wishman recounts the anecdote: "Knowing when to stop asking questions is sometimes learned from painful lessons of having gone on too long. Lincoln was fond of telling the story of the young lawyer who had asked one question too many: 'If you now admit not having seen the defendant bite the young man's ear, how can you tell this jury that he really did bite that ear off?' 'Because,' the witness answered, 'I saw him spit it out.'" Seymour Wishman, *Anatomy of a Jury: The System on Trial* (New York: Times Books, 1986), pp. 179–80.

5. Poindexter, the next witness to be called after North, also appeared with his attorney, although Schultz, Meese, and others who appeared after Poindexter did not make use of the North-Sullivan precedent.

6. *Joint Hearings,* North, pt. 1, p. 18.

7. Ibid., p. 21.

8. For example, in the following exchange between Liman and Poindexter, the interrogator makes a dramatic show of conceding ample space for the witness to elaborate on his answers. Afternoon session, June 19, 1987, ML/DB transcript. Beckler is Poindexter's attorney, and Hamilton is chairman of the House committee.

Liman: Did the President of the United States sign, that finding.

Poindexter: As I've testified before, he did (uhb)

Poindexter: [on or about the Fifth of December, ah- I'm vague on the date.

               [

Liman: [(When) (0.6)

Beckler: (uh) Mister Liman, I'm gonna ask you to just let him finish, I know you [have a
      lot of questions and we're gonna answer them *all,*

                                                                        [

(Liman):   [( )

Beckler: but don't interrupt please, "the end," you kn[ow that puts a little chill=

                                                        [

Liman: [Mister Bekl-

Beckler: =on this witness.

Liman: Misteh B- Mister Beckler, I've tried not to interrupt (though) I did not intend to
      and I apologize. Sometimes it's not clear whether the witness has finished his answer,
      and I ts-

      [saw, when I interrupted, that I had, and I apologized (to)
      [

Beckler: [(All right) we have plenty of time [here. Now we're not in a rush.

                                              [

Hamilton: [Counsel, uh

Hamilton: Counsel, may I suggest to you that uh when you have a comment or
    objec[tion that you address it=
       [
Beckler: ['Scuse me (Mr. Hamilton)
Hamilton: =to the [chair and not to the counsel and not to members.
Beckler: [
                [I'm very sorry about that
Beckler: Yes [(Mister Hamilton)
       [
Hamilton: [that- I think that will be helpful. Thank you.

Liman's apology is interesting for its extreme deference: he defends his "unintentional interruption" by saying, "sometimes it's not clear whether the witness has
finished his answer." Indeed, it seems plausible in conversation-analytic terms that
Poindexter's utterance—"As I've testified befo:re, he did uh::b"—constituted a complete answer to the question, so that Liman had every "right" to begin speaking at
that point. Moreover, he immediately cut off his incipient question ("what") and
yielded the floor to Poindexter when the witness continued his utterance. In effect,
Beckler's objection took issue with an "interruption" that Liman had already retracted, yet Liman accepted Beckler's accusatory characterization of his utterance
and apologized for that "interruption." Perhaps we should not take Liman's deference too seriously, as its very excess rhetorically dramatizes the interrogator's
claim to be undertaking a fact-finding inquiry in which witnesses are allowed every
chance to give complete, unconstrained testimony. Considering the intense public
scrutiny and the committee's explicit aim to rise above partisan politics, Liman can
be said to be conducting an interrogation where the effort to squeeze a confessional
truth from Poindexter and his political allies hinges on the continued production of
an "unconstrained" dialogue. Before Poindexter's appearance, the committee interrogators, especially Liman, were publicly and sometimes viciously criticized. Poll
results indicated that a large proportion of the audience believed the interrogators
had been unfair to the witnesses, and, according to committee members William
Cohen and George Mitchell, "thousands of letters, telegrams and phone calls started
flooding our offices. They complained about Liman's hair, abrasiveness, and religion. [Richard] Secord [who testified at the outset of the televised hearings] was a
patriotic Anglo-American. Liman was a nasty New York lawyer—translate as "New
York Jew." Cohen and Mitchell, *Men of Zeal: A Candid Inside-Story of the Iran-
Contra Hearings* (New York: Hill and Wang, 1988), p. 75.

9. Inouye, the Senate committee chairman, denied the motion because twenty
copies of the statement had not been delivered to the committee at least twenty-four
hours in advance. After much wrangling, and with the support of several Republicans on the committee, Sullivan gained a concession for North to read the statement

on the second day of his testimony. By then it was a moot point, since North was able to deliver his statement in piecemeal form as stirring, speech-like answers during the morning session of his first day of testimony. Further negotiations pertained to North's bid to give an exemplary "slide show" in support of Reagan administration efforts to solicit private donations to the cause of the Nicaraguan contras. After much wrangling, North was allowed to show his slides without a projector and to describe them as he peered at them with overhead lights.

10. See Anita Pomerantz, "Telling my side: 'Limited access' as a 'fishing' device," *Sociological Inquiry* 50 (1980): 186–98.

11. C. Wright Mills, *The Sociological Imagination* (Oxford: Oxford University Press, 1959), p. 6.

12. The notion of the "virtual participant," one who straddles the fence between cultural membership and analytic detachment, is borrowed from Habermas. See his *The Theory of Communicative Action,* 1:102–41. For a critical discussion of the origins and significance of the concept of the virtual participant in Habermas's work, see David Bogen, *Order Without Rules: Critical Theory and the Logic of Conversation* (New York: SUNY Press, 1996).

13. See Peter Novick, *That Noble Dream: The "Objectivity Question" and the American Historical Profession* (Cambridge: Cambridge University Press, 1988).

14. Conversation analysts (see Methodological Appendix) have developed Harvey Sacks's work on stories, mainly by identifying and describing sequential techniques through which participants in conversations set up the telling and continuation of stories, and the ways in which storytellers calibrate what they say in light of reciprocal moves by their recipients. A systematic treatment of this aspect of Sacks's work on stories can be found in Amy Shuman, *Storytelling Rights: The Uses of Oral and Written Texts by Urban Adolescents* (Cambridge: Cambridge University Press, 1986).

15. Daniel K. Inouye and Lee H. Hamilton, *Report of the Congressional Committees Investigating the Iran-Contra Affair, with the Minority View,* abridged ed. (New York: Times Books, 1987), p. 156.

16. Afternoon session, July 7, 1987, in *Joint Hearings,* North, pt. 1, pp. 51–52.

17. For a description of particular aspects of collaborative storytelling, see Gene Lerner, "Assisted storytelling: Deploying shared knowledge as a practical matter," *Qualitative Sociology* 15 (1992): 247–72.

18. For an example in a criminal case, see Augustine Brannigan and Michael Lynch, "On bearing false witness: Perjury and credibility as interactional accomplishments," *Journal of Contemporary Ethnography* 16 (1987): 115–46.

19. Although Dorothy Smith's work on what she calls "textually mediated discourse" opens up the topic of how textual formats enter into and organize communicative actions, our approach differs from hers in at least one significant respect. Smith contrasts embodied experience—the actual location of the "knower"—from text-mediated discourse, which omits, or rules irrelevant, the situationally located

details of situated experiences, feelings, and activities. She then identifies the former with womens' experience, and the latter with relations of ruling dominated by
men. (See Dorothy Smith, "Sociology from women's experience: A reaffirmation,"
Sociological Theory 10 (1992): 88–98.) In our approach, narratives of experience do
not correspond to a body's "actual experience" (among other things, they can be
fictional), nor are they "owned" by or associated with specific categories of agents.
Instead, the relevant identities are dialogically contingent assemblages of available
character types and membership categories. Similarly, although texts and textually
mediated modes of communication may be modern, to us it seems that in contemporary Western societies texts (and modes of objectified discourse, more generally)
no longer can be associated unequivocally with relations of ruling. In the dialogue
between North and the committee interrogators, it is unclear at the moment which
male voice more closely represents relations of ruling, since North's "experiential"
resistances can be traced back to a division between different "ruling" factions.

20. Harvey Sacks, *Lectures on Conversation,* ed. Gail Jefferson (Oxford: Basil
Blackwell, 1992), 2:483.

21. Ibid.

22. Ibid. For clarity, here we have reedited the more literalistic version that appears in the published volume: "It's in that sort of way that an event which, in the,
quotes, objective reality, has the current teller figuring altogether incidentally. . . ."

23. A genre of "human interest" news story presents various "ordinary" testimonies in answer to questions like, "Where were you when Kennedy was shot?"
Such stories rely on the fact that interviewees and readers can recognize, and find
interest in, a report of the very sorts of experiential details that are typically not part
of a public news report.

24. The report sometimes quotes excerpts from testimony, or it mentions that
witnesses' versions differed, but these versions are subsumed within the overall
narrative of events.

25. See Sacks, *Lectures on Conversation.* For a concise synthesis of fragments of
these lectures, see Sacks, "On doing 'being ordinary,' " in *Structures of Social Action: Studies in Conversation Analysis,* ed. J. M. Atkinson and J. C. Heritage (Cambridge: Cambridge University Press, 1984), pp. 413–529.

26. *Joint Hearings,* North, pt. 1, pp. 51–52.

27. Sacks, *Lectures on Conversation,* p. 454.

28. Wayne Beach, "Temporal density in courtroom interaction: Constraints on
the recovery of past events in legal discourse," *Communication Monographs* 52
(1985): 1–18; and Wayne Beach and Phyllis Japp, "Storifying as time-travelling: The
knowledgeable use of temporally structured discourse," in *Communication Yearbook 7,* ed. Robert Bostrum (Beverly Hills, Calif.: Sage, 1983), pp. 867–88.

29. See, for example, the section on stories in the Methodological Appendix, in
which we describe Sacks's analysis of a story about an incident at a department

store. Sacks points out that, although the scene could in principle be described differently, for the storyteller the presence of the police is conveyed as a natural, "legitimate" component of the scene described.

30. See Charles Goodwin, "The interactive construction of a sentence in natural conversation," in *Everyday Language: Studies in Ethnomethodology*, ed. G. Psathas (New York: Irvington Press, 1979).

31. See W. L. Bennett, "Storytelling in criminal trials—a model of social judgment," *Quarterly Journal of Speech* 64 (1978): 311–28.

32. Max Gluckman, "The reasonable man in Barotse law," in *Order and Rebellion in Tribal Africa* (New York: Free Press, 1963), p. 189. Also see R. M. Emerson, *Judging Delinquents* (Chicago: Aldine, 1969), pp. 192–201.

33. Richard Eggleston, *Evidence, Proof and Probability* (London: Weidenfeld and Nicolson, 1978), pp. 164–65.

34. Morning session, July 7, 1987, ML/DB transcript.

35. Ann Wroe, *Lives, Lies, and the Iran-Contra Affair* (London: I. B. Taurus, 1991), p. 243, cites testimony at the hearings by North's secretary, Fawn Hall, in which Hall describes an interchange with a lawyer who coached her to reply "We shred every day" when asked about the shredding. This is another instance of North's having sustained an apparent strategy that was disclosed in earlier testimony at the hearings.

36. North testimony, morning session, July 7, 1987, *Joint Hearings,* North, pt. 1, p. 19. For another analysis of these same passages, see Timothy Halkowski, " 'Role' as an interactional device," *Social Problems* 37, 4 (1990): 564–77.

37. Morning session, July 14, 1987, in ibid., pt. 1, p. 22.

38. Afternoon session, July 14, 1987, in ibid., pt. 2, p. 190.

39. Ibid.

40. On later occasions North professed to be astonished by his becoming a subject of a criminal investigation, arguing that this betrayal by his administration colleagues motivated him to reveal more to the committee than he otherwise would have.

41. The actual and potential fragility of North's characterizations of persons and agencies in his stories also covered his very appearance *in uniform* at the hearings. It might fairly be said that Lt. Col. North should have appeared at the hearings in his role as Mr. North, a staff member of the civilian NSC (indeed, John Poindexter chose to appear in civvies, although the term of address "Admiral" was used during the hearings and on the official transcripts). North's uniform, with its display of honorific medals and insignia, together with his erect posture and military mannerisms, raised the salience of "military officer" in a transparent attempt to neutralize the implication that he and other civilian employees of the White House conducted covert actions illegitimately. As many who witnessed the audiovisual spectacle of the hearings noted, North's testimony was not a text told by an invisible narrator; it

was a narrative "told in uniform" where the sense, credibility, and plausibility of the narrator's stories were infused by his explicitly displayed identity and military bearing. Neither was it a narrative told by a warm-bodied person, since for major elements of the public "Ollie" was a talking torso whose biography and identity became larger than life on a six-day televisual miniseries. Although the apparent success of this narrator in uniform indicates a conventional respect for the paired identities "Ollie North in his role as Lt. Col. North," North's "right" to wear the uniform was initially contested and the fact that it served his purposes in the end was a hard-won outcome of his performance on-camera.

42. Sacks, *Lectures on Conversation*, p. 234.

43. Ibid., p. 235.

44. Ian Hacking, *Rewriting the Soul: Multiple Personality and the Sciences of Memory* (Princeton, N.J.: Princeton University Press, 1995), p. 218.

6. MEMORY IN TESTIMONY

1. Ludwig Wittgenstein, *Philosophical Investigations,* trans. G. E. M. Anscombe (Oxford: Basil Blackwell, 1958), sec. 305. Also see Wittgenstein, *Zettel* (Oxford: Basil Blackwell, 1967), secs. 608 and 610.

2. Francis Yates, *The Art of Memory* (Chicago: University of Chicago Press, 1966).

3. John Sweeny, "The British connection," *Observer* (London) Nov. 7, 1993, p. 20. For a summary account of the Scott inquiry and other amusing examples of testimony by hapless civil servants, see Richard Norton-Taylor, "Truth and big guns," *Guardian Weekend,* Feb. 18, 1995, pp. 22–27.

4. For an elaborate treatment of the organizational production of information control, see Erving Goffman, *The Presentation of Self in Everyday Life* (Garden City, N.Y.: Doubleday Anchor, 1959).

5. Harold Garfinkel uses the expression "perspicuous instances" to describe actual settings of practical action in which a scholarly theme of interest (in this case memory) becomes subject to an immanent, practical treatment. Garfinkel recommends on-site investigation of the relevant practical expertise as a way of yielding radical insight into classic social-science topics. Garfinkel, "Respecification: Evidence for locally produced, naturally accountable phenomena of order, logic, reason, meaning, method, etc. in and as of the essential haecceity of immortal ordinary society (I)—an announcement of studies," in *Ethnomethodology and the Human Sciences,* ed. Graham Button (Cambridge: Cambridge University Press, 1991), pp. 10–19.

6. *Esquire* in its 1987 annual Dubious Achievements Awards issue tallied more than one hundred instances of the *Contra Mantra* for each of its award recipients. Senators William Cohen and George Mitchell counted 184 instances of Poindexter saying he could not recall events about which he was questioned (*Men of Zeal: A*

Candid Inside Story of the Iran-Contra Hearings (New York: Penguin, 1988, p. 195). A newspaper article headlined "Reagan retains charm but not his memory" declared that the former president claimed not to remember 124 times during a videotaped deposition recorded for Poindexter's trial (*Los Angeles Times,* Feb. 23, 1990, p. 1, cited in Michael Schudson, *Watergate in American Memory* (New York: Basic Books, 1992), p. 175. Such counts were used to indicate a collective failure of memory by key witnesses, but in practice it must have been difficult for the journalists to keep such precise tallies, since "I don't remember" is but one of a range of locutions through which witnesses profess not to recall, recollect, remember incidents or details located within incidents, or recognize particular formulations of events whose occurrence was not disputed.

7. Mitchell and Cohen, *Men of Zeal,* p. 163.

8. David E. Rosenbaum, *New York Times,* Dec. 17, 1980, quoted in Paul Ekman, *Telling Lies: Clues to Deceit in the Marketplace, Politics, and Marriage* (New York: Norton, 1985), p. 30. Mitchell and Cohen in *Men of Zeal* quote Nixon telling H. R. Haldeman and John Dean, "Just be damned sure you say 'I don't remember; I can't recall; I can't give an honest answer to that that I can recall.'" Quoted from transcript of March 21, 1973, "Transcripts of Eight Recorded Presidential Conversations," Hearings Before the House Committee on the Judiciary on H. Res. 803, A Resolution Authorizing and Directing the Committee on the Judiciary to Investigate Whether Sufficient Grounds Exist for the House of Representatives to Exercise Its Constitutional Power to Impeach Richard M. Nixon, May–June 1974, Serial No. 34, p. 120.

9. Ekman, *Telling Lies,* p. 30.

10. An exception was former Reagan assistant Michael Deaver, who was convicted of perjury for testifying under oath that he could not recall key aspects of his lobbying activities after leaving the White House. As a line of defense to account for such extraordinary memory lapses, Deaver claimed that his alcohol problem had fogged his mind as well as his ethical judgment. This claim was rejected by the court. (Mitchell and Cohen, *Men of Zeal,* p. 204).

11. Ethan Hoffman and John McCoy, *Concrete Mama: Prison Profiles from Walla Walla* (Columbia: University of Missouri Press, 1981), p. 139.

12. Wittgenstein, *Philosophical Investigations,* sec. 5.

13. John Searle, among others, overlooks this conventional possibility when he writes, "if I ask you a yes/no question, then your answer, if it's an answer to the question, has to count either as an affirmation or a denial of the propositional content of the original question." Searle, *Speech Acts* (Cambridge: Cambridge University Press, 1968), p. 8.

14. Jeff Coulter, "Two concepts of the mental," in *The Social Construction of the Person,* ed. K. J. Gergen and K. E. Davis (New York: Springer, 1985), pp. 132ff. For a study of a particular way in which "forgotten" items can be implicated, and rela-

tionally organized in conversation, see Charles Goodwin, "Forgetfulness as an interactive resource," *Social Psychology Quarterly* 50 (1987): 115–31.

15. John Henry Wigmore, *Evidence* (Chadbourn rev. ed., 1970), p. 1061.

16. Michael H. Graham, "The confrontation clause, the hearsay rule, and the forgetful witness," *Texas Law Review* 56 (1978): 156 (emphasis in original).

17. Ibid., pp. 161–62.

18. Ibid., p. 170.

19. Afternoon session, July 7, 1987, ML/DB Transcript, pp. 26–27.

20. Ibid.

21. Ekman, *Telling Lies*, p. 30.

22. Ibid. Ekman's discussion of these examples focuses on salience, or "memorability," of the events in question, but he does not directly acknowledge the importance of the occupational categories and associated responsibilities for information.

23. Jeff Coulter, *Rethinking Cognitive Theory* (New York: St. Martin's Press, 1983), p. 135.

24. See Garry Wills, *Reagan's America* (New York: Penguin, 1988), p. 465.

25. See Kenneth Burke, *A Grammar of Motives* (Englewood Cliffs, N.J.: Prentice-Hall, 1945).

26. Mitchell and Cohen (*Men of Zeal,* p. 197) observe that Poindexter's frequent pipe smoking "unwittingly produced a metaphor for his testimony."

27. Afternoon session, July 17, 1987, ML/DB transcript.

28. Ulric Neisser, "John Dean's memory: A case study," *Cognition* 9 (1981): 1–22.

29. Ibid., p. 10.

30. Ibid., p. 21.

31. The traditional view of memory is also challenged, though in a less radical way, in a set of influential experimental studies on eyewitness recall. See Elizabeth Loftus and Geoffrey Loftus, "On the permanence of stored information in the brain," *American Psychologist* 35 (1980): 409–20; Elizabeth Loftus, "Leading questions and the eyewitness report," *Cognitive Psychology* 7 (1975): 560–72.

32. This criticism is made in Derek Edwards and Jonathan Potter, "Ulric Neisser's memory," chap. 2 of *Discursive Psychology* (London: Sage, 1992), pp. 41–42. Also see David Middleton and Derek Edwards, "Conversational remembering: A social psychological approach," in *Collective Remembering,* ed. D. Middleton and D. Edwards (London: Sage, 1990), pp. 35–38.

33. Edwards and Potter "Ulric Neisser's Memory" cite Molotch and Boden's analysis of Sen. Gorney's interrogation of Dean. Senator Edward Gorney, a Nixon partisan on the Senate committee, repeatedly seized on points of ambiguity and inaccuracy in Dean's testimony in an effort to demonstrate Dean's lack of credibility. Harvey Molotch and Deirdre Boden, "Talking social structure: Discourse, domination and the Watergate hearings," *American Sociological Review* 50 (1985): 273–88.

34. See Schudson, *Watergate in American Memory.*

35. For a critique of representationalist theories of memory, see A. J. Cascardi, "Remembering," *Review of Metaphysics* 38 (1984): 275–302.

36. Wittgenstein (*Philosophical Investigations,* sec. 187) provides examples of how what a speaker says he could or would have done in the past is as much a matter of claiming a competence or moral status as the recalling of an incident. For a discussion of relevant aspects of counterfactual conditionals, see Malcolm Budd, "Wittgenstein on meaning, interpretation and rules," *Synthese* 58 (1984): 312. For an examination of a rape case in which questions about counterfactual possibilities come up, see Paul Drew, "Contested evidence in courtroom cross-examination: The case of a trial for rape," in *Talk at Work: Interaction in Institutional Settings,* ed. Paul Drew and John Heritage (Cambridge: Cambridge University Press, 1992), p. 478.

37. Afternoon session, July 7, 1994, ML/DB Transcript.

38. In the history of science the injunction to avoid "Whig historiography" is prominent in Thomas Kuhn's discussion of phlogiston theory, where he admonishes his readers not to use up-to-date chemistry texts as a basis for deciding what Priestley, Lavoisier, and their contemporaries were "observing" when they heated red calyx of mercury. *The Structure of Scientific Revolutions* (Chicago: University of Chicago Press, 1962).

39. Afternoon session, July 7, 1987, ML/DB transcript, p. 37.

40. See Augustine Brannigan and Michael Lynch, "On bearing false witness: Perjury and credibility as interactional accomplishments," *Journal of Contemporary Ethnography* 16 (1987): 115–46.

41. Coulter, *Rethinking Cognitive Theory,* p. 135, introduces the idea of entitled forgettings.

42. *Joint Hearings,* North, pt. 1, p. 24.

43. See chap. 4; also Timothy Halkowski, "'Role' as an interactional device," *Social Problems* 37 (1990): 564–77.

44. Graham ("The confrontation clause," p. 162) asserts that "Feigned lack of recollection more frequently constitutes a tacit admission rather than a denial of the prior statement." Whether or not this is so, interrogators rarely have the advantage of knowing if a witness is feigning particular disavowals of recall.

45. Wills, *Reagan's America,* p. 464.

46. Morning session, July 7, 1987, ML/DB transcript.

47. See Alec McHoul, "Why there are no guarantees for interrogators," *Journal of Pragmatics* 11 (1987): 455–71.

7. THE DOCUMENTARY METHOD OF INTERROGATION

1. Harold Garfinkel, *Studies in Ethnomethodology* (Englewood Cliffs, N.J.: Prentice-Hall, 1967), p. 16.

2. After much wrangling among the members of the committee, North was allowed to present the slide show on contra aid, but he was denied the use of a

projector. He thus described each slide, while holding it up to the light.

3. For a discussion of the uses of the record in a related media spectacle, see Lena Jayyusi, "The record shows . . .': Fact and disagreement in the Bush/Rather interview," presented at World Congress of Sociology, Madrid, July 1990.

4. *Joint Hearings,* North, pt. 1, p. 11.

5. The exchange took place in a succession of articles: Jacques Derrida, "Signature, event, context," trans. Samuel Weber and Jeffrey Mehlman, *Glyph* 1 (1977): 172–97; John Searle, "Reiterating the differences: A reply to Derrida," *Glyph* 1 (1977); and Derrida, "Limited Inc a b c . . ." *Glyph* 2 (1977). The two articles by Derrida are reprinted in his *Limited INC* (Evanston, Ill.: Northwestern University Press, 1988).

6. See chap. 3 for a discussion of the early moments in the opening session.

7. William S. Cohen and George J. Mitchell, *Men of Zeal: A Candid Inside Story of the Iran-Contra Hearings* (New York: Penguin, 1988), pp. 153ff.

8. Morning session, July 7, 1987, *Joint Hearings,* North, pt. 1, p. 16.

9. Ibid., p. 23.

10. Ibid., p. 46.

11. For an illuminating discussion of the idea of an "occasioned corpus," see Don H. Zimmerman and Melvin Pollner, "The everyday world as a phenomenon," in *Understanding Everyday Life: Toward the Reconstruction of Sociological Knowledge,* ed. Jack D. Douglas (Chicago: Aldine, 1970), pp. 80–103.

12. The actual and possible nonexistence of particular documents was no less significant than the existence of the documents the committee had in hand. For example, at one point North alleged, "I assured Admiral Poindexter—incorrectly it seems—that all of those documents no longer existed" (*Joint Hearings,* North, pt. 1, p. 19).

13. Quoted in Scott Armstrong (executive ed.), *The Chronology,* a report by the National Security Archive (New York: Warner Books, 1987), pp. 335–36. Also see Daniel K. Inouye and Lee H. Hamilton, *Report of the Congressional Committees Investigating the Iran-Contra Affair,* abridged ed., ed. Joel Brinkley and Stephen Engleberg (New York: Times Books, 1988), p. 199. In the committee report the sentence mentioning "Nir" and the end section on "Col Q" buying the hostages are deleted.

14. Erving Goffman's studies of "impression management" provide numerous examples of how performers of everyday episodes and their audiences orient to a distinction between deliberately projected characteristics and systematically hidden agendas. Various "slips" and "unmeant gestures" evidence a difference that "forces an acutely embarrassing wedge between the official projection and reality." Goffman, *The Presentation of Self in Everyday Life* (New York: Anchor Books, 1959), p. 52.

15. Goffman in ibid. (pp. 42–43) finds passages from Adam Smith that discuss the difference between self-aggrandizing performance and actual character. Smith, *The*

Theory of Moral Sentiments (London: Henry Bohn, 1853), p. 88. The epistemic consequences of this difference were also codified as maxims about truth-telling in seventeenth- and eighteenth-century English "courtesy literature." Steven Shapin, *A Social History of Truth* (Chicago: University of Chicago Press, 1994), esp. chaps. 3 and 5.

16. For a discussion of how a division of labor becomes readable at a glance from a documentary surface, see R. Anderson and W. Sharrock, "Can organisations afford knowledge?" *Computer Supported Cooperative Work* 1 (1993): 143–61.

17. Morning session, July 7, 1987, Lynch/Bogen transcript; also see *Joint Hearings,* North, pt. 1, pp. 13–14.

18. Garfinkel, *Studies in Ethnomethodology,* p. 78. Karl Mannheim originally used the terms "documentary interpretation" to describe a distinctive method of historical analysis. Mannheim, "On the interpretation of *Weltanschauung,* chap. 11, *Essays on the Sociology of Knowledge* (London: Routledge and Kegan Paul, 1952), pp. 33–83. Garfinkel respecified this method by treating it as an embedded feature of "lay" as well as "professional" reasoning.

19. "Repair" is discussed in Emanuel A. Schegloff, Gail Jefferson, and Harvey Sacks, "The preference for self-correction in the organization of repair in conversation," *Language* 53 (1977): 361–82. A more general discussion of "remedies" is provided in Erving Goffman, *Forms of Talk* (Philadelphia: University of Pennsylvania Press, 1983), pp. 199–200.

20. See Augustine Brannigan and Michael Lynch, "On bearing false witness: Credibility as an interactional accomplishment," *Journal of Contemporary Ethnography* 16 (1987): esp. pp. 132ff., on "minimalist agreements."

21. The question is designed in accordance with a "preference for agreement" discussed by conversation analysts (see Methodological Appendix). Consider an alternative way of phrasing such a question: "that doesn't mean that you are telling Mr. McFarlane, that Admiral Poindexter . . . had asked that you prepare a paper for the President, does it?" In this case, the question foreshadows a "no" answer rather than a confirmation of the "meaning" suggested by the question. See Harvey Sacks, "On the preference for agreement and contiguity in sequences in conversation," in *Talk and Social Organization,* ed. G. Button and J. R. E. Lee (Clevedon: Multilingual Matters, 1987), pp. 54–69. Also see Anita M. Pomerantz, "Offering a candidate answer: An information-seeking strategy," *Communication Monographs* 55 (1988): 360–73.

22. This sequence is discussed early in chap. 1.

23. Two senators on the committee wrote that North benefited from the televisual format because he was able to enlist popular support while glossing over the difference between the specific instances of covert activity, shredding, and the like that were supported by official policy and those that were unlicensed and used in an uncontrolled way. Cohen and Mitchell, *Men of Zeal,* pp. 162ff.

24. Morning session, July 7, 1986, *Joint Hearings,* North, pt. 1, p. 20.

25. Ibid., p. 23.

26. Ibid., p. 17.

27. Stanley Fish, *Doing What Comes Naturally: Change, Rhetoric, and the Practice of Theory in Literary and Legal Studies* (Durham, N.C.: Duke University Press, 1989), p. 37.

28. Afternoon session, July 7, 1987, ML/DB transcript, p. 18.

29. Ibid., pp. 18–19.

30. Inouye and Hamilton, *Report of the Congressional Committees,* p. 159.

31. Afternoon session, July 7, 1987, ML/DB transcript, p. 24.

32. See Anita Pomerantz, "Descriptions in legal settings," in Button and Lee, *Talk and Social Organization,* pp. 226–43.

33. Derrida, "Signature, event, context." Paul Ricoeur similarly speaks of the text's "career" escaping "the finite horizons of its author" and having "broken its moorings to the psychology of its author." Ricoeur, "The model of the text: Social action considered as a text," *New Literary History* 5 (1973): 95.

34. Wagner-Pacifici (citing Ricoeur) shifts from emphasizing the author's psychology to delineating a cultural sociology of readers. Textual fragments "released" from the central parties in a political crisis are positioned by organized factions of readers into the dramatic frame of the unfolding crisis. Robin Erica Wagner-Pacifici, *The Moro Morality Play: Terrorism as Social Drama* (Chicago: University of Chicago Press, 1986), p. 206.

35. Afternoon session, July 7, 1987, ML/DB Transcript.

36. In conversation-analytic terms, there is no such sequential reversal, since North's question can be heard as initiating an "insertion sequence" within the overall Q&A structure. Emanuel A. Schegloff, "Notes on a conversational practice: Formulating place," in *Studies in Social Interaction,* ed. D. Sudnow (New York: Free Press, 1972), pp. 76ff.

37. Roland Barthes, *Camera Lucida: Reflections on Photography,* trans. Richard Howard (New York: Hill and Wang, 1988), p. 85.

38. Afternoon session, July 7, 1987, Lynch/Bogen transcript, p. 23.

39. Justice William Brennan, dissenting opinion, in *Calif. v. Green:* 399 US at 152, quoted in Michael H. Graham, "The confrontation clause, the hearsay rule, and the forgetful witness," *Texas Law Review* 56 (1978): 175 n. 117.

40. Afternoon session, July 9, 1987, *Joint Hearings,* North, pt. 1, pp. 237–38.

41. Committee members William Cohen and George Mitchell (both senators from Maine, Cohen a Republican and Mitchell a Democrat) supported Liman's insistence when they later wrote that "[n]o trial court in the country would have permitted North to examine material while testifying without permitting the opposing attorney to examine it as well, regardless of its origin." They added, however, that Liman lacked support from many of the committee members and did not pursue the matter. *Men of Zeal,* p. 161.

42. Unattributed Chinese maxim, cited in Edward W. Clearly (general ed.), *McCormick's Handbook of the Law of Evidence*, 2d ed. (St. Paul, Minn.: West, 1972), p. 18.

43. The significance of "literary inscriptions" for the dissemination of facts and the stabilization of cultural fields was introduced in the context of science studies by Bruno Latour and Steve Woolgar, *Laboratory Life: The Social Construction of Scientific Facts* (London: Sage, 1979; Princeton, N.J.: Princeton University Press, 1986). Latour develops the theme further in his *Science in Action* (Cambridge, Mass.: Harvard University Press, 1987); and "Drawing things together," in *Representation in Scientific Practice,* ed. M. Lynch and S. Woolgar (Cambridge, Mass.: MIT Press, 1990).

CONCLUSION: A CIVICS LESSON IN THE LOGIC OF SLEAZE

1. The videotape of this event provided the focus of a special issue of *Research on Language and Social Interaction* 22 (1988/89). See also Lena Jayussi, " 'The record shows . . .': Fact and disagreement in the Bush/Rather interview," presented at World Congress of Sociology, Madrid, July 1990.

2. Judy Keen, "Watergate whistle blower talks about it 20 years later," *USA Today,* international ed. Aug. 8, 1994, p. 4A.

3. H. R. Haldeman, *The Haldeman Diaries: Inside the Nixon White House* (New York: Putnam, 1994).

4. Lawrence Walsh, *Final Report of the Independent Counsel for Iran/Contra Matters—United States Court of Appeals for the District of Columbia Circuit,* vol. 1, *Investigations and Prosecutions;* vol. 2, *Indictments, Plea Agreements, Interim Reports to Congress, and Administrative Matters:* vol. 3, *Comments and Materials Submitted by Individuals and Their Attorneys Responding to Volume I of the Final Report* (Washington, D.C.: U.S. Government Printing Office, 1994), subsequently published as *Iran-Contra: The Final Report* (New York: Times Books, 1994).

5. Theodore Draper, "Walsh's last stand," *New York Review of Books,* March 3, 1994, p. 30.

6. Ethan Bronner, "Poindexter's Iran-contra trial opens," *Boston Globe,* March 9, 1990, p. 10.

7. See Walsh, *Final Report,* pp. 121–22 (book version), for a discussion of the North appeal. The key point in the appeal ruling was that testimony by prosecution witnesses had been "colored" by North's immunized congressional testimony.

8. R. W. Apple, Jr., "The pardons: Bush etches place in history," *New York Times,* Dec. 25, 1992, p. A23. Also see Draper, "Walsh's last stand"; Walsh, *Final Report,* p. 473.

9. Jeffrey Toobin, "Ollie's next mission," *New Yorker,* Dec. 27, 1993–Jan. 3, 1994, p. 64.

10. Richard Harwood, "The Clintonites' behavior isn't funny," *International Herald Tribune,* Aug. 17, 1994, p. 7.

11. For a detailed analysis of testimony at the trial of the police officers in the Rodney King case, see Charles Goodwin, "Professional vision," *American Anthropologist* 96 (1994): 606–33.

12. For an interesting news report elaborating on some excerpts of testimony that might have been written by Lewis Carroll, see Richard Norton-Taylor, "Truth and big guns," *Guardian Weekend* (London), Feb. 18, 1995, pp. 22–27. For example, one senior official, when questioned about why he had failed to acknowledge a key bit of government knowledge when testifying at an earlier trial, is quoted as saying, "I think there was an element of mutual reinforcement of belief or misunderstanding . . . I quite simply misled myself on what I thought the situation was" (p. 25).

13. Frank Rich, "Just the standard-bearer if they want a holy war," *International Herald Tribune,* June 10, 1994, p. 9.

14. Christopher Hitchens, "Minority report," *Nation* August 22–29, 1994, p. 187, for example, strung together a series of colorful epithets to describe North as "a drug-running, blood-encrusted pathological liar and proto-fascist."

15. Leslie Phillips, " 'Ollie's army' charges forward: There seems no middle ground for followers and foes of North," *USA Today,* international ed., June 14, 1994, p. 7A.

16. See J. A. Barnes, *A Pack of Lies* (Cambridge: Cambridge University Press, 1994).

17. Haynes Johnson, *Sleepwalking Through History* (New York: Anchor Books, 1991), p. 368. Johnson attributes the quoted viewpoint to committee chairman Daniel Inouye.

18. In his account of the collective memory of Watergate, Michael Schudson identifies such a "collective lesson in civics culture" with mainstream conservative and liberal-constitutionalist views, but not with the more radical right and left interpretations. Schudson, *Watergate in American Memory* (New York: Basic Books, 1992), p. 29.

19. Ibid., p. 27. This lesson seems to have been applied with a vengeance by Nixon's political descendants during the Whitewater investigation of President Clinton.

20. Roland Barthes, *Mythologies* (New York: Hill and Wang, 1972), p. 17.

21. Albert Jonsen and Stephen Toulmin, *The Abuse of Casuistry: A History of Moral Reasoning* (Berkeley: University of California Press, 1988), pp. 9–10. For a detailed account of how jurors in a particular case contended with the tension between formal legal demands and their vernacular sense of justice, see Douglas Maynard and John Manzo, "On the sociology of justice: Theoretical notes from an actual jury deliberation," *Sociological Theory* 11 (1993): 171–93.

22. See Michel Foucault, *Power/Knowledge: Selected Interviews and Other Writings, 1972–1977* (New York: Pantheon, 1980).

23. Jonsen and Toulmin, *Abuse of Casuistry,* p. 11, speak of the "disrepute" into which the ancient concept of casuistry fell. Where it once described a technical area of ethics devoted to regulating ethical judgments in circumstances that are not readily covered by clear ethical principles, it became a "slur," describing a more "sinister" mode of application where exercises in sophistry enable dubious actions to be justified by reference to principles and conflicts between applicable principles.

24. Yaron Ezrahi, "Technology and the civil epistemology of democracy," *Inquiry* 35 (1993): 12–13.

25. See Michael Rogin, *"Ronald Reagan," The Movie: And Other Episodes in Political Demonology* (Berkeley: University of California Press, 1987); and Gary Wills, *Reagan's America* (New York: Penguin, 1988).

26. See, for example, John Keegan's account of Caesar's description of battle in *The Face of Battle* (London: Penguin, 1976), pp. 62ff.; regarding Churchill, see Clive Ponting, "Truly a self-made man," *The Times* (London), higher education supplement, July 8, 1994.

27. Jean Beaudrillard, *Simulations* (New York: Semiotext(e), 1983); Guy Debord, *The Society of the Spectacle,* trans. D. Nicholson-Smith (New York: Zone Books, 1992).

28. This is related to the interactional "preference" system discussed in the Methodological Appendix. See Harvey Sacks, "Everyone has to lie," in *Sociocultural Dimensions of Language Use,* ed. M. Sanches and B. G. Blount (New York: Academic Press, 1975), pp. 57–79.

29. See Erving Goffman, *Strategic Interaction* (Philadelphia: University of Pennsylvania Press, 1969).

30. Cartoonists and journalists played on this analogy between King Henry's utterance and President Reagan's management style; see Ann Wroe, *Lives, Lies, and the Iran-Contra Affair* (London: I. B. Taurus, 1991), pp. 114ff. For an interesting account of the Thomas à Becket story (although not the particular phase of it discussed here), see Victor Turner, *Dramas, Fields, and Metaphors: Symbolic Action in Human Society* (Ithaca, N.Y.: Cornell University Press, 1974).

31. Wroe, ibid., describes at great length the intricate strategies employed by Reagan administration subordinates through which they anticipated orders that were never given, thus enabling the "commander in chief" honestly to disclaim knowledge and responsibility. Interestingly, Wroe's account of these strategies relies heavily on the public testimony at the Iran-contra hearings. They were so effective that, even after they were revealed in the testimony, they continued to enable the deniability they initially set up. For a more technical discussion of promises and questions, see E. A. Schegloff, "On some questions and ambiguities in conversation," in *Structures of Social Action: Studies in Conversation Analysis,* ed. J. M. Atkinson and J. C. Heritage (Cambridge: Cambridge University Press, 1984), pp. 28–52.

32. See Fredric Jameson, "Postmodernism or the cultural logic of late capitalism,"

New Left Review 146 (1984): 53–92; Mike Featherstone, "In pursuit of the postmodern: An introduction," *Theory, Culture & Society* 5 (1988): 195–215.

33. For a discussion on this point, see Donna Haraway, "'Gender' for a Marxist dictionary: The sexual politics of a word," chap. 7 of *Simians, Cyborgs, and Women: The Reinvention of Nature* (New York: Routledge, 1991), pp. 127–48.

34. Jonson and Toulmin, *Abuse of Casuistry*, p. 157.

35. Jacques Derrida, "Limited inc. abc," *Glyph* 2 (1977): 162–254.

36. Representation is used here both in the sense of political representation of a constituency or people and representation in discourse. See Hannah Pitkin, *The Concept of Representation* (Berkeley: University of California Press, 1972). For a theoretical exploitation of this double sense of political/epistemic representation, see Bruno Latour, "Postmodern? No, simply amodern. Steps towards an anthropology of science: An essay review," *Studies in History and Philosophy of Science* 21 (1990): 145–71.

37. Jürgen Habermas, "The normative content of modernity," *The Philosophical Discourse of Modernity* (Cambridge, Mass.: MIT Press, 1990), p. 337.

38. In the committee report the discussion of "covert action in a democratic society" quickly shifts from a "fundamental" discussion of the propriety of covert actions to procedural questions about congressional accountability and oversight. Daniel K. Inouye and Lee H. Hamilton, *Report of the Congressional Committees Investigating the Iran-Contra Affair* (New York: Times Books, 1988), pp. 333ff.

39. Niklas Luhmann makes a more resigned comment about the collusiveness associated with scandals: "one can get the impression that the state bureaucracy is constructed as a social network with the main aim of ensuring that nothing happens when something does happen." Luhmann, "Politicians, honesty and the higher immorality of politics," *Theory, Culture & Society* 11 (1994): 35.

40. See, for instance, J. Maxwell Atkinson and Paul Drew, *Order in Court* (London: Macmillan, 1979); Paul Drew, "Contested evidence in courtroom cross-examination: The case of a trial for rape," in *Talk at Work: Interaction in Institutional Settings,* ed. Drew and John Heritage (Cambridge: Cambridge University Press, 1992), pp. 470–520; and Augustine Brannigan and Michael Lynch, "On bearing false witness: Perjury and credibility as interactional accomplishments," *Journal of Contemporary Ethnography* 16 (1987): 115–46.

41. Luhmann, "Politicians, honesty and the higher immorality of politics."

42. James Der Derian, "Arms, hostages, and the importance of shredding in earnest: Reading the national security culture (II)." *Social Text* 22 (Spring 1989): 79–91.

METHODOLOGICAL APPENDIX: POSTANALYTIC ETHNOMETHODOLOGY

1. The major initiatives and research policies of ethnomethodology are outlined along with a series of exemplary studies in Harold Garfinkel, *Studies in Ethno-*

methodology (Englewood Cliffs, N.J.: Prentice-Hall, 1967; Oxford: Polity Press, 1986).

2. In Richard J. Hill and Kathleen Stones Crittenden, *Proceedings of the Purdue Symposium on Ethnomethodology* (Purdue, Ind.: Institute for the Study of Social Change, Department of Sociology, Purdue University, 1968), pp. 6–7. Also see Harold Garfinkel, "On the origins of the term 'ethnomethodology,'" in Roy Turner (ed.), *Ethnomethodology* (Harmondsworth, Penguin, 1974), pp. 15–18; and John Heritage, *Garfinkel and Ethnomethodology* (Oxford: Polity Press, 1984), pp. 4–5.

3. Harold Garfinkel and Harvey Sacks, "On formal structures of practical actions," in *Theoretical Sociology: Perspectives and Developments,* ed. J. C. McKinney and E. A. Tiryakian (New York: Appleton-Century-Crofts, 1970), pp. 345ff.

4. Jürgen Habermas criticizes ethnomethodology for its absent (or concealed) normative stance, and he attempts to make explicit the normative validity claims that he argues are fundamental to all communicative action. Habermas, *The Theory of Communicative Action,* vol. 1, *Reason and the Rationalization of Society,* trans. T. McCarthy (Boston: Beacon Press, 1984). For a countercritique, see David Bogen, "A reappraisal of Habermas's *"Theory of Communicative Action* in light of detailed investigations of social *praxis," Journal for the Theory of Social Behaviour* 19 (1989): pp. 47–77.

5. Harvey Sacks, "Notes on methodology," in *Structures of Social Action: Studies in Conversation Analysis,* ed. J. M. Atkinson and J. C. Heritage (Cambridge: Cambridge University Press, 1984), pp. 21–27.

6. Garfinkel, *Studies in Ethnomethodology,* p. 34.

7. Victor Turner, *Dramas, Fields, and Metaphors: Symbolic Action in Human Society* (Ithaca, N.Y.: Cornell University Press, 1974), pp. 78–79. Turner's four-stage scheme of social drama is applied in a study of the kidnapping and murder of Aldo Moro, in Robin Erica Wagner-Pacifici, *The Moro Morality Play: Terrorism as Social Drama* (Chicago: University of Chicago Press, 1986). For an amusing application of a scheme developed from Turner, see Bruce Lincoln's analysis of "provocative inversions" produced by Duchamp's ready-mades and the serial arrangement of wrestling matches on a British professional wrestling card. Lincoln, *Discourse and the Construction of Society* (Oxford: Oxford University Press), chap. 9.

8. Turner, *Dramas, Fields, and Metaphors,* p. 96. Turner's narrative of the twelfth-century confrontation between Thomas à Becket and Henry II is artfully told, but at times he seems to endow the "root paradigm" with a mystical agency, such as when he says (perhaps with some poetic license) that during the future archbishop's darkest moments "courage came back to Becket from the paradigm glowing redly in his mind, the *via crucis* pattern of martyrdom" (p. 84).

9. See Peter Winch, "Nature and convention," in *Ethics and Action* (London: Routledge and Kegan Paul, 1972), p. 65.

10. Jeffrey C. Alexander and Philip Smith, "The discourse of American civil society: A new proposal for cultural studies," *Theory and Society* 22 (1993): 151–207.

11. Ibid., pp. 162–63.

12. Ibid., p. 188.

13. Ibid., p. 190.

14. C. Wright Mills, "Situated actions and vocabularies of motive," *American Sociological Review* 5 (1940): 904–13.

15. These provide one answer to the question "What are cultural studies?" See J. Hillis Miller, *Illustration* (Cambridge, Mass.: Harvard University Press, 1992), pp. 13–14.

16. Ludwig Wittgenstein, *The Blue and Brown Books* (New York: Harper and Row, 1958), p. 18. Also see Wittgenstein, *Philosophical Investigations* (Oxford: Basil Blackwell, 1958), sec. 109.

17. Wittgenstein, *Blue and Brown Books.*

18. See Pierre Bourdieu, *The Logic of Practice* (Oxford: Polity Press, 1990).

19. For a discussion of problems associated with ascribing "tacit beliefs" and "presuppositions," see Stephen Turner, *The Social Theory of Practices* (Oxford: Polity Press, 1994), pp. 34ff.

20. Harold Garfinkel, "Respecification: Evidence for locally produced, naturally accountable phenomena of order, logic, reason, meaning, method," in *Ethnomethodology and the Human Sciences,* ed. G. Button (Cambridge: Cambridge University Press, 1991), p. 12.

21. Garfinkel, *Studies in Ethnomethodology,* p. 68.

22. Alfred Schutz, "Concept and theory formation in the social sciences," in *Collected Papers* (The Hague: Martinus Nijhoff, 1962), 1:48–66.

23. Talcott Parsons recognized this problem when he was developing his theory of social action, and in a bold (but ultimately unconvincing) move he asserted that his "unit act" contained all the essential ingredients internal to the concept of social action. Parsons, *The Structure of Social Action* (New York: Free Press, 1949 [1937]), see esp. vol. 1, chap. 1.

24. See, for example, Button, *Ethnomethodology,* p. 12.

25. This point is well-argued with respect to the vernacular concept of motives, in W. W. Sharrock, W. W. and D. R. Watson, "What's the point of 'rescuing motives'?" *British Journal of Sociology* 34 (1984): 435–51.

26. See Garfinkel, *Studies in Ethnomethodology.* His program of "respecification" is outlined in Garfinkel, "Respecification."

27. For a critique of the assumption that the production and understanding of language imply the existence of an underlying "theory" of meaning, see G. P. Baker and P. M. S. Hacker, *Language, Sense, and Nonsense* (Oxford: Basil Blackwell, 1984).

28. For a review of the various lines of ethnomethodological study, see Douglas

Maynard and Steven Clayman, "The diversity of ethnomethodology," *Annual Review of Sociology* 17 (1991): 385–418. For an extensive bibliography of published research in ethnomethodology, see B. J. Fehr, J. Stetson, and Y. Mizukawa, "A bibliography for ethnomethodology," in *Ethnomethodological Sociology,* ed. J. Coulter (London: Edward Elgar, 1990).

29. There is now a large corpus of conversation-analytic work of which the most often cited study is Harvey Sacks, Emanuel Schegloff, and Gail Jefferson, "A simplest systematics for the organization of turn-taking in conversation," *Language* 50 (1974): 696–735. For our purposes, Sacks's transcribed lectures remain the richest available source of insights and examples concerning the social organization of linguistic phenomena. *Lectures on Conversation,* ed. Gail Jefferson (Oxford: Basil Blackwell, 1992).

30. This is a contentious issue among ethnomethodologists and conversation analysts. Heritage, *Garfinkel and Ethnomethodology,* and Maynard and Clayman, "Diversity of ethnomethodology," emphasize the threads of continuity between ethnomethodology and conversation analysis, whereas we have argued in favor of a "postanalytic" ethnomethodology that breaks with the formalistic tendencies. See M. Lynch, *Scientific Practice and Ordinary Action: Ethnomethodology and Social Studies of Science* (New York: Cambridge University Press, 1993), chap. 6; and M. Lynch and D. Bogen, "Harvey Sacks' primitive natural science," *Theory, Culture, & Society* 11 (1994): 65–104.

31. These studies include J. M. Atkinson and Paul Drew, *Order in Court: The Organisation of Verbal Interaction in Judicial Settings* (London: Macmillan, 1979); Wayne A. Beach, "Temporal density in courtroom interaction: Constraints on the recovery of past events in legal discourse," *Communication Monographs* 52 (1985): 1–18; D. R. Watson, "Some features of the elicitation of confessions in murder investigations," in *Interaction Competence,* ed. George Psathas (Washington, D.C.: International Institute for Ethnomethodology and Conversation Analysis and the University Press of America, 1990), pp. 263–95; Douglas W. Maynard, *Inside Plea Bargaining: The Language of Negotiation* (New York: Plenum, 1984); Michael Moerman, "The use of precedent in natural conversation: A study of practical legal reasoning," *Semiotica* 9 (1973): 193–218; and Anita M. Pomerantz, "Descriptions in legal settings," in *Talk and Social Organization,* ed. Graham Button and J. R. E. Lee (Clevedon: Multilingual Matters, 1987), pp. 226–43.

32. Other "systems" that are frequently discussed in the conversation-analysis literature are turn-taking organization and the organization of repair. These are relevant to our study, but we have not presented a summary of them here in order to keep our lesson brief and to the point. See Sacks et al., "A simplest systematics," for an outline of these systems, and Lynch and Bogen, "Harvey Sacks' primitive natural science," for a critical review.

33. For further discussion of technical aspects of how the preference system

operates for invitations, see Judy A. Davidson, "Subsequent versions of invitations, offers, requests, and proposals dealing with potential or actual rejection," in Atkinson and Heritage, *Structures of Social Action* (Cambridge: Cambridge University Press, 1984), pp. 102–28. Other "preference" systems are discussed in Anita Pomerantz, "Agreeing and disagreeing with assessments: Some features of preferred/dispreferred turn shapes," in Atkinson and Heritage, *Structures of Social Action,* pp. 57–101; Harvey Sacks, "On the preference for agreement and contiguity in sequences in conversation," in Button and Lee, *Talk and Social Organization,* pp. 219–25; Harvey Sacks, and Emanuel Schegloff, "Two preferences for the organization of reference to persons in conversation and their interaction," *Everyday Language: Studies in Ethnomethodology,* ed. George Psathas (New York: Irvington Press, 1979), pp. 15–21; and E. A. Schegloff, G. Jefferson, and H. Sacks, "The preference for self-correction in the organization of repair in conversation," *Language* 53 (1977): 361–82.

34. Sacks, "On the preference for agreement," p. 58.

35. Ibid., p. 57. By "yes—" or "no—," Sacks means an utterance that begins with yes or no (or a semantic equivalent) and then continues.

36. Ibid., p. 62.

37. Ibid., p. 64.

38. Ibid., p. 66.

39. From Michael Lynch, *Art and Artifact in Laboratory Science* (London: Routledge and Kegan Paul, 1985), p. 204. (Example originally supplied by Gail Jefferson.)

40. For research on an occasion where the "preference for agreement" is suspended or inverted, see M. H. Goodwin, "Aggravated correction and disagreement in children's conversation," *Journal of Pragmatics* 7 (1983): 657–77.

41. A two-volume set of the lectures is available (Sacks, *Lectures on Conversation*). See especially the fall 1971 series of lectures on stories.

42. An early discussion of the transformation of descriptions of "life-in-society" into professional accounts of social order is presented in chap. 2 of Garfinkel's, "Parsons' primer: 'Ad hoc uses,' " unpublished manuscript, University of California, Los Angeles, 1960.

43. See Gail Jefferson, "Sequential aspects of storytelling in conversation," in *Studies in the Organization of Conversational Interaction,* ed. J. Schenkein (New York: Academic Press, 1978), pp. 219–48; Charles Goodwin, *Conversational Organization: Interaction Between Speakers* (New York: Academic Press, 1981); Marjorie H. Goodwin, " 'Instigating': Story telling as social process," *American Ethnologist* 9 (1982): 799–819.

44. See Emanuel A. Schegloff, "Notes on a conversational practice: Formulating place," in Sudnow, *Studies in Social Interaction,* p. 97.

45. From Harvey Sacks, "On doing 'being ordinary,' " in Atkinson and Heritage, *Structures of Social Action,* transcript on p. 420.

46. The mention of clock time is interesting here, less as an "objective" point of reference than as an index for its "member relevance" as end of the workday.

47. Sacks, "On doing 'being ordinary,'" p. 423, points out that in a subsequent conversation between Jean and another witness to the scene, "the colored lady" is re-identified as an "employee," thus transforming the sense of the scene implied by Ellen's story.

48. Ibid., p. 218.

49. Sacks, "Conveying information; story-connective techniques; recognition-type descriptors; 'first verbs'; understanding; differential organization of perception," *Lectures on Conversation,* p. 185.

50. Sacks, "'Fragile' stories; on being 'rational,'" *Lectures on Conversation,* pp. 504–11.

51. See R. P. McDermott and Henry Tylbor, "On the necessity of collusion in conversation," *Text* 3 (1983): 277–97. The "complicity" between teller and recipient is established not only by virtue of who the persons are to each other; as Jefferson, Sacks, and Schegloff point out, a storyteller can progressively solicit and check out a recipient's "affiliation" to potentially sensitive or offensive details in a story over the course of his telling the story. The version of the story will thus be elaborated or censored depending on the recipient's show of interest and affiliation. See G. Jefferson, H. Sacks, and E. A. Schegloff, "Notes on laughter in the pursuit of intimacy," in Button and Lee, *Talk and Social Organization,* pp. 152–205. A related organizational matter concerns how talk about personal troubles or otherwise intimate matters is progressively introduced in a story, or series of story rounds. See Gail Jefferson, "On stepwise transition from talk about a trouble to inappropriately next-positioned matters," in Atkinson and Heritage, *Structures of Social Action,* pp. 346–69.

52. Sacks, *Lectures on Conversation,* pp. 505–6.

53. Ibid., p. 505.

54. See, for example, the collections of studies edited by Deirdre Boden and Don Zimmerman, *Talk and Social Structure* (Oxford: Polity, 1991), and Paul Drew and John Heritage, *Talk at Work: Interaction in Institutional Settings* (Cambridge: Cambridge University Press, 1992).

55. Atkinson and Drew, *Order in Court;* Doug Benson and Paul Drew, "'Was there firing in Sandy Row that night?': Some features of the organisation of disputes about recorded facts," *Sociological Inquiry* 48 (1978): 89–100; Augustine Brannigan and Michael Lynch, "On bearing false witness: Perjury and credibility as interactional accomplishments," *Journal of Contemporary Ethnography* 16 (1987): 115–46; Douglas Maynard, *Inside Plea Bargaining: The Language of Negotiation* (New York: Plenum, 1984); Anita M. Pomerantz, "Descriptions in legal settings," in Button and Lee, *Talk and Social Organization,* pp. 226–43.

56. Heritage, *Garfinkel and Ethnomethodology,* p. 78.

57. Sacks, Schegloff, and Jefferson, "A simplest systematics," p. 731. When described in this highly abstract way, the term "conversation" loses the more restricted connotation of a polite or convivial interchange among peers.

58. See Don Zimmerman and Deirdre Boden, "Structure-in-action: An introduction," in Boden and Zimmerman, *Talk and Social Structure,* p. 21. Note that E. A. Schegloff has contested such interpretations of conversation analysis, and his arguments have proved persuasive. Schegloff, "Between micro and macro: Contexts and other connections," in *The Micro-Macro Link,* ed. J. Alexander, B. Giesen, R. Münch, and N. Smelser (Berkeley: University of California Press, 1987), pp. 207–34.

59. See, for example, Don Zimmerman and Candace West, "Sex roles, interruptions and silences in conversation," in *Language and Sex: Difference and Dominance,* ed. Barrie Thorne and Nancy Henley (Rowley, Mass.: Newbury House, 1975); Hugh Mehan, *Learning Lessons: Social Organization in the Classroom* (Cambridge, Mass.: Harvard University Press, 1979); Kathy Davis, *Power Under the Microscope* (Dordrecht: Foris, 1988); Candace West and Angela Garcia, "Conversational shift work: A study of topical transition between women and men," *Social Problems* 35 (1988): 551–75.

60. A. W., McHoul, "Why there are no guarantees for interrogators," *Journal of Pragmatics* 11 (1987): 455–71.

61. See Jürgen Habermas, *Communication and the Evolution of Society,* trans. T. McCarthy (Boston: Beacon Press, 1979); *The Theory of Communicative Action;* and *Moral Consciousness and Communicative Action,* trans. C. Lenhardt and S. Weber-Nicholson (Cambridge, Mass.: MIT Press, 1990). See also S. Benhabib and F. Dallmayr (eds.), *The Communicative Ethics Controversy* (Cambridge, Mass.: MIT Press, 1990). To date, Habermas has accorded Sacks et al.'s model little more than a procedural role in organizing speech, having failed—we must presume—to have detected the substantive ethical content of that model. See *Theory of Communicative Action,* 1: 325–27.

62. See, for example, Harvey Molotch and Deirdre Boden. "Talking social structure: Discourse, domination and the Watergate Hearings," *American Sociological Review* 50 (1985): 273–88.

63. Emanuel A. Schegloff, "From interview to confrontation: Observations of the Bush/Rather encounter," *Research on Language and Social Interaction* 22 (1988–89): 218.

INDEX

MICHAEL LYNCH is Professor of Sociology in the Department of Human Sciences at Brunel University. He is the author of *Art and Artifact in Laboratory Science: A Study of Shop Work and Shop Talk in a Research Laboratory*, and *Scientific Practice and Ordinary Action: Ethnomethodology and Social Studies of Science*, and coeditor (with Steve Woolgar) of *Representation in Scientific Practice*. He also has written numerous articles for journals and books on social and cultural studies of science, social problems, and sociological theory.

DAVID BOGEN is Assistant Professor of Sociology at Emerson College in Boston, Massachusetts. His book, *Order Without Rules: Critical Theory and the Logic of Conversation*, will soon be published by SUNY Press. He has written a number of articles for journals and books on topics in social theory, communication studies, and social problems.

Library of Congress Cataloging-in-Publication Data

Lynch, Michael, 1948–

The spectacle of history : speech, text, and memory at the Iran-contra

hearings / Michael Lynch and David Bogen.

p. cm.—(Post-Contemporary Interventions)

Includes index.

ISBN 0-8223-1729-X (cloth : alk. paper). — ISBN 0-8223-1738-9

(paper : alk. paper)

1. Iran-Contra Affair, 1985–1990. 2. Legislative hearings—United

States. I. Bogen, David, 1960– . II. Title.

E876.L96 1996

973.927—dc20   95-41410

                                                                            CIP